Science and Innovation

NEW HORIZONS IN THE ECONOMICS OF INNOVATION

Series Editor: Christopher Freeman, *Emeritus Professor of Science Policy, SPRU – Science and Technology Policy Research, University of Sussex, UK*

Technical innovation is vital to the competitive performance of firms and of nations and for the sustained growth of the world economy. The economics of innovation is an area that has expanded dramatically in recent years and this major series, edited by one of the most distinguished scholars in the field, contributes to the debate and advances in research in this most important area.

The main emphasis is on the development and application of new ideas. The series provides a forum for original research in technology, innovation systems and management, industrial organization, technological collaboration, knowledge and innovation, research and development, evolutionary theory and industrial strategy. International in its approach, the series includes some of the best theoretical and empirical work from both well-established researchers and the new generation of scholars.

Titles in the series include:

Science and Innovation

Rethinking the Rationales for Funding and Governance

Edited by

Aldo Geuna

Senior Lecturer, SPRU – Science and Technology Policy Research, University of Sussex, UK

Ammon J. Salter

Research Fellow, SPRU – Science and Technology Policy Research, University of Sussex, UK

W. Edward Steinmueller

Professor, SPRU – Science and Technology Policy Research, University of Sussex, UK

NEW HORIZONS IN THE ECONOMICS OF INNOVATION

Edward Elgar
Cheltenham, UK • Northampton, MA, USA

Published by
Edward Elgar Publishing Limited
Glensanda House
Montpellier Parade
Cheltenham
Glos GL50 1UA
UK

Edward Elgar Publishing, Inc.
136 West Street
Suite 202
Northampton
Massachusetts 01060
USA

A catalogue record for this book
is available from the British Library

Library of Congress Cataloguing in Publication Data

Science and innovation : rethinking the rationales for funding and governance /
edited by Aldo Geuna, Ammon J. Salter, W. Edward Steinmueller.
    p.   cm. — (New Horizons in the economics of innovation)
    Includes index.
    1. Federal aid to research. 2. Science and state. I. Geuna, Aldo, 1965–
II. Salter, Ammon J. III. Steinmueller, W. Edward (William Edward) IV. Series.

Q180.55.G6 S35 2003
338.9′26—dc21

2002034677

ISBN 1 84376 109 2 (cased)

Printed and bound in Great Britain by MPG Books Ltd, Bodmin, Cornwall

Contents

PART III   MODELS OF RESEARCH FUNDING

Figures

Tables

Contributors

Cristiano Antonelli, University of Turin, Italy.

Michel Callon, CSI – École des Mines, Paris, France.

Fabrizio Cesaroni, St Anna School of Advanced Studies, Pisa, Italy.

Wesley M. Cohen, Carnegie Mellon University, Pittsburgh, PA, USA.

Robin Cowan, University of Maastricht, The Netherlands.

Paul A. David, All Souls College, Oxford, UK and Stanford University, CA, USA.

Dominique Foray, IMRI and University Paris Dauphine, Paris, France.

Alfonso Gambardella, St Anna School of Advanced Studies, Pisa, Italy.

Aldo Geuna, University of Sussex, Brighton, UK.

Bronwyn H. Hall, University of California, Berkeley, USA.

Nicolas Jonard, CNRS, BETA, Strasbourg, France.

Louise C. Keely, University of Wisconsin, USA.

Patrick Llerena, University Louis Pasteur, Strasbourg, France.

Ben R. Martin, University of Sussex, Brighton, UK.

Mireille Matt, University Louis Pasteur, Strasbourg, France.

Frieder Meyer-Krahmer, University Louis Pasteur, France and FhG-ISI, Germany.

Richard R. Nelson, Columbia University, New York, USA.

Jason Owen-Smith, University of Michigan, Ann Arbor, USA.

Fabio Pammolli, University of Florence, Italy.

Keith Pavitt, University of Sussex, Brighton, UK.

Walter W. Powell, Stanford University, CA, USA.

Massimo Riccaboni, University of Siena, Italy.

Ammon J. Salter, University of Sussex, Brighton, UK.

Véronique Schaeffer, BETA, University of Strasbourg, France.

W. Edward Steinmueller, University of Sussex, Brighton, UK.

Paula E. Stephan, Georgia State University, GA, USA.

G.M. Peter Swann, University of Manchester, UK.

John P. Walsh, University of Illinois at Chicago, IL, USA.

David A. Wolfe, University of Toronto, Canada.

Acknowledgements

This book is the result of a collaboration developed within a European Union sponsored network on new rationales for the public funding of research. The network brought together a diverse group of academic and policy experts to explore new models for the funding and governance of science. The network met in Paris and Brighton over a two year period, and culminated in the international conference 'Rethinking science policy: analytical frameworks for evidence-based policy' held at the University of Sussex, 21–23 March, 2002. Financial support for the network was provided by a research grant (ref. HPV1CT1999900006) from the STRATA programme of the European Union Directorate General Research. This grant allowed authors to meet and discuss research ideas and evidence of relevance for the emerging policy framework at both the European and Member-state levels.

The book has benefited from the energetic and proactive interest of Mike W. Rogers, the project officer in the European Commission. Mike provided a steady flow of information and perspectives from the European Commission and other research groups about the evolving content of the European Research Area (ERA) which helped to inform and structure our discussions.

We would also like to acknowledge the members of our network who are authors of contributions to this volume, as well as Cristiano Antonelli, Bronwyn Hall, Keith Pavitt, Paula Stephan and David Wolfe for their commentaries. Networks work best when they realize a collegial and congenial working life, a goal which we achieved in this effort – largely as a consequence of the equanimity and gentility of our colleagues. The book has also gained from comments and suggestions made by all the participants in the 'Rethinking science policy' conference. We would also like to thank Hugh Cameron, Jane Calvert, Paul Nightingale and Richard Stankiewicz for their participation in the network.

This book would have not been successfully completed without the editorial talents of Cynthia Little. Her invaluable and painstaking work in editing the contributions, in bibliographical research (aided by Amira Driscoll), and organizing production of the final manuscript of this book, is greatly appreciated.

Brighton, 1 October, 2002
A.G. A.S. E.S.

General introduction

> The epochal innovation that distinguishes the modern economic epoch is the extended application of science to problems of economic production. (Kuznets 1966, p. 9)

> Basic research provides most of the original discoveries from which all other progress flows. (United Kingdom Council for Scientific Policy 1967)

> The credit for our recent success really goes to the powerful system we have generated to create new knowledge and develop it into technologies that drive our economy, guarantee our national security, and improve our health and quality of life. (President's Council of Advisors on Science and Technology 2000, p. 1)

During the second half of the twentieth century, advanced industrial countries made unparalleled public investment in exploring what Vannevar Bush (1945) termed 'the endless frontier'. Combined with charitable and private investment, this investment constructed a number of 'powerful systems' for generating new knowledge and harnessing them to invention. This book is about the evolution of these systems, our changing understanding of their composition and operation and the lessons this offers for conceiving and implementing science and technology policy.

In times of turbulence or rapid change in the past the practices and understandings seem to have been more straightforward. In recent years, many within the scientific community have longed for the consensus that governed science policy following the Second World War. Few, however, would wish to reinstate one of the principal conditions supporting this consensus, the imperative of using science to fuel military races that could be lost but never won. Even well before this imperative was fundamentally altered by the events of 1989, however, the consensus supporting public investment in science and the tenets that had been established to govern this investment had already begun to fray.

The decline of belief in three fundamental principles has been central to the unravelling of the consensus. First, it was believed that scientific knowledge is gained through processes of investigation independent of its application and, therefore, relies upon institutions with a central interest in the pursuit of knowledge without regard to its immediate practical application. The accumulation of scientific discoveries originating in corporate research laboratories, from the transistor and the identification of the background radiation from the 'big bang', to the sequencing of human and other genomes, reduce the credibility of this belief. Even though it is possible to explain the mechanisms that generated these examples as exceptional, the veil of science's independence has been torn.

Second, while it was understood that the application of scientific knowledge could lead to danger or harm, it was widely believed that the scientific enterprise itself was innocent of these misapplications and therefore did not require external governance or review. Although scientists remain among the most trusted of all groups in public opinion surveys, they have not escaped a relative loss of public sympathy resulting from the accumulation of catastrophes in the application of science and the growing perception that the threat of even larger catastrophes is a product of scientific investigation. In addition, for many the extension of research into the natural and medical sciences raises ethical concerns on which no broad consensus exists and that, therefore, are inevitably a source of controversy, leading to loss of confidence in scientists' self-governance. While there continue to be many questions about how science should be governed and by whom, the common belief now is that science does need to be governed.

Third, it was believed that the processes governing scientific performance and reputation principally relied upon the capacities and energies of individual scientists and therefore that these processes could be relied upon to provide reliable guides to the allocation of resources. The decline in this belief is linked to the unravelling of the two previous beliefs and to the general distrust in many industrialized countries of elites and authority. Rather than consensus that scientists are pursuing a 'higher' interest in truth or public interest, the suspicion has grown that scientists (like almost everyone else) may be pursuing more conventional personal interests such as fame or money. For many scientists the decay of practice and belief in the principle that science pursues 'higher goals' is particularly troubling as it represents an attack on the cultural values that still motivate them. One measure of this is the 1969 exchange between US Senator John Pastore and Robert Wilson, the founder of Fermilab. When Pastore asked about the value of high-energy physics research in the support of national defence, Wilson replied, 'It has nothing to do directly with defending our country, except to make it worth defending'. For some, including many scientists, Wilson's reply is a spirited defence of the cultural value of science; for others it is an expression of the indifference of scientists to social need.

The military imperative, which had gradually faded from the rationale of first resort to a lower standing, collapsed entirely as the Berlin Wall came down. This has left only a few fundamental rationales for public science that remained safe from the declines in belief about scientific enterprise. One is the perceived centrality of science in supporting social needs such as health care and the safeguarding of the environment. Another is the opportunity to support domestic industrial competitiveness by supporting the generation of knowledge for eventual commercialization. A third and perhaps less central rationale for the public support of scientific enterprise, is that it is an essential component of advanced scientific training, through either the renewal of the skills and knowledge of university teachers or the provision of training in research for their students. None of these rationales supports the conclusion that the scientific community alone should govern investigation. Nor do they provide much basis for the pursuit of science as a cultural ideal, as an expression of a distinct set of values or the pursuit of aims that are governed by the search for fundamental knowledge or truth.

While some may lament these developments or look for ways to reverse the tide of public belief or some of its consequences, the contributors to this book have another goal in mind. They are seeking to identify what is happening and what is likely to happen as a result of the changing rationales for funding and governing science. The means that they employ to investigate these developments and potentials all reflect the view that science may be viewed as a social system with actors, structures and incentives that are rapidly evolving. This evolution is marked by a degree of stress or pressure. The dissipation of practice and belief in the several principles has reduced the autonomy of scientific organizations and increased efforts to establish methods for assuring their accountability. Predictably, the governance models used in other contexts have been extended to science – renewals of interest in cost–benefit accounting for public investments in science, efforts to 'commodify' scientific output by modifications in the definition of intellectual property rights and more explicit efforts to measure the quantity and quality of scientific outputs, are all symptoms of the efforts to apply managerial methods to the governance of science. Such efforts are likely to have mischievous and unintended effects. It is in this context that we introduce the idea of rethinking the underlying rationales for funding and governance.

The dominant economic theory of science established by Nelson (1959) and Arrow (1962) is based upon, and played a significant role in buttressing, the view that science requires independent public institutions. The central feature of this theory is that the information represented by scientific outputs has the feature of a 'public good' – it is, in principle, available to all – and, additionally, that because it is information, its use would not suffer from congestion effects, a conspicuous feature of other public goods ranging from roads and harbours to clean air and salubrious beaches. A minor lacuna in this theory was the requirement that there be some mechanism for recovering the costs of developing potential applications from the use of this publicly available scientific information, lest it 'sit on the shelf'. The mechanisms of intellectual property rights, first mover advantage and commercial secrecy were, however, likely to be adequate.

Nelson (1959) and Arrow (1962) provide the answer to the question, 'why is the market system unable to produce scientific information as it does other information outputs?'. Their answer is that it will produce such outputs, but that their amount will be smaller than is socially desirable. This is simply because any particular private actor contemplating an investment in scientific research will produce only as much as he or she is able to directly employ and capture the returns from creating – an amount that is likely to be less than is socially desirable. Unfortunately, the theory does not provide a means of assessing how *much* less or the problems of accountability would have been solved in the 1960s.

If private firms do not have adequate incentives to produce the appropriate amount of scientific information (and to distribute it throughout the economy), then it follows that this market failure is one in which it is proper for the government to intervene. Such intervention might range from subsidizing to commissioning the generation and distribution of scientific information. The specific assumption in Nelson's and Arrow's arguments, involving the universality of access to scientific information, also explains why extending the intellectual property rights to scientific information is unlikely to be a cure. While such an extension would increase private actor interest in making investments in generating scientific information, it would also raise the costs to other firms wanting to use this information far above the costs of its reproduction, again ensuring that too little science would be employed in the economy with deleterious consequences for output and productivity growth.

As with many arguments, the reliability of Arrow's and Nelson's conclusions depends upon the assumptions. Several of these assumptions need to be qualified in the light of intervening experience with the operation of the scientific system. The separation between scientific and technical knowledge production must be relaxed to consider the potential for complementarities between technological and scientific information. In other words, the progress of science may depend upon the advance of technology. The concept of a socially optimal amount of scientific information, therefore, cannot be separated from the decisions governing the production of technological knowledge. At first glance, this would seem to strengthen the Arrow and Nelson arguments. Greater outputs of scientific information will yield a more rapid rate of technological progress and, therefore, further strengthen scientific advance. The problem is that technological knowledge is not likely to be a public good that is freely available as an input into the production of new science. The asymmetry in access between scientific and technological knowledge provides a motive for linking scientific and technological research efforts and institutions.

Further evidence of the motives for linking scientific and technological research projects and organizations has been provided by scholars examining scientific laboratory experience. Collins (1982) notes the difficulty of replicating results based only upon published results. The replication of scientific knowledge, particularly at the early stages of new discoveries, may require the exchange of personnel as well as publication. It is certainly possible that the linkage between technological and scientific research is as important. The participation of corporations in scientific research and networks of researchers suggests further motives for linkages, such as the need to publish in scientific journals to gain effective access to the scientific community. If knowledge transfer problems are significant, existing channels for the publication of scientific information, for example, scientific journals, cannot be viewed as the solution to the problems of improving access to knowledge – linkages between research efforts and institutions need to be fostered.

The drawing of scientific and technological research into closer interaction suggests an alternative model for the science system, one based upon a 'network' of distributed knowledge. Some parts of this network may function effectively by employing the traditional social norms of 'open science', which emphasize that open disclosure is directly linked to the competition for scientific priority, the identification of the first discoverer of new scientific results (Dasgupta and David 1994). Other parts of the network may require the negotiation of exchange between those developing knowledge, either because they have not disclosed this information or because they are unable to disclose it effectively. While both types of networks are subject to the problems of market failure described by Arrow and Nelson, the 'negotiated access' part of the network is also subject to further market failures resulting from failures in coordination, transaction or knowledge discovery, that is, the identification of things worth knowing. These factors may be collectively termed 'scientific network failure'.

Analysing scientific network failure focuses attention on the scope of knowledge exchange and the possibilities of missing nodes or transfer agents that might bridge the parts of the network that do not regularly interact. It also suggests that some types of scientific knowledge may be exclusively exploited for a period of time by a limited number of participants. For example, if a particular line of scientific research, such as an investigation of the chemistry of proteins produced by the human endocrine system, is likely to have a specific applicability to the derivation of new pharmaceuticals it is conceivable that interested actors will identify each other and act either as an interest group supporting government funding for such research or as a 'club' to privately finance such research. To the extent that such clubs include all of the actors that might make use of such knowledge, the social welfare losses identified by Arrow and Nelson will not appear, even though the information that they produce does not circulate generally within society. The creation of such network structures serves a similar purpose to those served by intellectual property rights in that the costs of establishing them must somehow be recouped and passed on to those consuming the goods and services produced using the knowledge that the club produces or exchanges. In the search for ways to accomplish the aim of recouping the costs of network formation or the conduct of research, all of the traditional mechanisms of cartelization – restriction of membership, control of prices and output and monitoring of behaviour – are likely to be employed.

Gibbons et al. (1994) have suggested that the network of distributed scientific knowledge is a new mode for the operation of the scientific system and that it is in the process of displacing the traditional system in which universities and government research laboratories held a favoured position. It is possible to identify the creation of new organizational forms and methods of finance for the generation and distribution of scientific results. As yet, however, there is little systematic evidence for assessing the contributions of these new organizations to the knowledge base of science or their performance relative to older organizational forms. What does appear to be clear is that corporations, particularly the growing share of those that depend upon technological advances for sustaining their competitiveness and productivity improvement, are seeking wider and more effective access to a broader range of scientific and technological knowledge. In many cases, achieving this access may require active participation in scientific networks, both to support the interaction between their scientists and scientists working in public institutions and to provide better absorptive capacity for new knowledge (Cohen and Levinthal 1990).

The coexistence of a traditional public good and the newer network structure of science is the context that the contributors to this volume address. Each part takes up one of the primary questions posed by the evolving context in which science is funded and governed. The contributions in Part I further elaborate the evolving context of the policy environment focusing on the changing role of the university (Martin, Chapter 1), the challenges to existing structures of scientific expertise by extensions in the scientific network (Callon, Chapter 2) and the specific issues posed for network organization by the growing interdisciplinarity of research (Llerena and Meyer-Krahmer, Chapter 3). Commentaries by Pavitt and Wolfe challenge the contributors and extend the scope of the discussion.

In Part II, the changing relationships among actors are examined, principally using empirical research methods. Each of these contributions examines a piece of the larger puzzle, illustrating the scope of the new research that will be required to fully understand changes in the organization and performance of the science system. Both characterizing the changing nature of linkages between industrial and publicly funded research (Cohen, Nelson and Walsh, Chapter 4) and assessing their performance (Cesaroni and Gambardella, Chapter 7) are essential for understanding what may be expected. In addition, it is important to assess how the specificities of national context (Llerena, Matt and Schaeffer, Chapter 5) and the domain of scientific investigation (Riccaboni, Powell, Pammolli and Owen-Smith, Chapter 6) influence the evolving structure and performance of the science system. In their commentaries, Stephan and Steinmueller identify some of the key contributions and their limitations as well as identifying some of the unmet research needs in this area.

Part III develops the theory of the distributed knowledge system. The models developed in this part take up the new assumptions suggested by the network model of the science system and trace their implications for the design of collaborative alliances (David and Keely, Chapter 8) and the development of collaborative arrangements through individual initiative (Cowan and Jonard, Chapter 9). The pivotal role of new funding mechanisms is taken up for the cases of club good production (Swann, Chapter 10) and specific public programmes aimed at encouraging the formation of such clubs (Foray, Chapter 11). The commentaries of Antonelli and Hall extend the argument and identify further areas worthy of theoretical examination.

In the conclusion, we return to the overarching issues identified in this introduction and summarize some of the key findings in the chapters comprising this volume that are relevant to policy discussions, such as the emergence of the new European Research Area framework for guiding the next round of European Union funding for scientific and technological research.

REFERENCES

Arrow, K.J. (1962), 'Economic welfare and the allocation of resources for invention', in Richard R. Nelson (ed.), *The Rate and Direction of Inventive Activity*, National Bureau of Economic Research, Princeton, NJ: Princeton University Press, pp. 609–25.

Bush, V. (1945), *Science: The Endless Frontier: A Report to the President on a Program for Postwar Scientific Research*, Washington, DC: United States Office of Scientific Research and Development, National Science Foundation (reprint 1960).

Cohen, W. and D.A. Levinthal (1990), 'Absorptive capacity: a new perspective on learning and innovation', *Administrative Science Quarterly* **35**(1), 128–52.

Collins, M. (1982), 'Tacit knowledge and scientific networks', in B. Barnes and D. Edge (eds), *Science in Context: Readings in the Sociology of Science*, Cambridge, MA: MIT Press, pp. 44–64.

Dasgupta, P. and P.A. David (1994), 'Toward a new economics of science', *Research Policy* **97**(387), 487–521.

Gibbons, M., C. Limoges, H. Nowotny, S. Schwartzman, P. Scott and M. Trow (1994), *The New Production of Knowledge: The Dynamics of Science and Research in Contemporary Societies*, London: Sage.

Kuznets, S. (1966), *Modern Economic Growth: Rate, Structure and Spread*, New Haven, CT and London: Yale University Press.

Nelson, R.R. (1959), 'The simple economics of basic scientific research', *Journal of Political Economy* **67**(June), 297–306.

President's Council of Advisors on Science and Technology (2000), 'Wellspring of prosperity: science and technology in the US economy, www.ostp.gov/html/wellspring.pdf.

United Kingdom Council for Scientific Policy (1967), *Second Report on Science Policy Cmnd 3420*, London: HMSO.

PART I

The Evolving Research Policy Environment

Introduction

Science policy, in common with most other aspects of public choice, is the result of a multistage and interactive exchange between the processes of determining purposes and setting goals, defining programmes and implementing them, and reforming rules and evaluating outcomes. Each of these processes is, in the first instance, influenced by the localized politics of institutions and actors that are directly concerned with the organization and conduct of scientific research.

Throughout much of its history, the localized politics of scientific institutions and actors have been separated from the wider society. In the early history of science, this separation was maintained by societal disinterest or hostility towards scientific enterprise. In more recent times, the separation has been maintained by a series of social contracts in which scientists preserved a degree of independence and received a growing share of social resources in exchange for services rendered to the education, defence and health of their fellow citizens and to industry.

In discussing science as a social institution it is also natural to recall that the institution of 'patronage' played an important early role. Patronage continues to appeal to many scientists' desire for self-determination within a 'republic of science' whose institutions only partly overlap with those of the electoral democracies that have become the new patrons of science. Creating patronage for science, like other cultural institutions such as art and religion, involves appeals to aesthetic and ideological motivations. By adding claims of instrumental value, the republic of science has been able to expand well beyond the boundaries of charity.

Science's claims to instrumental value are the quid pro quo for the social contracts that have allowed it to expand. The first major expansion began in the nineteenth century with the creation of the Humboldt model. This model recognized the capacity of science to contribute to national prosperity and regional development when it was practised in a university setting that allowed the young to benefit from the scientific explorations of their elders and, to varying degrees, participate in these investigations. The second major expansion occurred following the Second World War, involving not only the dramatic increase in university enrolment, but also the commissioning of research in both universities and 'public' laboratories. This second expansion was foreshadowed by experiments in establishing public research institutions and in assigning specific research missions to universities, as early as the nineteenth century.

The history of the social contracts between science and government is the central theme of Ben Martin's (Chapter 1) examination, which focuses on the Humboldt model and the changing role of the university as the principal public research institution. Martin argues that the second expansion may be subject to retrenchment as the democratic institutions of society rebalance priorities between public investments. Moreover, he notes that the Humboldt model has not been, and need not be, the universal model for the public funding of universities. Instead, he argues that, from their earliest history, different species of universities have existed and that universities may find ways to adapt to a retrenchment of the second expansion of universities and even a gradual change away from the dominance of the Humboldt model. In doing so, a greater variety of university species is likely to emerge patterned on the liberal arts colleges of the US and the *grandes écoles* of France.

The Commentaries of Keith Pavitt and David Wolfe contest Martin's conclusions regarding a significant retrenchment from the second wave of university expansion. Both highlight the scale of the research enterprise that has been constructed in most of the Organisation for Economic Cooperation and Development (OECD) countries and the growing reliance on university research. Pavitt further questions whether the opinions that might lead to such a retrenchment are widely shared, attributing them instead to 'simplistic' views of public accountancy by government finance ministries. Pavitt and Wolfe both argue that universities have already achieved a central position in the knowledge-based economy as indicated both by the share of applied research that they conduct and by the continued enthusiasm of the larger companies for traditional models of university research. A substantial middle ground, in which major changes in the governance and funding of universities is possible, exists between the views of Martin and of Pavitt and Wolfe.

Michel Callon in Chapter 2 examines another facet of the republic of science, the question of who may qualify as a citizen of this republic. Callon contrasts the 'confined researcher' who has full citizenship rights and, more significantly, obligations with the 'researcher in the wild' who cannot endanger a citizenship that has never been granted. In a series of provocative examples, Callon reveals that researchers with full citizenship act not only to deny the scientific validity of non-citizen views, but also to deny them a voice in scientific debates.

These examples serve to highlight the potential for crisis in the governance of science. The legitimacy of science relies upon the perception that it has not been captured and confined by special interests. Public opinion surveys reveal that society retains a high level of trust in scientists relative to other professions. In part, this is the consequence of the perceived autonomy of scientists. If this autonomy is being employed to deny the values of open inquiry that scientists espouse as a tenet of their profession, this trust is likely to evaporate.

A common fear of opening scientific discourse to more voices is that these voices will mislead or distort understandings that require a systematic grounding in the methods and findings of science. As many historians of science have demonstrated, however, the construction of scientific consensus involves the suppression of contesting views. The uncomfortable conclusion of Callon's argument is that this process of suppression may also serve to de-legitimize and marginalize needed sources of variety in the discourse. The misleading conclusions and the distorted understandings thereby become the outcomes of the scientific discourse rather than what science dispels.

The third chapter in this part, by Patrick Llerena and Frieder Meyer-Krahmer, examines the changing geography of the republic of science. According to their argument the republic of science was once populated by disciplinary city-states whose walls provided safe havens for the production and circulation of knowledge. In recent years, however, the fields lying between these walls have proved to be more productive than the shops within the walls. One might then expect a migration outwards from disciplinary boundaries into the new interdisciplinary fields where opportunities await exploitation. In observations that recollect Callon's evocation of the 'confined' researcher, however, this migration is impeded by the existing systems for evaluating researcher's contributions and organizing research efforts.

Llerena and Meyer-Krahmer's chapter offers persuasive evidence for the proposition that interdisciplinary fields have become a major source of scientific discovery. Exploiting their potential, however, involves more than the individual researcher seeking to tap it. It is necessary to assemble researchers with distinct competencies and to establish a new discourse between them. This can only be done, they argue, through institutional reforms that allow more flexible organization of research. In their case study of University Louis Pasteur (ULP) in Strasbourg, one of the most important institutional reforms is restructuring the linkage between teaching and research. This is accomplished at ULP by offering new courses of study at the postgraduate level and by systematically introducing students to the values and processes of interdisciplinary research in their postgraduate training.

The reforms that Llerena and Meyer-Krahmer describe have important implications for the organization and governance of research. They highlight the importance of changing the criteria by which researcher performance is evaluated if disciplinary boundaries are to be overcome. They also indicate that interdisciplinary research involves the construction of new institutions that may need to be above a threshold size to achieve success. Assuming these conclusions are accurate, they have far-reaching consequences for the structure of funding of university research efforts.

The chapters in Part I share a common theme in considering the constraints that govern scientific enterprise. For Martin, these constraints arise from changes in the funding priorities of the state accompanied by growing demands to expand the delivery of teaching. These changes compel universities to evolve by making strategic choices within the constraints under which they must operate. For Callon, the constraints of central interest are those that the scientific establishment creates for itself by regulating the legitimacy of competing voices. Failing to mitigate these constraints may undermine the authority and trust that science holds in public opinion. For Llerena and Meyer-Krahmer, the constraints are the disciplinary rigidities that were erected to encourage rigour and to support the evaluation of researcher performance. In each of the chapters, however, it is also possible to see opportunities for responding to these constraints and this is their greatest contribution.

1. The changing social contract for science and the evolution of the university

Ben R. Martin

1 INTRODUCTION

According to some (for example, Ziman 1991, 1994, 2000; Pelikan 1992), science and the university are under threat. As we move towards a more knowledge-intensive society, academics face pressures to link their work more closely to the needs of the economy and society with (it is feared) potentially adverse long-term consequences for scientific research and for the university. This has been characterized (for example, by Guston and Keniston 1994a) as a fundamental change in the 'social contract' between science and the university, on the one hand, and the state, on the other, with the latter now having much more specific expectations regarding the outputs sought from the former in return for public funding. Others (Gibbons et al. 1994) have described it in terms of a transition from 'Mode 1' to 'Mode 2' knowledge production. This chapter argues that, if one adopts a longer-term historical perspective, then what we are witnessing appears to be not so much the appearance of a new (and hence potentially worrying) phenomenon, but more a shift back towards a social contract closer to the one in effect for much of the period before the second half of the twentieth century.

In what follows, we first consider previous versions of the social contract, in particular those embodied in the Humboldt university model and the contract set out by Vannevar Bush in 1945. After analysing the global driving forces subjecting the social contract to change, we examine the revised contract emerging over recent years. We identify some key questions that have been raised about these changes and their possible implications for science and universities. To answer these, we consider the process of historical evolution of universities, including the emergence of different 'species' of university reflecting their differing functions, ethos and relations with the surrounding environment.[1]

As we shall see, for much of the history of modern science, funds have been provided with a clear expectation that the work will result in specific benefits. Only for a period of a few decades after the Second World War was this former social contract relaxed, when governments were prepared to invest in science with much less precise and immediate expectations as to the eventual benefits. That period is now apparently ending.

2 HISTORY OF THE SOCIAL CONTRACT

The Humboldt Social Contract

While it is perhaps conventional to begin by focusing on the Vannevar Bush social contract which held sway for most of the second half of the twentieth century, it is worth looking first at the earlier social contract embodied in the Humboldt university model. In this, government assumed primary responsibility for funding the university (in contrast with earlier *ad hoc* funding arrangements). However, the key characteristic of the Humboldt model was the unity of teaching and research – the assumption that both functions had to be conducted within the same institution.

The Humboldt model subsequently spread from Germany to many other countries in the nineteenth and twentieth centuries – but not to all. In France, for example, universities and particularly the *grandes écoles* continued to concentrate on teaching while much of the academic research was carried out elsewhere in laboratories of organizations such as the Centre National de la Recherche Scientifique (CNRS) and the Institut National de la Santé et de la Recherche Médicale (INSERM) (see Schimank and Winnes 2000). The separation of teaching and research was even more pronounced in Eastern Europe. Nevertheless, by the second half of the twentieth century, there was a widespread belief among academics and others that the unity of teaching and research was essential to the university and to scientific knowledge production.

The Humboldt social contract, despite the reliance on the state for funding, was characterized by a high level of autonomy for both individuals and institutions. Academics were free to engage in research (typically spending 30–50 per cent of their time on this) and they were also free to choose their research topic. At the institutional level, in European countries (and some others but not the United States) governments provided general institutional funding for both teaching and research, leaving the university free to determine the allocation of resources across disciplines.

The Vannevar Bush Social Contract

The social contract that ran from 1945 to approximately the end of the 1980s is generally linked to Vannevar Bush and his 1945 report, *Science: The Endless Frontier*. A succession of scientific discoveries in the first half of the twentieth century together with several prominent applications of science during the Second World War gave rise to a belief in a simple linear 'science-push' model of innovation, beginning with basic research, leading on to applied research, then technological development and finally innovation. This model was set out in the Bush report.[2] The clear implication of the model was that, if government put money into the basic research end of the chain, out from the other end of the chain would eventually come benefits in terms of wealth, health and national security, although exactly what form those benefits would take and when they would materialize was unpredictable.

The linear model had the great merit of simplicity (even politicians could understand it!) as well as obvious financial convenience – it furnished a ready case for getting money out of governments.[3] It also implied that few 'strings' should be attached to the public funds provided to basic researchers, leaving them with considerable autonomy.

The social contract for the post-war period can be described as follows: 'Government promises to fund the basic science that peer reviewers find most worthy of support, and scientists promise that the research will be performed well and honestly and will provide a steady stream of discoveries that can be translated into new products, medicines or weapons' (Guston and Keniston 1994a, p. 2).

There were thus several essential characteristics of the Bush social contract. First, it implied a high level of autonomy for science. Second, decisions on which areas of science should be funded should be left to scientists. It therefore brought about the institutionalization of the peer-review system to allocate resources, a system used before the Second World War by private foundations that supported research. Third, it was premised on the belief that basic research was best done in universities (rather than government or company laboratories).

The Bush social contract proved very successful in the decades after 1945, especially in the United States. It contributed to large increases in government funding for science,[4] in the number of trained scientists and in research outputs (for example, publications in scientific journals).

3   GLOBAL DRIVING FORCES FOR CHANGE

Some time around the late 1980s (but perhaps slightly earlier in the UK and the US) we began to see the emergence of a revised social contract replacing that set in place by Vannevar Bush (Guston 2000). In this section, we consider the main forces bringing about that change.

One that was particularly important in the US was the end of the Cold War, resulting in a greatly reduced need for research in physical sciences and engineering. A related factor with similar consequences was dwindling enthusiasm for nuclear energy.[5] However, three factors that have been more global in their impact are increasing competition, constraints on public expenditure and the growing importance of scientific competencies.

Increasing Competition

We live in an ever-more competitive world.[6] Over the last 10–15 years, many more market-economy 'players' have emerged – in Asia, Eastern Europe, Latin America and elsewhere – greatly increasing the level of economic competition. Moreover, there are huge variations in labour costs (for example, by a factor of 100 or more between Germany and China) at a time when the process of globalization means that firms can much more easily shift resources and production between countries to benefit from lower costs or other local resources.

For industrialized countries, the key to success lies in continuous innovation to improve productivity and competitiveness. Consequently, new technologies such as information and communication technologies and biotechnology are becoming more important. These are heavily dependent on basic research for their development and exploitation, giving rise to the notion of the knowledge-based economy (for example, Stehr 1994), which in turn has led to pressures on science and on universities to help deliver that knowledge-based economy. Science is becoming more of a strategic competitive resource that nations believe they have to use to maximum advantage. Governments therefore need to have more explicit science policies. The open-ended Vannevar Bush social contract is hence no longer appropriate.

Constraints on Public Expenditure

At the same time, governments in many countries have been experiencing significant public expenditure constraints as they attempt to balance their budgets. Those constraints are likely to grow over time for various reasons including the ageing population and increasing costs of – and rising expectations concerning – health care, education and social welfare.[7] This trend is creating demands for greater accountability and for better 'value for money' from all areas of government spending, including that on science and universities. Consequently, assessment has become much more common (Geuna and Martin 2002).

Because of these expenditure constraints and the growing cost of research and development, no government can afford to do everything in science and technology, not even the richest. Governments now realize that they must be more selective – they must have explicit policies and clearer priorities for science. Choices have to be made. In the past, those choices tended to be made tacitly – they just 'emerged' from the policy process. Many governments now, however, are seeking to devise more systematic procedures for priority setting in relation to science and technology – for example, through technology foresight exercises (Martin and Irvine 1989; Martin 1995). Again, this runs counter to the Vannevar Bush social contract.

Increasing Importance of Scientific and Technological Competencies

A third key driver, closely linked to the first, is the increasing importance of scientific and technological competencies in the form of both knowledge and skills. This is certainly not a new trend. Over the latter part of the twentieth century, there has been a vast expansion of higher education – by a factor of 10 or more in terms of student numbers in many countries (see, for example, Mitchell 1992, pp. 881–3). Over the 1990s, however, scientific and technological knowledge has become even more of a strategic resource for companies and countries as well as for improving the quality of life. Scientific and technological skills or expertise are also becoming of ever-greater importance in relation to wealth creation and improvements in the quality of life. Here, matters are complicated by the fact that new technologies not only demand new skills; they also make old skills obsolete (arguably, at an increasing rate). This points to the need for continuous learning, with a shift away from the notion that the individual is educated only in the first 20 years or so of life to one of 'lifetime learning', a shift in which new technologies can make a major contribution.

The demand for new skills on the part of an ever-increasing proportion of the population to enhance their competitiveness in job markets underlies the determination of governments in many industrialized countries to shift from a relatively elitist system of higher education (HE) to a mass HE system. However, this raises a fundamental policy question. While governments may be willing to pay for large increases in HE teaching, are they prepared to pay for similar increases in the scale of academic research? If not, the inevitable consequence is either that not all academics or HE institutions can continue to do research, or that academics on average will spend less time on research and correspondingly more on teaching than previously. In either case, the end result is to break or substantially weaken a central aspect of the Humboldt social contract.

4   THE REVISED SOCIAL CONTRACT

These various forces for change mean that some time around the end of the 1980s (the exact timing varying across countries) saw the beginnings of a shift in the social contract for science and universities (Guston and Keniston 1994a, 1994b; de la Mothe and Halliwell 1997; Martin and Etzkowitz 2001). Faced with increasing competition and tighter financial constraints, governments now expect more specific benefits in return for continued investments in scientific research and in universities. In the case of the US, this revised contract has been described by a leading congressional figure in science policy as follows: 'The scientific community must seek to establish a new contract with policy makers based not on demands for autonomy and ever increasing funds, but on the implementation of an explicit research agenda rooted in [social] goals' (Brown 1992, quoted in Guston and Keniston 1994a, pp. 6–7). In other words, under the revised social contract there is a clear expectation that, in return for public funds, scientists and universities should address the needs of 'users' in the economy and society. They are also subject to much more explicit accountability for the money they receive.[8] In addition, implicit in the new contract is a more complex model of science and innovation than the previous linear model, unfortunately making it harder to persuade politicians of the merits of increasing public spending on research!

An alternative way of interpreting these changes is the Mode 2 thesis.[9] In an influential analysis of the changing nature of knowledge production in universities and elsewhere, Gibbons et al. (1994) have argued that we are witnessing a shift from Mode 1 to Mode 2. Mode 1 involves new knowledge being produced primarily within individual disciplines, mainly in universities and other academic institutes. There is little direct connection to societal needs and the results of the research are transferred at the end of the project to users who may or may not take up those results. There is also only fairly limited societal accountability required from those engaged in research; the obverse of this is that there is a considerable degree of autonomy for scientists to choose the problems on which to work.

Mode 2, by contrast, generally involves multi- or transdisciplinary research carried out in a growing variety of institutions (that is, not just universities) and with a blurring of the boundaries between the traditional sectors (university, industry, and so on) and also between science and society (Nowotny et al. 2001). Knowledge is increasingly being produced 'in the context of application' – in other words, with societal needs having a direct influence from an early stage and with relatively explicit social accountability for the funding received from government. In its strongest form, the claim of Gibbons et al. 'is that we are now seeing fundamental changes in the ways in which scientific, social and cultural knowledge is produced. . . . [T]his trend marks a distinct shift towards a *new* mode of knowledge production which is replacing or reforming established institutions, disciplines, practices and policies'.[10]

The implication here is that Mode 2 is new. However, Gibbons et al. are somewhat less convincing in terms of putting forward systematic evidence for such a new phenomenon (compare Weingart 1997; Godin 1998). As we shall see later, it is perhaps better to characterize this not so much in terms of the appearance of something new in the form of Mode 2, but rather a shift in the balance between the already existing forms of Mode 1 and Mode 2. Furthermore, while there has perhaps been relatively more Mode 2 taking place towards the end of the twentieth century than in previous decades, we may be merely returning to a balance between the two modes exhibited in earlier eras (compare Pestre 1997; Weingart 1997; Shinn 2000).

These various discussions about the future of science and the university raise a number of questions, which the remainder of this chapter will try to address.

- Are science and universities becoming more closely linked to societal needs? Or are we merely reverting to the situation of an earlier era?
- Is there more Mode 2 research now and, if so, compared with when?
- Is the social contract changing and, if so, compared with when? Is basic research under threat?
- Will the university survive in its current form? Is it threatened by new entrants?
- How great a threat is the separation of research and teaching in universities? Will the university remain a multifunction institution?
- Will science and universities become more central in the knowledge economy? If so, at what cost (if any) to their autonomy?

To address these questions, we consider an evolutionary model of the university, examining how it has adapted over time to its changing environment. Such a model may help us assess more systematically the prospects for the university and science in coming years.

5   ON THE ORIGIN AND EVOLUTION OF THE UNIVERSITY 'SPECIES'

Evolving Functions and Ethos of the University

Let us go back to the beginning – to the medieval university. Originally, this had two functions: teaching priests, public servants, lawyers and so on; and scholarship in a variety of disciplines (biblical, classical, medical, and so on). Over time, as the societal environment changed, so those functions evolved. With regard to teaching, there emerged two relatively distinct types of educational function, one being to develop the full potential of the individual student, the other to produce trained people with knowledge and skills useful to society, be they priests, administrators, physicians or whatever. Scholarship also evolved with two fairly fundamental changes. The first was that scholarship was broadened to include the creation of new knowledge – in other words 'research' – as well as the re-analysis and synthesis of existing knowledge. Second, a distinction emerged between two types of research – knowledge 'for its own sake' as opposed to knowledge to meet the needs of society.

These changes in the function of the university and its surrounding environment[11] were reflected in the emergence of different varieties and ultimately different 'species' of university. First, the medieval university was gradually transformed, emerging in Germany, for example, as the Humboldt university and in Britain as the Cardinal Newman university. The European model was later transferred to other countries, appearing in the United States as the 'Ivy League' university and in Japan as the imperial (and subsequently the national) university. Although there are significant variations between these national models (or 'varieties' to use Darwinian terminology), they can be treated as a single 'species', henceforth referred to as the 'classical university'.

Later on saw the appearance in Europe of a second species variously termed the technical college (or 'high school' or university), the institute of (science and) technology or the polytechnic. Again, this model was later transferred to the United States, Japan and elsewhere. While covering quite a range of 'varieties', these can likewise be grouped together as a single species, which we shall subsequently refer to as the 'technical university'.

Implicit in the 'classical' and the 'technical' university are two quite distinct conceptions of the nature and purpose of the university. According to the first, which might be termed the pure or 'immaculate' conception, the purpose of the university is education and knowledge 'for its own sake'. Set against this is the instrumental or utilitarian ethos of the 'technical university', according to which the role of the university is to create and disseminate useful knowledge and to train students with skills useful to society.

These rival conceptions were perhaps implicit from the start within the medieval university (compare Geuna 1998). However, over time the tensions between them led, in a process akin to speciation, to the emergence of two species, the classical and the technical university. In the former, with the Cardinal Newman version one had the 'ivory tower' of independent scholars producing knowledge for its own sake and passing it on to students to enable them to develop their full potential. In the Humboldt version were the additional features of the integration of teaching and research, and dependence on the state for funding.

As regards the technical university species, one of the earliest examples was the École Polytechnique set up to provide training for engineers and to meet the military needs of France. Besides subsequent *grandes écoles*, other examples include the technical 'high schools' in Germany and Switzerland, and the institutes of science and technology in Britain at Manchester and Imperial College, London. As noted above, this species was later transferred to other countries including the United States (with the formation of institutes such as Rennsselaer Polytechnic Institute, Massachusetts Institute of Technology [MIT] and Caltech), Italy (for instance, the polytechnics in Milan and Turin) and Japan (for example, the Tokyo Institute of Technology).

Although these have been the two main species of university, other relatively distinct species have emerged. For example, in the second half of the nineteenth century a new species[12] was created in the United States – the so-called 'land-grant' university – which was set up explicitly to meet regional needs, initially agricultural but later on industrial needs more generally. Other members of this 'regional university' species include the regional colleges in Europe which are seen as an 'engine' for the development of a region, especially economic and industrial development but perhaps also cultural (for example, in Sweden).[13] Another example of a new species is the Open University created in the UK in the 1960s and later copied in other countries, in which students receive most of their education at a distance.

In addition, the United States witnessed the creation of various hybrids. For example, Cornell University was set up as a cross between the Ivy League and the land-grant university. It should also be noted that not all universities took on a research function; in several countries, 'teaching only' institutions coexisted with 'full' universities combining teaching with research (and sometimes with research-only institutions). Examples of the 'teaching university' species include *grandes écoles* in France, *Fachhochschulen* in Germany, the former polytechnics in Britain, and the so-called 'liberal arts' colleges (although many teach science as well as humanities) in the United States.[14]

Coevolution of Different University Species

Within each national environmental 'niche', there have normally been two or more species of universities coexisting. In Germany, for example, the Humboldt universities coexisted with technical universities and *Fachhochschulen*. In France, there were universities and *grandes écoles*, and in Britain universities and institutes of science and technology and later polytechnics. In the United States, there was even more variety with Ivy League universities, land-grant universities, institutes of technology and 'liberal arts' colleges, not to mention hybrids like Cornell. In Japan, three types of university – national, prefectural (that is, state government) and private – have coexisted.[15] In each of those countries, there has been continuous tension between the rival ideologies, this tension being especially pronounced in the United States in the latter part of the nineteenth century. Eventually, the pure ethos came to dominate in the early part of the twentieth century, particularly in the prestigious institutions of North America and Europe. As Rosenberg and Nelson (1994, p. 338) observe: '[A]fter World War II . . . [there] was a shift of academic research toward the basic end of the spectrum and the development of a strong belief, at least in academia, that basic research is the proper role of the university'.

Yet although Mode 1 became the more prominent form of knowledge production in most universities, or at least the one accorded most visibility in the prevailing academic ethos, there was still much Mode 2 knowledge production taking place during this time. In the US, for example, over the second half of the twentieth century the great majority of research in universities was funded by the mission-oriented agencies such as the Departments of Defense, Energy and Agriculture, the National Institutes of Health and the National Aeronautics and Space Administration (NASA) rather than the basic research agency, the National Science Foundation (NSF).[16] This research was closely linked to meeting societal needs in the defence, energy, agriculture, health and space sectors. It was conducted not only in 'technical universities' but also in Ivy League as well as land-grant universities. Nevertheless, in the ideology of academic science that came to dominate during this time, the emphasis was very much on Mode 1 knowledge production and the pure or immaculate conception of the university.

6   RELATIONS AND TENSIONS BETWEEN FUNCTIONS

Teaching–Research Symbiosis – Reality or Convenient Myth?

For many, an essential feature of the university is the integration of teaching and research. Since the time of Humboldt, it has become conventional wisdom, even an article of faith, that research and teaching have to take place within the same institution. Yet there is surprisingly little rigorous evidence to support this belief, at least in relation to teaching at the undergraduate level[17] (Johnston et al. 1993; Schimank and Winnes 2000). According to the traditional rationale, there are mutual benefits between teaching and research. On the one side, in order to provide up-to-date teaching, lecturers need to be at the forefront of their research field. On the other, it is argued that teaching keeps lecturers broad in their interests; if they are not teaching, there is a danger that concentration on research may result in them becoming ever more specialized while the broadening influence of teaching may provide a positive stimulus to their research. There is some circumstantial evidence at both the individual and the institutional levels to support this conventional justification for having teaching and research combined in one institution. There is also evidence of the dangers of not combining the two – especially from the academy institutes in Eastern Europe where the lack of involvement in teaching may have been one factor that contributed to many of them becoming rather stagnant research institutions.

However, there are also prominent counterexamples of leading institutions where research and teaching are not combined. There are numerous excellent research-only institutes like the Max Planck institutes, CNRS laboratories, Medical Research Council laboratories in the UK and the US National Institutes of Health. Likewise, there are some very good 'teaching universities' such as the French *grandes écoles* and US 'liberal arts' colleges (although some of these have developed a research capability over the years).

Consequently, it is perhaps more productive to view the combination of undergraduate teaching[18] and research as a relationship that brings both benefits (in the form of synergy) and costs (if one is devoting time and energy to teaching, there is less of both of these for research, and vice versa) with some tension between them. In some circumstances the benefits may outweigh the costs, but in others they may not. One cannot automatically assume that the benefits of combining teaching and research will always be greater than the costs, as the conventional ideology of academic science would maintain. Nor is it essential that undergraduate teaching and scientific research should always be combined in higher education institutions. If it were, then one might have expected *all* 'liberal arts' colleges in the United States to evolve over time from teaching-only institutions to research universities as the volume of research funding available from the government grew. However, many have deliberately chosen to remain teaching universities, demonstrating that good quality undergraduate education does not depend on the existence of research.

The Two Traditional Functions (Teaching and Research) versus the 'Third Mission'

Next, let us consider the relationship between the two traditional functions of the university – teaching and research – and the 'third mission' of contributing to the economy, which has become more prominent under the revised social contract of the last decade. Here, the conventional academic ideology is that this third function may damage both teaching – through an overemphasis on short-term specific skill needs as opposed to a broader education – and also research – because of an overemphasis on short-term applied research to the detriment of long-term basic research.

Again, there is little rigorous systematic evidence for or against this belief. There is certainly some anecdotal evidence to support it but also some running counter to it. For example, in the case of teaching, at French *grandes écoles* where teaching is geared to such specific skills as civil engineering or administration, these institutions nevertheless provide a high-quality education that remains useful to the students over many years. As regards research, technical universities such as Aachen, Imperial College and Zurich have been engaged for many decades in research that addressed the needs of society but that has not apparently damaged their ability to conduct high-quality basic research. Likewise, leading US universities funded by the Department of Defense and the National Institutes of Health to carry out research aimed at meeting national needs in relation to defence and health have been responsible for some of the best basic research.

Moreover, it is not just in the twentieth century that the third mission of contributing to the economy and society has coexisted within universities with teaching and research. Indeed, towards the end of the nineteenth century, the third function was perhaps even more pronounced than it is today (Etzkowitz 1997, pp. 141–3). For example, in German universities (and later at the turn of the century in Japanese universities), engineering departments worked closely with companies in the mechanical, civil, chemical and subsequently the electrical engineering sectors, often effectively acting as research laboratories for new companies with their research results being directly applicable to innovative products. This does not appear to have greatly curtailed their ability to conduct basic research.

In Britain and France, leading physicists such as Lord Kelvin and Marie Curie spent up to half their time working on industrial problems (see Pestre 1997), without apparently adversely affecting their basic research. In the United States, in the case of the land-grant universities, the 'social contract' embodied in the 1862 Morill Act involved giving them land in return for supporting the development of agriculture and the mechanic arts (Rosenberg and Nelson 1994, p. 325); again, this does not seem to have affected their ability to carry out basic research or to provide high-quality teaching. Indeed, many land-grant universities went on to become leading universities of the twentieth century.

Nor was the late nineteenth century atypical. Since the emergence of modern science, research funding (whether from monarchs, wealthy patrons, governments or companies) has often been linked with the expectations of benefits, for example, in the form of new or improved weapons, more accurate nautical almanacs (based on improved astronomical observations), better medical care and agriculture, improved engines, new chemicals and materials, new energy sources, new electrical devices and so on. Indeed, historians and sociologists of science have found few instances where expectations of economic or social benefits were not influential in shaping science (for example, Merton 1938).

In short, there is little convincing historical evidence that an emphasis on helping to meet the needs of society and the economy necessarily results in adverse long-term consequences for universities or scientific research.[19] Again, it is perhaps best to view the linking of university teaching and scientific research with addressing economic and societal needs as something that brings both benefits and costs. In some circumstances, the benefits may be outweighed by the costs, in others the reverse may be true as the examples listed above suggest. Furthermore, there may be differences across fields, resulting in more benefits and hence more emphasis on the external effects of research within technical and medical sciences than in natural and social sciences and humanities.[20]

7 SOME TENTATIVE CONCLUSIONS

Are Science and Universities Becoming More Closely Linked to Societal Needs? Or Are We Merely Reverting to the Situation in an Earlier Era?

Let us now attempt to provide some tentative conclusions to the questions set out earlier, the first of which concerns whether science and universities are becoming more closely linked to societal needs. This analysis has suggested that in many countries there has been a shift in the balance compared with the period from 1945 to the late 1980s when the relationship between the university teaching and research, on the one hand, and the needs of society, on the other, was weaker and less direct.[21] However, even during that period the links with societal needs were not as insubstantial as the dominant academic ideology might suggest. As we have noted, during the post-war period a large proportion of government-funded research in the United States and elsewhere was funded by mission-oriented agencies. Within classical as well as technical universities, much of the research was explicitly funded to address societal needs (compare Etzkowitz et al. 2000, p. 318), even though the rhetoric of that time suggested that autonomy was all-important to the university and to scientific research.

Nevertheless, as we have seen, there has been a shift over the last decade or so in the way in which science and universities are funded. One danger is that this will lead to an eventual decline in social welfare, with the welfare of future generations being sacrificed for current consumption. How significant is such a threat? This chapter has argued that since 1990 the situation has in several respects become much more similar to that prevailing in the late nineteenth century, with many universities taking up more explicitly the third mission of contributing to technological development, innovation, the economy and society more generally. Just as science and universities survived and indeed thrived under these challenges a century ago, so they should be able to adapt to their new and more central role in the knowledge-based economy and to take advantage of the opportunities that this brings without sacrificing their autonomy (compare Benner and Sandstrom 2000; Pearson 2000).

However, there is an important caveat here – namely that the changes to the financial and policy environment in which universities are embedded should be gradual and incremental. With marginal changes in the environment, robust organisms prevail. In contrast, more profound environmental changes induce biological stress in evolutionary systems and often cause irreversible changes that increase the vulnerability of species.[22] Policies pursued in relation to science and universities should therefore perhaps reflect the precautionary principle advocated in relation to policies affecting natural ecological systems.

Is There Now More Mode 2 Research than Previously? Compared with When?

One important characteristic of Mode 2 research is its multi- or transdisciplinary nature. In relation to this, we need to remember that there have always been multi- and interdisciplinary research activities. Science is a dynamic system consisting of both established disciplines and emerging interdisciplinary areas. What starts off as a new multi- or interdisciplinary area may over time evolve into a recognized discipline. There are numerous historical examples of this, for example experimental psychology emerging from a combination of anatomy and physiology with philosophy, or the formation of biochemistry from biology and chemistry. Cognitive science is a more recent example arising from a combination of several fields including psychology, philosophy, linguistics and computer science to form a new discipline. This continuous creation of new disciplines from interdisciplinary research activities has always been going on.

Likewise, research that is carried out 'in the context of application' (a second key characteristic of Mode 2 research) has always been present within universities, in particular in universities in Germany and the United States at the end of the nineteenth century. Similarly, there has always been some blurring of institutional boundaries, a third Mode 2 characteristic. The US land-grant university was set up to provide an agricultural extension service to farmers as well as to carry out the traditional tasks of teaching and research. Such blurring of institutional boundaries may be more common or more pronounced in the case of technical and medical sciences than in the natural sciences.

Nevertheless, during the twentieth century and particularly after 1945, Mode 1 came to be seen in academic ideology as the 'normal' form of knowledge production while Mode 2 was viewed as a less central or even 'deviant' form of research that posed dangers to the university as an institution. That period is now ending. Yet, while there may be more Mode 2 research today than during the period from 1945 to the late 1980s, the level is not necessarily greater than a century earlier.

Is the Social Contract for Science Changing? Compared with When? Is Basic Research under Threat?

As with the previous question, the answer would appear to be, 'Yes, the contract is changing but only compared with the period from 1945 to the late 1980s'. This then raises another question of whether that post-war period was merely a temporary and, in historical terms, comparatively brief phase. One possible interpretation, for example, is that the relative generosity of the state towards science and the willingness to provide funds to researchers without too many strings attached represented a reward to scientists for their contributions in helping to wage and to win the Second World War (for instance, for their work on the atom bomb, radar, penicillin, operations research and code breaking).

There are, of course, other historical factors at work. In particular, during the twentieth century, the assumption that the public and private spheres were separate was at its height. That assumption is now being displaced by a model of overlapping spheres (compare Etzkowitz et al. 2000), with several activities that in the twentieth century were viewed as solely government responsibilities now being organized on a joint public–private basis. In the case of science and of universities, this trend is reflected in the growing importance of patents (part public, part private), incubators for start-up firms, university 'spinoffs' and so on (ibid.).

However, such changes should not necessarily be seen as threatening to science. The history of modern science shows that many of the most important advances have come from work characterized by Stokes (1997) as falling within 'Pasteur's Quadrant' – that is, research that is *both* concerned with addressing some societal need and at the same time essentially fundamental in nature. In this respect, the traditional categorization of research as either 'basic' or 'applied' is misleading; it implies that research that is in some way linked to an application cannot also be basic in nature, in turn suggesting (erroneously) that greater concentration of effort on the former can only be at the expense of basic research.

Will the University Survive in its Current Form? Is it Threatened by New Entrants?

One of the questions to be considered is whether the university is under such severe threat that one must ask whether it has a future in its current form. In the light of this brief historical review, it is clear that the university has proved remarkably adaptable over the course of its long history. The environment in which it has operated has been in constant flux. There have always been new entrants – former technical colleges, further education colleges, more recently the Open University and other distance-learning institutions. However, universities have managed to evolve – to adapt to the changing environment and to new competition, perhaps by shifting the emphasis between their functions, perhaps by embracing new functions, occasionally even forming a new species. Indeed, they are so adaptable that there have been very few instances of the 'death' of a university.[23] Universities reproduce but they very rarely die!

Given this adaptability, we would expect the university to survive (compare Barnett 2000) but in some cases to take on new or modified forms – that is, new species or hybrids. One new factor here is the development of information and communication technologies. These are likely to lower substantially the barriers to entry confronting new entrants to the higher education sector, leading to more hybrids and more blurring of institutional boundaries and perhaps also to new species. Overall, we therefore expect to see far greater variety across higher education institutions. First, we shall continue to see general universities combining teaching and research. Second, there will be new hybrids – perhaps a hybrid of the traditional 'bricks and mortar' university with the Open University delivering a large proportion of its higher education at a distance, the so-called 'bricks and clicks' university.[24]

Third, there will be specialized universities, in particular teaching-only institutions although those may be the ones that prove most vulnerable to new entrants from the commercial sector. Research-only universities are also possible – some in the US are now almost research-only institutions.

Fourth, there will be new entrants. New private universities are beginning to emerge in Europe, particularly in Central and Eastern Europe but also in Germany (Pearson 2000). There are also likely to be more 'no frills' universities like Phoenix University, adopting the philosophy of the supermarket to 'pile them high, sell them cheap'. Commercial publishers and software companies are becoming involved in 'e-universities', and some consultancies are developing research and teaching capabilities which they may subsequently package and offer to others outside the company. There will probably also be more company universities; already certain large firms in the United States and Britain (for example, British Aerospace) have decided that the skill and training needs of their employees are so extensive and perhaps so specific that it is more effective to provide them through their own 'university' rather than using traditional universities.

A fifth possible development is the networked university, involving either vertical integration of further education colleges with a university to form an integrated supply chain, or horizontal integration of similar departments across several institutions working together and linked electronically. There may also be closer integration with research institutes like the Fraunhofer institutes and perhaps also the integration of some universities with consultancies to form another possible hybrid. A related possibility is growing numbers of mergers and acquisitions. Already in London, University College London (UCL) and Imperial College have taken over most of the previously freestanding medical research institutes. Likewise in Sweden, the Karolinska University in Stockholm, as part of a 'network' strategy to enhance its critical mass, has taken over nursing, social work and other professional schools across Sweden.

Lastly, we shall see the spread of the 'entrepreneurial university' species predicted by Etzkowitz (1997, 2002) – that is, institutions giving considerable emphasis to the third function of contributing to the economy as well as to teaching and research.

How Great a Threat is the Separation of Research and Teaching in Universities? Will the University Remain a Multifunction Institution?

As we have noted, there has always been a degree of separation between undergraduate teaching and research in some academic institutions. Consequently, to argue that such a separation represents 'the end of civilization as we know it', as some academics have implied, is to exaggerate the dangers. Most universities may remain multifunctional but certainly not all of them. Some may choose to focus primarily on undergraduate education (as many did during the twentieth century or earlier), some largely on research and graduate education. Others may embrace the third function of making more direct economic contributions and thereby become entrepreneurial universities. One relevant factor here is the apparently decreasing time lag between the creation and use of knowledge. This may encourage the convergence of certain 'classical' and 'technical' universities, swelling the population of the 'entrepreneurial university' species in which are combined the functions of knowledge creation, knowledge transfer (particularly through trained students) and knowledge exploitation – that is, the integration of the three functions of teaching, research and contributing to the economy.

However, it is important to restress the caveat set out in the section entitled 'Are science and universities becoming more closely linked to societal needs' above regarding incremental changes compared with more radical transformations. In the light of this as well as the limited and ambiguous evidence on the relationship between teaching and research, there is some merit in governments adopting a precautionary principle with regard to policies that affect that relationship. It is possible that the shift to give greater emphasis to research addressing societal needs may ultimately come to prove a 'government failure', the consequences of which, as with other public investments, may unfortunately take time to be revealed.

Will Science and Universities Become More Central in the Knowledge Society? At What Cost to Autonomy?

The analysis presented here suggests that the university will become more central as the economy and society become more reliant on knowledge. It will be responsible for generating not only intellectual but also economic and social capital. As we have seen in recent decades, many of the most successful innovative regions in North America and Europe have included entrepreneurial universities as an essential component (Pearson 2000, pp. 9–10). In coming decades, the university is likely to become an ever-more important ingredient in building the knowledge-based economy.

Will this come at the price of reduced autonomy? Benner and Sandstrom (2000) have considered this issue from the perspective of neo-institutionalist theory. They describe and contrast the two models by which university research has previously been funded. The 'autonomy model' is exemplified by the traditional research council emphasizing scientific quality, an international orientation and academic initiatives, reinforced by collegial reputational control and an orientation towards basic research. In contrast, in the 'interventionist model', the mission-oriented agency is at the centre, trying to re-orient academic research to industry's knowledge interests, with the funding agency acting as a proactive entrepreneur.

Benner and Sandstrom (ibid., p. 300) suggest that we are witnessing the emergence of a new organizational field that is a hybrid of traditional academic research and the knowledge-based economy, combining collegial recognition with entrepreneurialism and societal accountability. This 'transinstitutional model' has been emerging since the 1980s, combining elements of the above two models in an organizational form related to the triple helix of Etzkowitz and Leydesdorff. The new model is based on academic autonomy and initiatives taken by university researchers, but at the same time efforts are made to direct academics to modes of operation that address the needs of industry (ibid.).

> The main difference from the interventionist model is the catalytic rather than the regulating role of the funding agency. The intention is to develop trans-institutional norms for knowledge production, which evolve within a wide socio-economic network, involving academic and industrial interests in the regulation of research programs (ibid., p. 300).

As a consequence, the autonomy of the university may actually be strengthened as it becomes less dependent on government funding. The ability to establish more explicit policies than previously may mean that there is less accidental evolution than previously.

To sum up, we have seen how various driving forces are bringing changes in the relationship between science and universities, on the one hand, and the state, on the other. Science and universities are now expected to contribute much more to the development of the critical technologies that nations feel they need to be at the forefront of – the technologies that are often identified in national foresight or other priority-setting exercises (Martin and Irvine 1989; Martin 1995; Martin and Johnston 1999). What we are witnessing here is a significant shift in the social contract; there are now much more explicit and direct expectations that, in return for public funding, universities and researchers should endeavour to deliver greater and more direct benefits to society than they did in the period from 1945 through to the late 1980s.

While there are some who fear that these changes threaten the autonomy of the university and the basic researcher, the historical analysis presented above would suggest that what is involved may actually represent more of a shift back towards the social contract embodied in the nineteenth century in the institutes of technology and technical universities, and in the land-grant universities in the United States. If this is so, the fact that science and universities were able to survive and to adapt to the social contract then in place gives grounds for optimism that they can do so again in the twenty-first century.

NOTES

1. This section draws substantially on Martin and Etzkowitz (2001). The author is very grateful to Henry Etzkowitz for many of the historical examples discussed here. The chapter has also benefited from comments of those who attended the International Workshop on 'New Policy Rationales for the Support of Public Research in the EU' held in Paris on 3–4 May 2001, and from several points made by a referee. However, any errors are the responsibility of the author.
2. This was perhaps the first time that the linear model had been set down formally, although it had appeared in discussions at the end of nineteenth century (Godin 2000, p. 5).
3. A proper economic justification for the Bush social contract came later with the work of Nelson (1959) and Arrow (1962).
4. There were other important contributing factors in the US such as the arms and space race with the USSR and government decisions to wage 'war' on various diseases such as cancer.
5. Both these factors are obviously linked to another trend, namely the decline in importance of physical sciences compared with biomedical sciences.
6. In the light of the historical criticisms made later, one should perhaps qualify this statement to 'more competitive than over the period 1945–90'.
7. Another factor is that we may be reaching the politically acceptable limits to tax-raising; if a government attempts to extract taxes above a certain level, companies or affluent individuals may take their business 'off-shore' to a country where the tax regime is less burdensome, an option made much easier by growing use of electronic transactions.
8. Examples of this greater emphasis on accountability and evaluation include the Research Assessment Exercise (RAE) to which UK university departments have been subject since 1986 (Geuna and Martin 2002), and the application of the Government Performance and Results Act (GPRA) to research agencies and programmes in the US.
9. Another way of envisaging these changes is in terms of a shift to a 'triple helix' relationship between universities, government and industry – see Leydesdorff and Etzkowitz (1996 and 1998), and Etzkowitz and Leydesdorff (1998 and 2000).
10. Quoted on the back cover of Gibbons et al. (1994) – emphasis added.
11. For a more detailed discussion of the coevolution of the structure, function and external relationships of universities, see Martin and Etzkowitz (2001).
12. Some might dispute whether the land-grant university is really a separate species from the institute of technology. As in the biological kingdom, there is an element of ambiguity in such classification schemes.
13. S. Hemlin (private communication).
14. Over time, some of these 'teaching universities' began to develop a limited research capacity in certain areas where the resources were available to make this possible.

15. In many of these countries, these various species of universities have also coexisted with research-only institutions – for example, Max Planck institutes in Germany, CNRS laboratories in France, Research Council institutes in the UK, and federally funded research and development centres in the US.
16. NSF accounted for less than one-fifth of federal support over the post-war period (Rosenberg and Nelson 1994, p. 335).
17. For teaching at the postgraduate level, the interaction between teaching and research is much closer, and for doctoral students the research training, almost by definition, needs to be provided by active researchers in institutions equipped with appropriate research instrumentation and facilities. The discussion in this section is concerned primarily with *undergraduate* teaching and its relationship to research.
18. See note 17.
19. This is an area where more empirical research and analysis is clearly required.
20. S. Hemlin (private communication).
21. Sweden may be one exception here. The post-war decades were characterized by an unusually heavy emphasis on Mode 2 knowledge production with Swedish universities expected to contribute to meeting societal needs. However, in the last few years, there has been a reaction against this system and calls for a shift back towards the Humboldtian ideal (R. Stankiewicz, private communication).
22. I am indebted to a referee for this key point.
23. Some might contend that this is where the evolutionary model breaks down because universities do not die. However, there is at least one analogy in the biological world – the subterranean fungi that have survived for thousands of years without dying.
24. One example of this is the University of California, Santa Cruz, which, in addition to 10,000 'traditional' students, has 70,000 obtaining higher education delivered into their homes or offices (M.R.C. Greenwood, presentation at SmithKline Beecham Science Policy Workshop, London, 1997).

REFERENCES

Arrow, K. (1962), 'Economic welfare and the allocation of resources for invention', in R.R. Nelson (ed.), *The Rate and Direction of Inventive Activities*, Princeton, NJ: Princeton University Press, pp. 609–25.

Barnett, R. (2000), '"The university" is dead, long live the university', *The Times Higher Education Supplement*, No. 1422 (11 February), p. 14.

Benner, M. and U. Sandstrom (2000), 'Institutionalizing the triple helix: research funding and norms in the academic system', *Research Policy* **29**(2), 291–301.

Brown, G.E. (1992), 'The objectivity crisis', *American Journal of Physics* **60**(9), 779–81.

Bush, V. (1945), *Science: The Endless Frontier: A Report to the President on a Program for Postwar Scientific Research*, Washington, DC: US Government Printing Office (reprinted 1990, National Science Foundation).

de la Mothe, J. and J. Halliwell (1997), 'Research frontiers, institutional innovation and the management of instrumentation resources', in Irvine et al. (eds), Ch. 13.

Etzkowitz, H. (1997), 'The entrepreneurial university and the emergence of democratic corporatism', in Etzkowitz and Leydesdorff (eds), pp. 141–52.

Etzkowitz, H. (2002), *MIT and the Rise of Entrepreneurial Science*, London: Routledge.

Etzkowitz, H. and L. Leydesdorff (eds) (1997), *Universities and the Global Knowledge Economy: A Triple Helix of University–Industry–Government Relations*, London: Cassell Academic.

Etzkowitz, H. and L. Leydesdorff (1998), 'The endless transition: a "triple helix" of university–industry–government relations', *Minerva* **36**(3), 203–8.

Etzkowitz, H. and Leydesdorff, L. (2000), 'The dynamics of innovation: from national systems and "Mode 2" to a triple helix of university–industry–government relations', *Research Policy* **29**(2), 109–23.

Etzkowitz, H., A. Webster, C. Gebhardt and B.R.C. Terra (2000), 'The future of the university and the university of the future: evolution of ivory tower to entrepreneurial paradigm', *Research Policy* **29**(2), 313–30.

Geuna, A. (1998), 'The internationalization of European universities: a return to medieval roots', *Minerva* **36**(3), 253–70.

Geuna, A. and B.R. Martin (2002), 'University research evaluation and funding: an international comparison', submitted to *Minerva.*

Gibbons, M., C. Limoges, H. Nowotny, S, Schwartzman, P. Scott and M. Trow (1994), *The New Production of Knowledge*, London: Sage.

Godin, B. (1998), 'Writing performative history: The new *new Atlantis?*', *Social Studies of Science* **28**(3), 465–83.

Godin, B. (2000), 'Measuring science: is there "basic research" without statistics?', Project on the History and Sociology of S&T Statistics Paper No. 3, Observatoire des Sciences et des Techniques, Montreal.

Guston, D.H. (2000), *Between Politics and Science: Assuring the Productivity and Integrity of Research*, Cambridge: Cambridge University Press.

Guston, D.H. and K. Keniston (1994a), 'Introduction: the social contract for science', in Guston and Keniston (eds), pp. 1–41.

Guston, D.H. and K. Keniston (eds) (1994b), *The Fragile Contract*, Cambridge, MA and London: MIT Press.

Irvine, J., B.R. Martin, D. Griffiths and R. Gathier (eds) (1997), *Equipping Science for the 21st Century*, Cheltenham, UK and Lyme, US: Edward Elgar.

Johnston, R., J. Currie, L. Grigg, B. Martin, D. Hicks, E.N. Ling and J. Skea (1993), *The Effects of Resource Concentration on Research Performance*, National Board of Employment, Education and Training Commissioned Report No. 25, Canberra: Australian Government Publishing Service.

Leydesdorff, L. and H. Etzkowitz (1996), 'Emergence of a triple helix of university–industry–government relations', *Science and Public Policy* **23**(5), 279–86.

Leydesdorff, L. and H. Etzkowitz (eds) (1998), *A Triple Helix of University–Industry–Government Relations: The Future Location of Research?*, New York: Science Policy Institute, State University of New York.

Martin, B.R. (1995), 'Foresight in science and technology', *Technology Analysis and Strategic Management* **7**(2), 139–68.

Martin, B.R. and H. Etzkowitz (2001), 'The origin and evolution of the university species', *Journal for Science and Technology Studies (Tidskrift för Vetenskaps- och Teknikstudier, VEST)* **13**(3/4), 9–34.

Martin, B.R. and J. Irvine (1989), *Research Foresight: Priority-setting in Science*, London and New York: Pinter.

Martin, B.R. and R. Johnston (1999), 'Technology foresight for wiring up the national innovation system: experiences in Britain, Australia and New Zealand', *Technological Forecasting and Social Change* **60**(1), 37–54.

Merton, R.K. (1938), *Science, Technology and Society in Seventeenth Century England*, Bruges: St. Catherine's Press.

Mitchell, B.R. (1992), *International Historical Statistics Europe, 1750–1988*, London: Macmillan.

Nelson, R.R. (1959), 'The simple economics of R&D', *Journal of Political Economy* **67**, 297–306.

Nowotny, H., P. Scott and M. Gibbons (2001), *Re-Thinking Science: Knowledge and the Public in an Age of Uncertainty*, Cambridge: Polity Press.

Pearson, I. (2000), *Universities and Innovation: Meeting the Challenge*, London: The Social Market Foundation.

Pelikan, J. (1992), *The Idea of the University: A Re-examination*, New Haven, CT: Yale University Press.

Pestre, D. (1997), 'La production des savoirs entre académies et marché', *Revue d'Économie Industrielle* Special Issue: L'économie industrielle de la science, M. Callon and D. Foray (eds), **79**, 163–74.

Rosenberg, N. and R.R. Nelson (1994), 'American universities and technical advance in industry', *Research Policy* **23**(3), 323–48.

Schimank, U. and M. Winnes (2000), 'Beyond Humboldt? The relationship between teaching and research in European university systems' (manuscript).

Shinn, T. (2000), 'The "triple helix" and "new production of knowledge" as socio-cognitive fields', paper presented at the Third Triple Helix Conference, Rio de Janeiro, 26–29 April.

Stehr, N. (1994), *Knowledge Societies*, London: Sage.

Stokes, D.E. (1997), *Pasteur's Quadrant*, Washington, DC: Brookings Institution Press.

Weingart, P. (1997), 'From "finalization" to "mode 2": Old wine in new bottles?', *Social Science Information* **36**(4), 591–613.

Ziman, J. (1991), 'Academic science as a system of markets', *Higher Education Quarterly 12*, **45**(1), 57–68.

Ziman, J. (1994), *Prometheus Bound: Science in a Dynamic Steady State*, Cambridge: Cambridge University Press.

Ziman, J. (2000), *Real Science: What It Is, and What It Means*, Cambridge: Cambridge University Press.

2. The increasing involvement of concerned groups in R&D policies: what lessons for public powers?*

Michel Callon

1 A CHANGING STAGE

Institutions created during the second half of the twentieth century to manage and steer scientific and technical activities have entered into a period of long-term reconfiguration. As many historians have pointed out, these institutions, founded in the immediate post-war years and strengthened throughout the Cold War (Guston 2000; Mirowski and Sent 2002) were explicitly designed to enforce strict distinctions that could be characterized in a very sketchy way as follows:

- a neat division of roles between scientific experts (or specialists) and political authorities, with the former producing reliable and 'consensible' knowledge (what is possible) on which the latter base their decisions (what is desirable) (Ziman 2000);[1]
- the constitution of an ignorant public, incapable of entering into the abstract formalism of scientific knowledge (such as concepts of time and space in post-Newtonian physics) and whose support for science and technology requires constant education (popularization);
- the development of non-profit research strongly structured around public agencies and universities; this sector is specialized in what is known as basic research, that is, long-term and disinterested research that feeds into economic markets and their applied research and development laboratories;
- heavy investments by public agencies in major technological programmes that are either civil or military – military programmes being considered as an important source of technology for the rest of the economy; and finally
- the key role of physics and chemistry, the cornerstone of the Cold War configuration; the high level of maturity, diffusion and

formalization of these disciplines has made a powerful contribution to maintaining the domination of the linear innovation model.[2]

This Cold War institutional Configuration (CWiC) was given dual legitimization: first, from a political point of view in Vannevar Bush's famous book *Science: The Endless Frontier* (1945) and, second, from a more theoretical point of view, but much later (in the late 1950s), with the analytical framework proposed by Nelson and Arrow with their theory of science 'as a public good' (Nelson 1959; Arrow 1962). These two different but complementary justifications provided the CWiC with a solid base enabling it to better resist constantly renewed overflowings of all kinds, at least for a while. For there were (and still are) a large number of overflowings to contain. Those overflowings encompass all the courses of action, as well as their unexpected and sometimes (at least for a while) invisible effects, that could not be maintained within the existing institutional frames.[3] Pestre, in his sharp comments on Gibbons et al.'s Mode 2 (Gibbons et al. 1994), for example, rightly stresses the historical uninterrupted role of interactions, exchanges and hybridizations between sciences, markets and politics (Pestre 1997), contesting the assumption made by the authors that such interactions are new or at least much more intensive than in the past. But what is original in the CWiC is the explicit recognition of the unavoidable existence of these interactions and, simultaneously, the constant attempt to maintain, for rational and efficiency reasons, a strict separation between the scientific sphere on the one hand, and the economic and political sphere on the other. A lot of energy and effort was therefore needed to define and safeguard boundaries.

This institutional arrangement (which must be considered as a never ended project) which held for a few decades, is cracking up in front of us as overlaps and overflowings proliferate. One of the most noteworthy and telling pieces of evidence of this transformation is the multiplication of what sociologists have called socio-technical controversies on issues related to the environment, health, identity and food (global warming, pollution, food safety) (Jasanoff et al. 1995). The so-called 'mad cow crisis' (bovine spongiform encephalopathy: BSE) or (at least in Europe) the heated debates on genetically modified organisms (GMO), on the patentability of genetic materials or even on therapeutic cloning are but a few striking illustrations of this new phenomenon. Faced with these controversies, which are fuelled by profound uncertainties both on the state of knowledge and on the composition of the collective, a new decision-making model is emerging that redistributes expertise and political responsibility and challenges the strict division not only between the political and scientific spheres but also between those who know and those who do not, those who decide and those who are subjected to their decisions.[4] At the same time other radical changes are taking place, including: the decline of public technological programmes, and especially military ones; the increasing, and now widely accepted, importance of techno-economic networks or networks of innovation as a dominant form of organized markets that are based on strong interactions between laboratories, firms and consumers; the growing role of the life sciences, which are replacing the physical sciences as epistemological cornerstones and make blatantly meaningless the linear model.[5]

This current upheaval tends to undermine the CWiC and might lead to a deep reorganization of the relationships among science, economic markets and politics.[6] One of the central tasks for social sciences might be to make visible and understandable the emergence of new institutional arrangements. To achieve this goal a huge amount of work is still to be done. In this chapter I want to show that one way of starting this analysis is to reflect on the new role played by lay people, especially when they take part in public controversies about the direction and the 'social impacts' of science and technology. This entry point is a strategic one, because it is during these debates and the controversies they spawn that social actors critically analyse existing institutions and lay the foundations of new ones. Furthermore, these debates contribute to raising the question of new modalities of intervention by public powers and lead to a new rationale for public research policy.

In order to better grasp the new role of lay people, or of what I prefer to call 'concerned groups',[7] I first introduce the notion of confined research, borrowing from the historian C. Licoppe (Section 2). Confined research, one of the two cornerstones of delegative democracy as epitomized by the CWiC, has strengths that explain its remarkable achievements but also has severe limits. It is suggested that one strategy for overcoming the limits of confined research without losing its advantages is to encourage it to cooperate with research 'in the wild' (Section 3). But such a collaboration is not so easy in the CWiC. One paradox of this institutional framing is to simultaneously produce the emergence of concerned groups and to make difficult the expression of their identity and the organization of their collaboration with confined researchers. Because the number of concerned groups is growing dramatically (Section 3), the existence of hybrid forums, where socio-technical controversies take place should be recognized as well as the necessity for collaborative research between concerned groups and professional scientists (Section 4). Finally, concluding remarks propose new modalities of intervention for public powers – for all that they want to make easier – in the constitution and organization of hybrid forums and the dynamics of cooperation between researchers in the wild and confined research (Section 5).

2   CONFINED RESEARCH AS ONE OF THE TWO PILLARS OF DELEGATIVE DEMOCRACY

To assess the impact of socio-technical controversies and evaluate their implications, it is necessary to describe the framework in which they arise and which they call into question, that is, delegative democracy.

Delegative democracy is a form of representative democracy based on a double divide, which is in fact a *double delegation*[8] (hence, its name). Due partly to this double delegation, it is very difficult to take science and technology into consideration in political debate, and highly unlikely that this will be done. The first division is that separating ordinary citizens from their elected representatives; the second creates a virtually insurmountable boundary between specialists and lay people. There is clearly double delegation: citizens delegate their will and decision-making powers to their elected representatives; non-specialists rely on scientists and experts (be they located in profit or non-profit organizations) to produce and evaluate the knowledge on which decisions can be based. This mechanism not only produces a double divide, it also precludes any overlap between political issues and questions related to science and technology.

In this chapter, both for the sake of space and because the corresponding analyses are well known, I only briefly consider the first divide. We simply need to remember here that it is the product of a procedure consisting of five reductions. The first is based on wholesale exclusion of all those who cannot vote and are thus transformed into foreigners. The second equates the collective, thus limited, to a collection of individuals considered to be independent from one another, endowed with a will and an ability to make autonomous judgements; groups, as such, that have no say in the matter. The third reduction limits the capacity of these individuals to express themselves to the choice of one or more names of candidates on a list or even, in the exceptional cases of referenda, to a 'yes' or 'no' answer to a simple and general question. By a more or less complex statistical calculation, the fourth reduction substitutes a reduced population of representatives for the population of voter-citizens. Finally, the last one reduces to silence, for a predetermined period of time, those that at the end of this procedure have become the represented; it simultaneously grants those that have become their representatives a quasi-exclusive monopoly on discussion of any political topic. This quintuple reduction comprising the delegation through which ordinary, individual citizens are constituted and entrusting a general mandate to their representatives, creates a huge distance between those same citizens and the spokespersons to whom they have delegated the power to decide on the composition of the collective. It can lead to the constitution of a closed, black boxed, world of professional politicians who, supported by parties that mobilize strategic resources, compete with one another to capture votes and devise programmes aimed primarily at broadening their electoral market.

The second divide, between specialists and lay people, between scientific knowledge (episteme) and opinion (doxa), is more relevant here. Scientific laboratories are at the heart of this divide: by construction, the laboratory is the locus of an accumulation of expertise and a concentration of equipment and instruments, which derives its strength from this concentration but also from the distance it establishes between itself and the rest of the world and particularly from lay people (Latour 1987).

This confinement was not ineluctable and there is probably nothing definitive about it either, for it is not the only possible configuration of relations between science and society. It does nevertheless have a history, the main steps of which might usefully be recalled, in order to better understand its strengths and weaknesses.

There are several ways of recounting this history or, rather, these histories. I have opted for Licoppe's version, which is closest to scientific practices and to the question of the modalities of the construction of the public sphere in which scientific research is set and in which it participates (Licoppe 1996). Licoppe suggests distinguishing three main periods in the organization of the production and circulation of knowledge. These are the main stages in a trajectory leading to what I call the confinement of research and which corresponds to a progressive distancing from the world in which lay people live.

The first stage or regime is that of *curiosity*. It is opposed to the Aristotelian view of knowledge, in which real science (*scientia*) can be based only on empirical common-sense statements, that is, statements shared by all (or resulting from a series of inferences considered to be true by everyone, as in mathematics). Aristotelian philosophy contrasts *experimentum*, corresponding to what we would call the laboratory experiment in which unusual and singular facts are produced, and *experientia*, corresponding to what we call experience that everyone accumulates and shares with all other human beings. For an Aristotelian, *experimentum* is dangerous because, due to its unusual, extraordinary and artefactual nature, it will inevitably generate controversy and disagreement. We know that Thomas Hobbes used the same argument to discern a possible source of civil war and social disorder in experimental science. The curiosity regime had a standpoint diametrically opposed to that of Aristotelian philosophy. Scientists organized experiments (*experimentum*) that were always unique, unexpected events, never seen or heard of before. To establish their reality, the experiments, designed to be real shows, were performed in public in front of a gathering of gentlemen and scholars. This science was open to networks of erudite elite, shaped by aristocratic civility, who were difficult to contradict. They were witnesses of a show and guarantors of the authenticity of original results. The truth consisted of that which could be demonstrated, attested to by eye-witnesses that could be trusted (Shapin 1994; Dear 1995).

At the end of the seventeenth century, a new regime progressively appeared: new facts, produced by experimentation, were validated in the name of their *utility*. What counted then was the replication of experiments and the regularity of results without which no dissemination would be possible and no use conceivable. Instruments and metrology became key requirements making this distant replication and constant movement of specialists between laboratories possible. The curiosity regime aimed for the construction and validation of isolated facts. The *utility* regime strove to achieve the multiplication of stable, reproducible and controllable facts.

The end of the eighteenth century witnessed the emergence of the regime of *exactitude*, characterized above all by the need to show that measurements corresponded as precisely as possible to simple and universal laws based on theory (the utility regime and the implicit obsession with reproducibility naturally led to the elaboration of laws and principles intended to capture these regularities). This required the production of increasingly sensitive instruments for measuring. One of the consequences of this race for ever-more powerful and precise instruments was a phobia about 'interference', experienced by all scientists. Since the bodies of the experimenters, or their assistants or those of members of the public were likely to disturb the instruments, especially sensitive ones, these were confined to laboratories and shielded by screens. The thermometers calibrated by Antoine Lavoisier were protected in a double boiler and double shield. Charles Coulomb's balances were so sensitive that the presence of the public disturbed them irremediably, so that his experiments had to be conducted in non-public spaces – in short, in private – if they were to succeed. While Coulomb was burying his instruments in the basement of the Observatory to get away from lay people, Giovanni Cassini expressed the need for this confined research marvellously well:

> I had had all entrances to this place blocked in advance, with the exception of a storeroom leading onto it but I had that closed off with a door; I thus had an underground cabinet in a vast enclosure where, in silence and total isolation, I could carry out these observations since I was always alone (Licoppe, 1996, p. 273).

Everything is said clearly and concisely. The modern schema of confined research, withdrawn, cut off from the world and consequently precise and effective, was born and, at the same time, its necessity was explained and justified. This was the beginning of the withdrawal of researchers. Doors and windows were blocked, as researchers and trained technicians, surrounded by powerful calibrated instruments, isolated themselves from the rest of the world. Far from the public and its trivia, specialists formed communities in which technical debates could take place. They were thus protected from the prattle of lay people who had no idea what they were talking about – and who could hardly know what they were talking about, since they were deprived of those laboratories cut off from the world and without which no scientific knowledge worthy of the name could be produced. The separation had never been so distinct. It can be summarized in a series of terms subsequently used to define science: purity, precision, exactitude, distance. This evolution was to reach its climax in the decades of the Cold War, when the alliance of scientists and militaries was to transform this confinement into the isolation of an ivory tower.

This history, considered very briefly, is interesting in more than one respect. It highlights the fact that confined research, in which specialists organize complicated manipulations using precise, powerful and calibrated instruments, is only one possible way of organizing research, one of the three steps so far in a historical process. The first corresponds to the establishment of an initial separation, the fundamental divide between *experientia* and *experimentum*, common experience and laboratory experiment. In the *experimentum* regime, the main aim was to produce something extraordinary, singular, never before seen, unheard of, as a contrast to the routine of *experientia*. At the starting point of any scientific approach is there not this decisive action through which a problem is shown, through which a questioning, an enigma or an oddity is made visible, perceptible? Formulating problems, that is, etymologically-speaking, setting an unexpected obstacle on paths crossed thousands of times, is compulsory for any scientific undertaking. Horton expressed this strikingly well when he characterized Western science by its compulsive partiality for everything monstrous (Horton 1967). That is what research feeds on: monstrous phenomena!

Transforming these monsters into something normal, in other words, making reproducible in different places that which is initially singular and local, is the second stage. To achieve that goal it is necessary to build metrological networks to calibrate instruments, and then to compare measurements and sometimes establish a general principle. In this way, a community is gradually formed, consisting of specialists sharing the same techniques and embodied knowledge, and capable of comparing and evaluating their experiments, and of building on the results obtained. Finally, in the last stage confinement verges on obsession: researchers establish their headquarters in closed laboratories, shielded from the public, where they peacefully carry out purified experiments without any risk of disturbance by troublesome parasites who could hinder their race towards ever-greater power and exactitude. All that is left for them to do is to leave their laboratories, to present their results and show that their distant exile has not been sterile.

Problematizing, that is, breaking away from common experience by making original phenomena perceptible, and to make them perceptible, inviting a public excited by the novelty; constructing a research collective that shares the same instruments and is capable of reproducing the phenomena on which it works. As well, cutting oneself off from the world, closing oneself in a laboratory to study things in depth and then returning to the world all the stronger for it: by showing that this confined research is but a stage in a multistep process, Licoppe invites us to discover the constant movements, the continuous interaction between specialists and the world around them. By unfolding that which has been folded, history shows us that the laboratory is simply a piece in a far bigger whole, a stage in a long sequence of comings and goings. Laboratories are both distant from the world and caught in a network of interaction and interdependencies, the traces of which are found in the genealogy of confined research.

The confinement of research and the professionalization of political representation are the two main features of delegative democracy. The establishment of this dual separation is the fruit of a long history and heavy investments, especially institutional. It is easy enough to understand how this delegative democracy resulted in the extreme configuration of the Cold War, of which it was, in a sense, the bedrock. The creation of an ignorant public that constantly has to be educated and of consumers that are content to choose between the goods offered to them, and the separation between science, governments and markets would have been impossible without this double divide and double delegation (Bensaude-Vincent 2000). It is owing to these two divisions that delegative democracy established, and has been trying to maintain and reinforce, divisions between ordinary citizens and political spokespersons, and between specialists and non-specialists, and ended up imposing the two roles of the scientist and the political decision-maker (see Figure 2.1). The most important point to note here is the crucial part played by confined research in the constitution of double delegation.

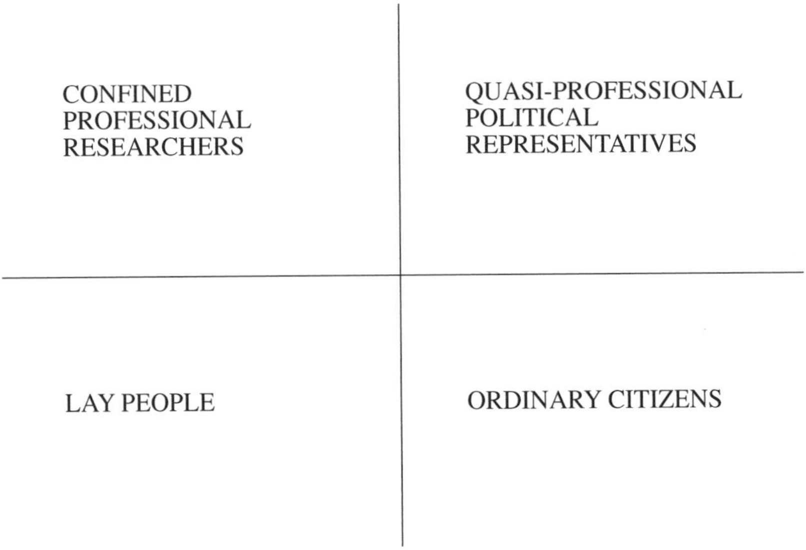

CONFINED PROFESSIONAL RESEARCHERS	QUASI-PROFESSIONAL POLITICAL REPRESENTATIVES
LAY PEOPLE	ORDINARY CITIZENS

Figure 2.1   Delegative democracy: CWiC

3   THE NEED FOR COOPERATION BETWEEN CONFINED RESEARCH AND RESEARCH IN THE WILD OR HOW TO ENRICH DELEGATIVE DEMOCRACY

The reader will certainly have perceived the symmetry of the procedures on which delegative democracy is based: two massive reductions, two black boxings, two exclusive delegations and two glaring distinctions. The first separates specialists from lay people[9] while the second widens the gap between professional politicians and ordinary citizens; two separations that generate two populations that did not exist before. It is in fact the very act of delegation – that by which lay people rely on specialists for knowledge production or by which ordinary citizens entrust their representatives to compose the collective on their behalf – that creates *both* lay people *and* ordinary citizens and, with them, their corollaries, *both* specialists *and* representatives. This double delegation tends to limit debate on the state of knowledge to professional researchers, and debate on the composition of the collective to no less professional spokespersons, even if leakages have always taken place but on a smaller scale. In order to make this drastic restriction possible, so that people agree to this voiceless silence, an extraordinary and fertile invention was needed: confined laboratories to contain uncertainties on the state of knowledge, and parliaments to contain uncertainties on the state of the collective. The uncertain *dêmos* has been replaced by the individual under the dual and reassuring figure of the lay person and the ordinary citizen.

The double delegation has tremendous advantages. Delegation to specialists, in particular, affords considerable power to transform the world.[10] In fact the confinement of the laboratory that places it at a distance from the world does not prevent it from acting on the world – on the contrary. The history recounted by Licoppe enables us to understand this paradox: it is by moving away that the scientist accumulates power. The *Translation* model formalizes this dual movement, highlighting not only its strengths but also its weaknesses and its limits (Callon 1986, 1987, 1992, 1994).

Translation Theory shows that the laboratory is at the centre of a three-fold movement: *Translation 1* (T1) which reduces the world, the macrocosm, and transports it into the microcosm of the laboratory, thus effecting a change of scale that allows a shift from the formulation of complex problems to that of problems that are easier to treat and solve; *Translation 2* (T2) which, in the laboratory and the research collective to which it belongs, submits the microcosm, a model of the macrocosm, to questioning, so that it can be written and discussed, through the production of inscriptions (Latour 1987) and, lastly, *Translation 3* (T3) which makes it possible to disseminate the transformations achieved during *Translation 2* in order to reconfigure the world, the macrocosm. This model is now sufficiently well known for me not to have to describe it in detail. It explains the remarkable strength and effectiveness of confined research. If *Translation 1* is conducted well, in other words if the world is realistically reduced, then the laboratory becomes a tremendously powerful lever to act on it. The detour organized by confined research opens the field to improbable and sometimes spectacular reconfigurations that trigger profound changes in the collective (Figure 2.2). But this power has a price. The distancing can go as far as a clear break and ends up producing powerlessness and even paralysis. The *Translation model* might prove useful to understand how such an 'induced effect' could happen.

In the following paragraphs I suggest both the reality of these limits and how, for T1, T2 and T3, they are overcome through the intervention of those I have called researchers in the wild.

Translation 1, as shown in my text on scallops, is based on the fundamental mechanism of problematization through which actors are interested in research and through which the laboratory becomes an obligatory passage point (OPP) (Callon 1986). In fact a research programme starts with the identification and formulation of a problem. Take these problems away from science and it soon becomes sterile. This phase of problematization is

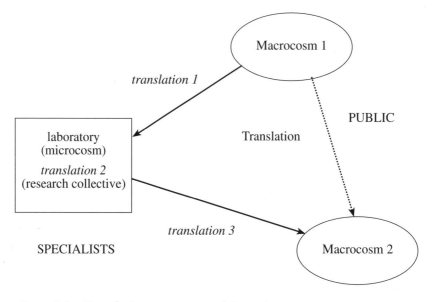

Figure 2.2   Translation as a structural dynamics

critical, for on it depends the laboratory's capacity to survive in the long run. Often controversial, it can involve a wide diversity of groups, in greater or lesser disagreement on their formulation. The circle of actors participating in the problematization phase has broadened spectacularly in recent years. That is why, for reasons that appear clearly in the following section, lay people increasingly convey problems whose treatment requires research. They constitute what I propose to call the 'concerned groups', concerned by the modalities of scientific and technical development and its orientation and management. I shall simply mention a few examples.

The first is drawn from the work of P. Brown (Brown 1992). He shows how, in the 1980s, residents of the small county of Woburn in Massachusetts progressively became aware of the increasing number of cases of infant leukaemia. These observations were made by several groups of people unrelated to one another, which gave them a degree of robustness. This oddity, this monstrous phenomenon, as Horton would have said, drew the attention of the population and ended up becoming a preoccupation, a shared problem. Faced with the exceptional, the singularity of the unexpected, explanations were sought. In this type of case the investigation, whether conducted by lay people or specialists, strives to reconstruct causal links. All those concerned were confronted with a series of inexplicable misfortunes that affected them personally. How could the death of a loved one be accounted for? How could a sense be found for this leukaemia that struck innocent children? Without an explanation, all these ordeals in the course of multiple human lives would end up making the existence of those they hurt absurd. Faced with the question, 'Why is it our children who die and not those in the neighbouring county?', the families threw themselves headlong into the exploration of causal links, in a kind of epidemiological study focused entirely on establishing connections, on revealing relations of cause and effect. They soon discovered the presence of industrial dumping grounds and the existence of polluting substances – and then nothing could stop them. Like good researchers, good investigators, the parents assumed that this epidemic was due to the presence of these pollutants and their effects on their children's health. People spoke about it and grouped together. They formed a community, no longer of peaceful citizens sharing the same territory and managing the same local institutions, but a community that had integrated into its daily existence the presence of pollutants that participated in collective life by impacting on inhabitants' health day after day. The waste had been outside the community, expelled from the collective, confined to dumping grounds which had ended up becoming invisible; and here it was again in sight, a member in its own right – for worse rather than for better – of a community that realized that it had been living with this waste for a long time without knowing it. The group became more and more tightly knit, as if the sudden awareness of the presence of toxic waste had strengthened the social link and produced solidarity between individuals who, until then, had had only tenuous links between them. People started reading, asking questions, exchanging information. They spoke to officials, met scientific experts and tried to acquire knowledge on the supposed effects of this toxic waste on the lives of residents in the surrounding areas.

The residents turned this search for causes into their own cause. They revealed new facts, showed the correlation between facts, and compiled databases that naturally did not yet exist. They referred the matter to government experts who (unsurprisingly?) concluded that there was nothing strange or freakish: 'Move on, there's nothing to see. All these so-called problems are just collective hallucinations'. And since experts are also human beings, they added, in all good faith: 'We understand your emotion and we share your grief'. Who understood whom? The group thought it understood that the official experts understood nothing. It commissioned its own experts and filed lawsuits. The case was reopened. Studies were launched, public debates organized. The hypotheses and methods of analysis were discussed extensively and openly. Months passed and results started to accumulate. A cancer register was established. A five-year study using retrospective and prospective data was launched, and a research programme on genetic mutations caused by trichlorethylene (TCE) was funded by the Massachusetts Institute of Technology. Moreover, the residents' action was not limited to the organization of a rigorous investigation only. The families ensured the continuity of the programme, the quality of measurements taken, the coordination of initiatives, and the formulation of new questions and new hypotheses. In short, to use civil engineering terminology, they played the part of the contractor and the project manager, both designing the programmes and managing them. There is nobody more obstinate, attentive, cautious and rigorous than a group of concerned people, even if they are wrongly labelled as lay people by defenders of delegative democracy, who want to know why they are enduring unbearable misfortune. From a strictly scientific perspective, this active and stubborn engagement ended up paying: the result was the discovery of TCE syndrome, which affects the immune, cardiovascular and neurological systems; a syndrome that, once identified, was shown to exist elsewhere.

This story, one among many others, shows that it would be absurd to contrast lay knowledge and scientific knowledge by using terms such as rationality and irrationality, objective knowledge and subjective beliefs. In this case the opposite is true. Conservatism, pusillanimity, the absence of intellectual openness and the refusal to accept unexpected events were on the side of the experts. Audacity, attention to new phenomena and a spirit of innovation were all qualities found in the lay people's camp. Confrontation was thus inverted. But very soon symmetry was restored, by the grace of the families who did not wish to humiliate the experts as certain experts sometimes arrogantly take pleasure in humiliating lay people. They tried to create a united front against their misfortune, to expand the research collective and to establish cooperation in which everyone was on an equal footing. Thus, the residents wanted to work not against the researchers but with them. It was because they deliberately took this standpoint that they ended up attracting attention to events that had slipped by unnoticed, that they aroused interest in their own problems, and that those problems were taken seriously enough for large-scale investigations to be launched.

This type of collaboration has probably never gone as far as in the case of neuromuscular diseases (Rabeharisoa and Callon forthcoming). Pointing out monsters to then absorb them into regularities that transform them into ordinary events: does this requirement at the base of scientific inquiry not apply literally to these children, suffering from muscular dystrophy which wracks their bodies and in some cases even affects their mental and intellectual faculties? Until recently the families hid their children, unable to tolerate them leaving the private sphere. In some cases their wish to hide them went so far as attempts to keep their tombs from being too visible or easily accessible. Doctors, the vast majority of whom were incapable of naming these diseases and proposing treatment, even of a palliative nature, and were themselves paralysed in the face of these families paralysed by worry, could find nothing better to say than: 'Don't get too attached or you'll suffer for nothing; your children are going to die'. For all of them these children were 'monsters'. It was said of them that they were degenerate, so different from other human beings that there was sometimes doubt as to whether they really were human beings in their own right. But they were 'freaks' that were hidden rather than being exhibited for study. Showing these 'freaks', making them exist as problems, was the painful but crucial decision taken by several families at the same time. Thirty years later, French muscular dystrophy patients participate in television programmes and are interviewed by journalists interested in their fate. They have been placed at the centre of clinical and biological research programmes, and science has done its job by putting back into causal determinations that which shocks because of its singularity. The problem has still not been solved but the 'monsters' have disappeared because they have become a subject of interest and have been recognized as a source of questions to which answers have to be found.

Without the families this *mise en science* would have been impossible; it required the creation of an organization and awareness campaigns aimed at the public authorities and medical institutions. Above all, as in the case of the Woburn residents, it was necessary for the patients and their families to engage themselves in what can be called, borrowing from Adam Smith, the previous accumulation of knowledge. The first step in the lengthy process through which a freakish phenomenon was transformed into an ordinary, common, usual one, consisted of making inventories of the 'monsters', comparing them and grouping them together into categories according to their similarities and differences. This classification took place just after the first public displays of the 'monsters' (the de-monstration of the monsters) that simply highlighted and increased their singularity. To put an end to that singularity and initiate scientific investigation, it was necessary to compare singularities so that the first regularities, until then invisible, would appear obvious even to the most uninformed observer. That was what the Woburn residents did by creating a database to demonstrate the repetitiveness of leukaemia cases. That was likewise what the families of muscular dystrophy patients did by embarking on vast investigations enabling them to itemize cases and collect standardized information. They also used what could be called proto-instruments enabling them to establish incontestable trajectories of the evolution of the diseases. These allowed them to show that the children lived up to a certain age, and to study the different phases of the disease. For this purpose the children were filmed and photograph albums were compiled, not just to capture a few fleeting moments of a waning life, for these records provided information and made repeated rigorous and objective observations communicable. The families, like those of Woburn, shaped what was to become their *experientia*, their shared experience that previously had not existed as such since everyone lived in isolation. It was on the basis of this *experientia* that *experimenta*, in other words experiments, could subsequently be conceived and carried out. Laboratory knowledge cannot thrive on sterile ground. Without this initial base, this fertile and nourishing soil, without the 'freaks' first shown then reduced to regularities, it would simply have been unthinkable. And, once again, as in the Massachusetts case, the movement to which the problematization corresponds draws its energy from a close mix of passion and reason: the film, worn out from being watched, showing the inexorable progression of the disease, revives the children and the pain of their loss while describing their symptoms and their evolution with clinical precision.

Popular epidemiology, previous accumulation of knowledge: in both cases the concerned groups – from the point of view of both their existence and their identity – took action to enable themselves to formulate the problems confronting them so that they could be dealt with by confined research. By performing these initial translations they were doing real research work, what we could agree to call research in the wild. An entire group was involved in this research and identified with its implementation and the interpretation of results. No unquestionable delegation was accepted, which is why the research can be qualified as 'in the wild'.

This research in the wild is also present and active in the course of *Translation 2*. T2 coincides with the establishment of a research collective composed of laboratories in which experiments and results are produced and discussed. As social scientists, and thanks to a growing number of empirical studies, we are now fully aware of the fact that groups of concerned lay people can be involved in this collective and its organization, both directly and/or indirectly.[11]

How are they directly involved? Research by Steve Epstein on the history of social movements related to the AIDS epidemic highlights the way in which patients took part in clinical research (Epstein 1996). How is the efficacy of a new molecule assessed? The usual answer derives from strict observance of a protocol, established and codified a long time ago, which stipulates rules for the selection of patients or healthy subjects on whom the molecule is to be tested, and which also requires double-blind trials (Marks 1997). For these trials two groups are formed: one is given the molecule for testing while the other receives a placebo, that is, an inactive molecule. Neither the patients nor the doctors treating them know which group is receiving the drug or the placebo. These rules have been devised over time with the intention of guaranteeing the objectivity of tests. They aim at eliminating subjective biases of both doctors and patients, biases which, given the importance of mental and psychological factors when it comes to health, can influence the efficacy of the treatment. While these rules may be objective, they are nevertheless in potential conflict with certain ethical considerations. First, under cover of scientific appearance, the concept of representativeness hides choices of a purely moral nature. Why, for example, exclude certain categories of patients? Can lifestyles, attitudes towards health care and disease, and biological characteristics not vary from one group to the next? Why, as is frequently the case, are women and African Americans or other minorities under-represented in clinical trials? These questions are at once scientific, political and moral. By wanting to consider at all costs that every sick body is equivalent to every other sick body, we end up being unable to grasp differences of efficacy and prevent certain groups from benefiting from possible chances of recovery or remission promised to those who were chosen for the tests. Another question, related to the preceding one, is raised when initial indications seem to show that the tested molecules are effective. Should one then maintain the administration of placebos, thus depriving the patients concerned of a chance of better health? Certain patients' organizations had radical answers to these two questions: it is unacceptable, they claimed, to exclude from scientific investigation minorities who are thus outcasts in two ways, just as it is unacceptable to continue the administration of placebos when one knows that treatment is available. Scientific objectivity, they added, does not warrant the death of a person for the sole aim of ensuring that one of his or her chance companions, chosen by the luck of the draw, can be healed or have a better lot. In all these respects the patient organizations raised unusual questions, developed arguments and put pressure on the relevant authorities (Barbot 1998).

But they also became involved in ongoing debates and revived others. Take the case of the controversy over the way in which to conduct drug tests. The specialists develop two contrasting points of view: pragmatic and purist. The former consider that it is unrealistic to want to purify the protocol, that is, to impose subjects who have received no treatment prior to the trial. To assess the real efficacy of a new molecule, they claim, one has to get as close as possible to reality which is never pure and is always dirty and disordered; in other words, medicine never deals with 'clean' patients who have never taken treatment. The latter consider that, on the contrary, in order to have 'clean' answers one has to purify the protocols as much as possible and select patients who are 'unpolluted' by previous treatments. This point of view causes certain patients to be eliminated, in fact certain groups of patients, which, in the eyes of the organizations' leaders, results in de facto segregation. This debate running throughout the scientific and medical community is exemplary; it clearly shows the tension between laboratory research which is confined and wants to work on purified objects–subjects, and research in the wild which is confronted with compound, impure, polluted realities.[12] Beyond this opposition we see another issue emerging. When knowledge acquired on purified objects seeks fields of application in the real world and tries to maintain the conditions of its effectiveness, it has to require that patients themselves be 'purified' if they want to be healed. We are bordering here on a process of normalization, and the associations are worried, or rather, some of them are, for patients' spokespersons are divided. Some of them become more radical than the most radical specialists and argue for the strengthening of existing protocols. In their view this is the only way of really knowing what a molecule is worth. Others support those who defend the most pragmatic approaches. The *kriegspiel* can start based on very complicated and changing alliances between subgroups of patients and subgroups of physicians and biologists (Barbot 2002). This example shows that not only are the concerned groups of lay people in a position to participate in the research collective, they are also, like all good researchers, at odds over the research strategies to develop.[13]

As the nuclear example shows, this involvement can take different forms. The concerned groups do not necessarily engage personally in the research collective. They practise critical vigilance, especially by paying for the services of experts whom they introduce into the collective. In this case the critique formulated by lay people concerns the constitution of the research collective and its functioning, for all the rules in the world, all institutional norms, are not enough to guarantee the existence of this open science, rightly celebrated in the textbooks of Mertonian-style sociology of science (Merton 1973). For reasons that are easily understood, in certain cases a research topic can be appropriated by a small group of researchers working outside all peer control, often in total secrecy. Confined research then becomes closed research. The only way of transforming it into open research in which the diversity of strategies and approaches is represented, is by broadening the collective by introducing what we usually call counter-experts, or by creating new laboratories and using new instruments. This strategy has been constant in the nuclear case. If we take the French case, which is the one with which I am most familiar (although similar episodes took place in other countries), an example is the creation of the Crii-rad[14] at the time of the Chernobyl accident: French experts, on the basis of measurements on which they had a monopoly, affirmed that the radioactive cloud – probably dissuaded from entering our territory by fearsomely efficient customs officials – had ended up docilely agreeing to bypass France.

It took the mobilization of groups outside this closed and quasi-secret collective for these results and hypotheses to be discussed.

Lay people can therefore participate in the research collective, in the debates running through it and in the choices it makes. Sometimes their participation is direct, as in the case of AIDS. But, as in the nuclear case, it may also be indirect. In this case either the concerned groups, through their vigilant presence, urge researchers to exercise more and more caution and conscientiousness, or these groups call on experts to practise this vigilance on their behalf and to create a forum for discussion. Concerned groups, when they have control of financial resources, might act as genuine decision-makers imposing their scientific or technological choices on professional researchers (Rabeharisoa and Callon 1999).

In these conditions, why not consider that lay people, whether allied to experts or not, act as veritable researchers when they take part in the very process of scientific investigation? Like T1, T2 can be enriched by the involvement of concerned groups.

With *Translation 3* starts the return journey from the research collective to the outside world. How can one ensure that what has been achieved in a laboratory can be spread, reproduced and applied elsewhere? How can one transform the world after manipulating and reconfiguring it on a reduced scale in a laboratory? The answer is well known: by turning the world into a laboratory. For the world to behave as in the research laboratory, one simply has to transform it so that at every strategic point there is a 'replica' of the laboratory, that site where the phenomena under study can be controlled. It is worth pausing for a moment on this mechanism, for it runs counter to many received ideas on what is usually called the application of knowledge. In order to understand how researchers in the wild intervene in this process, let me briefly recall the notion of 'laboratorization' (Knorr-Cetina 1995).

Let us follow Bruno Latour and his account of one of the many return journeys of the great Louis Pasteur, back into the real world (Latour 1996). If Pasteur was great, it was precisely because he was able to 'see' big and to master the third part of the translation, that which, from the original laboratory, gave him access to and a grip on the world. Owing to the anti-diphtheria serum developed in his laboratory, Pasteur, or rather Doctor Roux who took over from him, thought that he could eradicate the epidemic. He obviously still had to convince doctors who until then had, for good reasons, been opposed to Pasteur's work and the different vaccinations he had developed. As Bruno Latour drily points out: 'a vaccination takes a doctor's patients away. And a doctor may be a disinterested guy who wants to take care of humanity, but the fewer patients there are the fewer doctors there will be!' (Latour 1996, p. 30). But the research programme on the anti-diphtheria serum was totally different: it interpreted doctors' interests and expectations positively, instead of confronting them head-on. The administration of a serum to a patient implies that a diagnosis is first carried out, and that is, in this context, a medical act and one of a doctor's exclusive prerogatives. Here then was a discovery that enriched doctors' competencies and scope of action and, consequently, that was to enrich them financially too! To be able to administer the serum, doctors had to agree to a few changes to their surgeries, to transform them into annexes of the Pasteur Institute. They also had to be trained and, therefore, demanded training in the methods and know-how of bacteriology. Each doctor set up a lab in his surgery, acquired a microscope and learned to use it. Doctors invested, underwent training, transformed their surgeries as they transformed themselves, probably estimating that the reconfiguration of their competencies *and* their profession *and* their identity was worth the try. This reconfiguration was also beneficial to the patient and the Pasteur Institute, which was to confirm the diagnoses and sell the serums. A network of tightly interdependent interests was thus woven. There were of course opponents, recalcitrant elements, but they were swept along with the tide. The laboratory expanded by reconfiguring all those who wanted to have it at hand. The difference between the world before T1 and the world after T2 and T3 was this sudden proliferation of laboratories and, with them, the techniques and entities they transported and the interests and projects they promoted. We notice the strategic character of the utility regime, as defined by Licoppe,[15] for the laboratories first had to be reproduced within the research collective for them to be able to be launched in the world at large, like Christopher Columbus's caravels setting off to conquer the New World. The expression 'laboratorization of society' does not mean that society is reduced to a vast laboratory, but that laboratories which frame and pre-format possible actions are set up in various places. This movement is continuous, for not only are new areas of action thus opened up by the establishment of new laboratories, but those already in place are replaced by new laboratories that make existing ones obsolete.

Laboratorization is a never-ending undertaking, constantly being worked on. Let's leave the Pasteur Institute to its transformation of French society in the late nineteenth century and turn to the genetic consultation service at a large Paris hospital. Only twenty years ago this service did not exist. Patients with muscular dystrophy, for example, ended up there after being turned away by all existing services, in their quest for a proper diagnosis or at least a name for their disease. Then the Généthon was developed and genes were identified. The service started taking samples from worried mothers and sending them to a central laboratory for genetic diagnosis concerning either the mother or the embryo she was carrying. Within a short while, instead of relying on outside researchers, the service acquired sequencers. It now performs diagnostic tests itself and even tries to identify the genes implicated in unstudied genetic diseases. The service employs its own researchers capable of working on proteins and their functions, and of screening molecules to stimulate deficient genes. The laboratory is now in the doctor's surgery; this is no longer only the replication of existing laboratories but the edification of a new type of laboratory close to users. Molecules are discovered, such as the one making it possible to curb the progression of Friedreich's ataxia (a severe neuromuscular disease). The life and identity of doctors but also of patients is changing radically once again, and even more profoundly. Clinicians become researchers, day after day transferring competencies acquired in the laboratory into their consultations and prescriptions; and patients, instead of seeing themselves as isolated individuals, incapable of having any control over their own fate, are learning the origin of their own suffering and becoming able, above all, to master the conditions of procreation.

This proliferation of laboratories, constantly starting over and over again, is becoming spectacular. Motor cars, for example, are microcosms straight out of firms' research departments. The factory that produces compact disks, the one that prepares vectors for gene therapy and the one that processes highly radioactive waste, all closely resemble laboratories that master the knowledge and technologies they use. Each one of us, in the most commonplace daily routines, thus uses laboratories constructed and disseminated by research collectives who have brilliantly mastered T1, T2 and then T3.

It is to this process of laboratorization of society that the expression 'social acceptability of technologies' refers: does society agree to be laboratorized? Would concerned actors agree to live in, or to pass through, the laboratories that have been prepared for them? Yet between the world in which these groups live and that of laboratories, irreducible gaps can still be sustained. Since this point is now well documented, I shall therefore limit myself to an example drawn from the classic study by Bryan Wynne of sheep farmers in Cumbria in the UK (Wynne 1996).

To answer the above question, let us pause a little longer in the nuclear field and go to the surroundings of the Sellafield reprocessing plant. In the early 1970s, British sociologist Brian Wynne tells us, the inhabitants of this area observed what seemed to them to be an abnormally high rate of infantile leukaemia. The experts consulted reassured them that nothing abnormal was happening at Sellafield. Yet the inhabitants were not convinced; they were sure that something strange was happening to them. They therefore decided to organize epidemiological tests themselves. The results of these tests received extensive media coverage one day in 1983 when the BBC broadcast a programme showing the reliability of the residents' observations. This programme highlighted the web of lies and secrets in which officials were entangled. An official inquiry was eventually launched. It confirmed the excess of leukaemia but without attributing any particular cause to the phenomenon. In the history subsequently rewritten, the role of lay people in the identification and formulation of the problems is purely and simply obliterated; it is decided that everything started with the official inquiry. Up to this point there is nothing different from the Woburn case except – and this is important – the 'elimination' of residents in the Sellafield area who found themselves dispossessed of a history of which they were the origin. Confined science is so allergic to parasites in general and to intrusions by non-experts in particular that it readily rewrites history! We recall the photographs 'touched up' by Stalinists so that people who had been physically eliminated would also disappear *in effigy*. It was to Sir Douglas Black, someone with a good reputation in every respect, that the idea and the paternity of the inquiry were attributed. Once the facts were established, all that remained was to find their cause. The people concerned were not to worry, for somewhere experts in white coats were attending to their problems.

But it was not because they were reduced to silence in the public sphere that the residents stopped thinking, expressing themselves and passing judgements or having feelings. It took a disaster, an accident, for that which was supposedly eliminated to re-emerge into full view. The officials thought that trust had been restored, when in fact the inhabitants had simply been denied the right to express themselves. They thought that the people were reassured, but they had only been reduced to silence – temporarily. The incident that was to bring lay people back into the picture occurred in 1986, a few miles from the first site, in the area of the Windscale nuclear power plant. We recall that 1986 was the year of Chernobyl. The radioactive cloud which, as we all know bypassed France (!), did not spare England. It forced the British authorities to regulate the commercialization of mutton from sheep bred in Cumbria. This was the beginning of a story that is not unrelated to the previous one and that was to bring research in the wild and confined research into conflict. It provides ideal ground for whoever wants to understand the difficulties awaiting experts in their undertaking to 'laboratorize' the world.

The decision taken by the agriculture ministry to ban the sale of sheep threatened the fragile economy of the areas concerned. Fears were, however, largely allayed when representatives from the ministry announced that the ban would be lifted within three weeks. To justify this decision they referred to the opinions of experts who considered that radioactive caesium, the cause of the contamination, would disappear from the environment and the bodies of sheep within twenty days. But this good news was short-lived. In July 1986 the ban was extended, for tests revealed that the contamination had neither disappeared nor even diminished. It was then decided to sell the sheep, not for slaughter but to be transferred, after being marked, to other pastures where their contamination would gradually disappear. The experts kept urging and encouraging the farmers to hold out; even if they lost money it would soon all be over.

It soon became clear that the decision to impose a three-week embargo was based on a serious mistake by the scientists. Yet this mistake was to be revealed only after several months of debate and complementary research. The experts' prediction ('Wait for twenty days and the contamination will disappear') corresponded to prior observations elsewhere, on alkaline soil. They had seriously underestimated the local, singular nature of the Cumbrian hills where caesium, which disappeared elsewhere, remained active and mobile. Knowledge considered to be transposable because produced according to a laboratory research model, proved to be particular and non-transposable. The Cumbrian grasslands fell outside the framework constructed by the experts. The real world is always more complex and diverse than that represented in laboratory models. Successive translations lose certain variables along the way, some of which prove to be of secondary importance while others are crucial back in the real world. That is what happened with the geology of Cumbria.

But an 'overflowing' never happens alone. The grasslands in which the contamination persisted were, as indicated above, in the areas surrounding the Sellafield reprocessing plant. The inhabitants of the area, unlike the experts, did not have a short memory. They were expelled from the official history written by Sir Douglas Black but history caught up with the learned lord; the lay people reappeared on the group photo. The specialists were confronted by those more specialized than themselves, and the file was reopened. A number of people started wondering about long-term contamination due to the activities of the plant, which may have been concealed by the experts. Suddenly a series of phenomena were explained: the excess of leukaemia that had officially been noted and the contamination that failed to correspond to scientists' predictions. There was nothing unreasonable about such a hypothesis since a serious fire had damaged the plant in 1957. Several sheep farmers (and who could offhandedly dismiss their hypotheses?) started to say that Chernobyl was a pretext, a false cause. Could everything not be imputed to the fire? Admittedly, the theory holds together – and the experts knew it. They all answered, without a shadow of doubt, that it was easy to determine whether caesium, which remained radioactive, came from Chernobyl or from the fire, by comparing measurements of the isotopes which had a different half-life. Measurements were taken and the experts' judgement was passed, clear and conclusive like a court decision: the radioactivity was, without any shadow of doubt, due to Chernobyl.

Despite the scientists' reassurance – perhaps even because of it – the farmers remained sceptical. The specialists had already been wrong once and it hardly seemed unreasonable to think that they might be again. Subsequent developments proved that their fears were grounded. Several months later the experts recognized that the radioactivity observed was partly due to Chernobyl and partly to what they modestly called 'other sources'. Another reason for the farmers' scepticism was that a reliable analysis would have required data prior to 1986. But, despite repeated requests from them and their representatives, these data were never provided. The authorities eventually admitted that no such data existed, implicitly confessing that they had not done their work properly. This arrogant certitude against a background of secrecy could only be met by mistrust. Basically, the most serious problem, in the farmers' eyes, was not so much that the experts had made mistakes, or even that they had failed to do their work properly, but that they had hidden all that behind the assurance that their status as scientists or experts gave them. The worst was obviously that they refused to see that the real world, that of farmers and sheep, of calcareous hills where a nuclear plant had burned one foggy night in 1957, that of Cumbria under clouds from Chernobyl, was not so simple that it could be contained in the knowledge produced, at a distance, by a confined laboratory. What reinforced the farmers' grim foreboding was that at one point the experts, distraught, asked for their help in measuring the radioactivity. The measurement campaign was organized by the experts without prior consultation with the farmers who were considered simply as assistants, barely capable of taking readings on an instrument. But the farmers knew that the scientists' study did not correspond to the geographical reality of their pastures, which consisted of heterogeneous areas that could not be reduced to a single climatic or environmental variable. 'They [the experts] cannot understand that. They think that a farm is a farm and a sheep a sheep'. At another stage the war-weary researchers suggested that the farmers let their flocks graze on other pastures that seemed less contaminated. The farmers had the same disabused reaction: 'The experts think that you stand at the bottom of the hill and that by waving your handkerchief the sheep race down to you. I've never heard of a sheep that'll eat straw!'.

This inability of the experts to enter into the details of in-depth knowledge needed for a sound understanding of phenomena was even more striking when it came to conducting real experiments. One such experiment, for example, was aimed at measuring the effect on sheep of bentonite sprayed on the grasslands. The farmers immediately remarked that no reliable conclusion could be drawn from these experiments: 'their' sheep were not used to being penned in, so that this would in any case upset their metabolism and affect their health. After a few weeks the experiments were discontinued, without the researchers having deigned to listen to the farmers at any stage.

During these various episodes different forms of know-how came into conflict. The local, multidimensional, variable nature of the phenomena was beyond the confined science of the specialists. They did not see that the world at large flowed over into their laboratory knowledge on all sides; even sheep turned out to be wild beasts that were difficult to control and contain. The farmers, on the other hand, owing to their own capacity for observation and memorization, had sound knowledge of that world. When the experts went into the field they were blind to such differences; they failed to perceive the logic of T3. At best, they ignored the concerned groups, in this case the farmers; at worst, they held them in contempt, accused them of irrationality and archaism, and considered them as natives hoodwinked by strange beliefs or representations of the world. The researchers believed that a sheep is a sheep; the farmers knew full well that this type of tautology is a serious mistake. It is in this gap between the two that possible cooperation between research in the wild and confined research can be set. It is because the specialists cannot see it that they stumble against an obstacle that they are unable to overcome.

Through this conflict of knowledge, there is also a conflict of identities at play. Cooped up in their laboratories and in their plans for collection and processing of data, scientists simply ignore the concerned groups, first by obliterating them, by keeping them quiet, and then by not listening to them when they speak. They reduce to non-existence a group with its experience, know-how, practices, investigation methods, and lifestyle in its environment. They deny the identity of these groups, everything that makes their richness, their feeling of existing, of being part of a world where they occupy a place.

This example indicates a third possible point of entry for concerned groups into research work: adaptation. We now know that *adopting* means *adapting*. All studies on innovation have shown the importance of the involvement of end users in the implementation of new technologies or new know-how (Lundvall 1988). I am simply generalizing this point. Between the laboratory and the real world, compromises have to be negotiated to take into account realities, identities, convictions and emotions, all badly reduced by confined research, badly translated because often not translatable, in laboratories. Sometimes this adaptation work is easy because concerned groups are visible and influential; sometimes concerned groups are simply ignored because they are emerging, weak and not yet visible enough: in this case a straightforward laboratorization of society might be opposed, often in a rather noisy or even violent manner, by groups seeking to be heard and taken into consideration (Callon 1999). Here again the concept of research in the wild is useful. It is not possible to do things by force; one cannot impose laboratories which, to impose the problems they know they can solve, undermine the interests and identities of the people for whom they are intended, usually ignoring the legitimacy of those same people's questions and problems. These laboratories must open up to the actors concerned or, rather, agree to cooperate with them because these additional investigations, even if they are likely to be at least partially conducted by confined research, should be organized and carried out essentially in the field, in real life.

What conclusion can be drawn from all this? Confinement enables research to have considerable strength and efficacy but is also constituently responsible for a number of weaknesses and limits. It has the disadvantages of its advantages. These weaknesses are the direct result of translation in which the laboratory withdraws from the world to be able to act on it more effectively. They appear at three stages: in the problematization phase; during the organization and the orientation of the research collective at work; and in the return phase with the transportation and replication/adaptation of laboratories. These weaknesses are revealed when the players that I have called emerging concerned groups enter onto the scene in each of these three phases. It is they who help to highlight these weaknesses and who try to compensate for them. They demonstrate the existence and necessity of research in the wild that enhances and completes confined research rather than being a substitute for it. This research in the wild is increasingly unavoidable when the concerned groups multiply and make themselves heard. If it is not to implode, confined research has to open up to these new actors and to engage in what I suggest calling 'cooperative research'. In this latter type of research, confined research and research in the wild cooperate at each (or at least at one or two of the three) critical stage(s) in the translation process (Figure 2.3). Its practical modalities are still to be invented and tested.

4   HYBRID FORUMS AND THEIR ORGANIZATION

In Section 3, I focused on the (constructed) distance between confined research and lay people, and on the resulting problems: this break makes it difficult for concerned groups to be taken into account and makes their participation in research problematical. This exclusion is particularly strong

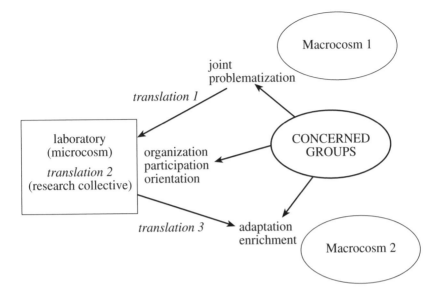

Figure 2.3   Research in the wild entry points

due to the second divide that delegative democracy establishes between ordinary citizens and their political representatives. The political arena (as configured in the delegative/Cold War model), is not ready to receive farmers contesting results concerning their sheep, just as it is not prepared to hear patients infected by the AIDS virus or suffering from muscular dystrophy, or the inhabitants of areas around dumping grounds who challenge the measurements taken by confined research. Or, should we say, it will require a long effort of mobilization and awareness in the public sphere before these voices are heard and recognized and the collaborative research process is finally set in motion. Having no social and political existence, and having great difficulties in existing at all, a concerned group has no chance of becoming a partner with confined research. Delegative democracy is a powerful machine that excludes from the political sphere and the sphere of knowledge production any groups not composed of legitimate specialists or of individual citizens with a clear view of their interests, of the risks they run and, more generally, of what they want and of who they are.

The time comes when a quantitative threshold is reached. The emerging concerned groups, which still have an uncertain and fragile identity, challenge the institutions of a delegative democracy whose procedures fail to take their views into account. As the pressure mounts, there is no alternative but to rebuild the procedures and institutions. In my view, this point has been

reached in many Western countries and especially in Europe. I see the proliferation of what sociologists call socio-technical controversies, as proof of this.
These controversies bring onto the scene increasing numbers of groups with
ill-defined identities, demanding a true involvement in research policies and
political debate.[16] As shown in the few examples I have given, they are strug-
gling towards the recognition of research in the wild and its cooperation with
confined research as well as towards the design and enforcement of other
modalities of consultation and representation. I am not just referring to existing, well-defined lobbies or organizations, but rather to the continuous proliferation of interests and demands that are unrecognized and no better
known than the outcome of current research. What is behind this proliferation which is produced by those social and scientific uncertainties?

The answer is known.[17] The more techno-sciences become a key factor
in our societies, the more the unforeseen consequences of their development and implementation proliferate. In the following I shall comment on
two that are directly linked to economic market functioning: *overflowing*
and *exclusion*. Both explain, at least partly, the increasing number of socio-
technical controversies and the role played by concerned groups in their
dynamics (Callon forthcoming).

Examples of overflowing abound in various domains. Take the food
industry. The mad cow crisis is a good illustration. The organization of
research and innovation trajectories led to the proliferation of prions that
threaten consumers and challenge eating habits, the organization of agriculture, and so on. In the case of the environment, the issues of nuclear and
non-nuclear waste management and of climate change are obvious examples. In the field of health, we have the debate generated by the hepatitis C
vaccination. These overflowings correspond to what economists usually
call negative externalities.[18] The groups concerned by these overflowings
may be large or small (for example, all consumers or only the people living
near a dump); they may already exist as consolidated groups with a legitimate spokesperson (for example, the inhabitants of towns situated near air-
ports, and their municipalities) or simply be loose groups of unrelated
individuals who suddenly learn that they share the same fate (for example,
workers poisoned by asbestos) and then progressively acquire a collective
identity that totally reshapes their individual identities (what they are and
want, their interests and the needs they express). The emergence of these
'hurt' groups is directly related to the appearance of overflowing, to its
extent and to the identification and characterization of its consequences
(on the living conditions of a particular group). As suggested in the preceding section, this characterization always involves some degree of commitment by the actors themselves (vigilance, first investigations and so on) and
consequently a very early mobilization of research in the wild.[19]

Exclusion concerns 'orphan' groups who feel left out, excluded from the logic of scientific and technical development and from the benefits it produces for some. Muscular dystrophy is a perfect example, as are the so-called orphan diseases. The term 'orphan' is very relevant to describe these exclusion mechanisms. The claim and demands here are not to be excluded from progress and its harmful effects or to be protected from the negative consequences of science and technology but, on the contrary, to be more closely involved in it. These exclusion mechanisms are steadily increasing, especially with the upsurge of network technologies and the crucial question they raise: that of access.[20]

Socio-technical controversies raise the increasingly urgent problem of the distribution of overflowings and exclusions that are massively the consequence of the modalities of coordination between techno-sciences and economic markets in the Cold War institutional Configuration. These overflowings are the countereffect of the rigid frame imposed and progressively strengthened by delegative democracy. Institutional divisions have been taken to their extreme. Society is seen as being composed of separated spheres. Efforts are constantly made to redraw and reinforce boundaries between experts and lay people, political representatives and ordinary citizens, academic science and applied science, science and power, power and the market. To be sure, the framing has never been perfect, always tolerating a degree of overflowing, provided it is neither too visible nor too frequent or contagious. The best frontiers are not completely impervious and should not be if they are to be effective.[21] There is nothing more normal than for experts and scientists to advise cabinet ministers on what to do, and for industrialists to tell academic researchers what they should look for and political decision-makers what they should decide. Each sphere has to be articulated to the others, and in this perspective overlapping and 'leakage' allow the system to function as a whole. However, in delegative democracy, and until recently, these limited overflowings and encroachments rarely go so far as to transgress the double divide – particularly the one keeping confined research at a distance, far from lay people. The constitution of an ignorant public that needs to be educated is one of the cornerstones of delegative democracy. But what socio-technical controversies and the emergence of concerned (hurt or/and orphan) groups in the public arena show, is one of the limits of the traditional separation between an ignorant public, sentenced to remain so, and an elite with the monopoly on true knowledge. These overflowings and exclusions reveal concerned groups who have difficulty existing on the political scene and are massively excluded from the production, circulation and implementation of knowledge and, furthermore, who challenge these divisions. This exclusion seems no longer to be accepted and becomes increasingly illegitimate.

The multiplication of *orphan groups* and *hurt groups* might be related to the rigidity of the institutional framing established by the double delegation: socio-technical controversies are the outcome of this double exclusion which is resisted by a growing number of concerned groups who enter into the public space and start to discuss the techno-sciences and to assert their own identities.

As I have shown elsewhere, and as many studies on socio-technical controversies confirm, the institutional arrangements (such as the market internalization of externalities) usually implemented to find acceptable solutions to these overflowings or exclusions and to the inequality they spawn, are largely ineffective. One of the main reasons for this inadequacy is the pervasive existence of uncertainties. Who is concerned? How? To what extent? With what effects? On what causal chain? Nobody knows the final answers to these questions. They must progressively be found through successive iteration. Economic calculation of interests, implied by internalization, is thus impossible in such situations (Callon 1998b). Political debate coupled with cooperative research is the only way to explore identities, identify demands, stabilize (at least for a certain time) interests and open up the way to acceptable compromises: it can no longer be avoided or postponed.

From this point of view, socio-technical controversies can be seen as a blueprint for this new type of political debate. More precisely, as shown by several studies, they constitute a powerful tool for collective experimentation and investigation that progressively, by trial and error, paves the way for a possible (even temporary) stabilization of identities, interests and knowledge (Callon et al. 2001).

Furthermore, the dynamic of these controversies, provided their development is not impeded, can be described as a joint process of investigation and learning which is characterized by:

- the continuous and progressive identification of actors who discover that they are concerned by projects under discussion; the exploration of the problems posed and of all problems considered, by the actors concerned, to be related to them; the exploration of the realm of possible options and the solutions to which they lead;
- the learning resulting from interaction between specialists' expertise and lay people's expertise; learning that leads beyond institutionalized representations to the mutual discovery of emergent and evolving identities, which are forced to take one another into account and simultaneously to change.

To sum up, socio-technical controversies are the melting pot where our societies are partially reshaped and transformed, and where scientific, technical and social uncertainties about externalities and identities are progressively reduced.

I must emphasize that controversies are not limited (at best) to open and friendly discussions or (at worst) bitter debates, aiming overtly at the production of an agreement. They are more than that. Socio-technical controversies tend, by trial and error, by progressive reconfiguration of problems and identities, to reveal a common world that is not only inhabitable but also liveable and alive, not closed in on itself but open to new explorations and new learning. The challenge, for the actors, is not only to express themselves or to interact, or even to reach compromises; it is not only to react, but also to build. They constitute what can be called socio-technical creative processes (Rip 1986; Cambrosio and Limoges 1991).

Controversies take place in public spaces that we suggested calling 'hybrid forums' (Callon et al. 2001): forums, because they are open spaces where groups can discuss technical choices concerning the collective; hybrid, because these groups and the spokespersons who claim to represent them are heterogeneous – consisting of experts, politicians, technicians and lay people who consider themselves to be concerned – and because the types of issue and problem addressed vary widely, from ethics to economics and law, through molecular biology, genetic engineering, physiology, or atomic physics and electromagnetism.[22]

By facilitating the development of this exploration and learning, hybrid forums help at least partially to overcome the two main divides characterizing our Western societies: that which separates specialists and lay people, and that which divides ordinary citizens from their institutional representatives, the dual divide. In hybrid forums these distinctions and the resulting asymmetries and exclusions are scrambled. Lay people dare to intervene in technical issues; citizens group together to elaborate new identities and express them, replacing their usual spokespersons by closer and more open representatives. It is owing to this dual transgression that overflowings, still unidentified, are made visible and manageable. The hybrid forum is thus an elucidation device. The only price to pay to use it is acceptance of the challenge to the two great divides. The actors engaged in socio-technical controversies, when they establish a new hybrid forum, clearly lay their cards on the table: 'We refuse the experts' monopoly and want to take part in cooperative research programmes! We want to participate directly in the political debate on the questions that our representatives either ignore or deal with without consulting us!'.

Each particular hybrid forum (on BSE, GMO, AIDS therapies, muscular dystrophies and so on) is a new enterprise, a place for testing forms of organization as well as procedures intended to facilitate cooperation between specialists and lay people and to make visible and audible emergent groups without official spokespersons. The actors' task is particularly difficult since they are confronted with two monopolies: the production of scientific and technical knowledge; and political representation. Without a minimum of formalism and guarantees, hybrid forums would be doomed to fail, nothing more than a demand soon forgotten. But this failure would have serious consequences for representative democracy. It is therefore urgent to assess the procedures that could enhance delegative democracy and make it more open to and willing to take into consideration, socio-technical controversies.

Experiences in the organization of hybrid forums have multiplied over the past twenty years. Forums exist on a local, national and soon transnational scale. The list of procedures that have been or are still being tried and tested is well known: consensus conferences, citizen panels or juries, focus groups, scenarios workshops and so on. Each of these procedures is incomplete and partial, taking into consideration only some aspects of the more general question of how to organize hybrid forums. But comparative studies by political scientists and sociologists make it easier to grasp the conditions of efficiency of these procedures and the modalities of their implementation (Joss 1999).

The inventory that we compiled suggests that it is relevant to classify these procedures in terms of two criteria (Callon et al. 2001). The first distinguishes procedures in relation to their lesser or greater capacity to facilitate collaborative research, that is, cooperation between confined research and research in the wild (three modalities are considered, depending on whether this collaboration concerns T3, T2 + T3, T1 + T2, or T1 + T2 + T3). The second criterion classifies procedures in relation to their capacity to allow concerned groups to express themselves and to organize dialogue in which interests and identities are likely to be debated. One could say of these procedures that they are all the more dialogic when they allow intense cooperative investigation between concerned groups and specialists, and simultaneously facilitate debate and mutual adjustments between concerned groups and other actors engaged in the collective and when they provide foundations for the political decision-making process.

5   PUBLIC ACTION

With the new emerging configuration, the role of public powers is doomed to a dramatic change. As suggested by economists and the editors' introduction to this work, the rationale for their intervention in the economic sphere has been deeply transformed. But it would be a serious mistake to limit the analysis to economic issues. As I tried to show in this chapter, the strong connections between techno-sciences and economic markets contribute to the multiplication of overflowings and exclusions, and the emergence of hurt/orphan groups who participate in the setting up of hybrid forums. Those groups call into question, explicitly or implicitly, the two divides on which delegative democracies are based. They urge, in particular, decision-makers to organize cooperation between confined research and research in the wild, but also to implement procedures allowing them to express and negotiate their emerging identities and worries. As they encourage networking between economic agents and professional scientists, public powers cannot but intervene and facilitate the organization and the functioning of those hybrid forums. The central question is now: how can the government contribute to the establishment of a new innovation regime in which innovations are socially acceptable because they are sociotechnically designed and implemented? To answer this question, a lot of work remains to be done. In the following, I would just like to indicate some of the most unusual possible lines of intervention.

My thesis is as follows: there can be no technical democracy or, in other words, no taking into account of science and techniques in democratic procedures and institutions without: (a) explicit recognition of the existence of constantly emerging concerned groups; (b) the existence of procedures intended to facilitate the expression, discussion and collective negotiation of these groups' identities; (c) the establishment of incentives and structures aimed at encouraging, developing and funding collaborative research in all its forms; and (d) the construction of public spaces in which identities and research are discussed simultaneously.

The rise of technical democracy requires institutional innovations aimed at the organization of hybrid forums. In our book we give a first inventory of these innovations together with a set of criteria for evaluating them (Callon et al. 2001). To give an idea of the radical transformations implied by the emergence of these new institutional configurations, I shall give some hints about possible consequences of government interventions. Here, simply as a more specific example, are some proposals concerning possible actions by public powers to facilitate the development and the organization of hybrid forums.

Promotion of the Identification and Exploration of Overflowings and Exclusions

This involves, in particular, a right guaranteeing the protection of whistle blowers but also, more generally, the organization of and support for all kinds of monitoring devices. We can imagine, in particular, the duty that researchers may have to indicate the doubts and suspicions they have on the effects (ethical, political or ecological) of a particular research project or programme on which they are working. This duty would be coupled to their protection against possible reprisals from their superiors. It also implies that the conditions of industrial secrecy must be seriously revised so that in times of crisis access is allowed to all useful information and knowledge (Chateauraynaud and Torny 1999).

In addition, a solid base should be given to the *associative movement* (by protecting it from interference from the public authorities and markets) so as to promote the constitution and expression of concerned groups.

Organization of Debates on Economic Markets

As argued in this chapter, markets are at the heart of overflowings and exclusions. A market can be effective only if it is framed and if, at least for a while, overflowings and exclusions are not taken into account. But it is necessary to ensure that this exclusion is not permanent. The concerned groups must, in some or other way, be taken into account. Controversies on GMOs, BSE, mobile phones, nuclear wastes, therapeutic cloning raise the question of the innovation regime promoted by a certain form of market organization. With socio-technical controversies and hybrid forums, the organization of markets and especially of the research on which they are based become a subject of (political) debate that has to take into account (among others) points of view developed by *hurt groups* and *orphan groups*. The government has a key part to play in the organization of these debates, instead of only considering the question of the coordination between academic research and economic markets (Callon 1998a).

Invention of Structures Aimed at Facilitating Collaboration between Confined Researchers and Researchers in the Wild

Institutional mechanisms must be devised to facilitate and organize collaborations between research in the wild and confined research. Given the novelty of the issue, the first task is to take stock of the ongoing experimentation, particularly in the AIDS field (Barbot 2002).

But one of the most difficult questions is about the inevitable limitation of research freedom. This implies appropriate juridical work and reflection, but there is no reason why researchers should be the only citizens to benefit from a status of extraterritoriality as regards their freedom. We have to start accepting the idea that not all research is good. The argument of realism, according to which prohibitions cannot be general and that there will always be countries to contravene them and take advantage of them, does not hold; no progress on human rights would have been possible if this argument had been taken as an inviolable law. Accepting the possibility of limiting research freedom is one of the conditions for the rise of collaborative research.

Linking Research and Exploration of Identities

The possibility for concerned groups to back both sides, that is, cooperative research and discussion on their identity and interests, is crucial. It is by launching new research that a way out of a political dead-end can be found, and by reverting to the political debate that new research avenues can be opened. These back and forth movements are facilitated not only by coordination structures, but also by the existence of a public space in which scientists, associations and political parties can enter into debate with one another. Reflection on the organization of this public space and especially on the role of the media seems indispensable. It will obviously have to abandon the logic of the public understanding of science, of the deficit model, and get rid of the assumption that the public is ignorant and that journalists must limit themselves to acting as mediators between lay people and scientists (Wynne 1995). The structuring of the public sphere is totally different when it is agreed that concerned groups have their opinions on the modalities of knowledge production and when their identity is taken into consideration.

Finally, the procedures to be imagined, tested and implemented, will aim at taking into consideration concerned groups when they are emerging in order to facilitate the expression and the negotiation of their identities as well as their active engagement in cooperative research. But such a move does not mean the disappearance of delegative democracy with its institutions. Once concerned groups have been able to stabilize, at least for a certain time, their identities and to participate in the production of knowledge (which is finally considered as reliable enough to undertake new predictable and consequently disputable courses of action), they could be treated as previously existing actors. Since their interests and arguments have become visible and debatable, their wills and demands can explicitly be taken into account (and negotiated) in the construction of the collective. Such an articulation between the existing institutions of delegative democracy and the procedures aimed at organizing hybrid forums will have to be carefully tested and assessed. But what must be taken care of is this possibly open smooth evolution from constantly emerging new situations to more stabilized ones. It implies, among other things, that emerging concerned groups be encouraged to weave alliances with constituted actors that are interested in their demands and projects.[23] Barbot wonderfully illustrated such a configuration in the French case of AIDS research: different patient organizations have been able, thanks to the public power support, to enter into evolving and complicated alliances with public researchers and even private pharmaceutical firms. But this articulation still requires more experiences, reflections and debates. In this phase of institutional upheaval, the social sciences have their role to play both to facilitate this articulation by making more visible still invisible groups and to promote the capitalization and formalization of experiments by the actors themselves in the organization of hybrid forums.

NOTES

* I would like to thank K. Pavitt and an anonymous referee for their comments and suggestions. The usual disclaimers apply.

1. The Manhattan project is an emblematic example not only of the chain from the laboratory to the world at large but also of the stormy relations between science and politics.
2. I do not distinguish between the linear model and the interactive Kline–Rosenberg model. The latter is a variant of the former; it implies identifiable, purified activities among which increasingly complex interaction takes place (Kline and Rosenberg 1986). The Kline–Rosenberg schema is very instructive from this point of view: it multiplies the arrows and interactions to be taken into consideration to account for the complexity of configurations. But when there are too many arrows in a diagram it means that the elements constituting it are no longer relevant.
3. Economic externalities, be they positive or negative, are but an example of these overflowings. For an extended discussion of the tension between framing and overflowing, see Callon (1998b).
4. One of the most striking signs of this emergence is the pervasiveness of the discussion on the meaning of the so-called precautionary principle which deeply reconfigures the traditional relation between science and politics (Callon et al. 2001).
5. The consequence is twofold: first, because of their lesser mathematical formalism and abstraction, they facilitate a return of lay people into the sphere of knowledge production; and, second, since the object of their research concerns social and individual identities, they establish a strong link between political and scientific preoccupations.
6. For a very complete analysis of the relations between science and markets, see the recent review by A.J. Salter and B.R. Martin (Salter and Martin 2000) and also P. Stephan (Stephan 1996).
7. As I shall show, the notion of lay people refers to what I call delegative democracy, while the notion of concerned groups points to the emerging subversion of this institutional configuration.
8. Christian Delacampagne gives the following pragmatic definition of representative democracy. According to him: 'Representative democracy is theoretically a parliamentary democracy: parliaments are assemblies of men and women, more often men, chosen for their wisdom, whose deliberations are supposed to result in the best possible decision'. But, he notes: 'Even if the existence of parliaments is necessary, it is not sufficient'. According to him, three additional principles must be adhered to: 'The principle of *tolerance* which requires the state to guarantee free expression of beliefs and of political, philosophical or religious ideas on its territory, provided that these do not undermine public order. The second principle is that of the *separation of powers* to ensure the establishment of the rule of law, that is, to protect citizens from all forms of abuse and, in particular, the arbitrary use that those in power could be tempted to make of their authority. The third principle is *justice*: a democracy worthy of the name must not be limited to formal democracy, blind to inequalities dividing people; it must have a concrete goal of social justice' (Delacampagne 2000, pp. 19–21). There are different modalities of representative democracy, delegative democracy being but one of them.

9. This separation is broken down into a multitude of resulting divisions, for example, between consumers and industries.
10. As for political delegation, it endows an individual with inalienable rights.
11. For a presentation of this work, see Callon et al. (2001).
12. It explains why within laboratories the definitions of what counts as purified objects or subjects are controversial issues, confined researchers sometimes fighting against each other in the name of the supposed end users of their research outcomes.
13. This is a case of Mode 2, with competencies scattered throughout the public, for example, there are gay doctors and researchers. See also Nowotny et al. (2001) and their notions of weak or strong contextualization.
14. The Crii-rad is a laboratory created by antinuclear activists in order to control the official measurements of radioactivity. For a penetrating analysis of the history of the mobilization of concerned groups on nuclear issues in France, see Barthe (2000).
15. This regime must not be confused with the utilitarian approach developed by certain economists. The regime of utility is but one configuration among others and not a universal and a-historical pattern.
16. In that sense my position is different from U. Beck's analysis, which simply ignores the richness and the complexity of socio-technical controversies, reducing all the debates to a simple question of risks and fears (Beck 1992).
17. For a very cogent analysis, see Strathern (1999).
18. Techno-sciences obviously produce in the same time positive externalities. Groups who are concerned by them should be invited to take part in the debate, but later, once hurt groups have been provided with the opportunity of having their voice heard.
19. On the subtle mechanisms through which lay people become aware of emerging problems, see Chateauraynaud and Torny (1999).
20. See, in particular, studies on standards and enraged orphans, and for a controversial but stimulating description, Rifkin (2000). Orphan groups when they transform themselves into researchers in the wild might contribute heavily to creating opportunities for greater access and inclusion. This trend is well illustrated by the development of free sources that facilitate the cooperative research and trigger more generally the production of open software and systems.
21. Just as Merton noted that the black market, provided it did not become a rule, was a sign of good health, so too we can maintain that in delegative democracy the confusion of roles, provided it does not go too far, oils the wheels.
22. A list of actual hybrid forums is easy to establish: global warming, BSE, mobile phones, nuclear wastes, therapeutic cloning, gene therapy, drugs property rights and so on.
23. This point and its political implications are examined in detail in Callon (2002).

REFERENCES

Arrow, K.J. (1962), 'Economic welfare and the allocation of resources for inventions', in R.R. Nelson (ed.), *The Rate and Direction of Inventive Activity: Economic and Social Factors*, Princeton, NJ: Princeton University Press, pp. 609–25.

Barbot, J. (1998), 'Science, marché et compassion. L'intervention des associations de lutte contre le SIDA dans la circulation des nouvelles molécules', *Sciences Sociales et Santé* **16**(3), 67–96.

Barbot, J. (2002), *Les Malades en mouvements. La Médecine et la science à l'épreuve du SIDA*, Paris: Balland.

Barthe, Y. (2000), 'La mise en politique des déchets nucléaires. L'action publique aux prises avec les irréversibilités techniques', Paris: École des Mines de Paris, Thèse en Socioéconomie de l'Innovation.

Beck, U. (1992), *Risk Society. Towards a New Modernity*, London: Sage.

Bensaude-Vincent, B. (2000), *L'opinion publique et la science. A chacun son ignorance*, Paris: Les empêcheurs de penser en rond.

Brown, P. (1992), 'Popular epidemiology and toxic waste contamination: lay and professional ways of knowing', *Journal of Health and Social Behaviour* **33**, 267–81.

Bush, V. (1945), *Science: The Endless Frontier: A Report to the President on a Program for Postwar Scientific Research*, Washington, DC: US Government Printing Office (reprinted 1960, 1990, National Science Foundation).

Callon, M. (1986), 'Some elements for a sociology of translation: domestication of the scallops and the fishermen of St Brieuc Bay', in J. Law (ed.), *Power, Action and Belief. A New Sociology of Knowledge?*, London: Routledge & Kegan Paul, Sociological Review Monograph, pp. 196–229.

Callon, M. (1987), 'Society in the making: the study of technology as a tool for sociological analysis', in W. Bijker, T. Hughes and T. Pinch (eds), *New Directions in the Social Studies of Technology*, Cambridge, MA: MIT Press, pp. 83–106.

Callon, M. (1992), 'The dynamics of techno-economic networks', in R. Coombs, P. Saviotti and V. Walsh (eds), *Technological Change and Company Strategies*, London: Academic Press, pp. 72–102.

Callon, M. (1994), 'Four models for the dynamics of science', in Jasanoff et al. (eds), pp. 29–63.

Callon, M. (ed.) (1998a), *The Laws of the Markets*, London: Blackwell.

Callon, M. (1998b), 'An essay on framing and overflowing: economic externalities', in Callon (ed.), pp. 244–69.

Callon, M. (1999), 'The role of lay people in the production and dissemination of knowledge', *Science, Technology and Society* **4**(1), 81–94.

Callon, M. (2002), 'From science as an economic activity to socio-economics of scientific research: the dynamics of emergent and consolidated techno-economics networks', in Mirowski and Sent (eds), pp. 277–317.

Callon, M. (forthcoming), 'Economy of qualities, researchers in the wild and the rise of technical democracy', in F. Pammolli, (ed.), *Science as an Institution and the Institutions of Science*, Cambridge: Cambridge University Press.

Callon, M., P. Lascoumes and Y. Barthe (2001), *Agir dans un monde incertain. Essai sur la démocratie technique*, Paris: Le Seuil.

Cambrosio, A. and C. Limoges (1991), 'Controversies as governing processes in technology assessment', *Technology Analysis and Strategic Management* **3**(4), 377–96.

Chateauraynaud, F. and D. Torny (1999), *Les sombres précurseurs. Une sociologie pragmatique de l'alerte et du risque*, Paris: Éditions de l'EHESS.

Dear, P. (1995), *Discipline and Experience: The Mathematical Way in the Scientific Revolution*, Chicago: University of Chicago Press.

Delacampagne, C. (2000), *La philosophie politique aujourd'hui. Idées, débats, enjeux*, Paris: Le Seuil.

Epstein, S. (1996), *Impure Science: AIDS, Activism, and the Politics of Knowledge*, Berkeley, CA: University of California Press.

Gibbons, M., C. Limoges, H. Nowotny, S. Schwartzman, P. Scott and M. Trow (1994), *The New Production of Knowledge*, London: Sage.

Guston, D.H. (2000), *Between Politics and Science. Assuring the Integrity and Productivity of Research*, Cambridge: Cambridge University Press.

Horton, R. (1967), 'African traditional thought', *Africa* **1** and **2**, 155–87.

Jasanoff, S., G.E. Markle, J.C. Peterson and T. Pinch (eds) (1995), *Handbook of Science and Technology Studies*, London: Sage.

Joss, S. (ed.) (1999), 'Introduction: Public participation in science and technology policy', *Science and Public Policy*, Special issue **6**(5), 290–93.

Kline, S. and N. Rosenberg (1986), 'An overview of innovation', in R. Landau and N. Rosenberg (eds), *The Positive Sum Strategy*, Washington, DC: National Academy Press, pp. 275–306.

Knorr-Cetina, K. (1995), 'Laboratory studies: the cultural approach to the study of science', in Jasanoff et al. (eds), pp. 140–66.

Latour, B. (1987), *Science in Action. How to Follow Scientists and Engineers through Society*, Cambridge, MA: Harvard University Press.

Latour, B. (1996), *Le métier de chercheur, regard d'un anthropologue*, Paris: INRA.

Licoppe, C. (1996), *La formation de la pratique scientifique; le discours de l'expérience en France et en Angleterre (1630–1830)*, Paris: La Découverte.

Lundvall, B.Å. (1988), 'Innovation as an interactive process: from user-producer interaction to national systems of innovation', in G. Dosi, C. Freeman, R. Nelson, G. Silverberg and L. Soete (eds), *Technology and Economic Theory*, London: Pinter, pp. 349–69.

Marks, H. (1997), *The Progress of Experiment. Science and Therapeutic Reform in the United States. 1900–1980*, Cambridge, MA: Cambridge University Press.

Merton, R.K. (1973), *The Sociology of Science*, Chicago: University of Chicago Press.

Mirowski, P. and E. Sent (eds) (2002), *Science Bought and Sold: The New Economics of Science*, Chicago: University of Chicago Press.

Nelson, R. (1959), 'The simple economics of basic scientific research', *Journal of Political Economy* **67**, 297–306.

Nowotny, H., P. Scott and M. Gibbons (2001), *Re-thinking Science. Knowledge and the Public in an Age of Uncertainty*, Cambridge: Polity Press.

Pestre, D. (1997), 'La production des savoirs entre académies et marché. Une relecture historique du livre *The New Production of Knowledge*, *Revue d'Économie Industrielle* Special Issue: L'économie industrielle de la science, M. Callon and D. Foray (eds) **79**, 163–74.

Rabeharisoa, V. and M. Callon (1999), *Le pouvoir des malades: l'Association française contre les myopathies et la recherche*, Paris: Presses de l'École des Mines de Paris.

Rabeharisoa, V. and M. Callon (forthcoming), 'The involvement of patients in research activities supported by the French Muscular Dystrophy Association', in S. Jasanoff (ed.), *States of Knowledge: The Co-production of Science and Social Order*, Chicago: University of Chicago Press.

Rifkin, J. (2000), *The Age of Access. The New Culture of Hypercapitalism where All of Life is a Paid-for Experience*, New York: J.P. Tacher/GP Putnam's Sons.

Rip, A. (1986), 'Controversies as informal technology assessment', *Knowledge: Creation, Diffusion, Utilization* **8**(2), 349–71.

Salter, A.J. and B.R. Martin (2000), 'The economic benefits of publicly funded basic research: a critical review', *Research Policy* **30**(3), 509–32.

Shapin, S. (1994), *A Social History of Truth*, Chicago: University of Chicago Press.

Stephan, P.E. (1996), 'The economics of science', *Journal of Economic Literature* **34**(3), 1199–235.

Strathern, M. (1999), 'What is intellectual property after?' in J. Law and J. Hassard (eds), *Actor Network Theory and After*, Oxford: Blackwell, pp. 156–80.

Wynne, B. (1995), 'Public understanding of science', in Jasanoff et al. (eds), pp. 361–88.
Wynne, B. (1996), 'May the sheep safely graze? A reflexive view of the expert–lay knowledge divide', in S. Lash, B. Szerszynski and B. Wynne (eds), *Risk, Environment and Modernity. Towards a New Ecology*, London: Sage, pp. 44–83.
Ziman, J. (2000), *Real Science: What It Is and What It Means*, Cambridge: Cambridge University Press.

3. Interdisciplinary research and the organization of the university: general challenges and a case study

Patrick Llerena and Frieder Meyer-Krahmer

1 INTRODUCTION

It might be concluded, on the basis of studies of emerging technologies in the United States, Japan and Germany, that a series of technological changes are: drastically increasing costs of innovation; increasing the significance of inter-disciplinarity and the dynamism of overlapping technology areas; and producing an increasingly close relationship between basic research and industrial application, as well as a tighter meshing of research and demand. This chapter focuses on one of these changes – the growing importance of cross-, multi- and interdisciplinarity. In this chapter we use the last term to encompass all three, which reflects the fact that separating technologies is becoming more and more difficult. The overlaps between areas are often highly dynamic and seem – at least in some cases – to be the core drivers of scientific, technological and economic change. These phenomena have several consequences for the systems of innovation that are discussed in this chapter. These phenomena are not totally 'new', but they are indications of long-term structural change in the process of knowledge production and diffusion that may constitute a new set of paradigms for technological advance.

The purpose of this chapter is to analyse trends in this evolution of inter-disciplinarity and its impact on the university organization. The case of the University Louis Pasteur (ULP) in Strasbourg (France), where both authors are working and one has had a management role,[1] will be used to support the argument.

The chapter is structured in the following way. First, we shall delineate the main features of this investigation's context. In the second section we illustrate the increasing need for interdisciplinary research and the lack of such research in academia. Section 3 presents the conceptual framework used in this chapter and employs it in analysing the costs and benefits of interdisciplinary research and the forces driving this type of research. The fourth section will apply the argument to the case of a French research university, the University Louis Pasteur. The final part of the chapter draws conclusions about appropriate organizational structures in universities. These conclusions set out necessary changes in the traditional promotion of university/industry relationships as well as consequences for organization, communication, interaction, motivation and incentives within the public research world.

2 INTERDISCIPLINARY RESEARCH IN UNIVERSITIES: THE CONTEXT

Emergence of Interdisciplinarity: Empirical Evidence

It was widely believed that by the end of the twentieth century leading-edge research had become increasingly interdisciplinary (Metzger and Zare 1999). Many research institutions, universities and research funding organizations have begun to establish specific funding schemes or organizational settings to foster this type of knowledge production. Interdisciplinarity can be defined as direct or indirect use of knowledge methods, techniques and devices that are the results of scientific and technological activities in other fields. Because it is often difficult to distinguish interdisciplinary linkages from those that arise externally in the course of multidisciplinary or cross-disciplinary research, we shall use the term 'interdisciplinarity' to refer to all such linkages between disciplines.

As a starting point we focus on the available empirical evidence indicating the emergence of interdisciplinary knowledge production. Van Leeuwen and Tijssen (2000) studied the interdisciplinary dynamics of modern science on the basis of analysis of cross-disciplinary citation flows. They analysed the citation links between research papers from different scientific backgrounds, on the basis of citations given in research papers in a fixed set of 2,314 journals and used the citation data to track key trends in interdisciplinarity in worldwide science in the 1985–95 period. They show that more than two-thirds of the citations cross disciplinary boundaries. Their findings reveal noticeable increases in interdisciplinarity across a wide variety of disciplines. They also offer tentative evidence of the significant differences between disciplines in terms of their interdisciplinary orientation. The majority of the top-ranking disciplines belong to the biomedical sciences. The low scores of mathematics, astronomy and astrophysics confirm their traditional focus on mono-disciplinary basic research. Table 3.1 gives an overview of the cross-disciplinary citations (CDCs) according to top- and bottom-rated disciplines.

Table 3.1   CDC-related statistics of disciplines (within fixed journal set)

Discipline	CDC rate 1995 %
Top CDC rates	
Medical informatics	97.4
Mining and mineral processing	96.9
Information and library science	96.0
Vascular disease	95.1
Substance abuse	94.3
Mathematics – miscellaneous	94.1
Psychology	93.8
Geriatrics and gerontology	92.4
Biophysics	92.3
Research medicine	92.3
Public health	91.6
Bottom CDC rates	
Materials sciences – paper	56.2
Obstetrics and gynaecology	55.7
Biochemistry and molecular biology	54.0
Polymer science	53.8
Anaesthesiology	53.6
Agriculture – soil science	53.0
Ophthalmology	42.9
Mathematics	26.1
Astronomy and astrophysics	14.3

Source: Van Leeuwen and Tijssen (2000, p. 185).

In addition there is a series of case studies on the emergence of interdisciplinarity (Tijssen 1992; Rinia et al. 2001; Deppert and Theobald 1998; Bordons et al. 1999). These case studies range from natural and environmental resources as ecological–economic systems (Batabyal 2000) to autoimmune diseases and new drug development. In the case of interdisciplinarity in autoimmune diseases, Hinze (1999) assumes co-authorship to be an indicator of research collaboration. For selected European countries she found that something between 91 and 99 per cent of all publications were collaborative (with about 27 per cent involving international collaboration). Different collaboration strategies could be detected in nationally co-authored papers. For instance, Germany seems to focus more on intradepartmental collaboration, while France and Italy have stronger interinstitutional links. About 54 per cent of all publications are based on interdisciplinary collaboration, with an even higher share of interdisciplinary collaborations among the articles based on international collaborations.

Further examples of the emergence of interdisciplinarity are the modern methods of drug discovery and development. According to Reiss and Hinze (2000), the technological developments and achievements that contributed to the changing methods of drug discovery and development which emerged during the 1990s were: techniques for increasing the number of potential drug targets; new systems of screening; and techniques for increasing (by orders of magnitude) the number of chemicals with potential pharmaceutical activity. 'All in all, these changes are leading to a new scheme of drug discovery and development which is characterized by higher complexity and necessitates the interaction and integration of more different disciplines' (Reiss and Hinze 2000, p. 59). Figure 3.1 gives an overview of the new drug discoveries and developments and indicates their relevant disciplines.

Changing Needs for Interdisciplinary Research: Inherent Problems and Shortcomings of the Academic Setting

In the 1993 study 'Technology at the threshold of the twenty-first century' carried out by Grupp, it is stressed that technology at the beginning of the twenty-first century cannot be separated according to conventional disciplines. Regardless of how differently the paths of technology emerge, eventually they are all linked. An important finding of the TRACES study (a detailed discussion can be found in Schmoch et al. 1996a) is the clear recognition that important innovations often stem from the interaction of several previously unconnected streams of scientific and technological activity. For example, the research path of the development of the video recorder reveals that this particular innovation was the result of the merging of several streams of scientific and technological activity, including control theory, magnetic and recording materials, magnetic theory, magnetic recording, electronics and frequency modulation. Against this background, the authors of TRACES come to the conclusion that:

> Another important factor . . . was that of interaction between scientific disciplines and/or highly effective personal communication . . . Organizations which support and guide research must increase their emphasis on communication particularly among disciplines and between non-mission and mission-oriented research . . . The continued involvement of a variety of institutions would appear to be a worthwhile objective to help the need for diversity of research. (IIT Research Institute 1968, pp. 22–3; see also Irvine and Martin 1984, p. 20)

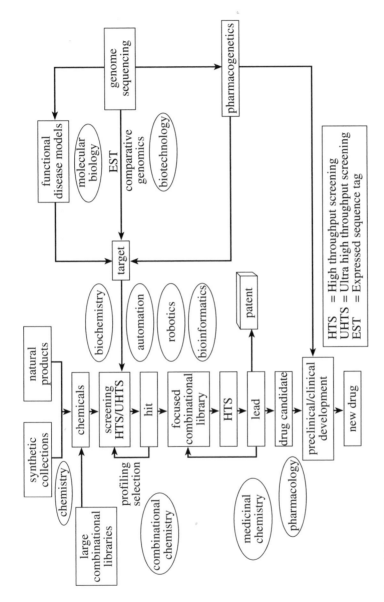

Source: Reiss and Hinze (2000).

Figure 3.1 *Overview of the new drug discoveries and developments and their relevance*

The intertwining between science and technology on the one hand, and between different technological areas on the other, requires new organizational and social innovations. This is also emphasized in Gibbons et al. (1994) who suggest that:

> [S]cientific and technological knowledge is coming to be produced in new ways . . . The familiar discipline-based, internally driven, individually-dominated structures that currently dominate the universities and the public sector laboratories are yielding to practically-oriented, transdisciplinary, network-dominated, flexible structures that are characteristic of the mode of organization of science and technology in the most advanced sectors. (Gibbons et al. 1994, p. 79)

Our view differs from that of Gibbons et al. because we assume that Mode 1 and Mode 2 knowledge production are coexisting, coevolving and interconnected.

The need for cooperation is expressed by scientists representing almost all branches of scientific activity. People like Heisenberg (1971), or von Weizsäcker (1978), philosophers, biologists and sociologists from different countries, commonly propose a joint effort by all disciplines to overcome the isolated development of knowledge production in favour of a broader-based strategy to tackle problems. Further reasons for interdisciplinarity (in Section 3 we refer to them as 'benefits') are as follows.

First, following Schmoch et al. (1996b), interdisciplinary research can be looked at from the perspective of a discipline-bound scientist who struggles with a specific research problem. He/she is searching for some kind of help from other disciplines that deal with related problems. Cooperation in this case aims at improving the process of knowledge production in a particular scientist's own discipline; it is efficiency increasing. Authors like Jantsch (1970) and Lenk (1978, 1980) point to the fact that the improvement of efficiency to solve problems within single disciplines remains crucial.

Second, and again following Schmoch et al. (1996b), there is a group of problems that have surfaced with the development of modern industrialized societies which economists call public goods, such as health, national security and the environment. As science took on the role of general problem-solver in the twentieth century, it is now expected that scientists will deliver solutions to such important problems for society. The range of these global problems, however, reaches far beyond the borders of single scientific disciplines. Consequently, scientists from various disciplines are forced to work together to find solutions (von Weizsäcker 1978; von Ditfurth 1984; Kocka 1987; Maier-Leibnitz 1992; Robson 1993). Probably because of the widespread public acknowledgement of these wide-ranging problems, national governments have undertaken initiatives for problem-bound interdisciplinary research on specific subjects. The book by van den Daele and Krohn

(1979) deals with the influence of government on national research agendas (especially in relation to interdisciplinary projects).

Schmoch et al.'s (1993) study on the theoretical and institutional background of the science and technology interface shows that knowledge transfer between science and industry takes various paths and urges cooperation from different disciplines and institutions. In this context, Grupp (1993) investigated the development and structure of technology at the threshold of the twenty-first century. What all these authors found contrasts sharply with traditional concepts of technology. The emerging technologies will no longer fit into common classification schemes because single technological developments are not evolving in isolation, but are the result of early and intensive networking between different areas of science and, thus, different disciplines. Consequently, new technological developments will not appear unless scientists and engineers from all disciplines work together. As in science, knowledge production is characterized by increasing interdisciplinarity. The overlapping areas are characterized by highly dynamic technological change as well as great economic importance (see Figure 3.2). Kodama (1992) calls this phenomenon 'technology fusion'.

The problems of interdisciplinary cooperation (referred to in Section 3 as 'costs') represent a diversity of factors: difficulties of communication,

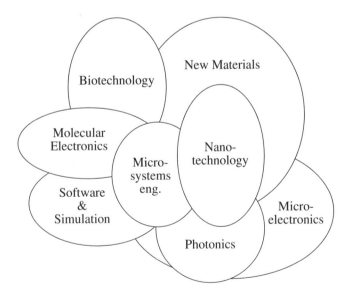

Source: Fraunhofer-ISI (Grupp 1993).

Figure 3.2   Technologies at the threshold of the twenty-first century

codes and language; discipline-specific theories, methods and reference systems; and finally the costs of establishing an absorptive capacity (Defila and Di Giulio 1996). Schmoch et al. (1996a) analysed these factors in further detail on the basis of case studies in the areas of medical lasers and neural networks. With regard to the disciplinary orientation, a strong tendency towards a division of research according to traditional disciplines even in interdisciplinary areas can be observed. In the case of medical lasers there is still a quite strict division between, on the one hand, technical, system-oriented research and on the other biomedical research. In neural networks the activities are generally divided into computer science and neuro-biology. A number of research areas, such as the natural or life sciences, are characterized by 'small' interdisciplinarity, with relatively close linkages between disciplinary methods and outlook. Research efforts in these areas bring together, for example, teams of physicists and electrical engineers or biologists and physicians. Only a few institutions have sought to integrate disciplines that are normally regarded as distant from one another. Where such integration has been pursued, the results have often led to substantial progress.

The results of these case studies confirm that industrial companies seem to find it relatively easy to organize interdisciplinarity. Companies, however, work in the applied part of interdisciplinary fields, where the disciplinary differences generally are not so great. For example, (see Schmoch et al. 1996a) the manufacturers of medical lasers have to integrate the work of physicists, electronic and mechanical engineers and precision machinists, but not physicians. Industrial research teams in neural networks generally consist of physicists, electrical engineers and computer specialists, but seldom biologists. The big interdisciplinary gaps between, for example, physics and medicine or computer science and biology, appear in the early stages of a new techno-scientific field and thus primarily at the level of basic research. As a consequence, academic institutions are initially confronted with problems of 'big' interdisciplinarity. The disciplinary structures in universities, however, are much more rigid than in industrial enterprises, and the introduction of interdisciplinary approaches in academic institutions creates a need for new types of organizations.

3   THE ANALYTICAL FRAMEWORK FOR INTERDISCIPLINARY RESEARCH INTERESTS IN UNIVERSITIES

To be able to develop the analysis further we need a representation of the process and stakes involved in this type of scientific evolution. Our purpose in this section is to propose a heuristic representation of the costs and benefits resulting from interdisciplinary research. To do this, we must be more specific about what we are representing.

The costs and benefits we are considering are those arising out of interdisciplinary research. Our purpose is to consider the university as a knowledge producer and active agent in the diffusion process. The benefits are the revenue (tangible and intangible, financial and non-financial) that the university can receive from conducting interdisciplinary research – one of them being to find solutions not only to industrial problems but also to societal ones such as health- and environmental-related issues. We assume that these benefits and costs can be represented on a similar scale and that there is a measure, of some kind, of the distance between disciplines. Finally, we assume that the benefits increase with disciplinary distance but at a decreasing rate; and that the costs increase at an increasing rate. The rationale behind this assumption is that the greater the diversity of the discipline involved in a research project, the more interesting and potentially fruitful will be the research but, at the same time, the more difficult will be the problems of communication, the mutual complementarities and cross-fertilizations.

Figure 3.3 represents the costs and benefits of interdisciplinary research, as a function of the 'distance' of the disciplines involved. Our reasoning starts from the situation represented by the two dashed lines representing the initial learning costs and benefits as a function of interdisciplinary distance. The figure illustrates that the largest net profit possible under the initial conditions is (1), where the gap between learning costs and benefits is greatest.

The arguments presented so far in this chapter offer several reasons why the learning benefits curve may be shifting upwards as depicted by the solid benefit curve in Figure 3.3. These reasons include:

1. the emergence of new science-based technologies, such as bio-informatics;
2. the increased interrelatedness of technologies (technology fusion); and, more importantly
3. the already mentioned trend of a significant shift from products to solution-oriented demand, which implies investment in focused, demand-oriented and interdisciplinary research.

As a consequence, even within a given institutional frame and incentive structure, there is an intrinsic interest in allowing for more interdisciplinary research or, as it is represented in Figure 3.3, a move from (1) to (2)

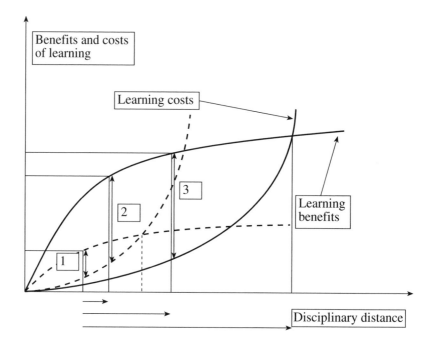

*Figure 3.3   A heuristic representation of the costs and benefits of
interdisciplinary research*

resulting from the greater benefits that can be achieved by moving outward
in disciplinary distance.

In the earlier sections of this chapter the argument was developed that
interdisciplinary research induces specific characteristics and costs. In fact,
some aspects of the institutional frame and of the incentive structure actually act as a deterrent to interdisciplinary research projects. This is particularly the case in universities and is the consequence of disciplinary
rigidities. If the evolution of the social needs requires greater interdisciplinarity, it is important to consider how the cost curve may be lowered and
displaced to the right as depicted in Figure 3.3 by the solid cost curve.

First, interdisciplinary research implies the de facto coexistence of strong
disciplinary expertise *and* interaction capabilities. The development of
interdisciplinary programmes will depend on one major factor: the existence of 'absorptive' capabilities, that is, the capability to interact in a constructive way with other disciplines. More generally this capability implies
the ability to understand the specific paradigm of other disciplines, that is,
to understand the procedures and algorithms used to select problems and
solutions, in a given scientific knowledge base. For research organizations

and the researchers themselves it is the ability to look outwards from their original disciplines and to absorb some of the reasoning and results from others. The development of such capabilities involves:

- at the individual level: specific training curricula, encouraging contact with other disciplines, but maintaining a strong disciplinary basis;
- at the institutional level: developing research programmes allowing for interactions between researchers from different disciplines, and considering interdisciplinary research as a real public good, relevant to societal needs, such as health and environment.

More generally the institutional framework should guarantee the symmetry of disciplines, and allow for interdisciplinary interactions. The institutional frame allows for a locus and forum for such interactions.

Second, the organization of research institutions and the incentive structure imposed on them and on individual researchers are essentially discipline oriented. In fact it is generally only disciplinary criteria and results that are recognized as being worthy, and careers for researchers are based on their disciplinary records. Interdisciplinary research is often seen as being second best and to be avoided by 'excellent' researchers anxious to build a career and reputation. The incentive structure, both at the individual level and at the research laboratory level, has to evolve, integrating and valorizing more positively (but not exclusively) the interdisciplinary dimension necessary to deal with particular research questions. From an economics viewpoint the incentive structure is one of the keys to influencing the knowledge production behaviour of individuals and organizations.

Third, an important part of the knowledge applied in research programmes, or at least during the duration of the research process itself, is tacit by nature. It is frequently the case that it is only once the results are obtained that the process of codification of both the process and the results begins. The institutional and organizational design must allow interactions to occur between disciplines, that is, between researchers from different disciplines, during the research process. Research institutions and organizations are responsible for the existence (or not) of communication patterns in the early stages of research programmes and projects and should develop means for early codification of intermediary results. They should allow access to the process of research and to non- or pre-codified knowledge. The development of interdisciplinary research is an additional argument for the development of strong rights of access to ongoing knowledge development with a rather weak system of property rights. It is necessary to 'ensure the dynamic efficiency of the innovative network and the development of a dynamics of creation and circulation of knowledge' (Cohendet and Meyer-Krahmer 2001, pp. 1563–91).

In Figure 3.3 the impact of these changes would correspond to a shift of the cost curve downward and to the right (from the dotted to the solid learning cost curve). As a consequence, the level of interdisciplinarity (or the distance between disciplines) involved in the research programme will increase, and there will be an increase in net benefits. In Section 4, the case of the University Louis Pasteur is used to illustrate a possible organizational solution that has been designed to favour the growth of interdisciplinary research and/or to create a more appropriate structure to satisfy changing scientific needs within research programmes.

4   CASE STUDY: UNIVERSITY LOUIS PASTEUR

University Louis Pasteur (ULP), located in Strasbourg, France, is historically a research university. The first major impulse of development came from the German Emperor, Kaiser Wilhelm, when the Alsace region was annexed to Germany, between 1870 and 1918. He redesigned both the infrastructure and research directions and organizations, based on Humboldtian principles, focusing on the natural and experimental sciences. The investments and focus were maintained when the university returned to French administration, with the addition of the life sciences after the Second World War. The reorganization of French universities after 1968 involved the constitution of three independent universities, University Louis Pasteur being one of them.

ULP is, in the French context, unusual, because of not only its history but also its structure. Since the nineteenth century, the main emphasis of the university has been on research (especially academic research) excellence and international openness. In fact, ULP is a medium-sized university in terms of number of students (16,500 in 2000), but receives the largest budget of the universities in France (almost €200 million including the salaries of public servants). Only 60 per cent of the budget is direct government subsidy (the national average being between 80 and 95 per cent). The main reason for these structural characteristics is that ULP is a large centre for medical and environmental analytical work. ULP conducts all the medical analysis for Strasbourg University Hospital and carries out environmental pollution analysis (principally in the areas of food and water), which is a secondary activity in terms of the budget it brings. The link with the University Hospital is essentially a heritage of the period of German administration, and is unique in France. It represents a budget of about €45 million.

Table 3.2   The faculties or similar components of ULP

Mathematics and computer sciences
Medicine
Chemistry
Physics
Pharmacy
Odontology
Life science
Psychology and educational sciences
Geography
Economics and management
Engineering schools in biotechnology, physics, chemistry and earth sciences
Professional institute for sciences and technology
Undergraduate technical institute

ULP is also usually characterized as a research university and, compared with other French universities, is internationally oriented. Twenty-seven per cent of the student population are postgraduate students, of whom about 30 per cent are foreigners. About 3,500 staff are engaged in research activities at ULP, including those personnel directly employed by the university and those working at the university that are employed by national organizations (for example, the Centre National de la Recherche Scientifique: CNRS, and the Institut National de la Santé et de la Recherche Médicale: INSERM). The research budget of ULP is about €35 million (civil servants' salaries, logistics and infrastructures not included). More than 50 per cent comes from external sources (public/private contracts), making it one of the most active university research contractors in the French university system.

The Organization of ULP Distinguishes between Teaching Activities and Research

Traditionally, teaching is organized in faculties. These faculties are essentially disciplinary (see Table 3.2). Heterogeneous disciplines are included in some curricula and some training programmes but in a rather marginal way, except either for very specialized professional training (in the environmental sciences, or production engineering) or for closely connected disciplines (clinical psychology and biology, for example). The main role of faculties is to organize training programmes (both academic and professional) and deliver nationally recognized degree courses, up to the master's level.

The organization changes somewhat when we consider postgraduate studies and especially doctoral studies. The structure is then trans-faculty and organized in doctoral schools. The doctoral schools are thus by definition interdisciplinary with the explicit goal of encouraging contacts between students engaged in the doctoral programme from different research areas, and delivering some common courses (especially those that are the most basic, or are of common interest). This organization is a first attempt to create some interaction between research groups and disciplines and it creates additional opportunities for interdisciplinarity.

Research activities, regarded in the Humboldt tradition to be a crucial activity, are organized in a different, though related, way to teaching.

ULP comprises 84 research units (or laboratories). The research units are not strictly or directly integrated in one particular faculty. Instead, they are, in the first instance, individually governed. In 1990, ULP decided to create a so-called research centre and/or a research federation, in other words groups of research units with common interests, focused around common research targets or objectives, research equipment and so on. In total, by 2000, ULP had defined 17 research federations. The role of the federation is to organize common research activities (seminars, conferences, technology transfer) and/or manage common services (libraries, equipment), to develop common research projects in the main domain of the particular federation. At ULP, most of the research federations are organizational structures relevant to the development of interdisciplinary research programmes.

The organizational frame of ULP has some consequences that can be interpreted in terms of our analytical framework. First, the initial training is focused on disciplines even if they are broadly defined, in order for young scholars to master at an advanced stage a core discipline of specialization. But as soon as a student is directed towards research activities (postgraduate studies) he or she is introduced to interdisciplinarity if not for their own research project, then in doctoral studies courses.[2] This type of doctoral training helps to lower some of the barriers of communication and to increase the common understanding of differentiated methodologies and techniques, and lower the cost curves represented in Figure 3.3.

The existence of organizations such as the federations, highly heterogeneous in terms not only of the disciplines involved but also in terms of activities and institutional identity and rationale, is an important factor in lowering the cost function, in order to increase the degree of profitability of interdisciplinary research programmes and to make it possible to tackle a group of problems, such as health, national security or environment, that have emerged as a result of the development of modern industrialized societies. In particular it enables research programmes to cross institutional boundaries and disciplinary frontiers.

An Example: The Molecules and Innovative Therapeutics Federation

The Molecules and Innovative Therapeutics (MIT) federation[3] is an interesting example – although very specialized, it is representative of the idea of the federation. It also demonstrates how the federation crosses the frontiers of the university itself, because it involves other national research institutes such as CNRS and INSERM.

The Molecules and Innovative Therapeutics federation is made up of six research units from ULP (EA in Figure 3.4), CNRS (UPR in Figure 3.4), INSERM (U in Figure 3.4) or a combination of ULP and CNRS (UMR in Figure 3.4). These units are organized around four competences: chemistry, protein engineering, screening and biology of interactions and cytometry. The federation has developed intensive collaborations with certain firms including HMR, Eli Lilly and Synthélabo, mostly through long-term contracts, or funding of PhD projects.

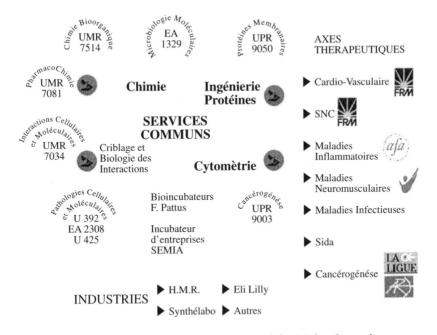

Figure 3.4   Presentation of the composition of the Molecules and Innovative Therapeutics research federation

MIT federation research projects address several major medical goals including treatments for AIDS and cancer, and have developed close relations with certain foundations and charities. They also provide the infrastructures to support start-ups (bio-incubator) and technology transfer. The MIT federation has strong connections with the Faculties of Pharmacy and Chemistry and the Engineering School in Biotechnology.

The main objective of the federations is to create an interdisciplinary research community encompassing computer scientists, biologists, pharmacists and chemists, developing applied research from basic and fundamental research on new drugs, in national public or university research laboratories or in start-ups.

This example shows, in particular, the institutional complexity that is needed to organize interdisciplinary research in the French context. The institutional, organizational and coordination costs are important and certain organizational devices have to be applied in order to minimize them: the federations at ULP serve this purpose.

The federations also allow for economies of scale and vertical integration of the research process, from fundamental research to final product (drugs, for example), with most of the necessary feedback loops and interactions being accomplished in-house.

The example of MIT shows also that the federations operate under very flexible and sometimes tacit rules of coordination and trust between the units and personnel involved. This is particularly important in terms of property rights, for instance. Very often the mutual rights and interests in getting access to the research in progress and to the results of the other members of the federation are higher than the individual interests linked to protection.

In fact, the MIT federation is a flexible organization that has emerged from ULP and operates as a coordination device for the new division of labour in knowledge production.

5   CONCLUDING REMARKS

The increasing importance of trans- and interdisciplinary research means that organizations must develop tools and organizational structures to integrate the intra- as well as the interorganizational knowledge in an efficient way. What are the appropriate means to exploit the *entire* knowledge base? This question has been discussed extensively in different science communities, for example, the management science literature (see von Wichert-Nick and Reger 1994). Trans- and interdisciplinarity calls for efficient horizontal coordination – the issue of science-based technologies for an efficient vertical coordination. A useful approach is Aoki's (1986) model, which links the level of the information structure to the level of the coordination mode and explains the necessary conditions and prerequisites for horizontal and vertical coordination. This model was aimed at the economic analysis of the organization of the firm. Essentially, it compares the relative efficiency of two information structures of the firm, the horizontal and vertical. Foray and Llerena (1996) used the model to discuss efficient information structures and coordination mechanisms in technology policy. It is the matching process of coordination structures (firms and policies) that is critical for interdisciplinary research.

During the 1990s, universities and research institutes established a specific organizational setting for interdisciplinary research. University research centres and institutes have been nominated as an important organizational locus or mechanism for interdisciplinary research collaboration. Lee (1999) studied 142 research centres engaged in energy or material research in engineering across 70 research-based universities in America. The study identified some important contexts and factors for interdisciplinary research collaboration. While the research centre size, the level of administrative integration and funding support were strongly associated with the potential for interdisciplinary collaboration, the establishment of interdisciplinarity as a mission of the research centre was likely to enhance the extent of interdisciplinary research carried out. An applied research orientation, along with a substantial presence of professional research staff, also encourages interdisciplinary activity. Disciplinary and faculty structures, however, were likely to be major barriers and inhibitors of interdisciplinary collaboration. Funding organizations also set up schemes to fund interdisciplinary research. Policansky (1999) studied the efforts of the national research council to support interdisciplinary problem-solving. Laudel (1999) studied the German science foundation (Deutsche Forschungsgemeinschaft) supporting interdisciplinary collaboration. Both studies demonstrate the importance for success of the incentive system, the organizational setting and the absorptive capacity.

An important consequence of the growing need for and extent of interdisciplinarity in science and technology policy is the necessary changes in organization, communication, interaction and motivation within the public research world. In science-based technologies, there is a need to identify new ways to link basic and applied research. In addition, fostering interdisciplinarity requires establishing better horizontal linkages between distinct disciplines. Interdisciplinarity is often confused in discussions of the integration or mixing of disciplines. It is essential to understand that first-class trans- and interdisciplinary research is highly dependent on the *disciplinary* quality of the scientists involved in such interdisciplinary research being first-class. Therefore, an efficient linkage between (and not the integration of) disciplines is crucial. Possible mechanisms of such linkages are:

- Organization of research: problem orientation in the case of easily definable social or industrial–technical problems. This demands new ways of organizing and managing research projects and researcher careers that differ from the inwardly-looking and discipline-bounded methods used at present.
- Better linkage of long-term application-oriented basic research with applied research would meet future requirements better. This could be achieved, for example, by an improved institutional network, cooperative research on specific subjects, new models of financing, improved communication and other assessment criteria.
- Team research: besides the currently predominant orientation of academic research towards individualized research setting, team research must be strengthened. The promotion of research groups is a good beginning here, as well as the setting-up of cooperatively managed institutes.
- Improved intra- and intersectoral mobility of researchers: on an international level and also between science and industry.
- Increased flexibility of research structures: more rapid take-up of new developments through relaxation of the present rigid public service rules and budget laws; deregulation of the academic administration; and networking of research institutions for a limited time, especially in an international framework (virtual research institutes).

More generally, the research structures need to strive for more openness, interaction and flexibility in actions and initiatives.

NOTES

1. In particular, Patrick Llerena has been Vice-President for both Industrial Relations and Finance and Development at ULP.
2. We do not consider here professional training, where the exposure to interdisciplinarity arises earlier.
3. More information can be found on the web site: http://www-ifr-glaustriat.u-strasbg.fr/Rech/rech.htm.

REFERENCES

Aoki, M. (1986), 'Horizontal vs. vertical information structure of the firm', *American Economic Review* **76**(5), 121–36.

Batabyal, A.A. (2000), 'An interdisciplinary research agenda for the study of ecological–economic systems in the American West', in *Resources Policy* **26**(2), 69–75.

Bordons, M., M.A. Zulueta and S. Barrignon (1999), 'Measuring interdisciplinary collaboration within a university: the effects of the multidisciplinary research programme', *Scientometrics* **46**(3), 383–98.

Cohendet, P. and F. Meyer-Krahmer (2001), 'The theoretical and policy implications of knowledge codification', *Research Policy* **30**(9), 1563–91.

Defila, R. and A. Di Giulio (1996), *Voraussetzungen zu interdisziplinärem Arbeiten und Grundlagen ihrer Vermittlung*, Basel: Birkhäuser.

Deppert, W. and W. Theobald (1998), 'Eine wissenschaftstheorie der Interdisziplinarität. Zur Grundlegung integrativer Umweltforschung und-bewertung', in *Umweltforschung quergedacht. Perspektiven integrativer Umweltforschung und -lehre*, Berlin/Heidelberg/New York: Springer pp. 75–106.

Foray, D. and P. Llerena (1996), 'Information structure and coordination in technology policy. A theoretical model and two case studies', *Journal of Evolutionary Economics* **6**(2), 157–74.

Gibbons, M., C. Limoges, H. Nowotny, S. Schwartzman, P. Scott, P. and M. Trow (1994), *The New Production of Knowledge*, London: Sage.

Grupp, H. (ed.) (1993), *Technologie am beginn des 21 jahrhunderts*, Heidelberg: Physica-Verlag (abridged: 'Technology at the beginning of the twenty-first century', *Technology Analysis & Strategic Management* **6**(4), 379–410.

Heisenberg, W. (1971), *Schritte über Grenzen. Gesammelte Reden und Aufsätze*, Munich: R. Piper & Co. Verlag.

Hinze, S. (1999), 'Collaboration and cross-disciplinarity in auto-immune diseases', *Scientometrics* **46**(3), 457–71.

Illinois Institute of Technology Research Institute (1968), *Technology in Retrospect and Critical Events in Science*, study for the National Science Foundation, Chicago: Illinois Institute of Technology.

Irvine, J. and B.R. Martin (1984), *Foresight in Science. Picking the Winners*, London: Frances Pinter.

Jantsch, E. (1970), 'Inter- and trans-disciplinary university: a systems approach to education and innovation', *Policy Sciences* **1**(4), 403–28.

Kocka, J. (ed.) (1987), *Interdisziplinarität, Praxis – Herausforderung – Ideologie*, Frankfurt: Suhrkamp.

Kodama, F. (1992), 'Technology fusion and the new R&D', *Harvard Business Review* **7**(4), 70–78.

Laudel, G. (1999), *Interdisziplinäre Forschungskooperation: Erfolgsbedingungen der Institution 'Sonderforschungsbereich'*, Berlin: Ed. Sigma.

Lee, S.-J. (1999), 'Interdisciplinary collaboration at university research centers and institutes in engineering: an analysis of organizational and environmental contexts and factors', unpublished D.Phil. dissertation, University of Oregon.

Lenk, H. (1978), 'Philosophie als fokus und forum', in H. Lübbe (ed.), *Wozu Philosophie?*, Berlin, New York: de Gruyter, pp. 35–69.

Lenk, H. (1980), 'Interdisziplinarität und die rolle der philosophie', *Zeitschrift für Didaktik der Philosophie* **1**, 10–19.

Maier-Leibnitz, H. (1992), 'Science and the humanities: a plea for interdisciplinary communication', *Interdisciplinary Science Reviews* **17**(2), 171–7.

Metzger, N. and R. Zare (1999), 'Interdisciplinary research: from belief to reality', *Science*, **283**(5402), 642–3.

Policansky, D. (1999), 'Interdisciplinary problem solving: the national research council', *Policy Sciences* **32**(4), 385–91.

Reiss, T. and S. Hinze (2000), 'Innovation process and techno-scientific dynamics', in A. Jungmittag, G. Reger and T. Reiss (eds), *Changing Innovation in the Pharmaceutical Industry – Globalization and New Ways of Drug Development*, Berlin, New York: Springer Verlag, pp. 53–65.

Rinia, E.J., N. van Leeuwen, H.G. van Vuren and A.F.J. van Raan (2001), 'Influence of interdisciplinarity on peer-review and bibliometric evaluations in physics research', *Research Policy* **30**(3), 357–61.

Robson, M. (1993), 'Interdisciplinary efforts are needed as researchers battle environmental threats', *The Scientist* **7**(7), 12–14.

Schmoch, U., S. Breiner, K. Cuhls, S. Hinze and G. Münt (1996a), 'The organisation of interdisciplinarity – research structures in the areas of medical lasers and neural networks', in G. Reger and U. Schmoch (eds), *Organisation of Science and Technology at the Watershed. The Academic and Industrial Perspective*, Heidelberg: Physica-Verlag, S. 267–398.

Schmoch, U., S. Hinze, G. Jaeckel, N. Kirsch, F. Meyer-Krahmer and G. Münt (1996b), 'The role of the scientific community in the generation of technology', in G. Reger and U. Schmoch (eds), *Organisation of Science and Technology at the Watershed. The Academic and Industrial Perspective*, Heidelberg: Physica-Verlag, S. 1–138.

Schmoch, U., E. Strauss, H. Grupp and T. Reiß (1993), 'Indicators for the scientific base of European patents', Report to the CEC (DG XIII), Karlsruhe.

Tijssen, R.J.W. (1992), 'A quantitative assessment of interdisciplinary structures in science and technology: co-classification analysis of energy research', *Research Policy* **21**(1), 27–44.

van den Daele, W. and W. Krohn (1979), *Geplante Forschung: Vergleichende Studien über den Einfluß politischer Programme auf die Wissenschaftsentwicklung*, Frankfurt: Suhrkamp.

von Ditfurth, H. (1984), *Wir sind nicht nur von dieser Welt*, Munich: Hoffman und Campe.

van Leeuwen, T. and R. Tijssen (2000), 'Interdisciplinary dynamics of modern science: Analysis of cross-disciplinary citation flows', *Research Evaluation* **9**(3), 183–7.

von Weizsäcker, C.F. (1978), *Der Garten des Menschlichen*, Munich: Carl Hanser.

von Wichert-Nick, D. and G. Reger (1994), 'The implementation of a learning organization for R&D management', in *Evolutionary Economics of Technological Change: Assessment of Results and New Frontiers*, Proceedings of the EUNETIC Conference, Strasbourg: European Parliament, pp. 1173–98.

Commentaries

KEITH PAVITT

Ben Martin and Michel Callon were both asked to launch a debate about important changes in science policy, and their chapters do this admirably. Martin's chapter (Chapter 1) concentrates on publicly funded science and Callon's chapter (Chapter 2) focuses on socio-technical controversies and scientific activities designed to reduce negative externalities. My comments have two objectives. First, to redress the balance towards continuity compared to change in science policy: my theme song is not Bob Dylan's 'Times, they are a'changing', but Shirley Bassey's 'A little bit of history repeating'. Second, to try to distinguish fads from facts, perceptions from practices: science policy is like managing in a changing and unpredictable world – important, difficult, not well understood, and therefore subject to swings in fashion.

1 Government Funding of Academic Research

In Europe, public policies towards academic research are, as the papers show, subject to competing perceptions. Going out of fashion are the models that are linear, and those based on Bush, Humboldt and the Cold War. In fashion are shifts from Mode 1 to Mode 2, to the triple helix, to the knowledge economy, and – more generally – towards a more explicit concern for practical utility. These apparent shifts need to be tested – as best we can – against actual practice in the support and practice of academic research and in its links with business and other users. The following picture emerges:

- *The substantial share of applied subjects* Although difficult to estimate precisely, applied subjects like engineering, medicine, geology and agricultural sciences continue to account for a high (that is, more than 50 per cent) share of academic research in leading OECD countries.
- *Continuing dominance of public funding* Public funding continues to dominate academic research (more than 90 per cent of the total) despite calls for more privatization and for closer links with corporate

users. A higher corporate share in a country is not associated with greater technological dynamism: it is, for example, higher in Belgium than in the US. Inputs and outputs of basic research are in general highest in those countries with strong commitments to corporate research and development (R&D): Switzerland, Scandinavia and the US.

- *Useful academic research is good academic research*   Systematic evidence from the US shows that the academic research that corporate practitioners find most useful is publicly funded, performed in the research universities, and published in prestigious refereed journals. Evidence from other countries is anecdotal but similar. In Germany, for example, the Humboldt model has in fact traditionally included strong corporate links with academic physics and chemistry, and the establishment of the *Technischehocheschulen*.

- *Evidence of 'widespread dissatisfaction' among corporate users is sparse*   Here the situation apparently varies widely among countries. In the UK, where critical rhetoric is among the strongest, it comes mainly from government sources (of which more below). In the US, companies like IBM have complained recently about the potentially harmful effects on future technological competitiveness of *reductions* in *public* support for *academic* research in the *physical* sciences.

These observations lead me to three conclusions. Academic research continues to be appreciated by technologically aware corporate practitioners. Most of the criticisms about lack of relevance come from government officials and politicians, especially from ministries of finance, often based on simplistic notions of public accountability. International differences in public policies reflect differences in the relative weight of these officials, compared to the weight of technologically dynamic business firms advocating strong public support for high-quality basic research. This explains the stronger public support given to academic research in the US, Switzerland and Scandinavia than in the UK.

Models simplify, and no one simple model is a sufficient basis for policy, although each may offer interesting insights. Thus Humboldt's prescription of the autonomy of academic research and its links with research training would be supported by many corporate practitioners, Modes 1 and 2 have been around for a long time and are complementary, and the origins in academic science of information and communication technology, biotechnology and modern materials give at least partial credence to the linear (*alias* Vannevar Bush) model.

Within this context, the following changes in academic science policy deserve further consideration:

- the internationalization (not globalization) of the links between academic research and corporate practice, reflected in the partial internationalization of corporate R&D, and of postgraduate research training and
- the increase in the direct usefulness of academic research in biotechnology and software, reflected in the increasing volume of university licensing and spinoff firms.

2 Socio-technical Controversies: Science to Reduce Negative Externalities

Michel Callon is right to identify the importance of socio-technical controversies in science policy. However, there are grounds for arguing that they are not new. For example, in the nineteenth century, scientists were heavily involved in actions to improve public health in the growing and insalubrious towns and cities, as well as safety and working conditions in mines and factories. More recently, and reflecting the growing direct links between science, technology and the increasingly destructive nature of weapons, they have become involved through the Pugwash conference and other mechanisms in the development and implementation of international treaties regulating the development and use of nuclear, chemical and biological weapons.

However, he is right to point to the growing importance of biology in such controversies and to the shift of concern from producers (workers) to consumers and residents. In addition, his insistence on the importance of 'reliable' science, properly validated through laboratory-based procedures, is supported (in this writer's view) by what happened during the recent major crisis of foot-and-mouth disease in the UK. In the best traditions of openness and democracy, many individuals and concerned groups had a point of view on its causes and required policies – and did not hesitate to express them publicly. Nearly all the opinions and recommendations were entirely predictable on the basis of either the ideology or material interests of those expressing them. One of the few exceptions was the government's chief scientist, who in the early stages publicly contradicted an elected minister by saying that the epidemic was not under control. Based on a number of epidemiological models, he also made public predictions about what would happen if various courses of action were followed, and these have turned out broadly to be correct. Whether the policies themselves were the correct ones is still a matter for debate. But properly validated science was able to get the dynamics of the epidemic right.

This brings me finally to two difficulties about what Callon calls 'translation' between socio-technical controversies and what laboratory-based science can do. The first is the inevitable difficulty of maintaining clear distinctions between science and politics. Institutions may not find it in their interest to be scientifically open and rigorous. Callon cites as an example the famous disappearance, according to government officials, of the Chernobyl radioactive cloud once it reached the frontiers of France; similar behaviour has been observed in Greenpeace and other groups that claim to represent consumers and residents. And even if the scientific experts genuinely try to be rigorous, the complexity of the subject matter may defeat them, when it involves multiple fields of expertise, and judgements that cannot be corroborated in the laboratory.[1]

The second difficulty is deciding who pays for laboratory science related to socio-technical controversies? In principle, the economic case for government support is much stronger than for so-called 'out-reach' activities to support the competitive and profit-making activities of private firms. In practice, the difficulties are many. As with the disappearance of radioactive clouds, governments may be part of the problem rather than the solution. And how to distinguish genuine controversies from special pleading? This is a rich field for debate and institutional innovation in science policy. In the meantime, pluralism in funding sources – including private charities and foundations – should probably be encouraged.

3   A Mild Warning about Change for its Own Sake

It is sometimes assumed that the new is by definition exciting, important, better and happening quickly; and (symmetrically) that the old (that is, what exists) should be changed, and that those defending it are inevitably the servants of special interests and inefficiency. This may indeed sometimes be the case, for example, in opposition to demonstrably better research practices, to exploring opportunities (or dangers) emerging from new knowledge or even to the acceptance of properly validated new knowledge itself.

In the case of science policy, some new opportunities and problems do deserve more serious consideration: for example, the increasing internationalization of links between research and technological practice, the 'massification' of higher education, the new technological opportunities emerging from university research, socio-technical controversies and the welfare and ethical problems associated with recent biomedical advances.

However, most of these processes have been happening progressively over a long period, and the same can be said about the 'knowledge' economy, the 'learning' economy and the 'new' economy. Coping with them does not require precipitate action. Above all, it does not justify tampering with or diluting the institutions that produce knowledge that John Ziman has called 'public' and 'reliable'. Both autonomous and open academic science (and related postgraduate training), and laboratory science, are not simply expressions of a scientific humanism and an enlightenment that some consider outmoded. They are also – as we have seen above – efficient vehicles for defining and solving contemporary problems. They should therefore be supported and protected by those who claim to be managing the present system, and also those who criticize it.

DAVID A. WOLFE

Despite the growing consensus that the industrial economies are becoming more 'knowledge based', there remains considerable disagreement over the implications of this development for the changing role of the universities in the creation and dissemination of knowledge. Knowledge-based economies are those in which the production, use and distribution of knowledge and information are critical to the process of economic growth and development. The innovation system in a knowledge-based economy encompasses the key functions of: knowledge production – developing and providing new knowledge; knowledge transmission – educating and developing human resources; and knowledge transfer – disseminating knowledge and problem solving (OECD 1996). In most industrial countries, the government funds between 20 and 50 per cent of research and development (R&D) and much of this funding is directed towards universities, although the actual proportion across the OECD countries varies. Universities act as a primary source of 'knowledge workers', as well as a primary source of the key factor of production – knowledge itself. A recent survey in *The Economist* goes even further, in arguing that the university acts 'not just as a creator of knowledge, a trainer of young minds and a transmitter of culture, but also as a major agent of economic growth: the knowledge factory, as it were, at the centre of the knowledge economy' (David 1997, p. 4).

At issue is the changing nature of the relationship between universities and the broader innovation system in which they are embedded, as well as the process of scientific investigation and discovery that underlies the knowledge production function. While firms are the primary source of commercially directed innovation, since the early 1980s private firms have expanded their research linkages with universities, partly in response to the rising cost of conducting R&D. This trend has coincided with increasing budget constraints on government and a decline in public funding for university-based research. The growing concern on the part of governments to facilitate the process of knowledge transfer within the innovation system has also generated greater pressure on universities to collaborate with private firms. This pressure, in turn, creates an internal tension between their roles in the development and transmission of knowledge (research and teaching) and that of transferring knowledge to other actors in the innovation system (OECD Secretariat 2000).

While the linkages between universities and private firms have grown over the 1980s and 1990s, agreement on the appropriate boundaries of their respective roles has not kept pace. One issue that underlies this confusion concerns the distinction between basic and applied research – and where primary responsibility for the performance of each should lie. Basic research seeks to widen the understanding of the phenomenon of a scientific field. The defining quality of basic research is the contribution it makes to the general body of knowledge within an area of science. In contrast, applied research is directed towards some individual or group or societal need or use. In its second annual report in 1952, the National Science Foundation defined the relationship between the two as a linear model involving the progression through a technological sequence leading eventually to product development, the final stage involving the systematic adoption of research findings into useful materials, devices, systems, methods and processes (Stokes 1997). Theoretical support for this model, and an underlying justification for government funding of basic research, was provided by the pathbreaking work of Richard Nelson and Kenneth Arrow in the late 1950s and 1960s. Nelson explained why many potential applications and new combinations of knowledge would not be fully explored or developed if the private firms undertaking the research captured the benefits for themselves, either by keeping the results secret or by exerting their property rights over the findings. Arrow extended this analysis by arguing that the output of basic research took the form of information that was expensive to generate, but effectively costless to reproduce and use, thereby exhibiting the qualities of a true public good (Pavitt 2001).

The linear model has been subject to considerable criticism and refinement since the 1980s. Stokes argues that positing a rigid dichotomy between basic and applied research misapprehends the fundamental nature of scientific research (Stokes 1997). Much scientific investigation is driven by concerns for both the expansion of knowledge and its potential use. The relationship between basic and applied research moves along parallel trajectories that intersect, but maintain their autonomy. Science often proceeds to a higher level of understanding with little regard to the implications for technological improvement, while much technological innovation involves narrowly targeted engineering or design changes, based on existing or well-understood science (ibid., p. 87). Branscomb argues in similar fashion that much of what is classified as applied research is really need-driven creative research into new kinds of materials, new processes or ways of exploring or measuring, and new ways of doing and making things, which he calls 'basic technological research' (Branscomb 1998).

Both use-inspired basic research and basic technological research may lead to commercializable products, but only a small portion of that research has such potential and the process frequently involves considerable time lags. Furthermore, much of the knowledge transfer from public research organizations to other parts of the innovation system is person-embodied. The effective exploitation of that knowledge depends on the capacity of firms to absorb and apply research results, not all of which are transmitted in a codified form. Knowledge is therefore not a freely available good, but involves a large tacit component of skills and capabilities embodied in people, products and procedures (Cohen and Levinthal 1990; Pavitt 1991; Senker 1995). These capabilities also depend on the specific institutional arrangements and cultural setting within which knowledge is disseminated – including the mechanisms for coordinating and organizing non-market dimensions of interfirm relationships, the nature of the financial system, the organization of the education and training system, and not least, the role of government policy. This constitutes the key contribution of the innovation systems literature (Lundvall and Maskell 2000).

All three of the chapters referred to above are concerned with changes in the social setting for the conduct of scientific research, but they downplay the extent to which these changes are conditioned by the institutional arrangements and cultural environments of national (and regional) innovation systems. Both Martin (Chapter 1) and Callon (Chapter 2) suggest that the 'social contract' for science forged in the aftermath of the Second World War saw society willing to fund massive investments in basic research in the expectation of long-term economic benefits, while leaving the principal research institutions, the universities, autonomy in the conduct of that research. The social contract had several critical implications for the conduct of science in post-war society: it implied a high degree of autonomy for the realm of science, vigorously reinforced by the 'boundary work' of the scientific community itself; it afforded 'expert' status to the role of scientists in the exercise of judgement about most matters relating to the conduct of scientific investigations and the application of the resulting knowledge; it privileged the role of the universities and other public research organizations as the principal sites for the conduct of scientific research (although these arrangements exhibited considerable national variation across innovation systems); and it assumed a strict separation between the sphere of science and that of politics and economics.

The chapters agree that many elements of this contract have been subject to increasing strain since the 1980s. This questioning is the outcome of a broader shift in the lines demarcating the university from other aspects of society, reflecting, in part, the massification and democratization of the post-secondary education system; a questioning of the universities and their individual disciplines as the sole, or even primary, source of scientific expertise; the growing internationalization of scientific communities facilitated by the adoption of information and communication technologies; a greater involvement of industry with university research; an increase in interdisciplinary research and a shift in the emphasis of government funding from basic to more applied research; and, finally, a greater expectation that university-based research will lead directly to commercializable results. This shift is reinforced by the political expectation that research funding be tied to broader public policy objectives about promoting national innovative capacity and increased competitiveness.

However, Martin maintains that if one adopts a longer-term historical view, this shift appears less like a new phenomenon than a return to the conditions that prevailed prior to the Second World War. In the late nineteenth century the expectation that universities would contribute to broader social and economic goals was widespread among some of the European universities, particularly those in Germany, as well as some in Japan. Even in the US, the land-grant universities established by the Morrill Act in 1862 were allocated many of these functions. Martin suggests that the post-1980s relationship between the universities and other actors in the innovation system more closely resembles this historical model than the one embodied in the post-war social contract for science. Yet, as Stokes and Branscomb suggest, and Martin acknowledges, the university system has been the locus of both basic and applied research over most of its history and, even at the height of the post-war period, much government funding was also directed at applied research. Martin concludes that the future university system may be characterized by a diversity of institutions with a greater variety of combinations of teaching and research functions, more networking among universities by electronic means, more interdisciplinary undertakings within institutions and a more entrepreneurial flavour. The university may even become more autonomous as its dependence on government funding is reduced.

The changing relationship between scientific expertise and the broader social and institutional settings within which science is conducted underlies Michel Callon's (Chapter 2) conception of 'research in the wild'. He argues that the institutions vested with responsibility for the conduct of scientific and technical activities in the second half of the twentieth century have entered a period of reconfiguration. The basic characteristics of these institutions included a clear division between the roles of scientific experts and political authorities; the exclusion of the public from sophisticated debates about the nature of scientific knowledge; the conduct of not-for-profit research in public sector agencies and universities; substantial investment by the public sector in major programmes for technology development, both civilian and military; and, finally, a key role for physics and chemistry in the conduct of research. A key aspect of the post-war configuration for scientific research was the attempt to maintain a strict separation between the sphere of research, on the one hand, and the economic and political sphere that provided funding for, and used, the outputs of that research, on the other. He argues that a new model is emerging that redistributes expertise and political responsibility, as well as challenging the strict division between the political and scientific and between the notions of those viewed as experts and those excluded from scientific debates due to a lack of expertise. The greater involvement of democratic publics in scientific debates, termed 'research in the wild', makes it difficult to exclude them. Research must be opened up to these new actors and they should be engaged in a process of cooperative research, where confined research and 'research in the wild' interact at each critical stage.

This cooperation will result in a new public space labelled hybrid forms – open spaces where a multiplicity of groups involving both expert and concerned lay people can debate technical choices that have a powerful impact on their collective well-being. Technical democracy, or taking account of science and techniques in democratic procedures and institutions, requires an explicit recognition of the legitimate role played by these concerned groups. The notion of cooperative research and hybrid spaces provides an alternative to the vision of scientific investigation that prevailed under the post-war social contract for science, yet it is surprisingly vague in terms of the implications of national (or regional) differences for this model and the extent to which existing political and institutional arrangements will support the conduct of cooperative research and the creation of hybrid spaces.

The chapter by Llerena and Meyer-Krahmer (Chapter 3) also deals with changes in the nature of the university as a research institution. They identify a number of changes impacting on the role of universities, including the increasing costs of innovation, the growing importance of interdisciplinary research, the overlapping of technology areas, an increasingly close relationship between basic research and industrial application, as well as a tighter integration of research and the demand for its results. They develop a framework for analysing the nature of interdisciplinary research in the changing university structure, which emphasizes three key elements. The first is that interdisciplinary research implies a de facto coexistence of strong disciplinary expertise and the capability for interaction among the distinct disciplinary traditions. This requires the presence of strong absorptive capabilities on the part of individual disciplines, as well as a capacity to exchange ideas in a constructive manner with other disciplines. The second point recognizes that the organization of research institutions and the incentive structure imposed on them are essentially discipline oriented. The third point is that a key part of the knowledge used in research programmes is tacit in nature. The institutional and organizational design for successful interdisciplinary research must allow for interactions between the disciplines and take account of the fact that much of the knowledge base of disciplinary research is tacit in nature.

Based on their case study of interdisciplinary research at University Louis Pasteur in France, they conclude that the growing importance of interdisciplinary research means that the institutions involved must develop new tools and organizational structures to integrate the interdisciplinary knowledge within them in an efficient way. The emerging science-based technology paradigm should not be seen as a return to the linear model, but rather to a more interactive view of the nature of technology transfer in the innovation system with more feedbacks and better linkages between public and private and basic and applied research. They characterize these knowledge flows as a 'two-way bridge' and argue that policies to strengthen the innovation system must enhance the organizational linkages to improve these flows.

The key changes discussed in these chapters – the changing relationship between the respective roles of private firms and universities in the performance of basic and applied research, the shifting boundaries between scientific expertise and concerned public groups and the increase in interdisciplinary research with its implications for the operation of universities and the wider innovation system – all involve changes in the prevailing institutional arrangements within the innovation system, but these arrangements exhibit distinct national (and regional) variations. Countries vary in the extent to which, and the sectors in which, they display a strong capacity to perform research and development and introduce new products and processes, due to the underlying structure of their innovation systems and the linkages between the elements of those systems. Similarly, the changes affecting the role of the university in the innovation system exhibit distinctive national variations; an effective understanding of the role must take account of these variations.

Recent changes in the character of the university system within the US innovation system illustrate this point. Although the post-war social contract set out the guiding principles for federal involvement with the funding of university research, the federal government was far from being the only player in that system. In fact, analyses of the changing role of the university in the US innovation system highlight a number of its key features. The post-war university system was highly decentralized in terms of the multiple sources of institutional control and sources of funding, both for ongoing operations, as well as for the conduct of scientific research. Closely related to this was the highly competitive nature of the university system, especially in terms of research funding. Competition for research funding placed continuing pressure on the universities to adjust their research priorities, policies and cost structures to the prevailing demand in the market for academic research. Third was the highly regional nature of the university system that ensured that the research activities of the universities were linked to the economic base of their regions (a legacy of the land-grant tradition), but also provided an important source of new knowledge and ideas for the stimulus of local industry. Finally, there was a linking of research activities and graduate teaching that contributed to the process of knowledge transfer from the universities to industry embedded in the tacit know-how of their graduates (Rosenberg and Nelson 1994; Feller 1999; Pavitt 2001).

Some of these features have been accentuated by more recent trends since the 1980s. Chief among these trends is the decline in the universities' share of national basic research performed, especially from 1995 to 1999, which parallels the dramatic increase in the share of basic research performed by private industry. This growth was linked to the economic boom in the US (and the increasing availability of venture capital as an alternative source of funding, especially for biomedical and biotechnology research) that may not be equalled in the current decade. The decline in the level of basic research performed by the universities as well as the rise in the proportion of research funded from the universities' own sources also reflected the drop in federal support for university-performed R&D. The other key trend is the rise in the level of federal funding for biomedical research through one principal agency, the National Institutes of Health, which may come to dominate federal funding of R&D to an even greater extent than the Defense Department did at the height of the Cold War. These shifts reflect the broad restructuring of the R&D system that has followed the end of the Cold War, as well as the impact of the 1990s economic boom on the funding and locus of research performance in the US innovation system (Mowery 2002). Thus, the changing role of the universities in the US must be analysed in the context of this broader restructuring of institutional arrangements in its national innovation system.

The preceding analysis highlights how the specificity of institutional arrangements within the national innovation system conditions the conduct of scientific research within its public research organizations. It also draws attention to the fact that some of the most important impacts of the national innovation system are felt at the local and regional levels. This insight is reinforced by a growing body of research that emphasizes the importance of proximity in the transfer of knowledge from the institutions that generate it to those that adopt and apply it. This research underlines the fact that the linkages and benefits from public investments in basic research are increasingly localized. Proximity to the source of the research is critical for the success with which new product innovations are transferred from the laboratory to commercial exploitation. While much of the research on which these findings are based rely on US data, a recent study using European data reports similar results. The most frequently cited explanation for this proximity effect is the need to gain access to tacit knowledge, or at least knowledge that is not yet codified. Conversely, the role of proximity declines when useful knowledge is available in a codified form. This suggests that proximity may be more important for the transfer of relatively new research results in science-based fields where personal access to those conducting the research is critical for the effective transfer of its insights (Feldman 2000; Adams 2001; Arundel and Geuna 2001). This has important implications for the development of local clusters and regional innovation systems, especially in the critical fields of biomedical and biotechnology research, if the broad trends described by Mowery at the national level continue.

These chapters provide a valuable contribution to the ongoing debate over the changing role of the university in the knowledge-based economy and the corresponding shift in the relationship between scientific expertise and the broader society. Two competing conceptions of the changes affecting the nature of science and the role of the universities are emerging from this debate – one that sees the process of knowledge creation, dissemination and application as increasingly complex, formalized and global; the other that sees it as intensely personal, experience (or tacit knowledge) based and proximate. Applying the insights derived from these contributions to the evaluation of the policy rationales for public support of research requires that we ground the general insights they afford in the institutional specificities of both national and regional innovation systems.

NOTE

1. Hence, according to Gilpin (1962) US scientists involved in nuclear policy in the 1950s thought they had technical disagreements, when they were in fact political.

REFERENCES

Adams, J.D. (2001), 'Comparative localization of academic and industrial spillovers', National Bureau of Economic Research Working Paper No. 8292, http://www.nber.org/papers/w8292.

Arundel, A. and A. Geuna (2001), 'Does proximity matter for knowledge transfer from public institutes and universities to firms?', Brighton: SPRU – Science and Technology Policy Research, University of Sussex, October.

Branscomb, L. (1998), 'From science policy to research policy', in L.M. Branscomb and J.H. Keller (eds), *Investing in Innovation: Creating a Research and Innovation Policy that Works*, Cambridge, MA: MIT Press, pp. 112–39.

Cohen, W.M. and D.A. Levinthal (1990), 'Absorptive capacity: a new perspective on learning and innovation', *Administrative Science Quarterly* **35**(1), 128–52.

David, P. (1997), 'The knowledge factory: a survey of universities', *The Economist*, 4 October, 2–22.

Feldman, M.P. (2000), 'Location and innovation: the new economic geography of innovation, spillovers and agglomeration', in G.L. Clark, M. Gertler and M.P. Feldman (eds), *The Oxford Handbook of Economic Geography*, Oxford: Oxford University Press, pp. 373–94.

Feller, I. (1999), 'The American university system as a performer of basic and applied research', in L.M. Branscomb, F. Kodama and R. Florida (eds), *Industrializing Knowledge*, Cambridge, MA: MIT Press, pp. 65–101.

Gilpin, R. (1962), *American Scientists and Nuclear Weapons Policy*, Princeton, NJ: Princeton University Press.

Lundvall, B.-Å. and P. Maskell (2000), 'Nation states and economic development: from national systems of production to national systems of knowledge creation and learning', in G.L. Clark, M. Gertler and M.P. Feldman (eds), *The Oxford Handbook of Economic Geography*, Oxford: Oxford University Press, Ch. 18.

Mowery, D. (2002), 'The changing role of universities in the 21st century US R&D system', in A.H. Teich, S.D. Nelson and S.J. Lita (eds), *AAAS Science and Technology Policy Yearbook 2002*, Washington, DC: American Association for the Advancement of Science, Part 7, available at www.aaas.org/spp/yearbook/2002/Ch.2S.pdf.

Organisation for Economic Cooperation and Development (OECD) (1996), 'Special Theme: The Knowledge-based Economy', in *Science, Technology and Industry Outlook 1996*, Paris: OECD, pp. 229–56.

OECD Secretariat (2000), 'Trends in university–industry research partnerships', *STI Review* **23**, 39–65.

Pavitt, K. (1991), 'What makes basic research economically useful?', *Research Policy* **20**(2), 109–19.

Pavitt, K. (2001), 'Public policies to support basic research: what can the rest of the world learn from US theory and practice? (And what they should not learn)', *Industrial and Corporate Change* **10**(3), 761–79.

Rosenberg, N. and R.R. Nelson (1994), 'American universities and technical advance in industry', *Research Policy* **23**(3), 323–48.

Senker, J. (1995), 'Tacit knowledge and models of innovation', *Industrial and Corporate Change* **4**(2), 425–47.

Stokes, D.E. (1997), *Pasteur's Quadrant*, Washington, DC: Brookings Institution.

PART II

New Actor Relationships

Introduction

The relationship between academic research and innovation rarely stands still. For instance, a variety of indicators of science and technology have shown that in the 1990s the link developed between academic research and industrial innovation became stronger. For example, Narin et al. (1997) found there was a threefold increase in the number of academic citations in industrial patents in the US through the mid-1990s. Much of this research leads one to question commonly held assumptions that academic research is separated from industrial practice. In fact, in recent years, it is becoming increasingly common to highlight the sheer complexity and multiplicity of social interactions that link academic research and industrial practice. The patterns of interactions that bind research to practice are diverse, often subtle and influenced by a wide mixture of social and economic factors.

Central players in reshaping understanding about the links between research and innovation are a number of new, path-breaking empirical studies of university and industry interactions (see Mansfield 1991; Klevorick et al. 1995). Chapter 4 builds on these past empirical studies, updating some of the results from the highly influential Yale survey. The original Yale survey showed that academic research was useful to industrial research and development (R&D) managers, detailing the interactions between disciplines and industries. It demonstrated that there is considerable variety across different industries in the way research influences industrial practice. In some sectors, for instance pharmaceuticals, the link between research and practice is tight, whereas in others the link is more indirect. An essential part of this analysis was the distinction between research that was directly useful and research that provided background knowledge for the firms' scientific and technological activities. Using this distinction, the study was able to document the importance of traditional disciplines, such as physics and mathematics, for a number of sectors (Klevorick et al. 1995).

Chapter 4 is not just a replication of the earlier Yale study; it is an extension and further elaboration of the Yale approach. It attempts to characterize the relationships between research and innovation in more detail. The chapter demonstrates that publicly funded research remains extremely useful for industrial firms in the US. This is an important finding and challenges the common contention that academic research is 'useless'. The chapter also explores the key channels of exchange between industry and academic research. It contradicts the conventional view that publicly funded research primarily generates new ideas for industrial R&D, finding instead that it contributes to *finishing* existing R&D projects.

Chapter 5 focuses on changes in the national system of research funding in France. It explores the unexpected consequences of changes in France's policies towards universities and research. Like many OECD countries in the 1990s, France developed a new policy environment to support the commercialization of publicly funded research conducted at universities. The new French strategy draws heavily on ideas that Steinmueller (see Commentary) characterizes as 'managerial' which contend that greater efforts are necessary to support the commercialization of university research. France's efforts to create new sources of funding that run alongside traditional support mechanisms for research and teaching as well as a series of measures are designed to encourage interaction between researchers and industry.

Despite the enthusiasm within OECD policy communities for commercialization of research, there is an ongoing and unresolved debate among science policy researchers about the merits of such policies (see Florida 1999). These efforts to support commercialization of university research have often been based on a desire to copy the perceived success of the US system. Pavitt (2001) argues that too often European and other OECD countries have drawn the wrong lessons from the US system. It is not the ability to commercialize technology that sets the US apart from Europe, it is the high levels of public support for basic research and the multiplicity of entrepreneurial funding agencies that target highly profitably new lines of inquiry, a point that Stephan reinforces (see Commentary). Like Pavitt, in Chapter 5 Llerena, Matt and Schaeffer are sceptical about new French policies. They directly challenge two main principles of the French policy reform – the first focused on the maintenance of the lack of university autonomy in managing staff and facilities and the other suggesting that entrepreneurial researchers will be able to derive considerable financial benefit from their research. They suggest that the new French reforms have only had a marginal impact on the state of university autonomy in France. They have not provided the universities with the freedom that was intended by the reform programme. Moreover, the authors suggest that the idea of the entrepreneurial researcher is largely a myth. They suggest a more radical agenda of reform, involving greater university autonomy and greater personal discretion for researchers to raise income from their research activities. For them, the current set of reforms still carries with it many of the limitations of past generations of French innovation policy, an overly bureaucratic and state-directed system of control.

Chapter 6 focuses on interactions between universities and firms in the life sciences in Europe and the US. The chapter brings together new evidence on collaborative R&D projects to explore the patterns of relations between public and private actors in the life sciences. It finds that the sets of network relations in the US are concentrated in regional clusters that span a number of drug development stages, a diverse range of organizations and numerous different disciplines. In comparison, European networks are less dense, more specialized and display greater geographic dispersal. In other words, the US networks are institutionally thick, involving considerable interaction across organizations and disciplines, whereas the European networks are institutionally thin, involving smaller numbers of actors in highly specialized communities. The authors suggest that the characteristics of the European networks limit universities' participation in commercially oriented R&D, undermining the economic potential of these university centres. However, the authors suggest that the US and European networks are profoundly influenced by the distinct cultural and institutional contexts in which they are located. Given these differences between Europe and the US, they argue that European research policy should not attempt to copy American policies. Rather, they suggest that European policy should be focused on developing a new set of network interactions between basic research and development, and among small firms and universities within Europe.

Chapter 7 is located in the tradition of the New Economics of Science. It seeks to characterize a science system through the methods and approaches of economic analysis. It deals with the tricky issue of evaluating research funding programmes. Previous research has found programme evaluation difficult because: (a) it is often hard to measure research performance; (b) many of the benefits of the funding are long term in nature; and (c) there is a strong selectivity bias, arising from the fact that *ex post* evaluations are usually conducted on research groups that have previously received research funds and therefore have been able to improve their qualifications for further funding. Cesaroni and Gambardella confront these challenges of evaluation in Chapter 7 by using several new combinations of economic techniques and new data. Their study is based on a comprehensive data set drawn from the Italian Research Council's programme for biotechnology and bioinstrumentation, which ran from 1989 to 1993.

In their approach, they assess the impact of funding on a research team's performance and the impact of several structural features of the team, such as size, location and so on, in shaping research performance. They find that the past performance of the principal investigator and collaborations with foreign research institutions play a key role in shaping the research performance of the project. However, they also find that research funding produces constant rather than increasing returns to scale, suggesting that incumbent advantage is limited, at the current scale of Italian research funding. It is therefore not possible to adopt a strategy of picking 'winners' as these researchers are located well away from the marginal project selected. The result of funding a greater diversity of projects and researchers may, however, be serving to preserve diversity and prevent the accumulation of advantages of incumbency.

REFERENCES

Florida, R. (1999), 'The role of the university: Leveraging talent, not technology', *Issues in Science and Technology*, **15**(4), 67–73.
Klevorick, A.K., R.C. Levin, R.R. Nelson and S.G. Winter (1995), 'On the sources and significance of interindustry differences in technological opportunities', *Research Policy*, **24**(2), 185–205.
Mansfield, E. (1991), 'Academic research and industrial innovation', *Research Policy*, **20**(1), 1–12.
Narin, F., K.S. Hamilton and D. Olivastro (1997), 'The increasing linkage between US technology and public science', *Research Policy*, **26**(3), 317–30.
Pavitt, K. (2001), 'Public policies to support basic research: What can the rest of the world learn from US theory and practice? (and what they should not learn)', *Industrial and Corporate Change*, **10**(3), 761–79.

4.   Links and impacts: the influence of public research on industrial R&D*

Wesley M. Cohen, Richard R. Nelson and John P. Walsh**

1   INTRODUCTION

This chapter reports findings from the Carnegie Mellon Survey on Industrial R&D on the contributions of university and government research labs – what we will call public research – to industrial innovation. By advancing our understanding of the contribution of public research to industrial R&D, we hope to deepen our understanding of the determinants of technological change broadly, and speak to assumptions that have guided policy discussions over the past two decades concerning the economic impact of public research.

Understanding the impact of public research on industrial R&D is central to understanding the innovation process itself. The so-called 'linear model' of innovation, reflected most notably in Vannevar Bush's (1945) *Science: The Endless Frontier*, conceived of industrial innovation as proceeding from basic to applied research and then to development and commercialization. In this traditional view, public research – particularly university research – proceeds upstream and independently of technological development, which, however, draws from the pool of research results. A richer characterization of the innovation process has been developed over the past two decades by scholars such as Gibbons and Johnston (1975), Kline and Rosenberg (1986), Nelson (1990) and von Hippel (1988), among others. This conception is of a more interactive relationship where public research sometimes leads the development of new technologies, and sometimes focuses on problems posed by prior developments or buyer feedback. In this view, industrial innovation emerges from a complicated process where fundamental research need not play an initiating role, or, at times, any role. In this study, we both build on and probe this perspective by considering the contribution of public research to technical advance in the context of the different sources and types of knowledge that may stimulate and inform industrial R&D.

In the post-Second World War period, the presumption that basic research proceeds independently of, but often drives, technological developments strongly coloured policy-makers' commitments to public research generally (even though public research also encompasses a good deal of applied research and development). Over the past two decades, motivated by fiscal constraints and stiffening international economic competition, numerous policy-makers have, however, effectively eschewed the linear model as they have encouraged universities and government labs to embrace the cause of technology commercialization. Reflecting the sentiment that public research is too distant from industry in the majority of industries (with the notable exception of biomedical research), policy-makers have called on universities and government R&D labs to make their science and engineering more relevant to industry's needs. The National Science Foundation has embraced this mission with the creation of the Science and Technology Centres, the Engineering Research Centres and other programmes that tie government support of university research to industrial participation. In order to stimulate regional economic development, numerous state governments have followed suit. Federal policy-makers have even changed the nation's intellectual property policy to increase incentives to commercialize public research (for example, the Bayh–Dole Amendment).

In this chapter, we use data from the 1994 Carnegie Mellon Survey (CMS) of Industrial R&D to characterize the extent and nature of the contribution of public research to industrial R&D. We first assess how public research stands relative to other sources of information affecting industrial R&D.[1] In this context, we report on how public research tends to be used in industrial R&D labs. Second, we consider the overall importance of public research, as well as that of specific fields of basic and applied research and engineering. Third, we consider the importance of the different pathways through which public research may impact industrial R&D, including publications, informal interactions, consulting, and the hiring of university graduates. Finally, we consider what roles different kinds of firms (for example, large versus small and start-ups versus established firms) play in bridging public research and industrial R&D.

In brief, our data suggest that public research has a substantial impact on industrial R&D in a few industries, particularly pharmaceuticals, and is generally important across a broad segment of the manufacturing sector. Like previous studies, we find that the contribution of public research to industrial R&D varies across industries. The uses of public research are also observed to vary. Consistent with a more interactive conception of the innovation process, our data show that public research is used at least as frequently to address existing problems and needs as to suggest new research efforts. The most important channels for accessing public research appear to be the public and personal channels (such as publications, conferences and informal interactions), rather than, say, licences or cooperative ventures. Finally, we find that large firms are more likely to use public research than small firms, with the exception that start-up firms also make particular use of public research, especially in pharmaceuticals.

2   BACKGROUND

Two decades ago, scholars concerned with the study of technological advance had a limited understanding of the impact on technical advance of the kind of research that was conducted at universities and government labs. The discussion at that time tended to involve an attempt to sort out 'demand pull' from 'opportunity push' as factors influencing technological advance, where 'opportunity push' was typically intended to capture the impact of new scientific and technological knowledge. Research that was 'upstream' relative to commercial application was seen as key to initiating new inventive efforts. Since that time, most scholars have come to understand that this view – the linear model – does not adequately characterize the role of fundamental understandings emerging from science or engineering.

Research by Gibbons and Johnston (1975), Klevorick et al. (1995), Mansfield (1991), Nelson (1990), Rosenberg (1992), Mowery and Rosenberg (1979), Rosenberg and Nelson (1994), Feller (1990), Hounshell (1996), Narin et al. (1997) and others have advanced our understanding of the role of public – particularly university – research in technological advance beyond the old debate about demand pull versus opportunity push. From this research, we learned that, while upstream research can spawn new research projects, downstream technical advances can also instigate and shape upstream research. Moreover, innovative efforts are often guided by perceptions of need and demand, although more fundamental understandings will often then shape how and with what success those efforts proceed.

As scholars were rethinking the linear model, policy-makers' presumption of the social value of public research was weakening. In this context, empirical economists began assessing the contribution of academic research to technical advance. Little consensus has emerged, however, on the extent or nature of that contribution. The 'Yale survey' – which laid the groundwork for the current study – found that firms in the majority of industries reported that the direct contribution of research conducted by universities and government R&D labs to their R&D activities was slight compared to sources within the 'industrial chain' (that is, firms in the industry itself, suppliers and buyers). Science in general was also widely reported to be relatively more important. Nelson (1986) and Klevorick et al. (1995) interpreted their findings to suggest that recent university research (that is, conducted in the prior 10–15 years) had little direct effect on industrial R&D outside of a few technologies such as drugs, other areas of medicine, sophisticated organic chemical products, and some areas of electronics. They argued that the impact of university research was none the less substantial, though indirect; that university research and science used in most industries' inventive efforts tended to be relatively mature and typically exercised influence through the more applied sciences and engineering fields or via the training of industry's scientists and engineers.

Using other methods and data sources, Mansfield (1991), Jaffe (1989), Adams (1990) and Narin et al. (1997) added other elements to the evolving picture. Mansfield's survey research study of 76 firms spanning information processing, electrical equipment and instruments, drug, metal and oil firms suggested that 10 per cent of new products and processes would have been delayed a year or more in the absence of academic research conducted within the prior 15 years. While relatively small, this impact was large in absolute terms, conceivably denying industry $24 billion in sales in 1985. Estimating the elasticity of corporate patenting with respect to university research to be as high as 0.6, Jaffe (1989) judged the influence of university R&D to be important overall and strongest in the drug industry. On the basis of a regression analysis of bibliometric data, Adams similarly finds the effects of academic R&D on manufacturing productivity to be important, though, in the case of academic research in the basic sciences, to take approximately 20 years to become manifest. More recently, using firms' patent citations to the scientific and engineering literature, Narin et al. (1997) concluded that the linkages between industrial R&D and current public research (conducted in either academia or government labs in the prior 10 years) grew dramatically between the late-1980s and early-to-mid-1990s.

Thus, Klevorick et al. (1995) find the direct impact of recent university research in most industries to be small when assessed relative to other sources of information or scientific knowledge generally. Not necessarily inconsistent with this evaluation, others find the impact to be substantial when assessed as elasticities or in absolute terms.

Further complicating the picture is the deepening of ties between public research institutions – particularly universities – and industry over the last two decades that may signify a recent change in the impact of public research. For example, US patents granted to universities increased from 589 in 1985 to 3,151 in 1998 (NSB 2000). During this same period (and especially during the 1980s), industry funding of university research increased from $630 million to $1.896 billion (NSB 2000). Moreover, ties between industry and universities have generally deepened, as reflected in the 60 per cent growth in university–industry R&D centres in the 1980s (Cohen et al. 1998) and the more than eightfold increase in university technology transfer offices between 1980 and 1995 (AUTM 1999).

Notwithstanding the different frames of reference and perspectives on the contribution of public research to technical advance, some understandings are reasonably solid. For example, there is broad consensus that while the linear model may capture key aspects of the innovation process in some settings, its applicability is limited. Previous studies also raise several questions. To the extent that academic research impacts industrial R&D, what are the channels of that impact? Also, how do industrial R&D labs actually use public research? What is the effect of firm size on the exploitation of public research, and do start-ups provide an important bridge between public research and industrial R&D? Using the CMS data, we now try to address these and related questions. At the outset, we note that our examination of the extent and nature of the contribution of public research to industrial R&D is incomplete. The innovation process is complex, often subtle and varies across industries, technologies and over time in ways that one survey cannot hope to reflect fully.

3 DATA

The data come from a survey of R&D managers administered in 1994. The population sampled are all the R&D units located in the US conducting R&D in manufacturing industries as part of a manufacturing firm. The sample was randomly drawn from the eligible labs listed in Bowker's *Directory of American Research and Technology* (1994) or belonging to firms listed in Standard and Poor's COMPUSTAT, stratified by three-digit SIC industry.[2] We sampled 3,240 labs and received 1,478 responses, yielding an unadjusted response rate of 46 per cent and an adjusted response rate of 54 per cent.[3] Our survey data are combined with published data on firm sales and employees from COMPUSTAT, Dun and Bradstreet, Moody's, Ward's and similar sources.

The survey provides several measures of the influence of public research on industrial R&D that allow us to examine different dimensions of that influence. As noted above, much of the literature relevant to this chapter focuses on the impact of university research on industrial R&D. In contrast, we ask respondents to consider the impact of research produced by universities *and* government research institutes and labs. Citations on US patents to the scientific and engineering literature provided by the National Science Board (1998) suggest, however, that of public research institutions, universities dominate in their impact on industrial R&D, suggesting, in turn, that our findings characterize predominantly the impact of university research.[4]

For the analysis in this chapter, we restricted our sample to firms whose focus industry was in the manufacturing sector and were not foreign owned, yielding a sample of 1,267 cases. This sample includes firms ranging from less than 25 to over 100,000 employees, with annual sales ranging from less than $1 million to over $60 billion. The median firm has 2,263 employees and annual sales of $412 million. The average firm has 20,263 employees and sales of $4.2 billion. The business units (defined as a firm's activity in a specific industry) range from fewer than 10 employees to over 50,000, with annual sales from zero to over $30 billion. The median business unit has 400 employees and $100 million in sales. The average business unit has 6,095 employees and sales of $2.1 billion. The average R&D intensity (R&D dollars divided by total sales) for the firms is 3.23 per cent. Presented in Table 4.1, the size distribution of our firms and business units, expressed in numbers of employees, shows that 35 per cent of our sample are 'small' firms with less than 500 employees (and almost 18 per cent have fewer

Table 4.1   Size distribution of business units and firms (by employment)

	Frequency	Percentage	Cumulative frequency	Cumulative percentage
(A) Business units				
Less than 100	262	24.2	262	24.2
100–500	302	27.8	564	52.0
500–1,000	114	10.5	678	62.5
1,000–5,000	229	21.1	907	83.6
5,000–10,000	71	6.5	978	90.1
10,000+	107	9.9	1,085	100.0
Frequency missing = 276				
(B) Firms				
Less than 100	215	17.7	215	17.7
100–500	212	17.4	427	35.1
500–1,000	64	5.3	491	40.3
1,000–5,000	229	18.8	720	59.1
5,000–10,000	111	9.1	831	68.2
10,000+	387	31.8	1,218	100.0
Frequency missing = 49				

than 100 employees). Over half of our business units have fewer than 500 employees.

In our survey, we asked R&D unit managers to identify the 'focus industry' of their R&D unit, defined as the principal industry for which the unit was conducting its R&D.[5] For the purpose of presentation in the tables, our observations are grouped into 34 ISIC groups which are aggregated at the two- or three-digit level and span the manufacturing sector. For some analyses, we disaggregate our data more finely into 64 industries, defined roughly at the three-digit SIC level.

4   SOURCES OF KNOWLEDGE USED IN INDUSTRIAL R&D

We begin our analysis by examining the importance of a broad range of information sources, of which the R&D conducted in university and government R&D labs is one. We asked respondents to indicate whether information from a source either suggested new R&D projects or contributed to the completion of existing projects over the prior three years. For each of these two functions, we listed a broad range of possible knowledge sources, including university and government R&D labs (that is, 'public research'), competitors, customers, suppliers, consultants/contract R&D firms, joint or cooperative ventures, and the firm's own manufacturing operations.

The 'linear model' suggests that upstream research – and hence the institutions of public research that conduct much of it – should play an initiating role as a key source of the ideas leading to industrial innovation. Our results suggest, however, that a preponderance of industrial R&D projects are initiated in response to information from buyers (consistent with von Hippel 1988) or from the firm's own manufacturing operations. In virtually all industries, our respondents listed buyers and the firm's own manufacturing operations as the predominant sources suggesting new projects, with 90 per cent listing customers and 74 per cent listing the firm's manufacturing operations. Also, as shown in Figure 4.1, knowledge from public research labs does not play the central role in suggesting new projects; 32 per cent of the respondents list public research as such a source, and in the majority of industries, public research plays only a modest role in suggesting new projects. In a few industries, however, public research was rated as a relatively important stimulus to the initiation of new R&D projects. With 58 per cent of respondents reporting public research as a source for new project ideas, the pharmaceutical industry is the most heavily influenced by public research by this measure. For suggesting new projects, public

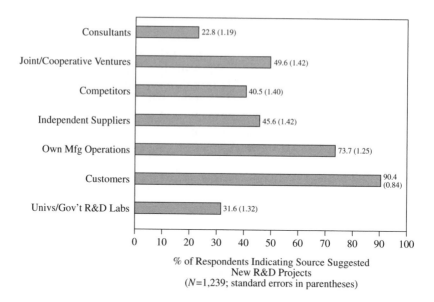

Figure 4.1   Information sources suggesting new projects

research is also relatively important in the petroleum, steel, machine tool, semiconductor and aerospace industries, each with 50 per cent or more of the respondents reporting public research as a source of new project ideas.

Figure 4.2 shows that the sources of information contributing to R&D project completion are less concentrated than those suggesting R&D projects. No one source so dominates as did buyers in the prior case. None the less, and consistent with the notion that downstream needs and feedback often guide industrial R&D (compare Kline and Rosenberg 1986), one source – namely the firm's own manufacturing operations – is more important than the others. About 78 per cent of the respondents report that knowledge from manufacturing operations contributes to R&D project completion. The key role of manufacturing operations as a knowledge source is unsurprising given its centrality to process innovation and the importance of 'manufacturability' for product innovation. The impacts of buyers and suppliers are now comparable, with close to 60 per cent of respondents reporting use of each.

As noted above, the 'linear model' of innovation would suggest that upstream research should principally suggest new project ideas. We observe, however, public research playing a slightly more important role overall as a knowledge source for R&D project completion rather than for project initiation, with 36 per cent of respondents reporting public research

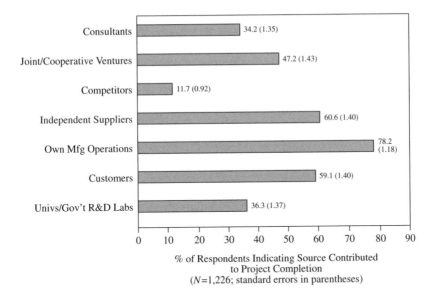

Figure 4.2   Information sources contributing to project completion

as a source of knowledge for this former function versus 32 per cent for the latter. This suggests that, at least as often as not, public research provides the means to achieve some technological goal, which itself emerges, if not from the firm's own R&D, then typically either from buyers' or the firms' own manufacturing operations. The industries where public research is relatively important in helping firms to execute projects (that is, with scores exceeding 45 per cent) include food, paper, drugs, glass, search/navigation equipment, car/truck and aerospace. Of these industries, drugs, car/truck and aerospace score the highest, all with scores above 55 per cent.

We observed above that the pharmaceutical industry stands out in the degree to which public research both suggests new R&D projects and contributes to R&D project completion. The pharmaceutical industry is also distinctive with regard to its sources of knowledge. For example, in response to a follow-up question about which of these sources was the *most* important, the drug industry was the only one where a majority of respondents did not list customers as their most important source of new project ideas.[6] Only 31 per cent of drug industry respondents listed customers as the most important source – the least of any industry (in contrast to 66 per cent for the whole sample, $p < 0.0001$, using Wilcoxon rank sum test), though 20 per cent listed public research as the most important (in contrast to 3 per cent for the whole sample, $p < 0.0001$). Regarding the sources contributing to the completion of R&D projects, where firms' own manufacturing operations tend to be most important (chosen by 32 per cent of the sample), only 19 per cent of drug industry respondents reported their manufacturing operations to be the most important knowledge source ($p <$ 0.05), scoring in the lowest quartile (along with three other chemical industries) of the 34 industries that span the manufacturing sector.[7]

We can only conjecture why customers and the firms' own manufacturing operations are less important as sources of knowledge for R&D in the drug industry as compared to others. Perhaps drug firms do not have to go to customers to determine what kinds of drugs will be most profitable, but can rely upon broad professional awareness of the relative incidence of different diseases and medical conditions to inform their expectations. With regard to the subordinate role of manufacturing operations, manufacturing processes have historically been rather routinized in the drug industry, at least until recently. Our data also suggest that if the linear model applies to any industry, drugs would be the best candidate, although even here feedback from customers (that is, patients and physicians) commonly stimulates upstream research.

Figures 4.1 and 4.2 show that public research plays a less important role as a knowledge source than a number of other sources. It is useful, however, to divide our consideration of knowledge sources between those that lie directly in what may be called the firm's vertical chain of production and sale, including suppliers, buyers and the firm's own manufacturing operations, versus those that do not. While the importance of public research never compares favourably to those sources of knowledge residing in the vertical chain (consistent with Klevorick et al. 1995), its importance is comparable to knowledge sources that lie outside of it, namely competitors, consultants/contract R&D firms and joint or cooperative ventures. In the aggregate results, joint/cooperative ventures (with other firms or universities) score consistently higher ($p < 0.0001$, using paired Wilcoxon rank sign test) than public research – around 50 per cent for both suggesting project ideas and contributing to project completion. Public research outscores, however, consultants/contract R&D as a source of knowledge for both suggesting new R&D projects ($p < 0.0001$) and contributing to project completion (n.s.).[8] Although rivals constitute a more important source for project ideas than public research institutions (41 per cent versus 32 per cent, $p < 0.0001$), public research institutions are markedly more important than rivals as a source of knowledge contributing to project completion – 36 per cent for public research versus 12 per cent, for competitors ($p <$ 0.0001), suggesting that the impact of public research on firms' R&D is at least comparable to that of rivals' R&D. To provide perspective on the importance of the contribution of public research to industrial R&D, con sider that empirical studies in economics suggest that 'R&D spillovers' from competitors (roughly comparable to our notion of information flows from rivals) contribute significantly to technical advance and productivity growth within industries (Bernstein and Nadiri 1989; Griliches 1992).

5 WHAT AND HOW MUCH DOES INDUSTRY GET FROM PUBLIC RESEARCH?

In our survey, we probed how public research contributes to technical advance in industry. The question is whether industry benefits from the creation of prototypes of, or idea-designs for, new products and processes, or rather from the less tangible and more intermediate input of disembodied knowledge. Scholars of technical advance, notably de Solla Price (1984) and Rosenberg (1992), have also highlighted another form of contribution of public research to technical advance in industry – the development of new instruments and techniques which find use in industrial R&D. Accordingly, we asked respondents to report the percentage of their R&D projects which, over the prior three years, 'made use' of the following outputs from public research: (1) research findings; (2) prototypes; and (3) new instruments and techniques.

For each category of output, Table 4.2 presents the industry averages weighted by respondent lab R&D spending.[9] Since the response scale is defined in terms of broad categories (below 10 per cent, 10–40 per cent, 41–60 per cent, 61–90 per cent, over 90 per cent), we use category midpoints to compute the percentages except in the lowest category, 'below 10 per cent,' to which we assign a value of 0 per cent.

Responses to the survey suggest that the contribution of public research to industrial R&D is principally via research findings, and this contribution is far greater than that of 'prototypes'. The weighted average for the percentage of R&D projects using prototypes generated by public research is only 8.3 per cent. Prototypes generated by public research fall in the 20–35 per cent range in only three industries (glass, TV/radio and motors/generators) and in the 10–20 per cent range in another three (drugs, machine tools and aerospace). In contrast, research findings were considered useful in 29.3 per cent of our respondents' R&D projects. As Table 4.2 shows, public research findings are judged to be useful in over a quarter of respondents' R&D projects in the petroleum, pharmaceuticals, chemicals (nec), aerospace, communication, search/navigation equipment, TV/radio and semiconductor industries. Our survey also finds the instruments and techniques developed by university and government labs to be useful to 22.2 per cent of industrial R&D projects. While not as pervasive in their impacts as

Table 4.2 *Use of public research outputs in industrial R&D*

Industry		Weighted percentage of R&D projects using output			
	N	Research findings	Prototypes	Instruments and techniques	
		Weighted means of midpoints			
1500: Food	80	16.0	1.1	15.0	
1700: Textiles	16	14.2	3.0	3.0	
2100: Paper	24	24.7	3.3	26.6	
2200: Printing/publishing	7	2.8	0.2	3.9	
2320: Petroleum	13	34.1	0.1	27.5	
2400: Chemicals, nec	57	28.9	5.8	28.0	
2411: Basic chemicals	33	22.6	0.6	17.5	
2413: Plastic resins	25	16.2	0.0	7.9	
2423: Drugs	54	41.4	12.3	35.4	
2429: Miscellaneous chemicals	25	19.3	9.9	9.4	
2500: Rubber/plastic	29	21.1	8.1	12.4	
2600: Mineral products	15	21.8	0.6	21.8	
2610: Glass	6	24.7	23.7	48.1	
2695: Concrete, cement, lime	6	7.7	0.0	11.6	
2700: Metal, nec	7	15.4	8.1	14.2	
2710: Steel	8	9.2	7.6	7.7	
2800: Metal products	35	3.6	1.4	3.3	
2910: General purpose machinery, nec	59	18.7	2.9	4.3	
2920: Special purpose machinery, nec	57	22.1	0.7	1.1	
2922: Machine tools	8	21.8	15.2	7.6	
3010: Computers	23	23.5	3.2	22.6	

3100: Electrical equipment	20	1.0	0.2	0.3
3110: Motor/generator	21	15.3	32.3	13.7
3210: Electronic components	22	3.2	1.5	3.2
3211: Semiconductors and related equipment	23	36.4	6.8	18.6
3220: Communications equipment	30	42.9	2.8	14.4
3230: TV/radio	7	45.3	23.9	46.8
3311: Medical equipment	66	17.7	2.4	6.3
3312: Precision instruments	32	12.9	6.3	13.3
3314: Search/navigational equipment	33	31.2	8.3	17.2
3410: Car/truck	8	21.4	7.3	14.8
3430: Auto parts	26	15.7	3.9	8.0
3530: Aerospace	42	28.6	13.4	24.9
3600: Other manufacturing	76	63.2	25.2	44.4
All	993	29.3	8.3	22.2

research findings, 20 per cent or more of R&D projects make use of such instruments and techniques across a range of industries, including drugs, petroleum, chemicals (nec), aerospace, glass, TV/radio and computers.

The response scale used here – namely the percentage of R&D projects using public research output – allows us to go beyond purely subjective or relative notions of importance by affording the opportunity to quantify – however crudely – the impact of public research in terms of the magnitude of industrial R&D affected. In the 1991–93 period, the US manufacturing sector performed an average of $88 billion (in constant 1992 dollars) of R&D per year. To the extent that our sample reflects the range of R&D-performing firms and industries in the manufacturing sector, and assuming that the percentage of projects using public research is equivalent to the percentage of R&D effort expended, our result that 29.3 per cent of industrial R&D projects used public research findings implies that an annual average of about $26 billion worth of industrial R&D used public research findings in the 1990–93 period. Similarly, our finding that 22.2 per cent of industrial R&D projects used instruments and techniques generated by public research implies that an annual average of almost $20 billion worth of industrial R&D used such instruments and techniques.[10] While we should interpret these estimates cautiously, the results suggest that the overall impact of public research on industrial R&D is substantial in absolute terms.[11]

6   WHAT FIELDS OF PUBLIC RESEARCH CONTRIBUTE TO INDUSTRIAL R&D?

Building on a question posed in the earlier Yale survey (Klevorick et al. 1995), we asked firms to evaluate, by field, the importance to their R&D (on a four-point Likert scale) of the contribution of public research conducted over the prior 10 years for each of 10 fields, including: biology, chemistry, physics, computer science, material science, medical and health science, chemical engineering, electrical engineering, mechanical engineering and mathematics.

Our first approach to using these responses to evaluate the importance of public research is to determine whether a preponderance of an industry's respondents (that is, >50 per cent) report public research to be at least moderately important (scoring at least three on a four-point scale). Table 4.3 presents, by industry, the percentage of respondents scoring each of the fields at least 'moderately important'. Consistent with the earlier Yale survey (Klevorick et al. 1995), we find that, of the basic sciences, only chemistry has a reasonably broad impact on industrial R&D, with over 50 per cent of industry respondents reporting it to be at least moderately useful in the food, petroleum, metals and several chemical industries, including drugs. To the extent that the other three examined fields of basic science, namely physics, mathematics and biology, are relevant, they tend to impact a specific industry. Biology is particularly important for pharmaceuticals, with 64 per cent of respondents reporting it to be at least moderately important, and physics is particularly relevant to semiconductors, with 62 per cent reporting it to be at least moderately important. Following Nelson (1986) and Klevorick et al. (1995), we note that the relatively low scores for the basic sciences other than chemistry do not mean that research in these fields is unimportant for technical advance, but that their effect may be expressed through the applied sciences and engineering fields that they inform.

As may be expected, more respondents consider research in the engineering fields to contribute importantly to their R&D than research in the basic sciences, except for chemistry. Table 4.3 shows that the impact of public research in chemical engineering is most apparent in the petroleum and selected chemical industries. The impact of public research in mechanical engineering is most evident in general purpose machinery, glass and somewhat in the transportation-related group of industries. Electrical engineering is considered to be particularly important across the range of industries concerned with electronics, including computers, semiconductors, communications equipment and instruments, as well as auto parts and glass.

Our findings on the impact of public research in the applied sciences suggest that the influence of medical and health science is strong in the drug and medical equipment industries. The impact of the other two applied sciences considered, namely materials and computer science, is much more pervasive – indeed more pervasive than any basic science or engineering field. More than half of respondents rate computer science research as at least moderately important in the glass, printing/publishing, communications equipment, search/navigation equipment, aerospace and, of course, computer industries. The field with the most pervasive direct impact on industrial R&D is materials science. Half or more of industry respondents scored materials science as at least 'moderately important' to their R&D activities in 15 of our 33 manufacturing industries, spanning the chemicals, metals, electronics, machinery and transportation equipment industries. If any discipline can be awarded the title of a 'general purpose' research field for the manufacturing sector, it is materials science.

When we identify industries in which a majority of respondents report some research field to be at least moderately important, we observe a pervasive impact of public research on industrial R&D. In 26 of the 34 industries, half or more of the respondents reported at least one public research

Table 4.3 Importance of public research, by academic discipline

Industry	N	Bio	Chem	Phys	CompSc	MatSc	Med	ChemE	EE	MechE	Maths
		Percentage of respondents indicating research 'moderately' or 'very' important									
1500: Food	94	38.3	51.1	6.4	40.4	21.3	29.8	34.0	9.6	14.9	8.5
1700: Textiles	23	8.7	43.5	13.0	39.1	43.5	4.4	34.8	8.7	8.7	13.0
2100: Paper	31	22.6	45.2	22.6	35.5	51.6	16.1	48.4	12.9	16.1	12.9
2200: Printing/publishing	12	0.0	50.0	8.3	50.0	25.0	0.0	41.7	25.0	33.3	8.3
2320: Petroleum	18	11.1	55.6	22.2	33.3	44.4	5.6	44.4	11.1	38.9	22.2
2400: Chemicals, nec	75	13.3	52.0	8.0	24.0	22.7	17.3	34.7	1.3	5.3	5.3
2411: Basic chemicals	42	14.3	47.6	7.1	23.8	23.8	16.7	40.5	2.4	4.8	2.4
2413: Plastic resins	30	13.3	56.7	13.3	30.0	50.0	6.7	46.7	3.3	3.3	6.7
2423: Drugs	70	64.3	74.3	7.1	30.0	26.5	75.7	22.9	5.7	5.7	4.3
2429: Miscellaneous chemicals	32	12.5	62.5	9.4	31.3	46.9	12.5	37.5	3.1	12.5	9.4
2500: Rubber/plastic	35	2.9	45.7	28.6	31.4	60.0	5.7	48.6	11.4	22.9	11.4
2600: Mineral products	19	10.5	26.3	21.1	31.6	68.4	5.6	31.6	15.8	21.1	15.8
2610: Glass	6	0.0	33.3	33.3	83.3	83.3	16.7	33.3	66.7	66.7	16.7
2695: Concrete, cement, lime	10	30.0	30.0	30.0	30.0	60.0	10.0	30.0	10.0	30.0	10.0
2700: Metal, nec	9	11.1	55.6	0.0	22.2	77.8	0.0	44.4	0.0	22.2	0.0
2710: Steel	10	10.0	0.0	20.0	20.0	40.0	0.0	20.0	30.0	30.0	10.0
2800: Metal products	51	2.0	15.7	14.0	27.5	45.1	5.9	23.5	18.0	28.0	7.8
2910: General purpose machinery, nec	79	1.3	13.9	10.1	29.1	53.2	5.1	21.5	26.6	59.5	10.3
2920: Special purpose machinery, nec	74	10.8	23.0	25.7	35.1	38.4	5.4	20.3	31.1	36.5	14.9
2922: Machine tools	11	0.0	0.0	0.0	36.4	36.4	0.0	0.0	27.3	36.4	0.0
3010: Computers	28	3.6	21.4	35.7	67.9	50.0	0.0	14.3	64.3	53.6	21.4
3100: Electrical equipment	23	0.0	13.0	8.7	8.7	21.7	8.7	8.7	17.4	21.7	8.7
3110: Motor/generator	24	0.0	4.2	12.5	29.2	41.7	0.0	4.2	58.3	33.3	8.3

3210: Electronic components	28	3.6	25.0	28.6	32.1	53.6	7.1	10.7	63.0	50.0	28.6
3211: Semiconductors and related equipment	26	11.5	46.2	61.5	46.2	76.9	11.5	30.8	65.4	42.3	26.9
3220: Communications equipment	37	2.7	8.1	29.7	54.1	27.0	2.7	5.4	70.3	37.8	24.3
3230: TV/radio	9	0.0	11.1	33.3	44.4	55.6	11.1	22.2	66.7	33.3	22.2
3311: Medical equipment	76	35.5	34.2	21.1	30.3	47.4	76.3	18.4	29.0	29.0	15.8
3312: Precision instruments	38	15.8	18.4	21.1	39.5	31.6	15.8	5.3	52.6	39.5	23.7
3314: Search/navigational equipment	41	2.4	12.2	34.2	53.7	41.5	4.9	12.5	68.3	43.9	36.6
3410: Car/truck	9	11.1	22.2	33.3	44.4	55.6	11.1	22.2	33.3	44.4	22.2
3430: Auto parts	34	2.9	14.7	23.5	41.2	54.6	2.9	20.6	50.0	58.8	23.5
3530: Aerospace	51	2.0	31.4	31.4	54.9	68.6	3.9	27.5	45.1	54.9	28.0
3600: Other manufacturing	97	4.1	25.8	17.5	38.1	45.4	13.4	18.6	28.9	39.2	13.4
All	1,252	14.5	33.7	18.6	35.9	42.6	17.8	25.2	27.4	30.2	14.0

field to be at least moderately important, and half or more of the respondents in 14 of the industries reported public research from at least two fields to be at least moderately important. If we compute the simple average of scores across respondents by field, a somewhat different picture emerges. One or more fields score an average of 3.0 or higher in only eight of the 34 industries, including drugs, semiconductors, medical equipment, communications equipment, aerospace, TV/radio, search/navigation equipment and glass.

Another way of summarizing these data is to ask whether there is any field of public research that is especially important for a firm's R&D. To evaluate the importance of these most important fields by industry, we compute the average of the maximum field scores by respondent (notwithstanding the field) across all respondents for each industry. On average, respondents rate the most important field of public research to be 'moderately important', as reflected in an average score of 3.04. Of the 34 industries, 21 report an average of this maximum score to equal at least 3.0. A handful of industries – drugs, glass, metals, computers, semiconductors and medical equipment – show scores of 3.30 and above.

Thus, the majority of our results on field-specific impacts suggest that public research conducted over the prior 10 years is critical to a handful of industries and is pervasively useful across the manufacturing sector.

Of all our survey questions regarding the influence of public research, the question discussed in this section most closely resembles one posed in the Yale survey (Klevorick et al. 1995) and offers the best opportunity for comparison. There are, however, some important differences between the two surveys' samples, questions and response scales. First, the CMS inquired about the importance of the research of universities and government labs and institutes, while the Yale survey inquired about university research alone. Second, we requested respondents to evaluate, by field, the importance of public research to *their own R&D activities* while the Yale survey asked respondents to report, by field, the relevance of university research to *technical progress for the respondent's industry as a whole*. Third, while both surveys use Likert scales, ours is four-point while the Yale survey's was seven. Fourth, the fields covered in the CMS are a subset of those covered in the Yale survey; our survey did not include geology, agricultural science, applied maths/operations research and metallurgy. Finally, the populations surveyed differed. The Yale survey covered only larger, public firms; the CMS provided substantial representation from small and private firms as well. While we can do little about the questions or response scales (other than rescaling), we can make the two samples more comparable by restricting ours to only the larger firms (with sales over $500 million). For the comparison, we also conform our industry definitions to the Yale industry definitions and restrict our attention only to those 33 of the 130 four-digit SIC level industries surveyed by the Yale team that have at least four observations in each sample.

To consider whether the two surveys yield different results, we make several comparisons. First, we compute the average of the maximum field scores by respondent (notwithstanding the field) for each industry. For 21 of the 33 'comparison' industries in the CMS, this average maximum score equals at least three of a maximum of four (reflecting 'moderate importance'). In comparison, for 23 of the 33 industries in the Yale survey, this average maximum score equals at least 5.25 (the rescaled equivalent to 3.0 in the CMS). When we compute simply the average score by field for each industry, 12 of the 33 industries in the CMS have at least one field attaining an average score of 3.0 or above, and 13 industries in the Yale survey have at least one field attaining an average score of 5.25. When we compare the number of industries in which half or more of the respondents reported at least one public research field to be at least moderately important, we again observe very similar results across the two samples.[12] Overall, the earlier Yale survey's findings of the field-specific influence of university research on industrial research appear to be comparable to those of the Carnegie Mellon Survey.

Can we conclude from this comparison that the extent of the contribution of public research to industrial R&D has changed little between 1983 when the Yale survey was administered and 1994 when the CMS was? Although our comparison provides little support for the position that the influence of public research has become more pervasive, we are reluctant to conclude that little has changed. Our comparison is necessarily based on the subset of industries where comparison was possible. Also, in light of the differences between the questions and response scales, any assessments of intertemporal changes in influence within industries are limited.[13] In any case, most of the results considered in this section suggest that, as of the mid-1990s, the contribution of public research to industrial R&D is widespread.

7   DIMENSIONS AND INCIDENCE OF INFLUENCE OF PUBLIC RESEARCH

In the prior three sections, we examined the influence of public research along different dimensions. We examined: (1) how public research affects industrial R&D in the sense of whether it suggests new R&D projects or contributes to the completion of existing ones; (2) the influence of three different types of output of public research, including research findings, instruments, and techniques and prototypes; and (3) the general importance of the impact on industrial R&D by research field, scored along a semantic scale. In this section, we consider how these three dimensions of influence relate to one another, and what those relationships suggest about the influence of public research more generally. To address these questions, we compute simple correlations across the different dimensions of influence, measured at the industry level for 64 industries defined at the three- or four-digit ISIC level.

Across the three dimensions of influence, at the industry level, we typically observe significant correlations in the 0.25 to 0.45 range.[14] One telling exception to this pattern, is that, between each of the three types of output from public research (research findings, instruments and techniques, prototypes) and the frequency with which public research contributes to the completion of existing projects, the correlations are low (around 0.10) and insignificant.[15] Given that public research importantly affects industrial R&D by contributing to R&D project completion, we interpret these weak relationships to suggest that public research may contribute to project completion in ways or forms that are not reflected in the three output types considered, namely research findings, prototypes, or instruments and techniques. These may include, for example, the kind of knowledge that is conveyed via interpersonal interactions like consulting or informal relationships.[16] If true, this implies that our estimated percentages of industrial R&D projects affected by the research findings or instruments and techniques originating from public research understate the overall impact of public research.

Given that our findings show that public research can do different things in different industries, it should not be surprising that it is not just the R&D of 'high tech' industries that benefits from public research. For example, among the six industries with 50 per cent or more respondents reporting public research as a source of new project ideas, we find steel, machine tools and petroleum – three industries considered to be 'mature'. Similarly, among the seven industries with 45 per cent or more of the respondents reporting public research contributing to the completion of existing projects, we find three other mature industries, namely food, paper and car/truck. To probe more systematically the relationship between our various measures of the influence of public research and industry innovative activity, we correlate our measures of influence with industry R&D intensity, measured as R&D weighted averages of business unit R&D expenditures to sales. As expected, the strength of the correlations vary considerably across the different dimensions of influence of public research, with the strongest relationships between industry R&D intensity and the percentage of industrial R&D projects making use of research findings ($r = 0.31$) or new instruments and techniques ($r = 0.29$) originating from public research. We observe the weakest relationship between industry R&D intensity and the degree to which public research contributes to the completion of existing projects ($r = 0.05$), which is not surprising if one considers that public research may partly substitute for a firm's own R&D.[17] If public research substitutes for industrial R&D and possibly obviates the need to undertake some R&D projects, then estimates of the percentage of R&D projects affected by public research outputs will only provide a partial, intermediate sense of the impacts of public research on technical advance. This provides yet another reason to believe that our estimates in section 6 of the impact of public research outputs on the share of industrial R&D projects may underestimate the overall effect of public research on technical advance and productivity growth.

8   PATHWAYS OF KNOWLEDGE FLOW

The Carnegie Mellon Survey evaluated how useful information moves from universities and other public research institutions to industrial R&D facilities. We asked our respondents to report on a four-point Likert scale the importance to a recently completed 'major' R&D project of each of 10 possible sources (or channels) of information on the R&D activities of universities or government R&D labs or institutes. The information sources considered include patents, informal information exchange, publications and reports, public meetings and conferences, recently hired graduates, licences, joint or cooperative ventures, contract research, consulting and temporary personnel exchanges. Table 4.4 presents the percentage of respondents indicating that a given channel is at least 'moderately important'. As shown, publications/reports are the dominant channel, with 41 per cent of respondents rating them as at least moderately important. Informal information exchange, public meetings or conferences, and consulting follow in importance, with aggregate scores for each of these channels in the range of 31 to 36 per cent.[18] After that point, there is a sharp drop-off in the scoring to another set of channels, namely recently hired graduates, joint and cooperative ventures and patents, with aggregate scores in the range of 17 to 21 per cent of respondents indicating these channels to be at least moderately important. Licences and personnel exchange are the least important channels, with scores of less than 10 per cent.

These aggregate scores show that the most important channels of information flow between public research institutions and industrial R&D labs are the channels of open science, notably publications and public meetings and conferences. Moreover, these channels, as well as the next most

Table 4.4 Importance to industrial R&D of information sources on public research

Industry	N	Patents	Pubs./ Reps.	Meetings or conferences	Informal interaction	Recent hires	Licences	Coop./ JVs	Contract research	Consulting	Personnel exchange
					Percentage of respondents indicating research 'moderately' or 'very' important						
1500: Food	93	9.7	51.6	37.6	44.1	21.5	10.8	22.6	30.1	46.2	7.5
1700: Textiles	23	13.0	26.1	26.1	21.7	21.7	0.0	13.0	8.7	13.0	0.0
2100: Paper	31	9.7	45.2	35.5	32.3	9.7	0.0	19.4	35.5	22.6	3.2
2200: Printing/publishing	12	16.7	33.3	25.0	16.7	8.3	8.3	0.0	16.7	25.0	0.0
2320: Petroleum	18	0.0	38.9	50.0	27.8	11.1	11.1	11.1	22.2	44.4	0.0
2400: Chemicals, nec	73	24.7	35.6	28.8	20.6	16.4	8.2	15.1	20.8	24.7	9.6
2411: Basic chemicals	41	17.1	36.6	26.8	39.0	17.1	2.4	14.6	17.1	34.2	2.4
2413: Plastic resins	28	14.3	35.7	32.1	21.4	21.4	0.0	3.6	10.7	14.3	0.0
2423: Drugs	68	50.0	73.5	64.7	58.8	30.9	33.8	41.2	52.9	58.8	8.8
2429: Miscellaneous chemicals	32	25.0	34.4	25.0	31.3	21.9	3.1	3.1	12.5	25.0	0.0
2500: Rubber/plastic	35	5.7	17.1	14.3	11.4	14.3	2.9	11.4	8.6	22.9	0.0
2600: Mineral products	19	5.3	26.3	21.1	21.1	31.6	5.3	10.5	10.5	26.3	10.5
2610: Glass	6	33.3	50.0	50.0	50.0	50.0	16.7	50.0	33.3	33.3	0.0
2695: Concrete, cement, lime	10	30.0	50.0	30.0	20.0	30.0	30.0	10.0	10.0	10.0	10.0
2700: Metal, nec	8	25.0	62.5	62.5	87.5	25.0	0.0	25.0	37.5	50.0	12.5
2710: Steel	11	18.2	36.4	54.6	45.5	18.2	18.2	36.4	54.6	36.4	18.2
2800: Metal products	51	19.6	25.5	13.7	25.5	17.7	7.8	13.7	9.8	21.6	3.9
2910: General purpose machinery, nec	76	15.8	30.7	26.3	30.3	14.5	7.9	10.5	13.2	31.6	1.3
2920: Special purpose machinery, nec	72	19.4	33.3	33.3	27.8	16.7	11.1	16.7	15.3	30.6	2.8

2922: Machine tools	11	9.1	36.4	45.5	45.5	18.2	0.0	9.1	18.2	36.4	0.0
3010: Computers	29	13.8	41.4	37.9	34.5	34.5	3.5	6.9	6.9	24.1	3.5
3100: Electrical equipment	23	8.7	30.4	21.7	21.7	0.0	0.0	8.7	13.0	8.7	0.0
3110: Motor/generator	25	4.0	40.0	36.0	44.0	12.0	0.0	20.0	12.0	28.0	4.0
3210: Electronic components	27	18.5	37.0	33.3	33.3	29.6	11.1	14.8	11.1	30.8	3.7
3211: Semiconductors and related equipment	25	20.0	60.0	48.0	54.2	36.0	12.0	20.0	20.0	40.0	4.0
3220: Comm. equipment	37	5.4	48.7	32.4	32.4	27.0	8.1	8.1	16.2	29.7	18.9
3230: TV/radio	9	22.2	66.7	33.3	33.3	33.3	11.1	33.3	22.2	22.2	11.1
3311: Medical equipment	74	27.0	40.5	36.5	47.3	18.9	17.6	23.0	23.0	44.6	6.8
3312: Precision instruments	39	23.1	46.2	41.0	41.0	10.3	12.8	18.0	7.7	33.3	5.1
3314: Search/navigational equipment	40	7.5	52.5	50.0	50.0	20.0	12.5	27.5	32.5	42.5	12.5
3410: Car/truck	9	33.3	33.3	11.1	33.3	11.1	11.1	22.2	33.3	22.2	11.1
3430: Auto parts	32	9.4	43.8	31.3	25.0	18.8	9.4	21.9	18.8	21.9	9.4
3530: Aerospace	49	14.3	57.1	51.0	55.1	20.4	8.2	40.8	36.7	40.8	6.1
3600: Other manufacturing	93	12.9	33.3	34.4	31.2	17.2	5.4	9.7	16.1	19.4	7.5
All	1,229	17.5	41.2	35.1	35.6	19.6	9.5	17.9	20.9	31.8	5.8

important channels of informal information exchange and consulting, are relatively decentralized in the sense that they do not typically reflect formal institutional links. With the exception of consulting, these most important channels are also not mediated through any sort of market exchange.

The relatively high score for consulting underscores the importance of this little-studied vehicle through which public research impacts industrial R&D. Both more and less R&D-intensive industries consider consulting to be important. Industries where over 40 per cent of respondents report consulting to be at least moderately important include food, petroleum, drugs, metals, semiconductors, aerospace and medical and other equipment.

Surprisingly, the hiring of recent graduates is of small importance overall. This result requires some elaboration. First, we are inquiring about the impact on industrial R&D of public research, not about the broader economic impacts of university training. Also, if one looks at the industry-level results, one observes recent graduates playing a somewhat important role relative to other channels in selected industries, notably in the electronic component, communications equipment and computer industries, although publications are still more important in these industries.

One assumption underlying current policy is that cooperative or joint ventures between universities and industry will encourage the use of academic research by industry.[19] Since, as noted above, our data reflect predominantly the impact of university research, they suggest that such cooperative ventures have typically not contributed as importantly to industrial R&D as other channels, at least not in any direct fashion. Exceptions to this overall pattern, where a third or more of our respondents report joint and cooperative ventures to be at least moderately important, include drugs (where all channels tend to be more important), glass, steel, TV/radio and aerospace. In some industries such as steel (where another channel, contract R&D, is an even more important channel than joint or cooperative ventures), such cooperative relationships may have become substitutes for industry R&D as upstream and corporate R&D have been cut back.

Intellectual property policy affecting public research has also changed over the past two decades. The Bayh–Dole Act permits universities, government research labs and other non-profit institutions to obtain patent rights to the output of federally sponsored research. The impetus behind Bayh–Dole and related legislation was the assumption that there was a stock of underexploited, valuable knowledge residing in universities and other research institutions receiving federal funding, and that patents would 'incentivize' the private sector to undertake the downstream R&D and related investment necessary for commercialization (Mazzoleni and Nelson 1998). Although our results cannot speak to the effects of patents and licensing on industry's incentives to use and commercialize public research, they suggest that licences and patents are subordinate means of conveying the content of that research to industry. Our data indicate that, even though the impact of public research is reasonably pervasive, patents and licences appear to be useful mechanisms of technology transfer in only a few industries. In most industries, patents and licences are not nearly as important as other channels for conveying public research to industry, including publications, conferences, informal information exchange, or consulting. Even in some high-tech industries reporting substantial public research impacts, such as communications equipment and aerospace, patents and licences achieved scores that were at best average. The main industry where patents and licences appear to be important for conveying public research is the pharmaceutical industry – with 50 per cent and 34 per cent of respondents reporting patents and licences, respectively, to be at least as moderately important as channels. Even here, however, informal channels and the channels of open science were still more important.

Thus, even if one accepts the premise of the Bayh–Dole Amendment that privatization of public research motivates industry to use it – which some scholars (for example, Mowery et al. 2000) do not – we should not assume that patents and licences provide the grist for the mills of industrial R&D. Rather, it is typically the public expressions of public research (that is, publications, meetings and conferences), or even informal interactions and consulting that centrally convey the content of that research to industry.

One question regarding the channels through which public research impacts industrial R&D is how the use of different channels, or at least the respondents' evaluations of their importance, relate to one another. To address this question, we conducted a factor analysis at the industry level. Presented in Table 4.5, the factor analysis shows the industry average scores for the channels loading on two factors. The channels that load on the first factor include publications, conferences and meetings, informal interaction, consulting, contract research and joint or cooperative ventures. Licences, the hiring of recent graduates and personnel exchange, load on a second factor. Patents do not load on either factor. The loadings on the first factor suggest that person-to-person interactions tend to be used with and perhaps complement more public channels such as publications or meetings. Indeed, prior work in the sociology of science suggests that direct exchanges often complement the published literature as a means of conveying information (Walsh and Bayma 1996). In the case of industrial R&D, such interactions may stem, for example, from an engineer seeing an article and then contacting the author about how the research might be used. Or, communications with faculty might point to published research of use to

Table 4.5 Industry-level factor analysis of channels-of-information flow
from public research to industrial R&D

Channel	Factor loadings	
	Factor 1	Factor 2
Publications/reports	**0.85**	0.04
Informal interaction	**0.84**	0.09
Public meetings or conferences	**0.84**	0.16
Contract research	**0.79**	0.23
Consulting	**0.70**	0.23
Joint or cooperative ventures	**0.63**	0.29
Patents	0.34	0.20
Personnel exchange	0.00	**0.70**
Licences	0.21	**0.69**
Recently hired graduates	0.25	**0.51**
Eigenvalue	*3.87*	*1.49*

the firm's R&D. We suspect that both processes are common and help explain the high correlations among these channels.[20]

In addition to examining the relationships across the channels of influence of public research, our survey data permit examination of the relationship between the importance of the different channels and how public research affects industrial R&D – that is, whether it suggests new R&D projects or contributes to the completion of existing ones. Table 4.6 presents the correlation coefficients between the industry average scores for the importance of each channel to a firm's R&D and the frequency by industry with which public research either suggests a new R&D project or contributes to project completion. We observe that the importance of the channels of consulting, contract research, public conferences and meetings are significantly and comparably correlated (that is, within 0.10 of one another) with both of these effects of public research. We find, however, much stronger correlations (in the range of 0.46 to 0.49) between the importance scores of publications, informal information exchange and joint/cooperative R&D projects with the contribution of public research to project completion than to the suggestion of new projects (in the range of 0.15 to 0.25). This finding suggests that industrial R&D personnel seek out academics, search the literature, or form cooperative ventures with public research institutions more commonly to address particular needs or problems than to generate new project ideas.[21]

Table 4.6   Correlations between importance of information channels and role of public research, by industry (N = 64)

Information channels	Role of public research	
	Suggests new R&D projects	Contributes to project completion
Patents	0.08	0.08
Publications/reports	0.23	0.49**
Public meetings or conferences	0.37*	0.46**
Informal interaction	0.25**	0.46**
Recent hires	0.55**	0.22
Licensed technology	0.20	0.28*
Cooperative/joint ventures	0.15	0.35**
Contract research	0.46**	0.56**
Consulting	0.45**	0.54**
Personnel exchange	−0.00	−0.05

Notes:
* Significant at the 0.05 confidence level.
** Significant at the 0.01 confidence level.

9   FIRM CHARACTERISTICS AND THE INFLUENCE OF PUBLIC RESEARCH

Having considered the aggregate and industry-level impacts of public research on industrial R&D, we now consider within-industry, cross-firm differences in those impacts. Following Link and Rees (1990) and Acs et al. (1994), we focus on whether there is a relationship between the degree to which a firm might exploit public research and its size. On the basis of an analysis of geographically defined, state-level industry R&D expenditures and university research expenditures, Acs et al. (1994) infer that small firms' R&D spending responds disproportionately more to university research, and conclude that small firms have a 'comparative advantage at exploiting spillovers from university laboratories'. For a sample of firms in machine tools, computing and aircraft and components, Link and Rees (1990) find that large firms are more likely to have ties to university research. However, their analysis of rates of return to R&D shows the returns to R&D of small firms' involved in university research to be higher than that of large firms, which they interpret to mean that small firms are able to transfer knowledge gained from their university research associations more effectively than larger firms.[22]

The CMS data offer a range of direct – though self-reported – measures of the knowledge inflow from university and government R&D labs. As described above, our data include percentages of firms' R&D projects that make use of public research, as well as whether or not knowledge from university or government labs either suggests new R&D projects or contributes to the completion of existing projects in the prior three years. We use an ordered logistic regression model to analyse within-industry variation in the percentages of R&D projects that use public research since the response scale is expressed as range intervals (that is, below 10 per cent, 10–40 per cent, 41–60 per cent, 61–90 per cent, over 90 per cent). We employ a logistic regression to analyse factors that might affect whether public research suggests new R&D projects or contributes to project completion because each of these two latter variables is binary (that is, yes/no). To focus on the effect of the within-industry variation of selected firm characteristics, we include 33 industry dummies to control for industry-fixed effects.

The key independent variable we consider is firm size, measured as log of firm sales. We believe that our sample is well suited to testing the impact of firm size since it includes firms from across the entire range of the firm-size distribution, with over a third of our sample firms having fewer than 500 employees, which is the conventional cut-off to reflect small firms. We also wish to consider whether public research affects technical advance particularly by influencing the R&D of start-up firms since start-ups are sometimes viewed as a key vehicle for transferring university research into commercial products.[23] Thus, we also include on the right-hand side a dummy variable, *START-UP*, signifying whether a firm is a start-up, defined as a firm that is no more than five years old, with fewer than 500 employees in 1993, and typically active in only one industry. Our analysis of the impact of public research on start-up firms is, however, limited. Because our sample was not designed to test the role of university research in start-up companies, we did not oversample start-up firms and so have relatively few observations – 22, which are concentrated in only three industries; five observations are in pharmaceuticals, four in computers, and four in medical equipment.

Presented in Table 4.7, the logistic regression results show a highly significant, positive effect of the log of firm size across all three dependent variables, suggesting that larger firms are more likely to use public research. One might argue that since larger firms tend to conduct more R&D and be involved in more R&D projects, one might expect that public research is more likely to suggest new R&D projects or contribute to the completion of existing ones for larger firms just on a random basis. Perhaps more informative, then, is the column (1) result that larger firms use public research in a larger percentage of their R&D projects.[24] In addition to the size effect,

*Table 4.7   Within-industry determinants of the influence of public research
(logit regressions)*

Dependent variable	1 % of R&D projects using public research	2 Suggesting new R&D projects	3 Contributing to R&D project completion
Intercept 1	−6.64**	−3.36**	−4.06**
	(0.54)	(0.56)	(0.55)
Intercept 2	−5.32**		
	(0.51)		
Intercept 3	−4.36**		
	(0.50)		
Intercept 4	−2.60**		
	(0.48)		
Log firm size	0.26**	0.23**	0.34**
	(0.05)	(0.06)	(0.06)
START-UP	1.23**	0.84[a]	1.52**
	(0.43)	(0.51)	(0.51)
Number of observations	1,193	1,186	1,176

Notes:
(1) Standard errors in parenthesis.
(2) Industry dummy coefficient estimates are omitted.
(3) [a]Significant at 10%; *Significant at 5%; **Significant at 1%.

we find a positive and significant coefficient estimate for *START-UP* in columns (1) and (3). *START-UP* is only significant at the 0.10 confidence level in column (2), suggesting that while start-up firms use public research in a greater percentage of their R&D projects than other firms and are more likely to use public research for completing existing R&D projects, they do not clearly rely more than other firms on public research as a source of new project ideas.[25]

To probe the role of start-ups in more detail, we ran a series of comparisons between start-up firms and the rest of our sample for the three industries where we have at least four start-up firms per our definition: drugs, computers and medical equipment. We use a non-parametric (Wilcoxon rank sum) test for differences in group means between start-ups and the rest of the firms in each industry.[26]

For the pharmaceutical industry, we find that start-ups are more closely tied to public research than established firms. For example, while about half of the non-start-up drug firms report public research suggesting new projects or contributing to existing projects, 100 per cent of start-up firms said yes to both questions ($p < 0.10$ for each). Comparing the percentage of projects that use the public research outputs of research findings, prototypes, or instruments and techniques, we again find that start-up firms score higher than more established drug companies. On average, 72 per cent of start-up firm projects made use of research findings, while only 36 per cent of established firm projects did ($p < 0.05$). For prototypes, the averages are 27 per cent for start-ups and 13 per cent for non-start-ups (n.s.). For instruments/techniques, start-ups are again higher (23 per cent v. 20 per cent) though the gap is small.[27]

For our other two industries, medical equipment and computers, the results on the use of public research by start-ups versus more established firms are mixed. For example, in medical equipment, established firms score higher on public research suggesting projects (36 per cent v. 25 per cent) and start-ups score higher on public research helping to complete projects (50 per cent v. 42 per cent), though neither difference is statistically significant. Medical equipment start-ups report a significantly greater percentage of projects making use of research findings (50 per cent v. 21 per cent, $p < 0.05$), prototypes (33 per cent v. 10 per cent, $p < 0.05$) and instruments/techniques (33 per cent v. 15 per cent, n.s.).[28]

For computers, evidence of a disproportionate use of public research by start-ups is weaker. For suggesting projects, there is no difference (25 per cent of start-ups v. 23 per cent of non-start-ups). For completing projects, 50 per cent of start-ups say, 'yes', versus 19 per cent of non-start-ups ($p < 0.20$). Ten per cent of start-up firms' projects make use of research findings, in comparison to 16 per cent of non-start-up firms' projects (n.s.). Five per cent of start-ups use prototypes versus 7 per cent for non-start-ups. And, only 5 per cent of start-up projects use instruments/techniques, compared to 15 per cent for non-start-up projects (n.s.).[29]

Thus, our comparison of start-ups and other firms in three high-tech industries shows that start-ups are most clearly tied to public research in the pharmaceutical industry. This should not be surprising, since the biotech start-up is the archetypical university, licence-based spinoff. For medical equipment and computers, the difference between start-up firms and established firms is less manifest. Across all three industries, as in the full sample regressions, start-ups are, however, more likely than established firms to use public research to complete existing projects than as a source of new project ideas.

The overall picture, therefore, is that larger firms are more likely to make greater use of public research, though start-up firms also benefit from public research, especially in pharmaceuticals.

10 CONCLUSION

The responses to our questionnaire suggest, on balance, that public research importantly affects industrial R&D in a broad range of industries, though often in different ways. It is sometimes a difficult matter to judge the importance of such an effect, and we do so in a number of ways. First, our data show that a large share – almost a third of industrial R&D projects for our sample firms – made use of research findings from public research, and over a fifth made use of instruments and techniques. Other evidence from our survey further suggests that the knowledge originating from public research is often conveyed outside of these particular forms of output, such as through consulting or informal communications, implying that the share of R&D projects affected by public research is likely to be even greater than that which make use of either the research findings or the techniques and instruments generated by public research. We also observed that the effect of the knowledge originating from public research on industrial R&D appears to be at least as great as the effect of that originating from rival R&D, and, as noted above, the empirical economics literature on R&D spillovers suggest intraindustry spillovers to be important to productivity growth. Most summaries of respondents' subjective evaluations of the importance of public research, broken down by field, also suggest that while public research is critical to a small number of industries, it is 'moderately important' across a broad swathe of the manufacturing sector. Although public research may be important in some absolute sense, we also find – as do Klevorick et al. (1995) – that its direct and immediate impact is much less, however, than sources of knowledge that lie more directly in the vertical chain of production and sale, including suppliers, buyers and the firms' own manufacturing operations.

Our survey also lends considerable support to the more nuanced, interactive conception of the innovation process advanced by Gibbons and Johnston (1975), Kline and Rosenberg (1986), von Hippel (1988) and Nelson (1990), where public research will sometimes lead technological development, but, more typically, downstream research and development or buyer input provide the impetus and guidance for what industrial R&D labs do. Consistent with this picture is the dominant role, noted above, of buyers and the firm's own manufacturing operations in either suggesting new industrial R&D projects or contributing to the completion of existing projects. Also consistent with this characterization is our finding that public research provides ways of solving problems at least as often as it suggests new project ideas.

Our survey yields other findings similar to those of the Yale survey. For example, we observe that the impact of public research, at least in most industries, is exercised through engineering and applied science fields – especially materials and computer science – rather than through basic sciences. Reflecting on the earlier Yale survey findings, Nelson (1986) and Klevorick et al. (1995) have cautioned, however, that the greater importance of more applied fields does not mean that basic science has little impact, but that its impact may be mediated through the more applied sciences or through the application of industrial technologists and scientists' basic scientific training to the routine challenges of conducting R&D.

We also find that there are some clear differences in the impacts of public research across industries. In this regard, the pharmaceutical industry stands out as an anomaly along many dimensions. There is no other industry where public research – and particularly a basic science (that is, biology) – is thought to be so relevant. Also, knowledge from buyers and firms' own manufacturing operations is less important to R&D in pharmaceuticals than in other industries, suggesting that the linear model may characterize the innovation process better in this industry than in others. Moreover, patents and licences are key means of conveying information from public research to industry in pharmaceuticals, partly reflecting the fact that patents are more effective in protecting inventions in drugs than in any other manufacturing industry (compare Levin et al. 1987; Cohen et al. 2000). Finally, the drug industry is one where start-ups clearly are more tied to public research than are firms in general.

In contrast to prior work (for example, Acs et al. 1994), we do not find that small firms disproportionately benefit from public research. Our regression results robustly show that large firms are much more likely to use public research. Although small firms in general exploit public research less, start-ups appear to use it more. While start-ups appear to differ from other small, established firms in the degree to which they benefit, our survey data do not tell us why. Perhaps some start-ups originate from universities and thus have strong pre-existing ties, or perhaps they are spinoffs from large firms and consequently benefit from the stronger ties that our data suggest exist between larger firms and the institutions of public research.

Two policy questions that come up repeatedly regarding university research is how much government support should it receive, and, second, should particular kinds of bridging mechanisms between universities and industry – such as university–industry cooperative ventures or technology licensing – be encouraged.

Although we cannot address the first question directly, our research suggests that the contribution of public research to industrial R&D is considerable and pervasive. Regarding the second question, our results on the channels of information flow between public research and industry suggest that the decentralized and longstanding channels of publications, conferences, informal exchange and consulting are the most important. We would suggest that, even when university–industry cooperative ventures or technology licensing between public research institutions and industry support technology transfer in an immediate way, encouragement of such bridging mechanisms should not come at the expense – as they occasionally do – of the other more important channels of open science noted above (compare Cohen et al. 1998).

The limitations of our study are numerous. First, our survey was designed to convey a sense of the more immediate impacts of public research. It was not our intent to discern the long-run effects of science or the training effects that may be universities' greatest contribution to technical advance. Thus, to the degree that we have identified impacts, our estimates should be considered conservative. Second, we have relied only upon one method in this study – a survey-based description. To arrive at more accurate and robust estimates of the impacts of public research, one should deploy numerous data sources and methods of analysis, including surveys, field studies and econometric analyses. Also, our analysis of start-ups is preliminary. Further research explicitly designed to compare start-ups to established firms is needed to examine their role. Also, based on a survey of firms at a point in time, our analysis cannot consider the role of public research in affecting the long-run evolution of industries, no less how industry itself shapes public research over time.

Overall, our results suggest that university research has a substantial impact on industrial research, that this impact is primarily through public and personal channels and that university research contributes to project completion as well as suggesting new projects. We also find substantial cross-industry differences, though few systematic differences between high-tech and more mature industries. These results suggest that both public research and industry product and process development progress through complex, intertwined processes, with public research sometimes driving industry R&D, but also providing knowledge that abets the progress of projects initiated due to information, needs and opportunities that originate from buyers, the firm's own manufacturing operations and other sources. We suspect that universities play this role not simply because they produce knowledge, but because, as pointed out by Goto (2000), they are also repositories thereof.

NOTES

*   Reprinted by permission, Wesley Cohen, Richard Nelson and John Walsh, 'Links and impacts: the influence of public research on industrial R&D', *Management Science*,

48(1), January 2002, pp. 1–23. Copyright 2002, the Institute for Operations Research and the Management Sciences, 901 Elkridge Landing Road, Suite 400, Linthicum, MD 21090, USA.

** The authors thank Diana Hicks, David Hounshell, Rob Lowe, David Mowery, Scott Shane, Jerry Thursby and other participants in the Georgia Institute of Technology Workshop on University Technology Transfer and Entrepreneurship for their comments. Principal research support was provided by the Alfred P. Sloan Foundation, and the Center for Global Partnership. Additional support was provided by Hitotsubashi University's Institute of Innovation Research.

1. We are using the word 'information' here to refer to the understandings, facts and theories that influence decision-making and problem-solving in industrial R&D.

2. We also oversampled Fortune 500 firms.

3. The results of a non-respondent survey showed that 28 per cent of non-respondents were ineligible for the survey because they either did no manufacturing or did no R&D. Excluding these from our denominator, as well as respondents who should not have been sampled, yields an adjusted response rate of 54 per cent of eligible respondents.

4. Citations on US patents to the scientific and engineering literature provided by the National Science Board (1998) distinguish between the influence on industrial R&D of university research versus that conducted by government. As of 1994, patent citations to publications originating from academia exceed those originating from the federal government by 5.7 times. This multiple varies, however, across fields, from 4.9 in the combined fields of biomedical research, clinical medicine and biology, to 8.4 in engineering and technology, suggesting that the impact of university research may be almost an order of magnitude greater than that of government research in industries outside the biomedical fields.

5. By identifying the focus industry for each lab, we reduce the measurement error that comes from having firms' responses reflect conditions in some ambiguous combination of the several industries in which they may be active.

6. For the food industry, 49.45 per cent chose customers.

7. At the same time, 19 per cent of our drug industry respondents claimed that public research, along with consultants/contract R&D, were the most important sources contributing to project completion. In contrast, the average for the total sample for public research is 5 per cent ($p < 0.0001$) and 7 per cent for consultants/contract R&D ($p < 0.0001$).

8. Given that some joint or cooperative ventures are between firms and public research institutions, we believe that the contribution of joint and cooperative ventures to industrial R&D partially reflects that of public research. This conjecture is supported by significant ($p < 0.01$), within-industry correlations between the contribution of university/government labs and that of joint/cooperative ventures both to suggesting new R&D projects ($r = 0.18$) and to R&D project completion ($r = 0.20$).

9. Weighting by R&D spending permits more accurate estimation of the overall impact of public research on industrial R&D, which requires, for example, giving the response of a $100 million R&D unit more weight than one that spends only a million.

10. Since projects using research findings and those using instruments and techniques derived from public research may overlap, we cannot aggregate the two types of impact.

11. To the extent that we oversampled large firms (among the R&D performing population) these estimates may be biased upward (see results on firm size below). However, since this is an R&D, and therefore size, weighted average, the inclusion of more small firms would likely have only modest effects on the averages. Also, while our sample represents the manufacturing sector broadly (since we stratified our sample by industry), this estimate is sensitive to the distribution of firms across industries since industries vary in their use of public research.

12. In 26 of the 33 comparison industries in the CMS, half or more of the respondents reported at least one public research field to be at least moderately important (scoring three out of a four-point scale). In the Yale survey, half or more of the respondents reported a score of five or six (on its seven-point scale) in, respectively 28 and 18 indus-

tries. Since the CMS number falls in the upper end of the range between the two Yale frequencies, the numbers appear to be similar.

13. To the extent that there is an expressed difference from the earlier Yale survey in the evaluation of the importance of public research based on these field-specific scores, it is difficult to determine whether the authors of the earlier study may have understated the scope of the impact of public research or whether, between the dates of the two studies, the importance of public research increased (as Narin et al. 1997, for example, believe).

14. The 'importance score' (out of a one- to four-point Likert scale) for that field of public research which is most important to an industrial lab's R&D is most highly correlated with the other dimensions of influence (in the 0.30 to 0.45 range).

15. In contrast, the correlations between the percentage of R&D projects affected by each of the three examined output types and the frequency with which public research suggests new projects are significant, in the range of 0.21 to 0.28.

16. Consistent with this conjecture, we observe strong industry-level correlations between the degree to which public research contributes to project completion and the importance of the channels of information flow between industrial R&D labs and public research of consulting and informal interaction (0.54 and 0.46, respectively). Also consistent with this conjecture, the channel of consulting is only weakly associated with the use of any of the three output types (all three correlations are 0.12 or less and n.s.). The pathway of informal interaction is, however, significantly associated with the use of research findings ($r = 0.28$).

17. If it only substituted for R&D, we would expect a negative correlation.

18. Thursby and Thursby (2001) similarly find that industry licensing executives identified publications and presentations, and especially personal contacts, as their most important sources for university technologies.

19. Since the 1970s, for example, we have witnessed the growth of the NSF's Science and Technology Centres and Engineering Research Centres, which tie government support for university research to industry participation. Stimulated by the example of such programmes and by the desire to tap into industry and tied government support, university–industry R&D centres have grown rapidly. Of the 1,056 estimated university – industry R&D centres existing as of 1990, almost 60 per cent were established in the prior decade and by 1990 they were the beneficiaries of almost 25 per cent of all government support of university research (Cohen et al. 1998).

20. Gibbons and Johnston (1975) similarly found that the technical literature and 'personal contact' were most beneficial to technological innovation when used together. Faulkner and Senker (1995) confirm this finding in their study of public sector research and industrial innovation in biotechnology, engineering ceramics and parallel computing. Jensen and Thursby (2001) similarly report that successful licensing of university technologies to industry typically requires, not only the licence, but additional input by the university-based inventor due to the embryonic state of development of the licensed technology.

21. The only pathway with an importance score more highly correlated with the contribution of public research to suggesting new projects is 'recently hired graduates with advanced degrees'.

22. Both of these papers were trying to consider why smaller firms' R&D productivity is greater than that of larger firms by appealing to the possibility that small firms rely more heavily on extramural research, and particularly university research, in lieu of internal R&D. Cohen and Klepper (1996) show, however, that the lower average R&D productivity of larger firms can easily be explained by the fact that larger firms simply undertake more R&D projects at the margin because, in most industries, they earn a higher return per R&D dollar due to their spreading of the fixed costs of R&D over greater levels of output. Thus, the differences in the average R&D productivity of larger versus smaller firms do not necessarily reflect any differences in R&D efficiency related to firm size, nor need they reflect greater exploitation of extramural knowledge flows on the part of smaller firms.

23. The Association of University Technology Managers 1999 Licensing Survey reports that 62 per cent of university licences were to small firms (12 per cent were to companies

started as a result of the licence), and that university research led to the founding of 344 companies (AUTM 1999).

24. We also find that larger firms are more likely to score higher on *MAXSCI* – the importance of public research from the most relevant field. The *MAXSCI* regression results are available upon request.

25. We checked to see if our results were robust to the inclusion of R&D intensity (measured as the ratio of business unit R&D employment over total business unit employment), the PhD/MD intensity of the lab, and the effort dedicated by the R&D lab to the monitoring or gathering of extramural scientific and technical information. All the results are robust, except for the already weak effect of '*START-UP*' in column 2, which becomes insignificant. These results are not featured due to the likely endogeneity of all three variables, and controlling for that endogeneity is beyond the scope of the present chapter.

    We also ran all specifications with *MAXSCI* as a dependent variable. These results suggest that start-ups are not significantly more likely to rate any field public research as more important. To consider the possibility that start-ups disproportionately focus on basic research, we created a new dependent variable, *MAXBASIC*, which is the maximum score among the basic research fields of biology, chemistry, physics and mathematics. We replicated the Table 4.7 regressions for this variable to see if start-ups score higher in terms of their use of basic sciences. While large firms use basic research more, the start-up effect is close to zero.

26. One might conjecture that, since we do not control for firm size in the analyses of the role of start-ups in the three industries, the association between start-ups and the influence of public research may appear to be weaker since start-ups tend to be small and larger firms tend to use public research more intensively (per our regressions). The qualitative results for the industry analyses are robust, however, even when we do control for firm size in logistic regressions run for each of the three industry samples.

27. Regarding the relative importance of the different channels through which knowledge may flow from public research to firms' R&D (for example, publications, conferences, licences and so on per Table 4.4), all score the same or higher for start-ups, reflecting the greater overall impact of public research on start-ups in the drug industry. There is, however, an especially notable difference with regard to the role of licensing, which scores on average 3.0 on a four-point scale versus a score of only 1.9 for non-start-up drug companies ($p<0.05$). Of the other channels of knowledge flow, joint and cooperative R&D projects and contract research also scored notably higher for start-ups, but with differences that were only weakly significant (for example, $p < 0.15$).

28. Regarding the importance of the channels through which public research may affect industrial R&D information, there is no clear difference in scores between start-ups and established firms in the medical equipment industry.

29. With regard to information channels, eight of the ten are more important to start-ups than to established firms, but only temporary personnel exchanges is significant (1.8 v 1.2, $p<0.15$), and the importance of licensing is nearly equal (1.5 for start-ups; 1.4 for non-start-ups).

REFERENCES

Acs, Z.J., D.B. Audretsch and M.P. Feldman (1994), 'R&D spillovers and recipient firm size', Review of Economics and Statistics **76**, 336–40.

Adams, J.D. (1990), 'Fundamental stocks of knowledge and productivity growth', *Journal of Political Economy* **98**, 673–702.

Association of University Technology Managers (AUTM) (1999), *AUTM*

Licensing Survey, Fiscal Year 1999 Survey Summary, available at http://www. autm.net/surveys/99/survey99A.pdf – last accessed 30 April 2002.

Bernstein, J.I. and M.I. Nadiri (1989), 'Research and development and intra-industry spillovers: an empirical application of dynamic duality', *Review of Economic Studies* **56**, 249–67.

Bowker Publishing (1994), *Directory of American Research and Technology*, New Providence, NJ.

Bush, V. (1945), *Science: The Endless Frontier: A Report to the President on a Program for Postwar Scientific Research*, Washington, DC: US Government Printing Office (reprinted 1990, National Science Foundation).

Cohen, W.M., R. Florida, L. Randazzese and J. Walsh (1998), 'Industry and the Academy: uneasy partners in the cause of technological advance', in R. Noll (ed.), *Challenges to Research Universities*, Washington, DC: Brookings Institution Press, pp. 171–200.

Cohen, W.M. and S. Klepper (1996), 'A reprise of size and R&D', *Economic Journal* **106**(July), 925–51.

Cohen, W.M., R.R. Nelson and J. Walsh (2000), 'Protecting their intellectual assets: appropriability conditions and why US manufacturing firms patent (or not)', Working paper no. 7552, Washington, DC: National Bureau of Economic Research.

de Solla Price, D. (1984), 'The science/technology relationship, the craft of experimental science, and policy for the improvement of high technology innovations', *Research Policy* **13**(1), 3–20.

Faulkner, W. and J. Senker (1995), *Knowledge Frontiers: Public Sector Research and Industrial Innovation in Biotechnology, Engineering Ceramics, and Parallel Computing*, New York: Oxford University Press.

Feller, I. (1990), 'Universities as engines of R&D-based economic growth: they think they can', *Research Policy* **19**(4), 335–48.

Gibbons, M. and R. Johnston (1975), 'The roles of science in technological innovation', *Research Policy* **3**(3), 220–42.

Goto, A. (2000), 'Japan's national innovation system', *Oxford Review of Economic Policy* **16**, 103–13.

Griliches, Z. (1992), 'The search for R&D spillovers', *Scandinavian Journal of Economics* **94**(3, Supplement), 529–47.

Hounshell, D. (1996), 'The evolution of industrial research in the United States', in R.S. Rosenbloom and W.J. Spencer (eds), *Engines of Innovation*, Boston, MA: Harvard Business School Press, pp. 13–86.

Jaffe, A. (1989), 'Real effects of academic research', *American Economic Review* **79**(5), 957–70.

Jensen, R. and M. Thursby (2001), 'Proofs and prototypes for sale: the licensing of university inventions', *American Economic Review* **91**(1), 240–59.

Klevorick, A.K., R. Levin, R.R. Nelson and S. Winter (1995), 'On the sources and significance of interindustry differences in technological opportunities', *Research Policy* **24**(2), 195–205.

Kline, S.J. and N. Rosenberg (1986), 'An overview of innovation', in R. Landau and N. Rosenberg (eds), *The Positive Sum Strategy*, Washington, DC: National Academy Press, pp. 235–306.

Levin, R., A. Klevorick, R.R. Nelson and S.G. Winter (1987), 'Appropriating the returns from industrial R&D', *Brookings Papers on Economic Activity* (Special Issue), 783–820.

Link, A.L. and J. Rees (1990), 'Firm size, university based research, and the returns to R&D', *Small Business Economics* **2**, 25–31.

Mansfield, E. (1991), 'Academic research and industrial innovation', *Research Policy* **20**(1), 1–12.

Mazzoleni, R. and R.R. Nelson (1998), 'Economic theories about the benefits and costs of patents', *Journal of Economic Issues* **32**(4), 1031–52.

Mowery, D.C., R.R. Nelson, B.N. Sampat and A.A. Ziedonis (2000), 'The growth of patenting and licensing by US universities: an assessment of the effects of the Bayh–Dole Act of 1980', *Research Policy* **30**(1), 99–118.

Mowery, D.C. and N. Rosenberg (1979), 'The influence of market demand upon innovation: a critical review of some recent empirical studies', *Research Policy* **8**(2), 102–53.

Narin, F., K.S. Hamilton and D. Olivastro (1997), 'The increasing link between US technology and public science', *Research Policy* **26**(3), 317–30.

National Science Board (NSB) (1998), *Science and Engineering Indicators – 1998*, Arlington, VA: National Science Foundation.

National Science Board (NSB) (2000), *Science and Engineering Indicators – 2000*, Arlington, VA: National Science Foundation.

Nelson, R.R. (1986), 'Institutions supporting technical advance in industry', *American Economic Review Papers and Proceedings* **76**, 186–9.

Nelson, R.R. (1990), 'Capitalism as an engine of progress', *Research Policy* **19**(3), 193–214.

Rosenberg, N. (1992), 'Scientific instrumentation and university research', *Research Policy* **21**(4), 381–90.

Rosenberg, N. and R.R. Nelson (1994), 'American universities and technical advance in industry', *Research Policy* **23**(3), 323–48.

Thursby, J.G. and M.C. Thursby (2001), 'Industry perspectives on licensing university technologies: sources and problems', *Journal of the Association of University Technology Managers* **12**, available at: www.autm.net/pubs/journal/00.

von Hippel, E. (1988), *The Sources of Innovation*, New York: Oxford University Press.

Walsh, J.P. and T. Bayma (1996), 'Computer networks and scientific work', *Social Studies of Science* **26**(3), 661–703.

5. The evolution of French research policies and the impacts on the universities and public research organizations

Patrick Llerena, Mireille Matt and Véronique Schaeffer

1 INTRODUCTION

It is now usually accepted that part (and for policy-makers increasingly so) of the justification for public research is its usefulness for society at large. The question is what is meant by 'utility' or 'usefulness'. Most of the economic debate understands both words in economic terms and, more precisely, that public research should be 'usable' in the short or long terms for the economic system, that is, for industry – by contributing to more effective production processes and/or new products, incorporating higher qualities and/or fulfilling new needs. In other words, public research should lead to 'innovation' in the Schumpeterian sense.

If we accept this point of view, the focus then moves to the design and the organization of the linkages between public research and industry. In this chapter we focus on the purposes and instruments available for policy in the context of the French innovation system and the implementation of these policies during the last few years.

The objective of this chapter is first to outline the recent evolution and challenges of French public research policies. The challenges arise from the internal evolution of the research system and research policy, a relative reduction of the resources devoted to public research, the increase in institutional complexity and the, at least partial, disappearance of traditional 'mission-oriented' policies. Instead, the public research system is urged to 'increase its socio-economic relevance', a development that introduces a further challenge to French research policies.

To address these challenges the French government implemented new policy tools and made institutional reforms during the 1990s, and particularly at the end of the decade. Most of the measures sought to compensate for the disappearance of large programmes and, simultaneously, to foster interactions between public and industrial research. In implementing these measures the government changed the legal framework for public/private collaborations and the modes of intervention employed by public policies.

Despite the relatively recent modifications to research policies, it is possible to make a preliminary critical assessment of the choices that were taken at the end of the 1990s, and this assessment is carried out in the second half of this chapter.

We first focus on the 1999 Innovation Law, which is a central element of the recent policy changes applicable to universities and public research institutions. The main objective of this law was to modify the institutional context of public research/industry collaborations and to encourage new industrial activities arising out of public research. We make a critical analysis of this law and develop arguments indicating the risks and unintended consequences of it.

The context of these changes was the recognition of a need for new tools and incentive mechanisms and a general willingness to depart from a 'mission-oriented policy', involving large national programmes and funding concentrated on relatively few scientific and technological areas and firms ('national champions'). Our contention is that these changes have had a marginal influence, particularly in relation to the much more important influences stemming from the general decrease in public commitments to research.

2   FEATURES AND EVOLUTION OF THE FRENCH RESEARCH SYSTEM AND POLICIES

The aim of this section is to present the characteristics of the French research system, in particular the public research system, and to clarify the context in which the 1999 Innovation Law was implemented, a context influenced by the challenges identified in the previous section. We also show how during the same period the French government adopted new orientations to its research and innovation policies and developed new tools but in the context of stringent financial constraints.

Characteristics of the Research Systems

A vast public research sector
In the French public research sector, it is particularly relevent to distinguish between civil and military research. In 1997, the public sector carried out

research to an approximate value of €11 billion (or 38.8 per cent of the total R&D), with civil research projects amounting to 86 per cent of this total.

The 20 public research organizations in France conduct 55 per cent of public sector R&D (employing 33 per cent of public sector researchers); the 160 universities and *grandes écoles*[1] carry out 27 per cent of R&D (employing 59 per cent of researchers); non-profit institutions account for 4 per cent of R&D (and employ 4 per cent of the researchers) and the defence sector accounts for 14 per cent of research (employing 4 per cent).

In terms of R&D human resources, the public research sector is large in France: in 1997, it employed 84,600 scientists or 55 per cent of all scientists of which 3,000 were employed in the defence sector, while the private sector employed 68,400 scientists or 45 per cent of all employed scientists.[2]

Concentrated private R&D

OECD (1999) reports that in 1995, 50 per cent of manufacturing R&D expenditure was in high-tech sectors (space and telecommunication equipment). Military purchases were a large proportion of this. The second particularity of French industry is that of R&D expenditure, in which a relatively small number of firms dominate the total. The 100 most important firms in terms of R&D expenditure account for 56 per cent of the R&D activity, employ 56 per cent of the researchers and 58 per cent of the total population employed in R&D. Two hundred firms conduct more than 75 per cent of industrial R&D and receive more than 90 per cent of public funds (tax credits excluded).

Existence of large research programmes

Innovation policy, at least since the Second World War, has been characterized by large public research programmes: telecommunications, electronuclear, space, civil aeronautics, electronics and so on. In the 1980s these research programmes accounted for about 51 per cent of the total civil R&D budget. The innovation policy was an archetypal 'mission-oriented' policy (Ergas 1987; Foray and Llerena 1996).

A set of specialized institutions

The focus on specific sectors and/or technologies was increased by the existence of mission-oriented public research institutions (for example, Office National d'Etudes et de Recherches Aerospatiales: ONERA; the Commissariat à l'Energie Atomique: CEA; Institut National de Recherche en Informatique et en Automatique: INRIA; the Institut de la Recherche Agronomique: INRA; the Institut National de la Santé et de la Recherche Médicale: INSERM). In addition, after the Second World War, France developed one main research institution, the Centre National de la Recherche Scientifique (CNRS), to compensate for the weak research activities in the state universities. Full-time researchers were employed by CNRS as civil servants. This institution took about 25 per cent of the national budget for civil R&D.

Thus the public research system in France is composed of public research institutions, universities and the *grandes écoles*, all relatively separate.

The overall organization of the French research system still corresponds to Chesnais's (1993) description:

> (1) the organization and funding of the largest part of fundamental research through a special institution, the CNRS, distinct from the higher education sector entities . . . (2) a dual higher education sector producing at least one type of senior technical person little known elsewhere, namely the *grandes écoles'* technical experts' elite of engineers cum industrial managers . . . and (3) a pervasive element of state involvement in the production not just of general scientific and technical knowledge, but often of technology *per se* in the form of patentable and/or immediately usable products or production processes. (Chesnais 1993, p. 192)

Recent Evolution of the System

The important evolution that took place in the 1990s did not change the structure of the system, instead it exacerbated its faults and produced a major challenge to its coherence.

Decrease in the proportion of public funding

France is in eighth position in terms of R&D expenditure as a proportion of GDP (2.2 per cent in 1998 compared to 3 per cent in Japan and 2.7 per cent in the US). However, certain features of the development of the R&D system in France must be taken into account. In the 1960s the national research effort stood at about 1.15 per cent of GDP. It reached a peak in 1990 of 2.42 per cent but since then has been decreasing to reach 2.2 per cent in 1998. More significantly, at the same time, the proportion of publicly funded research decreased from 70 per cent in the 1960s to 48 per cent in 1997. In addition, the research performed by public research organizations fell from 55 per cent in the 1960s to 40 per cent in 1997. The biggest decreases occurred in the early 1980s.

This general decline in the national effort to develop research, both public and private, took place at a time when the dominant discourse in the political arena was around the need for more innovation.

Decrease in and/or disappearance of 'large programmes'

In the 1990s there was a significant reduction in the number of 'large programmes'. For instance, telecommunication-related programmes disappeared with the privatization of France Telecom, while other programmes became of marginal importance. As Laredo and Mustar write:

> The total impulse effect of military programmes is greatly reduced. The large civil programmes with the exception of the space programme, no longer exist. The 1990s have thus seen the near disappearance of what has been seen as a central mode of state intervention in research during the post war period. (Laredo and Mustar 2002, p. 60)

Intertwining of institutions

Originally CNRS had its own research laboratories (*unité propre*), and the French research system was characterized by the separation between CNRS and the universities. Since the 1960s – and increasingly so during the 1990s – the universities and the CNRS have developed both associated and even joint (*unité mixte*) research units, in which personnel from both institutions work together in a unit which is evaluated as a single research unit. This evolution, combined with an important recruitment drive by the universities, means that (in terms of full-time equivalent) 'the research potential of universities is more than double that of CNRS' (Laredo and Mustar 2002, p. 61).

The Challenges for the French Public Research System

This evolution created important challenges to the researchers, to their institutions, the public administration and the policy-makers. Many of these challenges were unintended, in part because their implementation was uncoordinated. For example, the rapid and large personnel recruitments made by universities were undertaken to provide for teaching needs, with the development of research activities occurring as a byproduct. The consequence has been a growing incoherence in the research system. Public research had to develop with relatively fewer resources (both political and financial), and in a more complex institutional framework. The clear division of labour between institutions disappeared and the focus provided by the large programmes vanished and has had to be replaced by new modes of public intervention. However, the institutions themselves have not changed; nor has the related incentive structure. In particular, the implications of the growing number and institutional complexity of mixed research units have not been addressed: they are managed and receive incentives from at least two different institutional frameworks, that is, the university and CNRS. In fact, policy-makers and researchers have inherited the institutions, and the inertia of these institutions (Foray 2000), of the ministries and of the modes of setting priorities.

In addition to these challenges, which might be summarized by the slogan 'do better and do it more cheaply but in a more complex environment', further challenges have arisen from the evolution of the objectives that the research system is intended to address. The public research system is being urged to 'increase its socio-economic relevance'. These objectives are common to all industrialized countries (for example, Japan, see Fujisue 1998) and take on specific features in Europe (see Laredo and Mustar 2001a). The influence of these new objectives must also be included in any assessment of French research policies and their impacts on universities.

The 'European paradox' and the need for national measures

The 'European paradox'[3] arises from the conjunction of excellent European scientific performance (30 and 35 per cent of world and US publications, respectively) and the lower technological performance of Europe relative to that of the US or Japan, indicated, for example, by the respective shares in the patents granted both in the US and in Europe. The extent of this paradox differs between European countries due to the variety of national systems of innovation. This paradox is not apparent for instance in Germany or the Netherlands; it is stronger in the UK, Sweden and Spain, while France and Italy are fairly average.

The new policy tools being adopted as national measures in France must therefore be considered in a broader European context. At the European level, initiatives have been taken to avoid obstacles to innovation (Caracostas and Muldur 2001). On the basis of the Green Paper on Innovation published by the European Commission in 1995, an Action Plan for Innovation was elaborated in 1996, which stressed three major objectives: to strengthen the links between research and innovation; to develop a culture of innovation; and to adapt the administrative, legal, financial and fiscal environment. These policies have been implemented and have produced a general tendency to implement similar and complementary measures at the national level (see Meyer-Krahmer 2001).

The French context

The new policy in France is also a response to the specifically French failing of public research to interact with industry and to become a source of additional growth. Two particular reports highlighted this weakness.

The Guillaume report published in 1998, showed the weakness of the French innovation system in terms of linkages between academic and public research and the development of new economic activities. These weaknesses are analysed in comparison to the perceived performance of the US which is seen as a reference model.[4]

A set of official documents from the 'Cour des Comptes', in charge of public institutions and public expenditures, pinpointed two major problems in the French public research system – the absence of a property rights policy in public institutions and more generally a lack of competences. The research public institutions like the universities and CNRS generally do not reap significant return for the results of collective or contractual research projects with industry. In general, the property rights are claimed only by the industrial partner. In contrast with the US case prior to the Bayh–Dole Act, there was a legal framework to allow public research institutions to retain property rights arising from their research results (when significant government funds were employed to create the intellectual property). In most cases, however, institutions did not even consider this possibility.[5] The Guillaume report explains this as lack of competence and organizational structure to support the development of such activities in public research laboratories.

Research paid for outside the framework of institutional budgets, from the legal point of view, is a commercial activity and as such is subject to taxation, when conducted by universities and research organizations. However, for years no tax has been applied. Thus, universities have been able to develop commercial or quasi-commercial activities without taxation on the research services rendered by universities, which if performed by private sector actors would be taxed. This fact, which is of specific concern to the Cour des Comptes, has an important impact on the implementation process of some of the new policy measures.

3 REFORMS AND NEW TOOLS: AN ANSWER?

To face the challenges of the 1990s the French government implemented new policy tools and reforms. Most of the measures were concerned with compensating for the disappearance of large programmes while simultaneously attempting to promote further development of public research–industry interactions. These reforms included an innovation law which came into force on 12 July 1999 providing for:

- encouragement for the creation of new firms;
- an increase in the number of technological innovation and research networks; and
- financial and legal reforms to benefit innovative companies.

Basically the government changed the legal framework linked to public/private collaborations and the modes of intervention of public policies. Although these policy modifications have been made relatively recently, it is instructive to make a critical assessment of the reforms implemented at the end of the 1990s.

The July 1999 Innovation Law

The Innovation Law is one of the key elements in the general framework that the French government implemented to promote the diffusion of scientific results throughout industry. This law focuses on lowering the barriers to technology transfer from universities and public research institutions.

It is important not only to analyse policies, but also to assess their implementation and the difficulties encountered. Indeed, if we recognize that there is inertia in the evolution of institutions and that there are path dependencies in institutional change, then the initial phase and the processes of implementation are critical for the long-term success or failure of the policies. Policies are subject to the constraints of institutional and organizational evolution.

Mobility towards industry and the creation of firms by researchers: three main measures

A major obstacle to the development of interaction between academia and industry is the absence of any relevent incentive mechanism. See Table 5.1 for funding of academic research. One of the major objectives of the 1999 law is to put in place such incentives within an appropriate legal frame that allows financial benefits to public researchers, thereby increasing the incentives for researchers to participate in industrial collaborations compared with other activities having a more direct reward in academic prestige or advancement. Under the control of a national Commission de Déontologie (Ethics Commission), the law provides a variety of opportunities for researchers:

- to take secondment for a maximum of 6 years to set up a company to exploit the results of his/her research (§25.1 of the law);
- to stay in academia, while at the same time making a scientific contribution to a firm, with the possibility of becoming a shareholder up to a limit of 15 per cent of the shares in the firm benefiting from the scientific results (§25.2 of the law); and
- to stay in academia but be a member of the administrative board of a firm using the results of public research (§25.3 of the law).

These measures have been shaped in order to avoid conflicts of interest which are inherent in the commercial exploitation of scientific results (Etzkowitz 1996). Consequently, there is a limit to the financial interests a researcher can have in collaborating firms. The role of the Ethics Commission is to guarantee the interest of the state in the commercial exploitation of the results.

The employees (civil servants or not) of public research institutions, including universities, who wish to benefit by any of these measures, have to make an appropriate application. Each application is examined by the national Ethics Commission. The Commission assesses the suitability of each application – both in formal terms and in terms of public domain interest. Concerning the creation of a firm by the researcher (§25.1 of the law), the Ethics Commission demands proof (in the form of publications and/or patents) that the resulting firm will exploit mainly the results of the research of that particular researcher, produced during his/her working time as a result of his/her assigned tasks and function in the research organ-ization in which he/she is employed. The application must also attach any conventions or formal agreements between the created firm and the research organization; and these agreements should be negotiated and signed by someone other than the researcher. Finally, the new firm cannot be a subsidiary of an existing firm, that is, if existing firms are involved, they must have less than 50 per cent of the shares (financial institutions excluded). The last point is a significant signal of the 'entrepreneurial researcher model' that the public authorities had in mind when designing the law. This model has the potential to create problems. For example, it appears to require that venture capitalists operating 'incubators' can only take a minority position in the company.

Concerning both shareholdings up to the maximum of 15 per cent and scientific contribution to the activity of the firm (§25.2 of the law), the Ethics Commission tends to be wary of the possibility of personal inter-ests, incompatible with the scientific mission of the university. The firm's activities must be linked directly to the scientific expertise of the researcher, and must make use of that researcher's work. The contract between the firm and the research organization must not be signed by the researcher.[6] The researcher must not be directly or indirectly (through family members, for example) the effective manager of the firm. He or she is excluded from any direct decision-making processes in the firm. The Ethics Commission must be kept informed of all contracts signed between the research organization and the firm during the 5-year period over which such permissions are granted. Employing these criteria, the most appropriate applicant appears to be a civil servant researcher who is invited by an existing firm, with whom he/she has never worked before, to apply his/her research or transfer

Table 5.1   Performance and funding of research, 1996

Origin of funds	Type of laboratories: performance in MdF					
	Academic (Univ + CNRS)	Public total civilian	Military	Firms	VLE* /Coop	Total
Public civilian**	29.2	25.2	–	11.4	2.8	68.5
Public military	0.2	1.6	10.4	9.8	0.1	22.1
Industrial funds	1.0	2.8	–	89.7	–	93.5
Abroad (net R&D export.)	0.1	0.1	–	1.0	–	1.2
Total (MdF)	30.5	29.7	10.4	111.9	2.9	185.3

Notes:
Mdf = milliards de francs (billions of francs)
* Very large equipment.
** Including European Commission and regions.

Source: Based on OST (2000, p. 53).

a scientific contribution. In other words, these criteria may define a rather limited number of opportunities.

The cases examined by the Ethics Commission since 1999
This part of the law came into force in October 1999. By March 2001, 135 cases had been considered[7] of which 109 were approved, 18 rejected and 8 pending, awaiting additional information. Table 5.2 gives the classification of the 109 accepted cases.

The most common situation illustrated in Table 5.2 is researchers who wish to formalize their scientific contribution to an existing firm's activity by a formal contract, and some shares (up to 15 per cent).

The structure of the applications by scientific fields shows, not surprisingly, that the dominant fields are information and communication technology (ICT) and life sciences.[8] It is also not surprising that engineering is notable by its absence, this being the weakest field in French public research.

Of all the different French scientific institutions, the public research organizations are the principal exploiters of the new law. This is due to a lack of information in the very dispersed universities, and to the relative absence of specific administrative services supporting such initiatives. It is

Table 5.2   Structure of the 109 accepted cases

Objective	No. of cases	Scientific domain	No. of cases	Institutions	No. of cases
Creation of firms (§25.1)	41	ICT	55	Universities	39
Scientific contribution (§25.2)	58	Chemistry	5	Research organizations:	70
Administrative board (§25.3)	10	Life sciences	40	among which CNRS	32
		Social sciences	7	among which INRIA	16
		Engineering	2	others	22
Total	109	Total	109	Total	109

also due to the greater flexibility of university rules in designating 'expert advisers' to private firms. According to the 1936 regulations, university staff members can act as experts or consultants, with the only requirement being permission from the rector of the university.

The rejected cases are all justified for formal reasons. In six cases the application to set up the firm was made after the firm was already established. Two cases were excluded for content reasons, the Commission considering that the activity was not subject to 'transfer': one case was a pedagogical project (virtual campus) and the second was a project aimed at exploiting technological monitoring activities.

It appears that a well-designed and well-thought-out application is more likely to receive a positive decision. It is certainly too early to assess the real impact of this dimension of the law. A deeper analysis of the motives and backgrounds of the applicants would be interesting, in particular to see whether the early cases were a new phenomenon or were merely the regularization of already existing situations.

Strengthening Collaborations between Academic Research and Firms

The law is intended not only to facilitate the mobility of researchers and design appropriate individual incentive structures, but also to provide the organizational and administrative tools to strengthen the collaboration between academic research and firms.

The services for industrial and commercial activities

The 1999 law allows research institutions to create their own services for industrial and commercial activities (SAIC), in order to carry out services, to exploit patents or licences and to commercialize the products of their activities. SAIC is a response to different legal and administrative features of the French public system, which bar public research institutions from becoming involved in industry-related activities.

Some rules concerning the management of public budgets appear to act as a barrier to the development of relations between public research institutions and industry, for example, a priori expenditure control. SAIC allows public scientific organizations to have an internal budgetary structure, with a 'subsidiary' (specific and differentiated) budget, functioning under more flexible rules than the established public accounting system. Basically, the accounting rules will be similar to private ones, even though applied to a public research institution.

To be able to develop industry-oriented activities, the research institution needs complementary competences; for example, to undertake the implementation of a property rights policy or a commercial policy. SAIC allows the public scientific organization to hire non-civil service personnel with the required competences. This is a way to avoid the onerous national competition system involved in hiring civil servants in France. It also means that public research organizations may directly employ personnel with full participation in the national unemployment insurance system (called ASSEDIC). This was not the case in the past when universities had to cover alone the risks of unemployment for their 'contractual' employees. In other words, the 'contractual' employees had the same rights as private employees in firms, but the costs were covered directly by the university or the public research organization, and their non-civil service employees had to negotiate the substantial financial risks of unemployment. As a consequence, unless the research revenues were very secure, public organizations avoided hiring non-permanent research and staff members.

So SAIC is a new tool to allow public research institutions to organize their own technology transfer activities. It aims to simplify some of the procedures involved in the normal institutional and regulatory framework; however, the research institution is not obliged to take advantage of these new procedures. The only obligation for the research institution is to decide 'explicitly', that is, through a formal decision of its administrative board, how their technology transfer activities will be organized. As such, SAIC is a way of making explicit the technology policy in universities and public research institutions. It also makes them aware that these transfer activities are part of their mission.

But at the same time, the creation of SAIC has an impact on the internal 'power' and 'incentive' structures in universities. The introduction of a SAIC implies the centralization of the contractual and industry-oriented activities of the research unit and the faculties. In fact, all industrial contracts will have to be managed centrally at the university level. As a consequence, it induces (or at least has a strong tendency to induce) a major change in the internal power and incentive structure of the universities, in favour of the 'centre', that is, the rector level, as opposed to the research units or faculties. It is especially important to take this into account if we consider that universities – as a coordinated set of faculties and institutes – are a recent institution in France, created more or less successfully at the beginning of the 1970s.

As a matter of fact, the possibility of raising funds, in particular by the research unit itself, is considered (even if it is not true from the formal and legal point of view) as an insurance for research 'autonomy', in the face of the centralizing mechanisms of both the national and the university structures.

SAICs also have some fiscal relevance, because they increase the tax liability for revenues from commercial activities. All activities inducing benefits, including contractual research, should be taxed on a similar basis, as these activities are taxed when they are conducted by private entities, and the Ministry of Finance and Budget has long been wanting to collect those taxes. But the dispersion across university units (faculties, research units, research groups, functional departments and so on) of these types of activities, and the absence of an analytical accounting system in most public administrations, have made it impossible in practice to collect the majority of these taxes. The creation of SAIC, by introducing a unique locus in the universities for these activities and imposing a specific and separated accounting system, allows the evaluation of full costs the calculation of net benefits as well as the calculation of taxes which can be collected by the Ministry of Finance and Budget.

The implementation of SAIC is still (three years later) under discussion at ministry level. The obstacles to a final decision can largely be explained by the debate between the Ministry of National Education, Research and Technology (MENRT) and the Ministry of Finance and Budget, which have a kind of conflict of interest. Although taxation of formerly 'tax-free' activities will raise revenues, it will also act as a negative incentive to develop these kinds of industry-oriented activities.

Towards a Possible 'Externalization' of 'Useful' Research?

A first reaction to these difficulties, if not incoherencies, could be (and is in some universities) for universities to decide to 'externalize' their 'industrial and commercial activities', that is, their technology transfer activities. In particular universities could be (and sometimes are) tempted to create private subsidiaries outside the university to manage the 'useful' parts of their research. The universities would in this case exploit the opportunities opened by the law to create a specific and particular 'subsidiary' of the university responsible for all 'commercial and contractual' activities. In this case, the impact of the 1999 Innovation Law might appear quite paradoxical.[9]

Even if externalization does not occur, the difficulties of launching properly what can be considered as a major institutional change in French universities and public research organization will have major consequences for subsequent development. The organizational and institutional inertia was from the beginning a handicap for the reforms (and SAIC in particular) but the chaotic implementation process which has taken place since July 1999 has reinforced the handicap and hampered future implementation and diffusion.

The creation of incubators

To foster the creation of new technological firms and to commercialize the results of public research, the government decided to implement incubators and to allocate seed-capital. Incubator structures have been implemented in higher education and research organizations. They are a means by which such organizations can provide resources (premises, equipment, furniture) to new small firms or to projects of firm creation (in May 2000, 29 incubator projects had been created, equivalent to almost one per region). These resources, however, are provided free of charge. A subsequent regulation indicates precisely the type of financial arrangements that are possible for start-ups and incubators. This is a manifestation of a feature of the French public research system: a strong centralization of decisions and strong regulation by the central state.

The main conditions, which include both incentives and limitations to the development of industrial activities based on the results of the public research, are as follows.

Only very new (less than two years) and small firms (less than 50 employees and less than €50 million assets and less than €7 million turnover) are considered. A consequence of this regulation is that universities that had an active promotional policy to commercial activities and that welcomed start-ups before the new regulation will now have to 'expel' those that have had a degree of success. The firms must develop activities directly linked to the results derived from research in the laboratory, thus preventing high-tech firms from moving all of their operations to a campus. Support is limited to €100,000 per firm over a three-year period. The services include rents for the laboratories, equipment and scientific and managerial advice.

Shareholding and creation of private subsidiaries by universities

The French research institutions, and in particular the universities, have no financial autonomy. All major financial decisions have to be validated both by the Ministry of National Education, Research and Technology (MNERT) and the Ministry of Finance and Budget. In particular, this means that universities have no direct access to the financial markets, and have to undertake long and very uncertain discussions with the ministries in order to, for example, obtain loans to finance new infrastructure or equipment. As a consequence, French universities never (or exceptionally) use the financial and credit market: to have the funds needed to cover general costs means that they must accumulate a large operating capital.

In the same way they are not able to hold shares in businesses or to create private subsidiaries.

Before the 1999 Innovation Law, the possibility of becoming a share-holder or of creating private subsidiaries was limited for both universities and public research institutions to shares over 20 per cent. As a consequence, only a very few universities used this opportunity and created private subsidiaries. But some took simple shares in firms (in particular in start-ups linked to their research activities) of less than 20 per cent and generally only 1 to 2 per cent as a result of a decision by their administrative board. Although these cases cannot strictly be considered as creating a subsidiary, they could, none the less, provide commercially oriented and research-active universities with a way to lend support to start-ups.

The implementation of the 1999 Innovation Law has been complemented by means directed 'at facilitating the cooperation between universities and private structures'. The main focus of these is to eliminate the 20 per cent threshold and to require any request from the universities to be fulfilled within one month if no specific problems arise. In fact, it means that universities have to obtain the permission of the national ministry for any kind of industry participation – even marginal – including, for example, the case of start-up or incubator activities. Once again, practices that were locally controlled have been displaced in favour of central control with uncertain consequences as to incentives and outcomes.

Since 1982, research organizations and higher education organizations involved in research have had an explicit mission to direct their research towards commercial and industrial ends.[10] Each organization must define plans for 'valorizing' research that are adapted to its characteristics and create an appropriate structure for achieving these plans. The reforms undertaken at the end of 1990s are intended to support an additional effort towards integrating this mission in the development of universities and public research units. This section has illustrated how the process of implementation of the SAICs and some of the mechanisms that are supposed to facilitate the interactions might not work as intended. As previously noted, the new policies are still at an early stage of implementation and further evaluation will be needed.

Other Policy Tools

The 1999 Innovation Law was intended to alter the incentive structure and organizational possibilities both for individual researchers and for public research organizations and universities in order to increase interactions with industry. As noted earlier, during the same period, the French public research system has also had to deal with a relative decrease in financial resources and the disappearance of large research programmes. To further its goals of improving interactions and to mitigate some of the effects of the budgetary adjustments, the French government has developed a further set of policy tools.

The Fund for Technological Research

The Fund for Technological Research (Fonds pour la Recherche Technologique: FRT) is the main tool used to induce the emergence of part-nerships between public and private research. The objectives of the FRT are to provide a source of financial support for technological transfers from the public research organizations to industry. However, the amounts are margi-nal compared to the Civil Research Budget (6 per cent). Table 5.3 illustrates the distribution of this budget across different activities.

Table 5.3   The FRT budget

In million FFr	1999	2000
Regional actions	60	60
Technological innovation and research networks	352	510
National competition for the creation of innovative firms	100	100
Non-networks call for tender	40	0
EUREKA	50	50
Aeronautics	10	40
Incentive actions (incubators in 2000)	18	85
Subtotal	*630*	*845*
Space transfers	40	60
Total	670	905

Source: OECD (2001) *Outlook 2000.*

The technological innovation and research networks

A new institutional mechanism, technological innovation and research net-works (TIRNs), was implemented in 1998. The objective of TIRNs is to induce collaboration between public and industrial research laboratories in new technological fields. They are funded by some ministries, public research organizations and firms. The networks are in telecommunications, transportation, micro- and nanotechnologies, fuel cells, civil and urban engineering, human genomics, software technologies, new materials and technologies for health. It is notable that some of the domains were consid-ered as strategic in previous large programmes, such as telecommunica-tions. Others, like the national research programme on terrestrial transportation (PREDIT), are closely related to nationally important industries such as automobiles.

National competition for the creation of innovative firms
This competition has been launched every year since 1999 by the MNERT and about 500 projects received awards in the first two years. The final number of firms created is difficult to assess at this early stage.

National centres of technological research
These centres are set up by public research laboratories and industrial research departments of large companies and, in some cases, small and medium-sized enterprises. The idea is to concentrate human, financial and material resources in order to foster technology transfers and innovation, but also to reinforce local industrial development and to support teams working in TIRNs. Twelve of these centres were established in 2000.

The National Science Fund
The main objective of the National Science Fund is to support research efforts in priority sectors. It funds public or non-profit private organizations. A series of 'concerted incentive actions' comprise the framework for the National Science Fund and aim to generate new research disciplines designated as very important by the government. The fund amounted to €75 million in 1999 and grew to €106 million in 2000. Some programmes are more fundamental in the sense that they only involve public research teams, very often employing a multidisciplinary approach. Others are more 'needs' directed, for example efforts to induce cooperation between public research, industry and the medical sector. At present, 70 per cent of the National Science Fund is devoted to life sciences and more particularly to genomics.

In summary, there is a clear wish to forge new, or enhance existing interfaces between public research institutions and private firms. There is also a tentative move from a 'mission-oriented' policy towards a more 'diffusion-oriented' one. But the domains chosen for implementation are highly correlated with previous 'large programmes' (telecommunications, for example), and the large programmes continue to account for a major share of public research; 43.2 per cent of publicly funded R&D was related to either defence or large programmes in 1996 (see OST 2000, p. 59).

In the context of a general decline in the share of public funding for research, the new policy tools appear to have marginal effects in financial terms and in terms of reorienting research directions.

4 CONCLUSIONS

Our aim was to describe the recent evolution of the French research system and policies stemming from the 1999 Innovation Law and the new policy tools introduced in France during the 1990s.

These changes have occurred in conjunction with a relative decrease in the share of publicly funded research and a simultaneous increase in demands for the public research system to 'increase its socio-economic relevance', that is, pressures to adopt a more diffusion-oriented policy and to establish a new institutional framework for implementing this policy.

The policies conducted at the end of the 1990s were aimed at addressing these objectives. The 1999 Innovation Law was intended to change the incentive structures governing individual researchers as well as public research institutions and universities. The new policy tools are aimed at implementing a more 'diffusion-oriented' policy.

Compared to the United States, the French reforms presented in Section 3 provide elements that will facilitate the bridging between universities and industry:

- the 1999 Innovation Law provides some incentives for academic researchers to become entrepreneurs and also to help existing firms increase their scientific expertise;
- the national innovation networks will help to extend collaborations between public and private actors;
- the dominance of the National Science Fund by life sciences research seems to correspond to the US strategy (strong research abilities in a scientific area, near to market needs in a high-tech sector).

But some incentives are missing or are too weak, and the inertia of institutions suggests that the funds devoted to the new tools remain marginal compared to the continuing dominances of large research programmes and military research.

The analysis of the 'unintended' consequences of the 1999 Innovation Law leads us to reflect on the assumption that appears to underlie this law's enactment. The assumption motivating the law seems to be that increasing public research institution incentives to address 'social and economic concerns' would involve strengthening relationships with existing firms and creating new firms. This public research–private industry interaction would increase the revenues from the knowledge generated by public laboratories. This assumption seems to be reinforced by the relative decrease in public funding, and the consequent increased need for public research organizations to seek additional funding from the private sector.

In fact, the different measures, both the new policy tools and their legal features, are built around two major principles. A first principle is maintaining the lack of autonomy for universities in managing their 'endowments', in personnel (where most employment depends upon national competition), real estate (where the ministry controls equipment and building) and finance (where there is no direct access to financial and credit markets). The measures enacted in the last few years, particularly those involving legal and regulatory changes, are attempts to 'turn around' or at least change course in this absence of university autonomy. We conclude, however, that these are yet to have more than a marginal effect.

A second principle, which we believe is a myth, is that of 'an entrepreneurial researcher', or 'research unit' that is able to derive substantial resources and benefits from its current activities through the sale of research outputs: through patents, financial returns on company start-ups and the like.[11]

Given our critical views of the principles – first that the changes are relevant but of marginal effect and second that the entrepreneurial researcher or research is largely mythical – an open question remains about what alternative view might flow from our critique of these policy changes. An alternative approach could be based on opposite principles: complete autonomy of the universities with respect to their 'endowments'; and 'patrimonial' behaviour by researchers and research organizations that would seek 'rents' more than profits, out of the 'endowments', both directly or indirectly through, for example, research foundations.

From this perspective, universities and research organizations would behave more as 'rentier', trying to increase both their wealth and the revenue they get from it, in the long term; their wealth being real estate and financial, but also knowledge and human resources. They would in fact behave as 'capitalists' in the classical sense and not as 'managers' of revenue flows.

These concluding remarks are for the time being of course very speculative and are the subject for further research.

NOTES

1. To understand the specific role of the *grandes écoles* in France, see Chesnais (1993), but also Quéré (1999), Laredo (1999) and Laredo and Mustar (2001b).
2. See the annual report 'État de la recherche et du développement technologique', published by the Ministry of National Education, Research and Technology (MNERT 2000).
3. This 'European paradox' has been characterized and analysed in the *First European Report on Science and Technology Indicators* (European Commission 1994). The main aspects of this paradox are presented in Caracostas and Muldur (2001).

4. In the US, the transfers from public research to the private sector increased in the first half of the 1990s, measured in terms of patents and firm creation. From 1991 to 1995, the number of new patents more than doubled. In 1994 and 1995, 464 firms were created on the basis of licences given by universities. According to a study by the National Science Foundation, quoted by Guillaume (1998), almost 75 per cent of the patents taken out by American industry have a scientific reference to public research.
5. In February 2001, the incentives to individual researchers were increased. The inventor could get 50 per cent of the revenue of a patent (under the previous regulation this was only 25 per cent). But at the same time, the new rules stipulate quite precisely that it is 50 per cent of the net revenues, taking into account the direct cost linked to the management of the patent and licence. Knowing the importance of these costs, the real effect of the measure might be marginal if not negative.
6. Because it is forbidden for a civil servant to hold shares in a firm that he/she manages or with which he/she has signed contracts during the last five years.
7. Our discussion is based on the analysis by the ministry of the 135 cases examined by the Commission from October 1999 to March 2001.
8. This structure corresponds to the structure of property rights revenues from the universities studied by Mowery et al. (2001).
9. In Section 2 we mentioned the emergence of an increased institutional framework for mixed research units. The existence of SAICs specific to each institution (CNRS and the universities, for example) implies that a given research unit will formally depend on two SAICs and, as such, will eventually be subject to two different sets of procedures and rules, if not policies; either simultaneously or sequentially.
10. A letter to the rectors of universities, signed by the Minister of Education in charge of higher education, and the Minister of MNERT, dated June 2001, states that 'To play fully its role (in terms of attractiveness of the national territory in world competition), the public institutions must provide visibility and the traceability of their research, and control the exploitation of their results. They must protect them. Their property rights policy must also be targeted to a *fair return* on them and to the motivation of their . . . teams where the invention is coming from. Each researcher has a *duty* to ask himself the question about the protection before any diffusion' (emphasis added).
11. Even this view can be challenged in France with the evolution of returns to the inventor (see note 5), and at the university level in the US, see Mowery et al. (2001) on the net returns level and structure in the University of California (Berkeley) Stanford University and Columbia University.

REFERENCES

Caracostas, P. and U. Muldur (2001), 'The emergence of a new European Union research and innovation policy', in P. Laredo and P. Mustar (eds), *Research and Innovation Policies in the New Global Economy*, Cheltenham, UK and Northampton, MA, USA: Edward Elgar.

Chesnais, F. (1993), 'The French national system of innovation', in R.R. Nelson (ed.), *National Innovation Systems: A Comparative Analysis*, Oxford: Oxford University Press, pp. 192–229.

Ergas, H. (1987), 'The importance of technology policy', in P. Dasgupta and P. Stoneman (eds), *Economic Policy and Technological Performance*, Cambridge: Cambridge University Press, pp. 51–97.

Etzkowitz, H. (1996), 'Conflicts of interest and commitment in academic science in the United States', *Minerva*, **34**(3), 259–77.

European Commission (1994), *First European Report on Science and Technology Indicators*, Luxembourg: European Commission.

Foray, D. (2000), 'On the French system of innovation: between institutional inertia and rapid changes', Workshop on 'Innovation paradigm, the impact of economic ideas on RT policies', 4S/EASST Conference, Vienna, 27–30 September.

Foray, D. and P. Llerena (1996), 'Information structure and coordination in technology policy: a theoretical model and two case studies', *Journal of Evolutionary Economics* **6**(2), 157–74.

Fujisue, K. (1998), 'Promotion of academia-industry cooperation in Japan – establishing the "law of promoting technology transfer from university to industry" in Japan', *Technovation* **18**(6/7), 371–81.

Guillaume, H. (1998), *Rapport de mission sur la technologie et l'innovation, pour le compte du MENRST*, Paris: Ministère de l'Économie des Finances et de L'Industrie (MEFI), Secrétariat d'État à l'Industrie.

Laredo, P. (1999), 'S&T policy in EU countries and at EU level: towards complementarity roles', International Conference on 'Knowledge Spillovers and the Geography of Innovation – A Comparison of National Systems of Innovation', University Jean Monnet, Saint-Etienne, France, 1–2 July.

Laredo, P. and P. Mustar (eds) (2001a), *Research and Innovation Policies in the New Global Economy: An International Comparative Analysis*, Cheltenham, UK and Northampton, MA, USA: Edward Elgar.

Laredo, P. and P. Mustar (2001b), 'French research and innovation policy: two decades of transformation', in Laredo and Mustar (eds), pp. 447–96.

Laredo, P. and P. Mustar (2002), 'Innovation and research policy in France (1980–2000) or the disappearance of the Cobertist state', *Research Policy*, **31**(1), 55–72.

MENRT (Ministry of Education, Research and Technology) (2000), 'État de la recherche et du développement technologique', Projet de loi de Finance.

Meyer-Krahmer, F. (2001), 'The German innovation system' in Laredo and Mustar (eds), pp. 205–51.

Mowery, D., R.R. Nelson, B. Sampat and A. Ziedonis (2001), 'The growth of patenting and licensing by US universities: an assessment of the effects of the Bayh–Dole Act of 1980', *Research Policy* **30**(1), 99–119.

Organisation for Economic Cooperation and Development (OECD) (1999), *Études économiques de l'OCDE – France: politiques structurelles, recherche et innovation*, Paris: OECD.

Organisation for Economic Cooperation and Development (OECD) (2001), *Outlook 2000*, Paris: OECD.

Observatoire des Sciences et des Techniques (OST) (2000), 'Indicateurs 2000 – Rapport de l'OST', Directed by Rémi Barré, Economica, Paris.

Quéré, M. (1999), 'The French innovation system: some insights into the analysis of the institutional infrastructure supporting innovation', International Conference on 'Knowledge Spillovers and the Geography of Innovation – A Comparison of National Systems of Innovation', University Jean Monnet, Saint-Étienne, France, 1–2 July.

6. Public research and industrial innovation: a comparison of US and European innovation systems in the life sciences*

Massimo Riccaboni, Walter W. Powell, Fabio Pammolli and Jason Owen-Smith

1 INTRODUCTION

Public research systems in the United States and Europe are often compared with respect to their divergent levels of involvement in the private economy. The US research system, with its mix of both public and private institutions, has long played a significant role in conducting research that contributes to technological development and industrial performance (Geiger 1988; Rosenberg and Nelson 1994). Historically, this 'knowledge plus' orientation, in which high-quality public and academic research tends to be driven by 'joint goals of understanding and use' (Stokes 1997, p. 15) was contrasted to the European scene, where universities were believed to contribute more to knowledge for its own sake and to the preservation of distinctive national cultures (Ben-David 1977).

Over the past decade, the development of a number of key science- and technology-based industries – most notably information and communication technologies, and biotechnology – has helped spark economic growth. The United States has broad commercial leadership in a number of these new areas, and commentators suggest that US universities and research institutes played a significant role in this process (Mowery and Nelson 1999; Mowery et al. 2001). The diverse interfaces between US research universities and the private sector have been widely documented (Link 1999; Mowery 1999). Patenting by US universities increased nearly sevenfold over the 1976–98 period (Owen-Smith 2000) and licensing revenues from the sale of intellectual property have grown briskly as well. The science-based start-up firm has been the cornerstone of the commercial field of biotechnology, with university researchers playing a significant role as founders, consultants and members of scientific advisory boards.

In contrast, public–private relations in Europe have lagged behind, in part due to legal prohibitions in some countries against faculty collaboration with commercial entities and cultural predispositions against academic involvement with commerce. Since the late 1980s, however, European attention has shifted to technology policy and academic technology transfer (Howells and McKinlay 1999). In a climate of strong anxiety about European Union (EU) competitiveness in science-based industries, programmes developed following the Single European Act of 1987[1] encourage matches between universities/research institutes and firms, placing particular emphasis on quick delivery of tangible commercial results (Peterson and Sharp 1998).

Strong contrasts exist between European and US research infrastructures, however. Consider, as an illustration, differences in university organization and governance between the US and Germany. The US system is highly decentralized. Even public universities rely on diverse funding sources, including state and national governments, foundations and corporate supporters, tuition fees and gifts from alumni. Private universities, especially elite ones, are also supported by generous endowments. Financing of non-industrial research institutions is considerably more centralized within European nations, and this centralization entails more hierarchical control. For example, faculty members in the US have much more research independence at early career stages and academic scientists frequently move between universities in an effort to better their labour market position. In France and elsewhere on the continent, there is much less autonomy and mobility for younger scientists (Gittelman 2000). In addition, blurring boundaries between basic and goal-oriented research and increased competition for research support and funding enable greater mixing of disciplines in the US (Galambos and Sturchio 1998; Morange 1998). In Germany, a number of the highly prestigious Max Planck institutes are organized hierarchically around a single field, such as biochemistry, genetics or immunology. Elite research institutes in the US, such as Cold Spring Harbor, Salk or Scripps, routinely bring together faculty from multiple disciplines.

Against this background, in this chapter we build upon Owen-Smith et al. (2002) to undertake a broad comparison of linkages between research universities, public research institutes and the private sector in the field of the life sciences and analyse how differences in the pattern of these relationships have shaped the development of biotechnology in the United States and Europe. Over the last 25 years, the explosion of knowledge in molecular biology and genetics has generated a wide range of new medical opportunities. Because the relevant scientific knowledge and organizational skills are broadly dispersed, no single organization has been able to internally master and control all the competencies required to develop a new medicine (Powell et al. 1996; Pammolli et al. 2000; Orsenigo et al. 2001). Biomedicine, then, is characterized by extensive reliance on collaboration among many parties, including universities, research institutes, new biotechnology firms and mature pharmaceutical and chemical corporations (Arora and Gambardella 1994; Lerner and Merges 1998; Stuart et al. 1999; Arora et al. 2000). These varied combinations of organizations afford us the opportunity to analyse cross-national differences in the roles these diverse organizations play in the process by which biomedical research moves from non-industrial research laboratories to activities aimed at discovering and developing commercial applications.

The chapter is structured as follows, In Section 2 below, we sketch the institutional terrains in Europe and the US, which have shaped the division of labour in biomedical innovation. The research systems in the US and Europe are organized in qualitatively different ways, hence any comparison must be sensitive to variation on multiple dimensions. We use the methods of large-scale network analysis to capture these structural differences. Methods and data sources are discussed in Section 3. In Section 4, we present the comparative analyses, beginning with relational data on collaborative research and development (R&D) projects. We look at R&D projects that were originated by public research organizations (PROs),[2] and subsequently developed by an array of different types of organizations. The distribution shows US–European variation, as well as numerous cross-national linkages. To better understand these linkages, we examine the position of countries in the international network of collaborative R&D projects. We then view these national patterns more closely through an assessment of patent co-assignment relationships. We find, again, strong national-level patterns. In particular, our analyses point out the heterogeneity of the US system, on both scientific and organizational dimensions. We assess the implications of our findings in Section 5, stressing the dual importance of integrative capacity (that is, the ability to move back and forth from basic research to clinical development) and relational capability (that is, the ability to collaborate with diverse kinds of organizations). We conclude by noting that while many analyses of the biomedical systems in the US and Europe highlight differences in financial and labour markets and note key policy differences (for a review, see Gambardella et al. 2000), our work stresses the fundamental variation in the organization of the upstream R&D process.

2   TRAJECTORIES OF DEVELOPMENT IN THE US AND EUROPE

The canonical explanation for differences in the rate of development of US and European biomedicine is straightforward, emphasizing first-mover advantage in the growth of small, research-intensive US biotechnology firms. Along with the biotech boom, emphasis has been placed on the evolution of supporting institutions – ranging from federal policy initiatives (for example, the 1980 Bayh–Dole Act) to the availability of venture capital, intellectual property (IP) law firms and university technology transfer. We think this story is accurate, but incomplete. We focus, in contrast, on the upstream division of innovative labour. We highlight the importance of the underlying science and the diversity of organizations involved in R&D activities. Using data on public–private R&D relationships, we demonstrate that there are very different constellations of players in R&D networks in Europe and the US, and that these participants are engaged in different kinds of research and clinical activities. The contrasting stories are significant because our argument suggests that while legal and financial reforms and the availability of venture capital are necessary, these elements alone may not be sufficient to generate dense linkages between PROs and industry.

The United States is characterized by relationships between US PROs and firms located in dense regional clusters that span therapeutic areas, cross multiple stages of the development process, and involve diverse collaborators. In contrast, European innovative networks are characterized by sparser, more specialized relationships among a more limited set of organizational participants located in national clusters. Both US and European networks are geographically clustered, even if the EU picture appears to be more fragmented.[3] From these disparate starting points, European and US innovative networks branch out in divergent ways.

The science underlying biotechnology was developed in university and government laboratories. The leading centres of research in the new molecular biology were dispersed widely throughout advanced industrial nations.[4] Initial technological breakthroughs – most notably Herbert Boyer and Stanley Cohen's discovery of recombinant DNA methods and George Köhler and Cesar Milstein's cell fusion technology to create monoclonal antibodies – occurred in Californian and British universities, respectively. But from the outset, US universities and academic scientists actively worked to help create the biotechnology industry and reap rewards from their involvement (Liebeskind et al. 1996; Zucker et al. 1997; Mowery et al. 2001). Consequently, small science-based firms were initially located in close proximity to key universities and research institutes. In time, established pharmaceutical companies (EPCs) were also attracted to the field, at the outset collaborating with biotech firms in research partnerships and providing a set of downstream skills that were lacking in the R&D-intensive start-ups. Eventually, the considerable promise of biotechnology led nearly every EPC to develop, with varying degrees of success, both in-house capacity in the new science and a wide portfolio of alliances with small biotech firms (Arora and Gambardella 1990; Gambardella 1995; Henderson et al. 1999).

The early development of dedicated biotech firms (DBFs) created an initial advantage for the United States in biotechnology, as close contact between DBFs and universities had become commonplace by the mid-1980s. Important differences in the nature and level of support for academic life science research have also played a key role in shaping the comparative advantage of the US system (Gambardella et al. 2000).[5] The structure of the research system and the strategies pursued by funding agencies are crucially important. In the US, substantial R&D monies have been administered through the National Institutes of Health (NIH), which have supported significant interaction between the producers of fundamental biological knowledge and those involved in clinical research and drug development at public research centres and universities. Moreover, the US biomedical research system is characterized by numerous alternative sources of support, with selection mechanisms that complement the NIH and act according to different principles (Stokes 1997). These varied funding sources permit diversity to be explored.

In Europe, funding has tended to be administered at the central level, with strongly differentiated approaches apparent across countries. European funding patterns may have hindered the development of a critical mass, especially in smaller countries. In many cases, resources have either been spread among a large number of 'small' laboratories, or they have been excessively concentrated in the one or two centres of excellence. Support coming from the various European-wide programmes has only partially changed the situation. In addition, research funds are much less likely to support integration between basic science and clinical development.

European biomedical research has also been considerably less integrated with teaching. The relevance of the research–teaching nexus in fostering high-quality scientific research and integrating academic and industrial science should not be understated. In particular, the diffusion of molecular biology into general training in many European countries is a relatively recent phenomenon. Compared to the US, molecular biology research in Europe has tended to be confined to highly specialized university and research institute laboratories (Morange 1998). Particularly in continental

Europe, policies have been targeted mainly to creating specific organizational devices, such as science and technology parks, to manage technology transfer. These intermediary institutions may even increase the distance between universities and industry by introducing an additional layer to the relationship. We argue that these institutional differences in funding, and the relationships among research, clinical work and teaching, shape the structure of university–industry R&D networks in the US and Europe.

Partly as a consequence of the institutional differences sketched above, the founding of new biotechnology companies in Europe was more difficult. Rates of formation of start-ups are strongly correlated with the strength of university and public research institutes in the underlying science (Zucker et al. 1997). In the absence of small local firms, the large European companies turned to small American partners to tap new competencies as they struggled to catch up. Given the head start and faster rates of technological development in the US, European start-ups may have been pre-empted by American firms. Moreover, the more dominant large European pharmaceutical firms have had a pronounced effect on the development of European R&D networks, as these organizations serve a 'clearing-house' function for the development of more specialized innovations from national research clusters.

3   DATA AND METHODS

Analysing cross-national differences in organizational and institutional settings of innovative activities is most effectively accomplished with methods that visually represent these patterns of relationships. We are less interested in the attributes of individual research organizations and much more concerned with the linkages that structure innovation systems. Hence we utilize methods that capture these relational features graphically. We use graph-drawing techniques to examine key characteristics of life science knowledge networks.

We adopt a general analytical technique based on the theory of random fields (Ising 1925; Guyon 1994) to graphically display collaborative networks at the national, cross-national and organizational levels.[6] Specifically, we applied the Fruchterman–Reingold (FR) algorithm (1991) to simulate our network of collaborations as a system of interacting particles with repelling forces $\rho_{u,v}(x) = c_1^2/d(x_u, x_v)$ between every pair of nodes $u, v \in V$, and additional attracting forces $\alpha_{u,v}(x) = d(x_u, x_v)^2/c_1$ which are in place only between connected nodes, where $d(x_u, x_v)$ is the Euclidean distance of locations x_u and x_v of nodes u and v respectively. The parameter c_1 is set to $c_2\sqrt{A/n}$, where A is the desired layout area, n is the number of nodes and c_2 is an experimentally chosen constant. The FR algorithm aims to minimize the force of each node, which is equivalent to minimizing the energy U of the overall random field model:

$$U_{[u,v]}(x) = \begin{cases} |\alpha_{u,v}(x) - \rho_{u,v}(x)| & \text{if nodes } u \text{ and } v \text{ are connected,} \\ \rho_{u,v}(x) & \text{otherwise} \end{cases}$$

The FR algorithm is designed to find a stable configuration corresponding to a local minimum. In order to prevent the algorithm from resting in sub-optimal local outcomes and to improve the fit of the final configuration, we run the algorithm with several randomly chosen initial layouts. At the end, the drawings we present to illustrate our argument capture not only the pattern and density of collaborative activity, but also are a meaningful indicator of the extent to which such collaborations create actual clusters of tightly connected partners.

We draw on several complementary data sets to analyse European and US research organization–industry innovation networks for the period spanning 1988–2000. Patent and collaborative R&D project data sets are used to form the core of our analyses.

The Life Sciences Industry Database (referred to as BioBase) developed by Pammolli and Riccaboni surveys the economic and scientific activity of 11,656 private and public organizations active in the bio-pharmaceutical industry in Europe, North America and Israel.

BioBase provides detailed information on 17,734 pharmaceutical R&D projects set up worldwide for 1990–2001. Throughout this chapter we shall focus on the network of collaborative projects among organizations located in Europe, North America and Israel. As a whole, this network consists of 5,813 collaborative projects among 1,483 organizations. For each collaborative R&D project, the organization that originated a new pharmacologically active compound is distinguished from the organization(s) that licensed that patent for further development. In addition to this originator–developer distinction, BioBase offers detailed information about compound preferred names and synonyms, pharmacological actions, therapeutic indications, ATC classes,[7] patent and licensing information, countries of experimentation and commercialization, and monitors the whole history of project development (starting date; collaborative agreements; project suspended, discontinued, withdrawn; preclinical and clinical (I–II–III) tests; registration and market launch; patent filed, issued and expiry).

Moreover, BioBase draws upon 23,570 patents for therapeutically useful compounds or processes issued by major world patent offices (US, UK, Germany, France, Japan, Europe and the Patent Cooperation Treaty legal office) and assigned to the 90 most prolific research organizations worldwide.[8]

These 90 institutions represent more than 60 per cent of all patents in this sample. Thus, there is a natural cut-off point around 90, as the remainder of the distribution is very widely dispersed across hundreds of organizations. These patents were also coded according to the same pharmacological classification used for R&D projects.

Taken together, our data sources enable us to develop a comprehensive and novel view of patent co-assignment and collaborative networks involving European and US biotechnology firms, pharmaceutical corporations and PROs. Our data are broad in scope and involve thousands of relationships among multiple types of organizations, enabling us to map qualitative differences in public–private R&D networks in the life sciences.

4 ANALYSES: CROSS-NATIONAL NETWORKS AND ORGANIZATIONAL COMPETENCIES IN R&D

We begin by presenting an overview of general trends of international collaboration in drug development. We distinguish the roles of originators and developers, with the former responsible for the underlying basic science, focusing on the early stages of target identification/validation and drug discovery, and the latter handling downstream stages of R&D and subsequent manufacture and/or marketing. We identify originators as the organization that started the R&D project and, typically, held the relevant patent. Note that a variety of organizations – PROs, DBFs and EPCs – perform the roles of originating, developing, producing and commercializing new biomedical products.

Table 6.1 clearly shows that US organizations hold the lion's share of collaborative R&D projects both as originators (65.65 per cent) and as developers (57.16 per cent). In this respect, single European countries (United Kingdom, France and Germany) and even the European Union as a whole, lag far behind. Notably, the US research system looks both *central* and *large*. US *centrality* is reflected by the high volume of cross-national ties: European countries – with the exception of Italy – establish more than 50 per cent of their R&D collaborations with US partners. At the same time, the majority of US collaborations (53.26 per cent) are with US partners sustaining an enormous national market for technology. Moreover, the US is the only country in Table 6.1 with a large positive balance between the number of projects originated and developed, followed by a group of small Nordic countries (such as Sweden and Denmark), Canada and Israel. In contrast, firms in large EU countries reveal a marked predilection to act as developers of R&D projects originated abroad.

Despite the undisputed central role of the US system, Table 6.1 reveals

Table 6.1   Collaborative R&D projects originated and developed by country and partners' location

| | (1) Projects originated | | (2) Projects developed | | (1)–(2) | | Partners' location | | | | | | | |
| | | | | | | | National | | US | | EU | | Canada/ Israel | |
	No.	%	No.	%	No.	%	No.	%	No.	%	No.	%	No.	%
USA	3,816	65.65	3,323	57.16	493	8.48	2,481	53.26	–	–	1,979	42.49	198	4.25
UK	617	10.61	689	11.85	–72	–1.24	203	18.40	588	53.31	257	23.30	55	4.99
France	254	4.37	351	6.04	–97	–1.67	47	8.42	293	52.51	197	35.30	21	3.76
Germany	216	3.72	373	6.42	–157	–2.70	41	7.48	303	55.29	197	35.95	7	1.28
Switzerland	177	3.04	277	4.77	–100	–1.72	6	1.34	277	61.83	149	33.26	16	3.57
Canada	174	2.99	176	3.03	–2	–0.03	42	13.64	163	52.92	101	32.79	2	0.65
Italy	138	2.37	166	2.86	–28	–0.48	21	7.42	100	35.34	158	55.83	4	1.41
Denmark	95	1.63	82	1.41	13	0.22	5	2.91	89	51.74	69	40.12	9	5.23
Sweden	64	1.10	44	0.76	20	0.34	2	1.89	60	56.60	43	40.57	1	0.94
Netherlands	41	0.71	60	1.03	–19	–0.33	1	1.00	72	72.00	26	26.00	1	1.00
Israel	31	0.53	34	0.58	–3	–0.05	3	4.84	35	56.45	22	35.48	2	3.23
Other European countries	190	3.28	238	4.09	–48	–0.83	12	2.88	197	47.36	198	47.60	9	2.16
Total	5,813	100	5,813	100	0	0	2,864	–	2,177	–	1,417	–	127	–

Source: BioBase.

the existence also of a considerable intra-EU network of collaborations. If it is true that, as a mean, US partners account for 55 per cent of EU collaborations, about 42 per cent of total collaborations are subscribed within Europe and 3 per cent within Canada and Israel.

In a nutshell, data in Table 6.1 show that the US national innovation system in the life sciences is structurally central and quantitatively dominant in the cross-national R&D project network.

Table 6.2 helps to pinpoint the existence of remarkable differences between the US and the European networks. Table 6.2 distinguishes R&D collaborative projects according to the stage of signing. R&D collaborations are classified into three categories: preclinical, clinical development and marketing. It is straightforward to notice that organizations in large European countries tend to join a higher proportion of R&D collaborative projects in the final stage of marketing and commercialization, both as originators and as developers. Firms in Italy (76.81 per cent), Switzerland (53.11 per cent), Denmark (47.37 per cent), France (38.19 per cent), Germany (34.26 per cent) and other European countries (58.20 per cent) originate a considerably higher share of collaborative projects in the marketing phase as compared to organizations in Sweden (12.50 per cent), Canada (15.43 per cent), the US (17.36 per cent), Israel (18.75 per cent) and the Netherlands (19.51 per cent), which tend to participate in the network of R&D collaborations early on in the clinical and especially preclinical stages of development. The United Kingdom depicts an intermediate profile between North America and the Nordic EU countries on the one side, and continental Europe on the other. The overall picture looks slightly different by considering the proportion of collaborations subscribed as developers. Swiss and Danish companies tend to anticipate the stage of subscription as developers, while Swedish, Canadian and Israeli organizations tend to anticipate collaborations as originators.

Table 6.3 completes the description of the variety of roles and functions of the network of R&D collaborations for organizations located in different countries. More specifically, Table 6.3 reports the number and the percentage of collaborative agreements subscribed by public research organizations (PROs), dedicated biotechnology firms (DBFs) and established companies (ECs) in North America, Europe, Canada and Israel. According to the dominant representation of division of innovative labour in this domain, PROs tend to be originators, ECs play a fundamental role as developers and DBFs are positioned somewhere in between. Table 6.3 shows that this view is only partially correct, because of major differences among countries.

PROs play a fundamental role *both* as originators and developers in the US, the UK and Canada. In France and Israel they play a major role only

Table 6.2 Collaborative R&D projects originated and developed by country and phase of development

	Preclinical				Clinicals (I–II–III)				Marketing			
	Projects originated		Projects developed		Projects originated		Projects developed		Projects originated		Projects developed	
	No.	%*	No.	%**	No.	%*	No.	%**	No.	%*	No.	%**
USA	2,133	55.93	1,914	57.60	1,019	26.72	861	25.91	662	17.36	548	16.49
UK	293	47.33	350	50.80	172	27.79	191	27.72	154	24.88	148	21.48
France	107	42.13	147	41.88	50	19.69	70	19.94	97	38.19	134	38.18
Germany	82	37.96	142	38.07	60	27.78	106	28.42	74	34.26	125	33.51
Switzerland	45	25.42	108	38.99	38	21.47	71	25.63	94	53.11	98	35.38
Canada	109	62.29	94	53.41	39	22.29	53	30.11	27	15.43	29	16.48
Italy	14	10.14	23	13.86	18	13.04	24	14.46	106	76.81	119	71.69
Denmark	29	30.53	32	39.02	21	22.11	26	31.71	45	47.37	24	29.27
Sweden	47	73.44	19	43.18	9	14.06	7	15.91	8	12.50	18	40.91
Netherlands	19	46.34	30	50.00	14	34.15	18	30.00	8	19.51	12	20.00
Israel	14	43.75	11	32.35	12	37.50	6	17.65	6	18.75	17	50.00
Other European countries	41	21.69	63	26.36	38	20.11	57	23.85	110	58.20	119	49.79
Total	2,933	–	2,933	–	1,490	–	1,490	–	1,391	–	1,391	–

Notes:
* % of projects originated in any given Country.
** % of projects developed in any given Country.

Source: BioBase.

179

Table 6.3   Collaborative R&D projects originated and developed by country and organization type

	PROs				DBFs				ECs			
	Projects originated		Projects developed		Projects originated		Projects developed		Projects originated		Projects developed	
	No.	%*	No.	%**	No.	%*	No.	%**	No.	%*	No.	%**
USA	916	24.03	377	11.35	2,326	61.02	1,891	56.91	570	14.95	1,055	31.75
UK	143	23.18	86	12.48	264	42.79	177	25.69	210	34.04	426	61.83
France	46	18.11	20	5.70	61	24.02	50	14.25	147	57.87	281	80.06
Germany	12	5.56	20	5.36	56	25.93	29	7.77	148	68.52	324	86.86
Switzerland	16	9.04	11	3.97	10	5.65	11	3.97	151	85.31	255	92.06
Canada	51	29.31	19	10.80	115	66.09	149	84.66	8	4.60	8	4.55
Italy	10	7.25	8	4.82	3	2.17	10	6.02	125	90.58	148	89.16
Denmark	7	7.37	4	4.88	21	22.11	8	9.76	67	70.53	70	85.37
Sweden	2	3.13	6	13.64	35	54.69	16	36.36	27	42.19	22	50.00
Netherlands	1	2.44	5	8.33	23	56.10	17	28.33	17	41.46	38	63.33
Israel	10	32.26	1	2.94	15	48.39	9	26.47	6	19.35	24	70.59
Other European countries	28	14.81	12	5.15	67	35.45	57	24.46	94	49.74	164	70.39
Total	1,242	21.38	569	9.80	2,996	51.58	2,424	41.74	1,570	27.03	2,815	48.47

Notes:
* % of projects originated in any given Country.
** % of projects developed in any given Country.

Source: BioBase.

as originators, while Swedish PROs act mainly as developers. The picture looks completely different in continental Europe: PROs in Germany, Switzerland, Italy, Denmark and the Netherlands do not seem to contribute significantly to the network of collaborative R&D projects. In these countries most of the collaborative projects are originated (and developed) by established companies. In the first group of countries, the high degree of participation of PROs sustains a structural contribution of DBFs to the R&D network. North American DBFs are responsible for the majority of the collaborative R&D projects originated and developed in the US and Canada. DBFs play a significant role both as originators and developers in the UK, Sweden, the Netherlands and Israel while, despite the recent upsurge of the biotech sector in Europe, DBFs in continental Europe are confined to the role of originators (France, Germany and Denmark) or do not play a significant role at all (Italy and Switzerland).

In the US, dedicated biotech firms do the lion's share of the development work (nearly 55 per cent) on PRO-originated innovations. When a US PRO turns to a European partner, the large multinational corporation is the dominant option. In Europe, there are real differences in collaboration within and across nations. In local within-country collaborations, European PROs turn to DBFs and other PROs. But when collaboration occurs across European countries, the EPCs become the dominant partner. When European PROs reach across the Atlantic, US DBFs are the primary developers, especially for preclinical and clinical development. The picture that emerges is one of very different roles for small firms and large multinationals in Europe and the US. The large pharmaceutical firms are responsible for the bulk of cross-national collaborations in Europe, while the small biotech companies are the key developers in the US. We turn now to an in-depth examination of these organizational differences.

The country-level aggregate figures presented in Tables 6.1–3 do not tell the full story, however. R&D projects and patented biomedical innovations stem from the work of scientists and clinicians within specific organizations. Given the importance of non-industrial research centres in promoting scientific and technological progress in the life sciences, Figure 6.1 examines the upstream collaborative network among individual PROs to analyse relationships among organizations whose patenting activity drives the capability to participate in the network of R&D collaborative projects. Figure 6.1 is based on patent co-assignment networks among PROs. Each node is a university, research institute or hospital, and each tie represents one or more patent co-assignments between the organizations (see the legend in Appendix 6A.1). The relative spatial position of nodes is a reflection of the minimum-energy algorithm we employ using Pajek. Several features stand out in this image.

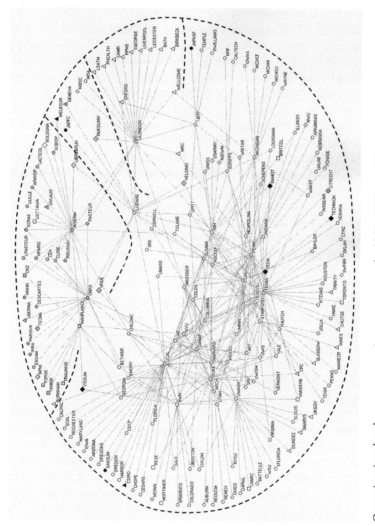

Figure 6.1   Organization-level patent co-assignment network, 1990–2001: public research organizations

Consider first the regional and national clustering of organizations (dashed lines). The tightly clustered French/German and UK research organizations on the right side of the figure and the densely connected US regions in the image's lower left-hand quadrant are the result of minimum-energy network drawing techniques and not of arbitrary placement. In addition to demonstrating the coherence of national and regional R&D systems, close inspection of patent co-assignment helps explain the causes of the US dominance apparent in Tables 6.1–3. Note the organizational homogeneity of the cluster of states in continental Europe (mainly German organizations on the left and French PROs on the right). Leading national institutes in France (INSERM, CNRS, Institut Pasteur) and Germany (Max Planck) play a pivotal role, while hospitals and universities are completely marginalized.[9] The United Kingdom (on the right) has a somewhat higher degree of institutional diversity, substantiated by the presence of both government and non-profit research and funding agencies (the universities of London and Oxford, the Medical Research Council and the Wellcome Trust).

Contrast these relatively isolated and homogeneous national clusters with the large and densely interconnected US network in the lower left quadrant of the figure, which is composed of tight, repeated interconnections among a diverse set of PROs. Elite universities (Harvard, MIT, the complexes of the University of California and Texas, Stanford and Johns Hopkins), research institutes (the Dana-Farber Cancer Center, Scripps, Sloan Kettering, the Salk Institute), and hospitals (Brigham & Women's and Massachusetts General) play central roles in innovative collaborations both within and across US regions. Connections across US regions and co-assignment ties linking geographically dispersed universities to the National Institutes of Health and other core institutions illustrate a public research system that also reaches across regions and organizational forms. Recall that these relationships represent patent co-assignments, a particularly close form of R&D collaboration. We argue that these systemic cross-national variations in the organization of early-stage research collaborations explain national differences in biomedical commercialization above and beyond variations in policies or later-stage technology transfer infrastructures. In Owen-Smith et al. (2002) we show that the structural clustering of European nations and US regions, and the consolidating effect of interregional ties in the US result from characteristics of the science underlying these patent co-assignment networks. Leading organizations in Europe are specialized innovators whose patents focus on specific sets of therapies and biological targets. The French institutes are specialized in therapeutic classes relating primarily to infectious disease and Aids research. German research institutes are more involved with hereditary cardiovascular diseases. The more dispersed and diverse UK institutions, for example, Cancer Research Campaign (CRC), Medical Research Council (MRC), and the British Technology Group (BTG) are somewhat broader in focus but still cluster in therapeutic classes largely related to cancer research. The greater breadth of the UK research system, and its higher degree of diversity compared to France and Germany, is coherent with the different profiles emerging from Tables 6.1–3. Major US PROs hold patents that span multiple substantive areas. In the US national innovation system, diverse public research institutions play the role of generalist innovators regardless of geographic location, though the prevalence of Boston- and California-based research organizations in the core suggests the importance of regional agglomeration.

Taken together, these differences in centrality (Table 6.1), phase (and degree of risk) of collaborative efforts (Table 6.2), organizational and relational roles (Table 6.3), network position and clustering in upstream R&D (Figure 6.1) are critical findings, suggesting that increases in scale alone will not alter the focus of R&D efforts because organizations typically engage in local searches, and would continue to patent and collaborate in those areas in which they are most skilled. In essence, then, we argue that one reason for greater integration across and within US regions can be found in the scientific overlap among generalist patentors. Alterations in the scale of patenting activity without corresponding shifts in this division of labour will not make the European system resemble its American counterpart. Instead, mere increases in scale might deepen specialization and heighten fragmentation among European national research systems.

To further our understanding of university–industry relationships, we insert now the private sector in our network representation. First, we take into consideration the patent co-assignment network as a proxy of joint research efforts in basic research and development (Figure 6.2; see legend in Appendix 6A.1). Next, we examine the network of collaborative R&D projects to compare the role of US and European institutions in supporting drug development towards the final market (Figure 6.3; see legend in Appendix 6A.2).

Figure 6.2 gives an extended representation of the patent co-assignment network, obtained by adding commercial entities to the network in Figure 6.1. Vertices, representing both public and private organizations, are distinguished according to their nationality by means of different shape/colour combinations (that is, white circles correspond to US organizations, black circles are Japanese ones, and grey triangles represent Swiss firms and institutions). To improve network legibility, vertices labels are reported only for *core* organizations.

First, we apply a *k-core* technique to identify the relevant core of the

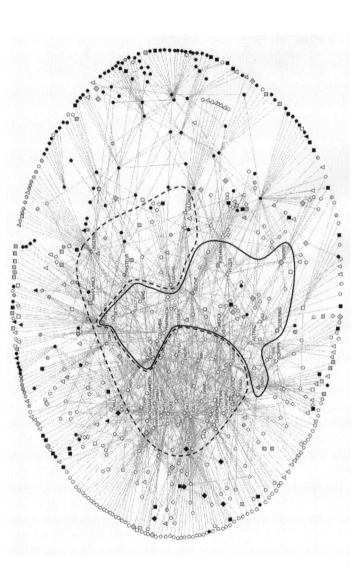

Figure 6.2   Organization-level patent co-assignment network, 1990–2001: public research organizations and commercial entities

graph. Technically, the *k-core* is a subgraph of a given network where each vertex has at least k neighbours in the same core. Then, we fix k equal to 5, to highlight leading organizations which take part in the tightly interconnected core of the net. Our investigation reveals two relational regions within the core. Most of the organizations within the first cluster, inscribed with a broken line, are PROs and DBFs. As in Figure 6.1, the core of the US research system concentrates on the left side while European leading institutions are on the right side. The second core region in Figure 6.2, delimited by a full line, includes all the most important pharmaceutical R&D corporations worldwide (Merck, Lilly, Pfizer, Aventis, Novartis, Glaxo, Roche, Pharmacia, AHP, Novartis, AstraZeneca, J&J and so on). Pharmaceutical corporations penetrate the centre of the university patent co-assignment network and break the weak US–European connections pinpointed in Figure 6.1.

Overall, US and European research systems are tightly interpenetrated, with US organizations playing a prominent role, and occupy the core of the university–industry complex. In contrast, firms and institutions in Japan tend to be closely related internally with very few linkages overseas. As a consequence, the Japanese research system plays a marginal role in the life sciences university–industry network. In extreme synthesis, we can identify three different relational strata corresponding to US, European and Japanese research systems, respectively. The US system is highly interconnected and central in the worldwide network of collaborations. The European system is broken into national systems and is highly dependent on the US systems which originate the majority of the R&D projects developed in Europe. Finally the Japanese system is highly interlinked but faces major difficulties to plug into the worldwide network of R&D collaborations.

Figure 6.2 reveals that major pharmaceutical companies play a fundamental role in supporting/obstructing the relational capabilities of PROs and biotechnology start-ups. There are three US DBFs (Amgen, Chiron and Human Genome Sciences) and a number of important US hospitals (Massachusetts General Hospital, Children's Hospital, Beth Israel Deaconess, Brigham & Women's Hospital) in the relational core as opposed to either DBFs or hospitals in Europe or Japan. In the last twenty years, many European multinational corporations experienced major organizational changes as a consequence of a sustained process of mergers and acquisitions (M&A). Most of them have since strengthened their linkages with the US research system (GlaxoSmithKline, AstraZeneca, Pharmacia Corp., Novartis). In this view, Aventis seems to represent an important exception to this picture. In 1998, Hoechst Marion Roussel and Rhône-Poulenc Rorer merged to form Aventis and located the headquarters of the holding company in Strasbourg. On the one hand Rhône-Poulenc has maintained important connections with the French research institutes (CNRS, INSERM, Institut Pasteur and Institut Merieux).[10] On the other hand Hoechst, as well as Boehringer Engelheim and Schering AG, are closely interlinked with the German research system. In addition to that, MPG and CNRS signed an important framework agreement for joint scientific research in 1981 to boost common R&D efforts within the European Union. As a result, Aventis play a pivotal role in structuring joint collaborative efforts between French and German PROs.

When we move to consider collaborative R&D projects, the structure of the network changes considerably (see Figure 6.3). First, the relationship between institutional and network proximity breaks down. Even though pharmaceutical companies still control the core of the net, the region delimited by a full line is now subdivided into four relational areas and in each subgraph established companies are mixed up with DBFs. In general, the network appears to be more interconnected, less hierarchical and the 5-core of the graph is no longer confined to the centre of the net.

Second, the relationship between geographical and relational proximity disappears too. Vertices of different shapes and colours appear to be distributed more or less randomly throughout the graph. Despite this apparent disorder, we can stress some major relational changes as compared to the patent co-assignment network in Figure 6.2. The relational area of European PROs, delimited in Figure 6.3 by a broken line, occupies a streaked region of the graph from the left (universities of London and Reading) to the right (Imperial Cancer Research). UK institutions now dominate the core of the European PRO network (British Technology Group, Imperial Cancer Research, Medical Research Council, universities of Oxford, Cambridge, London, Reading and Birmingham), while research institutions in continental Europe almost disappear (only the CNRS remains in the core).

More importantly, European PROs are almost completely detached by the commercial core of the net, which is completely surrounded by US institutions. In particular, three different US regions play complementary relational roles and can be said to be responsible for the success of the US system of innovation in drug development: the Bethesda complex (National Institutes of Health and, in particular, the National Cancer Institute, at the bottom), the Californian research system (the University of California Complex, Stanford, Salk Institute, Genentech and Chiron all disposed along the arrow on the left) and the Boston area (Children's and Massachusetts General hospitals, MIT, Harvard, Dana-Farber and Genzyme along the broken line arrow on the right). Once again, it is important to notice the high degree of institutional heterogeneity of

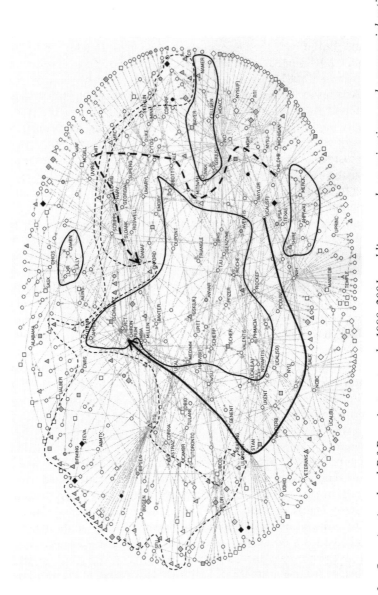

Figure 6.3   Organization-level R&D projects network, 1990–2001: public research organizations and commercial entities

the US research system both at the local and at the national levels. Moreover, contrary to most European PROs, US core institutions are present in both pre-development and development activities, revealing a tendency to integrate both fundamental and applied R&D within single institutions.

5 CONCLUSIONS

Our analyses of interfaces between non-industrial research institutes and firms in the US and Europe emphasize the importance of the division of innovative labour. We do not object to arguments that the United States' first-mover advantage was critical in establishing the trajectory of the field. But we supplement this explanation by stressing the diversity of actors involved and the varied roles played by scientific specialists and generalists. Without recognizing these elements in the context of an evolutionary trajectory shaped by distinct cultural and institutional contexts, European efforts to 'catch up' to the US by mirroring established policies and arrangements will likely be misguided. Central to the US system are two key factors: relational and integrative capability. A broadly diverse group of US organizations have established protocols in place for fostering research collaboration. Moreover, these alliances span organizations with different missions and serve to link basic research with clinical development.

The institutional structure of biomedical research evolved quite differently in Europe and the United States. The diversity of the US public research system, a highly mobile scientific labour force, and a host of regulatory and policy initiatives promoted widespread commercialization of academically originated research, largely through the founding of small biotechnology firms. In addition, the generalist technological role and integrative development profiles of US PROs have capitalized on scientific developments in molecular biology that more closely link goal-oriented therapeutic research with fundamental biological investigation. European universities developed competencies in molecular biology less quickly than specialized research institutes. The disciplinary focus of these institutes, combined with the centralizing effects of national R&D funding infrastructures and regulatory contexts, serve to limit universities' participation in commercially oriented R&D and concentrate R&D networks in specialized national clusters.

We also observe qualitatively different paths in the development of local centres of excellence in the US and Europe. In the former case, generalist regional clusters developed around PROs that integrated innovation and development work. These clusters planted the seeds of accumulative advantage as the regions attracted talented researchers, high-quality students, and increasing shares of R&D funding in addition to for-profit firms dedicated to the commercialization of new technologies. In Europe, national clusters of specialists may also have benefited from cumulative advantage in research funding and talent, but the funding sources were national rather than European, and research priorities and a community of local specialist firms may have deepened already narrow competencies rather than enabling broad exploration (see Owen-Smith et al. 2002). The role that European pharmaceutical corporations played as clearing-houses for innovations developed within these national clusters may also have mitigated against the broadening of regional scientific and organizational competencies.

Finally, notable differences in the constellation of organizations able to capture and develop innovations aided in pushing US and European industries in different evolutionary directions. We observe divergent roles played by PRO originators, DBFs and large pharmaceutical companies, which contribute to disparate industry outcomes in Europe and the United States. On this, our emphasis on the diversity of types of organizations and their multiple roles stands as a corrective to policy attempts to develop high-volume collaborations in Europe through copying American policies. Our focus on the division of innovative labour implies that European efforts to adopt US policies should be directed more at generating integration between basic research and clinical development and fostering extensive linkages among universities, small firms, and the heretofore dominant public institutes and large pharmaceutical companies.

NOTES

*   This chapter has been adapted from a previously published article: J. Owen-Smith, M. Riccaboni, F. Pammolli and W.W. Powell (2002), 'A comparison of US and European university–industry relations in the life sciences', *Management Science* **48**(1), 24–43.

This research was supported by grants from the Association for Institutional Research (Grants # 99–129–0, 00–129–1, Jason Owen-Smith, Principal Investigator: PI), the National Science Foundation (Grant # 9710729, W.W. Powell and K.W. Koput, PIs), the Merck Foundation (EPRIS Project, F. Pammolli, PI), the European Commission (Contract # SOE1–CT 98–1116, DG 12–SOLS: ESSY Project). We are grateful to audiences at Georgia Tech, Columbia University, the University of Gothenberg, the Centre de Sociologie des Organisations in Paris, the NPRNet Workshop in Paris, and the comparative workshop at Stanford's Institute for International Studies (IIS) for useful feedback. We thank Ashish Arora, Paul David, Bronwyn Hall, Hannah Kettler, Georg Kruecken, Richard Nelson, Keith Pavitt, Scott Shane, Deepak Somaya, Ed Steinmueller and Paula Stephan for their helpful comments. The chapter was a fully collaborative effort.

1. The Single European Act provided, for the first time, a legal basis for European R&D programmes (framework programmes) developed by the European Commission to complement national programmes and funds.
2. We define a PRO as any government research laboratory, public or private university, or non-profit or public research hospital or institute.
3. In the US, 37.2 per cent of dedicated biotech firms (DBFs) are located in California while Germany, the leading country in terms of number of DBFs, accounts for only 24 per cent of European companies. Even moving from a nation/state level to regions the picture does not change: 47.5 per cent of US dedicated biotechnology enterprises are concentrated in only three regions: San Diego, the Bay Area and Boston while to reach a comparable level of concentration in Europe, we must consider ten regions: Ile de France, Cambridgeshire, Greater London, Oxfordshire, Bayern, Berlin, Stockholm and Sydsverige, Basel, Central Scotland.
4. A survey of high-impact publications in molecular biology and genetics between 1988 and 1992 lists the Institut Chemie Biologique in Strasbourg, the MRC lab in Cambridge, UK, the Institut Pasteur in Paris, and the Karolinska Institute in Stockholm among the most prolific research centres. See *Science Watch*, July/August 1993, **4**(7), Institute for Scientific Information.
5. Pavitt (2000) estimates that the resources devoted to academic research in the life sciences in the US are 50 per cent larger than in Europe.
6. The theory of random fields provides a unified theoretical framework to cope with large systems of interacting agents both in natural and social sciences. The reader interested in the relationship between the theory of random field and graph-drawing techniques is referred to Guyon (1994), and Winkler (1995). A software package for large network analysis is available online at http://vlado.fmf.uni-lj.si/pub/networks/pajek. Pajek is used to analyse multiple types of large networks (Batagelj and Mrvar 2000; Albert et al. 2000).
7. The ATC classification has been developed and maintained since 1971 by the European Pharmaceutical Marketing Research Association. The 3-digit ATC designation is a widely accepted standard for classifying pharmaceutical products and is used by anti-trust authorities around the globe.
8. Information on the patents is found in *Patent Fast Alert*, published by Current Drugs, Ltd, London, UK.
9. Scientists at the CNRS or Max Planck may well have university laboratories, but the government institute is identified as their primary affiliation on the patents.
10. From 1991 to 1996, the French government invested FFr 820 million to create BioAvenir, a joint research programme with Rhône Poulenc (Lyon, France).

REFERENCES

Albert, R., H. Jeong, and A. Barabasi (2000), 'Error and attack tolerance in complex networks', *Nature* **406**(July), 378–82.

Arora, A. and A. Gambardella (1990), 'Complementarity and external linkages: the strategies of large firms in biotechnology', *Journal of Industrial Economics* **38**(4), 361–79.

Arora, A. and A. Gambardella (1994), 'Explaining technological information and utilizing it: scientific knowledge, capacity, and external linkages in biotechnology', *Journal of Economic Behavior and Organization* **24**, 91–114.

Arora, A., A. Gambardella, F. Pammolli and M. Riccaboni (2000), 'The nature and the extent of the market for technology in biopharmaceuticals', Paper presented at the 'International Conference on Technology Policy and Innovation: Economic and Historical Perspectives', Paris, 20–22 November.

Batagelj, V. and A. Mrvar (2000), 'Drawing genealogies', *Connections* **21**, 47–57.

Ben-David, J. (1977), *Centers of Learning: Britain, France, Germany, and the United States,* New York: McGraw-Hill.

Fruchterman, T. and E. Reingold (1991), 'Graph drawing by force-directed replacement', *Software – Practice and Experience* **21**, 1129–64.

Galambos, L. and J. Sturchio (1998), 'Pharmaceutical firms and the transition to biotechnology: a study in strategic innovation, *Business History Review* **72**, 250–78.

Gambardella, A. (1995), *Science and Innovation. The U.S. Pharmaceutical Industry During the 1980s,* New York: Cambridge University Press.

Gambardella, A., L. Orsenigo and F. Pammolli (2000), 'Global competitiveness in pharmaceuticals: a European perspective', Enterprise Papers, No. 1 (http://dg3.eudra.org/pharmacos/comdoc_doc.htm).

Geiger, R. (1988), *Research and Relevant Knowledge: American Research Universities since World War II,* New York: Oxford University Press.

Gittelman, M. (2000), 'Mapping national knowledge networks: scientists, firms and institutions in biotechnology in the United States and France', PhD Dissertation, New York University.

Guyon, X. (1994), *Random Fields on a Network,* Berlin: Springer.

Henderson, R., L. Orsenigo and G. Pisano (1999), 'The pharmaceutical industry and the revolution in molecular biology', in Mowery and Nelson (eds), pp. 267–311.

Howells, J. and C. McKinlay (1999), 'Commercialization of university research in Europe. Report to the Advisory Council on Science and Technology', Ontario, Canada.

Ising, E. (1925), 'Beitrag zur theorie des ferromagnetismus', *Zeitschrift Physik* **31**, 235–58.

Lerner, J. and R. Merges (1998), 'The control of technology alliances: an empirical analysis of the biotechnology industry', *Journal of Industrial Economics* **46**(2), 125–56.

Liebeskind, J., A. Oliver, L. Zucker and M. Brewer (1996), 'Social networks, learning, and flexibility: sourcing scientific knowledge in new biotechnology firms', *Organizational Science* **7**(4), 428–43.

Link, A. (1999), 'Public/private partnerships in the United States', *Industry and Innovation* **6**(2), 191–217.

Morange, M. (1998), *A History of Molecular Biology,* Cambridge, MA: Harvard University Press.

Mowery, D. (1999), 'America's industrial resurgence? An overview', in *U.S. Industry in 2000: Studies in Competitive Performance,* Washington, DC: National Academy Press, pp. 1–16.

Mowery, D. and R.R. Nelson (eds) (1999), *Sources of Industrial Leadership. Studies of Seven Industries,* New York: Cambridge University Press.

Mowery, D., R.R. Nelson, B.N. Sampat and A.A. Ziedonis (2001), 'The growth of patenting and licensing by U.S. universities: an assessment of the effects of the Bayh–Dole Act of 1980', *Research Policy* **30**(1), 99–119.

Orsenigo, L., F. Pammolli and M. Riccaboni (2001), 'Technological change and network dynamics. Lessons from the pharmaceutical industry', *Research Policy* **30**(3), 485–508.

Owen-Smith, J. (2000), 'Public science, private science: the causes and consequences of patenting by Research One universities', PhD Dissertation, University of Arizona.

Owen-Smith, J., M. Riccaboni, F. Pammolli and W.W. Powell (2002) 'A comparison of US and European university–industry relations in the life sciences', *Management Science* **48**(1), 24–43.

Pammolli, F., M. Riccaboni and L. Orsenigo (2000), 'Variety and irreversibility in scientific and technological systems', in A. Nicita and U. Pagano (eds), *The Evolution of Economic Diversity*, London: Routledge, pp. 216–39.

Pavitt, K. (2000) 'Academic research in Europe', SPRU Working Paper, no. 43, Science and Technology Policy Research, Brighton.

Peterson, J. and M. Sharp (1998), *Technology Policy in the European Union*, Basingstoke: Macmillan.

Powell, W.W., K.W. Koput and L. Smith-Doerr (1996), 'Interorganizational collaboration and the locus of innovation in biotechnology', *Administrative Science Quarterly* **41**(1), 116–45.

Rosenberg, N. and R.R. Nelson (1994), 'American universities and technical advance in industry', *Research Policy* **23**(3), 323–48.

Stokes, D.E. (1997), *Pasteur's Quadrant*, Washington, DC: Brookings Institution Press.

Stuart, T.E., H. Hoang and R.C. Hybels (1999), 'Interorganizational endorsements and the performance of entrepreneurial ventures', *Administrative Science Quarterly* **44**, 315–49.

Winkler, G. (1995), 'Image analysis, random fields and dynamic Monte Carlo models', *Applications of Mathematics* **27**, Berlin: Springer Verlag.

Zucker, L.G., M.R. Darby and M.B. Brewer (1997), 'Intellectual human capital and the birth of U.S. biotechnology enterprises', *American Economic Review* **88**(1), 290–306.

Appendix 6A.1   Organization-level patent co-assignment network, 1990–2001 (Figures 6.1 and 6.2)

COLOUR & SHAPE (NATIONALITY)
White: Circle – USA   Triangle – United Kingdom   Box – Canada
  Diamond – Italy/Spain
Grey: Circle – France   Triangle – Switzerland   Box – Germany
  Diamond – Other European countries
Black: Circle – Japan   Triangle – Australia/NZ   Box – Far East
  Diamond – Israel

Label	Organization
AFMYOP	Association Française Contre le Myophaties (FR)
AHP	*American Home Products (US)*
AMGEN	Amgen (US)
ARCH	Arch Development Corp. (US)
ARIZONA	University of Arizona (US)
ARKANSAS	University of Arkansas (US)
ASTRAZ	*AstraZeneca (UK-SE)*
AUBURN	Auburn University (US)
AVENTIS	*Aventis (FR-DE)*
BASF	*Basf AG (DE)*
BATH	University of Bath (UK)
BATTELLE	Battelle Memorial Institute (US)
BAYLOR	Baylor College of Medicine (US)
BETHISR	Beth Israel Deaconess Medical Center (US)
BIRKBECK	Birkbeck College (UK)
BMS	*Bristol Myers Squibb (US)*
BOEHRING	*Boehringer Ingelheim (DE)*
BOLOGNA	University of Bologna (IT)
BRANDEIS	Brandeis University (US)
BRITCOL	University of British Columbia (CA)
BURNHAM	Burnham Institute (UK)
BWH	Brigham & Women's Hospital (US)
CALPAC	California Pacific Medical Center (US)
CALTECH	California Institute of Technology (US)
CAMR	Centre for Applied Microbiology & Research (UK)
CANRC	Canada National Research Council (CA)
CDCP	Cent. Disease Control & Prevention (US)
CEA	Commissariat à l'Energie Atomique (FR)
CEDARS	Cedars-Sinai Medical Center (US)
CHILDH	Children's Hospital & Medical Center (US)
CHILDMC	Children's Medical Center Corp. (US)
CHIRON	*Chiron (US)*
CHOPE	City of Hope (US)

Appendix 6A.1   (continued)

Label	Organization
CHPHIL	Children's Hospital of Philadelphia (US)
CHUTQE	Coll. of the Holy & Undiv. Trinity of Queen Elizabeth (UK)
CNRS	Centre National de la Recherche Scientifique (FR)
COLDS	Cold Spring Harbor Lab. (US)
COLORADO	University of Colorado at Boulder (US)
COLUMBIA	Columbia University (US)
CORNELL	Cornell University (US)
CRC	Cancer Research Campaign (UK)
CSIRO	Commonwealth Scientific Industry Res. Org. (AUS)
CTRC	Cancer Therapy and Res. Center Res. Foundation (US)
CURIE	Institut Curie (FR)
DANAF	Dana-Farber Cancer Institute (US)
DESCARTES	Université L. Descartes (FR)
DKZ	German Cancer Institute (DE)
DUKE	Duke University (US)
DUNDEE	University of Dundee (UK)
EMORY	Emory University (US)
ENSAM	École Nationale Supérieure d'Arts et Métiers (FR)
FCHASE	Fox Chase Cancer Center (US)
FHUTCH	Fred Hutchinson Cancer Res. (US)
FLORIDA	University of Florida (US)
FORSK	Cancer-Forskningsfondet AF (DK)
FRAUNHG	Fraunhofer-Gesellschaft (DE)
GENEVA	University of Geneva (CH)
GEORGIA	Georgia University (US)
GLASGOW	Glasgow University (UK)
GSK	*GlaxoSmithKline (UK–US)*
HANSK	Hans-Knoll Institut (DE)
HARBOR	Harbor Branch Oceanographic Ins. (US)
HARVARD	Harvard University (US)
HELSINKI	Helsinki University (FI)
HGS	*Human Genome Science (US)*
HNMC	Hope National Medical Center (US)
HOUSTON	University of Houston (US)
HPARIS	Assistance Publique-Hôpitaux de Paris (FR)
HSICKC	Hospital for Sick Children (US)
ILLINOIS	University of Illinois (US)
INDIANA	Indiana University (US)
INNES	John Innes Center (US)
INRA	Institut National de la Recherche Agronomique (FR)
INSERM	Institut Nat. de la Santé et de la Rech. Médicale (FR)
INSGENR	Institute for Genomic Research (US)
IOWA	University of Iowa (US)

Appendix 6A.1 *(continued)*

Label	Organization
IOWAS	Iowa State University (US)
ISIS	*Isis Pharmaceuticals (US)*
J&J	*Johnsons & Johnsons* (US)
JAPFC	Japan Cancer Foundation (JPN)
JAPHSF	Japan Health Science Foundation (JPN)
JHU	Johns Hopkins University (US)
JOLLA	La Jolla Cancer Research Foundation (US)
LACTEOL	Lab. Lacteol Dr Boucard (FR)
LEICESTER	University of Leicester (UK)
LIBREBRUX	Université Libre de Bruxelles (BE)
LILLY	*Lilly (US)*
LIVERPOOL	University of Liverpool (UK)
LOUISIANA	Louisiana State University (US)
LPASTEUR	Université Louis Pasteur (FR)
LSHTM	London School of Hygiene and Tropical Med. (UK)
LUDWIG	Ludwig Inst. for Cancer Res. (US-DE-FI-BE-SE)
MAINECR	Maine Cent. Research (US)
MARYLAND	University of Maryland (US)
MASSGEN	Massachusetts General Hospital (US)
MAXPLANCK	Max-Planck Institute (DE)
MELBOUR	University of Melbourne (AUS)
MERCK	*Merck & Co. (US)*
MICHCF	Michigan Cancer Foundation (US)
MICHIGAN	University of Michigan (US)
MICHMI	Michigan Molecular Institute (US)
MICHSU	Michigan State University (US)
MILL	*Millennium (US)*
MIT	Massachusetts Institute of Technology (US)
MNHN	Musée National d'Histoire Naturelle (FR)
MORTIMER	Sir Mortimer B. Davis Jewish Gen. Hosp. (CA)
MRA	Microbiological Research Authority (UK)
MRC	Medical Research Council (UK)
MSINAI	Mount Sinai School of Medicine (US)
NCAROLINA	University of North Carolina (US)
NEBRASKA	University of Nebraska (US)
NEMCH	New England Medical Center Hospitals (US)
NEOUCM	Northeastern Ohio Univ. Coll. of Medicine (US)
NIBSC	National Institute Biol. Stan. & Cont. (US)
NIH	National Institutes of Health (US)
NJEWM	National Jewish Med. & Res. Center (US)
NNORD	*Novo Nordisk (DK)*
NOV	*Novartis (CH)*
NPHI	National Public Health Institute (FI)

Appendix 6A.1 *(continued)*

Label	Organization
NRF	Neurosciences Res. Foundation (US)
NTEXAS	University of North Texas (US)
NWU	Northwestern University (US)
NYU	New York University (US)
OHIOS	Ohio State University (US)
OKLAH	University of Oklahoma (US)
OREGON	State of Oregon (US)
OREGONS	Oregon State University (US)
OXFORD	Oxford University (UK)
PARISVII	Université Paris VII (FR)
PASTEUR	Institut Pasteur (FR)
PENN	University of Pennsylvania (US)
PENNS	Pennsylvania State Res. Found. (US)
PFIZER	*Pfizer (US)*
PHARMACIA	*Pharmacia Corp. (US-SE)*
RAMOT	Ramot University (IS)
RESE	Réseau d'évaluation et de surv. écologiques (CA)
RIJKSUNIV	Rijksuniversiteit Lieden (BE)
ROCHE	*Roche (CH)*
ROCHESTER	University of Rochester (UK)
ROCKEF	Rockefeller University (US)
ROUSSAY	Institut Gustave Roussy (FR)
RPMS	Royal Postgraduate Medical School (UK)
RWILLIAMS	Roger Williams Medical Center (US)
SALK	Salk Institute for Biological Studies (US)
SANSUM	Sansum Medical Research (US)
SCBIOP	S.té Civile Bioproject (FR)
SCHEPENS	Schepens Eye Research Institute (US)
SCHERING	Schering AG (DE)
SCRAS	S.té de Conseils de Recherches et d'Application (FR)
SCRIPPS	Scripps Institute (US)
SGEORGE	St George Hospital, London (UK)
SHRINERS	Shriners Hospitals for Crippled Children (US)
SLOANK	Sloan-Kettering Institute (US)
SLOUIS	St Louis University (US)
SMARYS	St Mary's Hospital Medical School (UK)
SRI	Southern Research Institute (US)
STANFORD	Stanford University (US)
SUNY	State University of New York (US)
SWFBR	Southwest Foundation for Biom. Research (US)
TECHNION	Technion R&D Foundation (IS)
TECMA	Technology Marketing Austria (AUS)
TEMPLE	Temple University (US)

Appendix 6A.1 *(continued)*

Label	Organization
TEXAS	University of Texas (US)
TEXHI	Texas Heart Institute (US)
TEXSYS	University of Texas System (US)
TJEFF	Thomas Jefferson University (US)
TORONTO	University of Toronto (CA)
TRINITY	Trinity College Dublin (IR)
TULANE	Tulane University (US)
UAB	University of Alabama at Birmingham (US)
UBERNA	University of Berna (CH)
UBOSTON	Boston University (US)
UCAL	University of California (US)
UKGOV	UK Government (UK)
ULILLE	Université de Lille (FR)
ULONDON	University of London (UK)
UMASS	University of Massachusetts (US)
UMINN	University of Minnesota (US)
UMISS	University of Mississippi (US)
UOTTAWA	University of Ottawa (CA)
UPITT	University of Pittsburgh (US)
USARMY	US Army (US)
UTAH	University of Utah (US)
UTRECHT	Utrecht University (UK)
UVLAUS	Université Vaudois Lausanne (CH)
UWASH	University of Washington (US)
UWIS	University of Wisconsin (US)
UWISM	University of Wisconsin-Madison (US)
VANDERB	Vanderbilt University (CA)
VERMONT	University of Vermont (US)
VIRGINIA	University of Virginia (US)
VRIJE	Vrije Universiteit (NL)
WAKEF	Wake Forest University (US)
WAYNE	Wayne State University (US)
WELLCOME	Wellcome Trust (UK)
WISTAR	Wistar Institute of Anatomy & Biology (US)
WSU	Washington State University (US)
YALE	Yale University (US)
YEDA	Yeda (IS)
YESHIVA	Yeshiva University (US)
YISSUM	Yissum (IS)

Note: Italicized organizations' names are companies.

Appendix 6A.2   Organization-level R&D projects network, 1990–2001
(Figure 6.3)

COLOUR & SHAPE (NATIONALITY)
White: Circle – USA   Triangle – Switzerland   Box – Canada
   Diamond – Italy/Spain
Grey: Circle – France   Triangle – United Kingdom   Box – Germany
   Diamond – Other European countries
Black: Circle – Japan   Triangle – Australia/NZ   Box – Far East
   Diamond – Israel

Label	Organization
A&MTX	Texas A&M Univ. System (US)*
ABBOTT	*Abbott Laboratories (US)*
AEINS	Albert Einstein Coll. of Medicine (US)
AHP(GI)	*American Home Pr. [Genetics Institute] (US)**
AHP(WA)	*American Home Pr. [Wyeth-Ayest] (US)**
ALABAMA	University of Alabama Res. Foundation (US)*
ANVAR	ANVAR (FR)
ASTRAZ	*AstraZeneca (UK-SE)**
AVENTIS	*Aventis (FR-DE)**
BAXTER	*Baxter International (US)*
BAYER	*Bayer (DE)*
BAYLOR	Baylor College of Medicine (US)*
BIOGEN	*Biogen (US)*
BIPSEN	*Beaufour-IPSEN (FR)*
BIRMING	Birmingham University (UK)
BMS	*Bristol Myers Squibb (US)**
BTG	British Technology Group (UK)
CAMBN	*Cambridge Neurosciences (US)*
CELLGEN	*Cell Genesys Inc. (US)*
CHILDHB	Children's Hospital, Boston (US)*
CHIRON	*Chiron Corp. (US)**
CNRS	Centre National de la Rech. Scientifique (FR)*
COLUMBIA	Columbia University (US)*
CORIXA	*Corixa Corp. (US)*
CORNRF	Cornell Biotech. Center for Adv. Tech. (US)*
CYTOG	*Cytogen Corp. (US)*
DANAF	Dana-Farber Cancer Institute (US)*
DUKE	Duke University Medical Center (US)*
DUPONT	*DuPont Pharmaceuticals Inc. (US)*
EMORY	Emory University (US)*
GENENT	*Genentech (US)*
GENZYME	*Genzyme Corp. (US)*
GEORGIA	Georgia University (US)*
GSK(UK)	*GlaxoSmithKline [Glaxo] (UK)**

Appendix 6A.2   (continued)

Label	Organization
GSK(US)	*GlaxoSmithKline [SmithKline] (US)* *
HARV	Harvard Medical School (US)*
HARV(BI)	Beth Israel Deaconess Med. Center (US)*
ICR	Imperial Cancer Research (UK)
ICR(F)	Imperial Cancer Research [Fund] (UK)
IDBIO	*ID Biomedical Corp. (CA)*
IVAX	*IVAX Corp. (US)*
LILLY	*Lilly (US)* *
LUDWIG	Ludwig Inst. for Cancer Res. (US-DE-FI-BE-SE)*
LXR	*LXR Biotech (US)*
MCGILL	McGill University (CA)
MDACC	MD Anderson Cancer Center (US)
MEDIMM	*MedImmune Inc. (US)*
MERCK	*Merck & Co. (US)* *
MGH	Massachusetts General Hospital (US)*
MICHIGAN	University of Michigan (US)*
MILLEN	*Millennium (US)* *
MIT	Massachusetts Institute of Technology (US)*
MIT(WH)	MIT [Whitehead Institute] (US)*
MRC	Medical Research Council (UK)*
NAMER	*Nycomed Amersham (UK)*
NCBC	North Carolina Biotechnology Center (US)
NCI	National Institute of Health [Cancer Inst.] (US)*
NIH	National Institutes of Health (US)*
NOVARTIS	*Novartis (CH)* *
NYSU	State University of New York (US)*
NYSU(F)	New York State University Res. Found. (US)*
NYU	New York University (US)*
OHIOS	Ohio State University (US)*
OXFORD	Oxford University (UK)*
PCOUNC	Population Council (US)
PFIZER	*Pfizer (US)* *
PHMACIA	*Pharmacia Corp. (US-SE)* *
RCT	*Research Corporation Technologies (US)*
READING	Reading University (UK)
ROCHE	*Roche (CH)* *
ROCKEF	Rockefeller University (US)*
ROSWELL	Roswell Park Cancer Institute (US)
RTI	Research Triangle Institute (US)
SALK	Salk Institute (US)*
SASK	Saskatchewan University (CA)
SCHER	*Schering AG (DE)* *
SCHERP	*Schering Plough (US)*
SCHWARZ	*Schwarz Pharma (DE)*

Appendix 6A.2 *(continued)*

Label	Organization
SCRIPPS	Scripps Research Institute (US)*
SERUM	Statens Serum Institut (DK)
SFU	South Florida University (US)*
SHIRE	*Shire Pharmaceutical (UK)*
SLOANK	Mem. Sloan Kettering Cancer Center (US)*
STAN	Stanford University (US)*
STEHLIN	Stehlin Foundation for Cancer Res. (US)
SUPERG	*SuperGen (US)*
TEMPLE	Temple University (US)*
TEVA	*Teva Pharmaceutical Ind. (IS)*
TEXAS	Texas University (US)*
TJU	Thomas Jefferson University (US)
TRIANGLE	Triangle Pharmaceuticals (US)
TULANE	Tulane University (US)*
UALBER	Alberta University (CA)
UBCOL	University of British Columbia (CA)*
UCAL	Univ. of California [n.c.] (US)*
UCAL(B)	Univ. of California [Berkeley] (US)*
UCAL(LA)	Univ. of California [Los Angeles] (US)*
UCAL(SD)	Univ. of California [San Diego] (US)*
UCAL(SF)	Univ. of California [San Francisco] (US)*
UCAMBR	University of Cambridge (UK)*
UFLOR	Florida University (US)*
UKENT	University of Kentucky (US)
ULONDON	University College London (UK)*
UMARYL	University of Maryland (US)*
UMINN	University of Minnesota (US)*
UOHIO	Ohio University (US)*
UPITT	University of Pittsburgh (US)*
UPRINC	Princeton University (US)
UPSA	*Bristol Myers Squibb [UPSA] (CH)*
UTENN	Tennessee University (US)
UTORONTO	University of Toronto (CA)*
UVIRG	University of Virginia (US)*
VALENTIS	*Valentis (US)*
VANDERB	Vanderbilt University (CA)*
VETERANS	Veterans Adm. Medical Center (US)
WAF	Wisconsin Alumni Res. Foundation (US)*
WSU	Washington State University (US)*
YALE	Yale University (US)*

Note: *Core organizations in both the patent co-assignment and the collaborative R&D project networks.

7. Research productivity and the allocation of resources in publicly funded research programmes

Fabrizio Cesaroni and Alfonso Gambardella*

1 INTRODUCTION

It is widely recognized that in recent years, many universities and other public research laboratories have generally been promoting efforts aimed at the exploitation of research results and their competencies (for the European case, see European Commission 1996). To this end, many different strategies have been implemented – for example, science parks, research consortia, licences, collaborations, spinoff companies and so on. In general terms, a change can be seen in the missions of public research centres towards more entrepreneurial activities (Etzkowitz et al. 1998). One of the factors that have boosted this trend is the decrease and change in funding sources for universities and other public research centres (Geuna 2001). None the less, the largest share of research funding to these organizations still comes from publicly funded research programmes, which allocate available resources among research groups according to specific objectives and goals – to achieve scientific excellence in specific fields, to create a critical mass of knowledge and research competency in specific areas, to promote the industrial transferability of research and so on.

The increasing budget constraints that governments in developed countries are facing in recent years have made this process of resource allocation to science increasingly questionable. Apart from the proportion of the public budget devoted to activities not directly linked to countries' economic performance and firms' profitability and productivity, what is mostly discussed is the possibility that institutional mechanisms of resource allocations have a direct impact on researchers' scientific production, and their long-term performance pattern (among others, see Dasgupta and David 1994; Stephan 1996). According to theorists of the New Economics of Science, if financial resources are allocated to researchers on the basis of their past scientific performance (that is, their scientific reputation), dynamic processes of cumulative advantage might emerge. In turn, the empirical fact that a small share of researchers is responsible for the largest share of scientific publications (Lotka 1926; de Solla Price 1963, 1976) might be the result of existing institutional mechanisms of selection and resource allocation, which tend to amplify the effects of heterogeneity of researchers' initial characteristics.

In parallel with the growing attention to processes of resource allocation to science, attention is being paid to methodologies of *ex ante* and *ex post* evaluation of funding programmes, through qualitative analyses, 'score and ranking' methods, econometric techniques, quantitative methods, normative and decisional models (Silvani 1998). Against this background, the objective of this chapter is to provide an econometric estimation of the production function of scientific outputs of research groups, and the impact of different allocations of resources among groups with different characteristics (for example, geographic location, past scientific performance, age of principal investigator [PI] and so on).

The empirical investigation is based on a funding programme launched by the Italian Research Council (Consiglio Nazionale delle Ricerche – CNR) in the field of biotechnology and bio-instrumentation (B&B), for the 1989–93 period. This was the first and broadest research programme launched in Italy in this field, to which almost all the research centres in Italy operating in the field of genetic engineering and biology applied for funding. The Italian scientific community in this field displays a distribution of (scientific and organizational) characteristics that are similar to those of foreign communities, and this makes the results of this study general, although the funding programme under study was in only one country. This chapter aims to go beyond the precise estimation of the parameters of researchers' production functions; it intends to present and discuss new econometric evaluation methodologies for such funding programmes.

In general terms, *ex post* evaluations of funding programmes encounter four main problems (Jaffe 2000):

- how to measure research output of funded research groups;
- how to identify and measure possible benefits spilling over from the funded group to other research groups;
- how to measure the impacts of funding on the research infrastructure of the funded research groups and assess their related long-term effects; and
- how to avoid selectivity bias, arising from the fact that *ex post* evaluations can only be conducted on selected research groups.

In this chapter we look specifically at this last point and consider different methodologies for dealing with the selectivity bias, using both parametric and semi-parametric estimations. Semi-parametric estimations have the advantage of comparing research units (or researchers) with similar scientific or institutional characteristics (for example, geographical location, institutional typology, PI's age, proposal's transferability, past scientific publications and so on). This allows the unobserved heterogeneity within each cell of research units (or researchers) created with this methodology to be reduced, and better captures the effects of selection. Compared to previous studies that analysed the same CNR B&B funding programme (Arora et al. 1998), the use of both parametric and non-parametric estimations makes the results more robust. Furthermore, in our study we had access to updated and new data, which means that our analysis is more complete. So, while in the 1988 study the authors used partial output data (that is, scientific publications obtained by the research units three years after the beginning of the programme), for our study complete output data were available. Furthermore, CNR provided us with the scores of the external referees who evaluated all the research proposals – giving us another variable to be included in the estimation methodology. It is worth noting that the use of referee scores added significant value to the analysis. Indeed, scores can be considered as an external measure of selection and the use of this measure in both parametric and semi-parametric estimations allows a partial solution to the unobserved heterogeneity associated with the selectivity problem. In fact, when we used referee scores in our estimations of the research productivity function, the results appeared to be more robust.

The chapter is organized as follows. In the next section (Section 2) we describe the dataset and variables used in the analysis. The third section concentrates on the selection and awarding phase, and discusses the use of referee scores as a proxy for selection. Section 4 first describes the theoretical model we used to derive the research productivity function for research units and estimates the parameters of the same equation using both parametric and semi-parametric estimations. These analyses allowed us to observe that, all else being equal, past publications are the best estimator of future scientific performance, while research grants show constant returns to scale in scientific output. The concluding section discusses the main results.

2   DATA DESCRIPTION

The empirical analysis was conducted using mainly information extracted from the research units' application forms in 1987, on the basis of which CNR selected which units would receive funding. Table 7.1 lists the

Table 7.1   Definition of variables

Variable	Definition
D_GRANT	Dummy equal to 1 if project has received a CNR grant
SCORE	Average referees' score of the project. Ranges from 1 (very poor proposal) to 4 (excellent proposal)
PRODUCT	Unit's Research Productivity (quality-adjusted number of output publications divided by the total grant received by CNR)
LPROD	Natural log of *PRODUCT*
PBEFORE10	Impact-factor of the PI's 10 best publications before the start of the project (PI's quality-adjusted input publications)
LBEFORE	Natural log of *PBEFORE10*
POTHERS	Impact-factor of the publications of other components of the research unit, before the start of the project (non-PI's quality-adjusted input publications)
LOTHERS	Natural log of *POTHERS*
COLLAB	Number of collaborations of the research unit with foreign non-profit institutions
LCOLLAB	Natural log of *COLLAB*
B_ASK	Research budget requested to CNR (in millions of ITL)
LASK	Natural log of *B_ASK*
AGE	Age of PI
LAGE	Natural log of *AGE*
SIZE	Size of research unit (no. of people employed)
LSIZE	Natural log of *SIZE*
D_PR7	Dummy for units in sub-Programme 7 (Bio-instrumentation)
D_TRANS0	Dummy equal to 1 if project's results are not supposed to be transferred
D_TRANS1	Dummy equal to 1 if project's results are supposed to be transferred to research institutions
D_TRANS2	Dummy equal to 1 if project's results are supposed to be transferred to not well-defined industrial sectors
D_TRANS3	Dummy equal to 1 if project's results are supposed to be transferred to specific firms
D_CNR	Dummy equal to 1 if research unit belongs to CNR
D_IND	Dummy equal to 1 if research unit is an industrial firm
D_UNI	Dummy equal to 1 if research unit is a university
D_OTHER	Dummy equal to 1 if research unit belongs to institutions other than CNR, universities and firms (i.e., foundations, other state-owned research institutes)
D_NORTH	Dummy equal to 1 if research unit is located in the north of Italy
D_CENTRE	Dummy equal to 1 if research unit is located in the centre of Italy
D_SOUTH	Dummy equal to 1 if research unit is located in the south of Italy

Table 7.2   Descriptive statistics

Variable	Obs	Mean	Std dev.	Min	Max
D_GRANT	809	0.4413	0.4968	0	1
SCORE	761	2.1853	0.8361	0	4
PRODUCT	344	0.2332	0.3112	0	2.497
PBEFORE10	815	21.3504	22.4402	0	139.5
POTHERS	701	21.8290	32.2752	0	222.338
COLLAB	856	1.3960	1.8495	0	16
AGE	853	52.2016	9.0886	0	85
B_ASK	853	365.0592	284.3212	25	4,224
D_PR7	858	0.1107	0.3139	0	1
D_TRANS0	854	0.0785	0.2690	0	1
D_TRANS1	854	0.3068	0.4614	0	1
D_TRANS2	854	0.2658	0.4420	0	1
D_TRANS3	854	0.3489	0.4769	0	1
D_CNR	857	0.1482	0.3555	0	1
D_IND	857	0.0362	0.1868	0	1
D_UNI	857	0.6383	0.4808	0	1
D_OTHER	857	0.1774	0.3822	0	1
D_NORTH	856	0.4755	0.4997	0	1
D_CENTRE	856	0.3376	0.4732	0	1
D_SOUTH	856	0.1869	0.3901	0	1

variables used in the analysis, and Table 7.2 shows descriptive statistics. The application forms reported information on groups' scientific capabilities, in terms of the PI's past publications related to the research topic (*PBEFORE10*), past publications on the same topic by other members of the research unit (*POTHERS*), number of scientific collaborations with foreign non-profit organizations, such as universities and other research laboratories (*COLLAB*), and degree of industrial transferability of the project. This last variable was included to help CNR assess the capability of the unit to promote a research activity whose results would be directly available to industrial firms.

CNR's explicit aim through the B&B programme was to encourage industrial transferability of research and, hence, applicants were asked to specify potential industrial users of their research. We codified those answers and created four separate dummies (*D_TRANS0* to *D_TRANS3*) representing increasing *ex ante* industrial transferability of the proposal. Thus, value 0 was assigned to those projects whose results were not intended to be transferred at all, values 1, 2 and 3 were assigned respectively to those intended to be transferred to other research institutions, to some not well-defined industrial sector (for example, pharmaceuticals or agro-chemicals industries), and to specific firms. Where units were able to indicate actual names of industrial users, their projects seemed to have real application opportunities, and hence they were awarded the highest value for transferability.

Concerning past publications (both of PIs and other members of the unit), application forms did not specify either the number of publications that applicants should indicate, or the period of time. Hence, crude information collected from application forms is not very comparable among research groups. In order to overcome this, we first employed the 1987 impact factor (IF) (as computed by the *Science Citation Index* – SCI) for the respective journals in which the units' publications appeared.[1] This can be considered as a sort of 'quality' measure of the publication. Then, we considered only the first 10 publications ranked in terms of impact factor. Note that some units provided a list of all the publications they had ever done on that topic, while others selected only the 'best' ones. Hence, by considering only the best 10, we were able to compare research units in terms of scientific capabilities.

From the application forms, we were also able to compile a set of structural indications concerning the research units and their composition. We considered unit size (*SIZE*) in terms of the number of researchers employed and directly involved in the project, the age of the PI (*AGE*), the location of the unit – distinguishing between those in the north of Italy (*D_NORTH*), in the centre (*D_CENTRE*) and in the south (*D_SOUTH*), and the institutional typology of the research units by identifying CNR (*D_CNR*), university (*D_UNI*), firms (*D_IND*) and other non-profit (*D_OTHER*) labs, and 'other' being mainly hospitals and foundations.

Table 7.3 summarizes sample characteristics in terms of the last two variables. As expected, most of the applications to the B&B project came from universities, which are the leading research institutions in Italy. CNR laboratories and other non-profit institutions constituted a similar group. Applications from firms were extremely small in number, demonstrating the poor development of the biotechnology sector in Italy. In terms of location, the geographical distribution of the applicants reflects the distribution of industrial, economic and scientific development of Italian regions, which decreases as you move from the north to the south. Almost half the applications were from northern research centres, one-third from the central area, and less than 20 per cent from the south (see Table 7.3).

CNR then supplied us with the list of units that were selected (*D_GRANT*), and the referees' scores (*SCORE*). Each proposal was scrutinized by up to three referees, who were required to assess different parameters concerning both the scientific competence of the research group

Table 7.3   Frequency tables

	Frequency	Percentage	Cumulative %
Locality			
North	407	47.55	47.55
Centre	289	33.76	81.31
South	160	18.69	100.00
Total	856	100.00	
Research unit			
CNR	127	14.82	14.82
Industrial firm	31	3.62	18.44
University	547	63.83	82.27
Other	152	17.74	100.00*
Total	857	100.00*	

Note: *Rounded.

(scientific and organizational capabilities, technical equipment, collaborations with other research groups), and the characteristics of the proposal (scientific and technological excellence of the research project, its capability to respond to B&B priorities, transferability of results). Furthermore, CNR was concerned with other elements, not directly linked to the scientific capabilities of the research unit or with the scientific excellence of the proposal, but more oriented towards issues of regional policy. Indeed, referees were asked to evaluate possible effects of the project on the growth of southern regions (the Italian Mezzogiorno), effects on the development of human capital, and the coherence and integration of single proposals with other national or multinational funding programmes. Referees were asked to assign a value from 1 (very poor) to 4 (excellent) for these elements. The variable *SCORE* thus represents the average value of evaluations assigned to any variable by the referees called to assess a single proposal.

Finally, CNR provided us with the list of publications produced by the selected units, together with the total budget awarded to those units. We combined these two variables in order to obtain an output measure. First, as in the case of *ex ante* publications, we weighted the output publications for quality, by considering the value of IF, a measure of the extent to which a journal is cited by other journals, of the journal in which the publication appeared. Next, we divided the quality-adjusted number of publications by the total budget awarded, so as to obtain a measure of research productivity (*PRODUCT*) for each unit. With this specification, the productivity variable measures the unit capacity for producing a scientific publication for any unit of money obtained.

This measure of performance clearly stresses the importance of scientific publications, compared to other possible outputs. In funding programmes like B&B in particular, in which industrial transferability was one of the supported objectives, different output measures could have been used (for example, number of patents, number of *ex post* collaborations with industrial partners, and so on). However, the reason for choosing scientific publications as the main research output was twofold. On the one hand, it is a more visible and measurable output, especially as parameters like IF are now available, which makes the results of different research groups comparable whereas patent statistics have only recently started to be collected, and it is even more problematic to compare collaborations with firms promoted by two different research units. On the other hand, although industrial transferability was one general objective of the B&B programme, most units had a clear scientific background and were part of the research system. Their aim was not to be involved in some more 'applied' research, but only to make the results of their research applicable for industrial purposes. Therefore, scientific publication clearly remained their primary objective. Indeed, studies on this same CNR programme (Potì et al. 1999) show that scientific publications were the main output of B&B, while other outputs (like patents, prototypes, methods, software and so on) were developed only secondarily.

3 THE SELECTION AND AWARDING PHASES

In 1987 CNR received 858 applications, of which 375 research groups were selected to receive an annual grant for the five-year period of the programme.[2] In making this choice, CNR took into account both scientific characteristics of groups and their proposals, the evaluations of the referees who assessed the proposals, and also some 'policy' objectives. As a first analysis of this process, Table 7.4 shows sample means for selected ($D\_GRANT = 1$) and non-selected ($D\_GRANT = 0$) units.

It emerges quite clearly that the scientific characteristics of the research groups played a critical role in CNR's decision. *PBEFORE10*, *POTHERS* and *COLLAB* were greater for the successful groups than for those that did not receive funding. The role of past performance is therefore evident. As discussed in studies on the processes of resource allocation for scientific programmes (among others, see David 1994), this opens up a problem of whether past publications are a measure of a researcher's knowledge capital, or simply his or her scientific reputation which, in turn, might be

Table 7.4　Sample means, **D_GRANT** *=0 and* **D_GRANT** *=1*

	D_GRANT=0		D_GRANT=1	
	Obs	Mean	Obs	Mean
SCORE	367	1.726	348	2.673
		(0.683)		(0.706)
PRODUCT	0		344	0.233
				(0.311)
PBEFORE10	427	14.587	343	29.529
		(16.979)		(25.552)
POTHERS	363	17.077	300	27.876
		(28.635)		(35.756)
COLLAB	451	1.100	357	1.846
		(1.528)		(2.168)
AGE	450	52.70	355	51.685
		(9.852)		(8.085)
B_ASK	451	334.989	357	410.915
		(297.308)		(268.412)
D_TRANS0	450	0.098	357	0.059
		(0.297)		(0.236)
D_TRANS1	450	0.347	357	0.261
		(0.476)		(0.439)
D_TRANS2	450	0.264	357	0.255
		(0.442)		(0.436)
D_TRANS3	450	0.291	357	0.426
		(0.455)		(0.495)
D_CNR	451	0.118	357	0.199
		(0.322)		(0.399)
D_IND	451	0.047	357	0.006
		(0.211)		(0.075)
D_UNI	451	0.645	357	0.639
		(0.479)		(0.481)
D_OTHER	451	0.191	357	0.157
		(0.393)		(0.364)
D_NORTH	450	0.444	357	0.515
		(0.497)		(0.501)
D_CENTRE	450	0.380	357	0.286
		(0.486)		(0.452)
D_SOUTH	450	0.176	357	0.199
		(0.381)		(0.399)

Note:　Standard deviation in parentheses.

affected by past levels of funding received by the same units.[3] In this latter case, if funding agencies such as CNR consider past publication tracks, but not past levels of funding, they might induce or reinforce path-dependences and give rise to state dependence in the production process, by which past success is rewarded with greater funding. This also increases the likelihood of future success. In this sense, units' past performance might be the result of external institutional mechanisms, rather than internal production capabilities.

At the same time, CNR's decision seems to be affected by the amount of funds required by research groups – B_ASK is greater for selected than for non-selected units – and by the proposal's degree of potential transferability. As shown by the four dummies related to this aspect, in the three cases of lowest transferability (D_TRANS0, D_TRANS1 and D_TRANS2) non-selected units show a sample mean greater than the selected groups. Only at the highest level do selected units have a greater sample mean than non-selected, showing that CNR has positively assessed, and then awarded a grant to, only those research groups with a clear notion of potential users of their research at the time of writing the proposal.

At the same time, the selection phase was influenced by policy concerns. These can be seen in the results related to units' institutional typology and geographical location. As far as institutional typology is concerned, while CNR research laboratories were advantaged, the opposite was the case for industrial and other non-profit research centres – D_IND and D_OTHER show sample means greater for non-selected than for selected units. This further reduced the presence of successful firm applications to only two units out of the 23 that put in an application.[4] The case of universities seems less defined. Sample means of the selected and non-selected are quite similar, showing that in this case non-policy arguments (like scientific capabilities) might have played a bigger role in their selection. Finally, in terms of location, the results in Table 7.4 show that only in the case of units located in the central regions was the number of non-selected units greater than the number of selected, while the opposite was the case for units in the northern and southern regions. While this result can be explained in part by the political interest of promoting scientific development in the Mezzogiorno, and thus a preference for units from those regions, it should be noted that past scientific performance of research groups from the central regions shows the lowest average levels. On average, $PBEFORE10$ for units located in the north is 22.29, for units located in the south it is 21.78, and for units in the centre it is (only) 19.77. In sum, geographical distribution of selected and non-selected groups might simply be the indirect result of other characteristics (such as past scientific performance), which are unevenly distributed among units located in different regions.

In order to take into account these kinds of interrelations among variables, we computed a multiple regression. Using a probit model, we regressed *D_GRANT* against the same set of variables discussed above. The results of this exercise are reported in Table 7.5. Most of the considerations discussed above were confirmed by these results. Hence, a unit's scientific background (mainly in terms of *PBEFORE10*), project transferability (mainly at the highest level), geographical location (especially if from the northern regions), and institutional typology (in the case of universities and CNR research laboratories) were key in determining selection. Equally important seems to be the size of budget requested, whose coefficient shows a value close to zero because of differences in the unit of scale – *B_ASK* is expressed in million lire.

Table 7.5   Determinants of selection (probit estimation)

Number of obs = 638	Pseudo $R^2 = 0.1400$	
LR chi^2(13) = 123.17	Log likelihood = -378.355	
Prob > chi^2 = 0.0000		

D_GRANT	*dF/dx*	Std error
PBEFORE10	0.0079	0.0012***
POTHERS	0.0002	0.0007
COLLAB	0.0237	0.0124*
AGE	−0.0009	0.0024
B_ASK	0.0003	0.0001***
D_TRANS0 [§]	0.0458	0.0856
D_TRANS2 [§]	0.0304	0.0570
D_TRANS3 [§]	0.1266	0.0517**
D_CNR [§]	0.1882	0.0738**
D_UNI [§]	0.1063	0.0580*
D_NORTH [§]	0.1063	0.0470**
D_SOUTH [§]	0.0508	0.0646

Notes:
([§]) *dF/dx* is for discrete change of dummy variable from 0 to 1.
* $p < 0.10$; ** $p < 0.05$; *** $p < 0.01$.

The results in Table 7.5 show the changes in probability of having *D_GRANT* = 1 for infinitesimal changes in each independent variable. So, for instance, all else being equal, having the highest level of project transferability increases the probability of being selected by 12.66 per cent. Similarly, CNR units have an 18.82 per cent higher probability of being selected than other institutions, and universities 10.63 per cent. Also units located in the northern regions, all else being equal, have a probability of being selected higher by 10.63 per cent compared to others.

An interesting aspect of the selection process is the role of the referees' evaluations. As indicated in the previous section, CNR submitted all the applications to up to three referees, who were asked to assess the proposals and give a score based on a set of parameters related to the scientific competence of the research groups and to the characteristics of the proposals themselves. The results of these evaluations are synthesized in the *SCORE* variable. Hence, in their award decision, CNR took account of both the characteristics of units and their proposal, and the referees' evaluations, which presumably correlated to the same characteristics. In order to analyse this aspect, we tried to regress *SCORE* against the same set of variables that we used in the probit analysis of selection. The results are reported in Table 7.6.

Table 7.6   SCORE *as proxy for selection (OLS estimation)*

Number of obs = 611	R-squared = 0.1427	
F(13, 597) = 7.65	Adj R-squared = 0.1241	
Prob > F = 0.0000	Root MSE = 0.76666	

SCORE	Coef.	Std error
PBEFORE10	0.0071	0.0015***
POTHERS	−0.0009	0.0011
COLLAB	0.0576	0.0173***
AGE	−0.0079	0.0034**
B_ASK	0.0003	0.0001**
D_TRANS0	0.2080	0.1339
D_TRANS1	0.1150	0.0841
D_TRANS3	0.1758	0.0809**
D_CNR	0.3902	0.1129***
D_IND	−0.2138	0.2843
D_UNI	0.1612	0.0874**
D_NORTH	0.0620	0.0703
D_SOUTH	−0.1250	0.0944
_cons	1.9857	0.2091***

Note: * $p < 0.10$; ** $p < 0.05$; *** $p < 0.01$.

Table 7.6 shows that *SCORE* is highly correlated with most of the variables considered in the selection process. In particular, *SCORE*'s values seem to be strongly linked to a PI's quality-adjusted past publications, to the number of foreign non-profit collaborations, to the highest level of transferability, and to the institutional typology of the research group, especially in the cases of CNR laboratories and universities. Thus, in looking at how research proposals were selected for funding, we can look at single variables and *SCORE* interchangeably, because they measure the same effect (that is, selection). Hence, in analyses on groups' research productivity reported in the next section, we considered the selection process either by reporting the set of variables discussed in this section, or simply the *SCORE*. As will be seen, the results are quite comparable.

4   ESTIMATION OF RESEARCH PRODUCTIVITY

Assumptions

In this section, we analyse groups' research productivity and how it is influenced by the amount of budget granted by CNR and groups' past scientific performance. In particular, we aim at isolating and measuring the effects of both research funding and past publications on research output. This task is not easy. As discussed previously, there are two orders of problems to deal with. First, for the empirical analysis of research output, information is available only on selected units, and none for the non-awarded groups. This determines a typical sample selection problem, which can be overcome by applying appropriate econometric techniques. Second, in determining the effect of groups' scientific capabilities – as measured in terms of past publications – on research output, we know that past publications are, in turn, affected by levels of funding received in the past. However, while tracks of past publications are publicly available – applicants were required to report such information on the application form – information on past levels of funding is not usually available. In order to overcome this we used the following procedure.

We first considered the stock of publications produced by a single research unit in a given time period as a function of the stock of funding received by the same unit and of the track of past publications that the unit produced in past time periods:

$$P_{jt} = B_{jt}^{\alpha} \, P_{jt-1}^{\beta} \, Z_j^{\gamma} \, e^{\varepsilon} \tag{7.1}$$

where:

P_{jt} is the stock of publications produced by unit j at time t;
B_{jt} is the stock of research funding received by unit j at time t;

P_{jt-1} is the stock of publications produced by unit j at time $t-1$, that is, without considering publications directly imputable to the participation in the last funding programme;

Z_j is the vector of other parameters influencing research output;

ε is the error term.

If we consider the derivative of (7.1) by B, we obtain:

$$PR_{jt} = dP/dB = \alpha \ B_{jt}^{\alpha-1} \ P_{jt-1}^{\beta} \ Z_j^{\gamma} \ e^{\varepsilon} \qquad (7.2)$$

where the ratio dP/dB can be considered as the additional production of publications (marginal product) by unit j given the additional level of resources provided by the last funding programme. In the case of the B&B programme that we are analysing in this study, the dP/dB value can be considered as the units' scientific production in terms of quality-adjusted publications divided by the amount of funds granted by the CNR to selected units. Hence, this value can be considered a measure of a unit's research productivity at time t (PR_{jt}), since it expresses the level of output produced for any unit of financial resources received. Equation (7.2) can be expressed in logarithmic terms:

$$\ln PR_{jt} = \ln \alpha + (\alpha - 1) \ln B_{jt} + \beta \ln P_{jt-1} + \gamma \ln Z_j + \varepsilon. \qquad (7.3)$$

In the case of the B&B funding programme under study, all values included in equation (7.3) are available, apart from B_{jt}. Indeed, we do not know all the previous histories of selected units, so neither do we know the total levels of funding that they have received in the past. In order to make equation (7.3) estimable, we further made the hypothesis that the value of B_{jt} is proportional to the size of the research group, in terms of number of people employed. As a partial justification for this assumption, it is intuitively reasonable to say that the larger the amount of research funds received in the past, the higher the possibility of creating a wider research group. Note that the number of people employed in the research group is different from the number of equivalent person months for the same research group. Usually, the number of person months is directly associated with the specific research project to be exploited in one funding programme, and might vary from one programme to another whereas the number of people in a research unit is usually more stable over time and presumably increases as the unit receives more funds. With this assumption, the (7.3) can be rewritten as:

$$\ln PR_{jt} = \ln \alpha + (\alpha - 1) \ln S_{jt} + \beta \ln P_{jt-1} + \gamma \ln Z_j + \varepsilon \qquad (7.4)$$

where S_{jt} is the unit's size expressed as number of people employed. Hence, equation (7.4) represents the productivity function that has been estimated. In this specification, what we were interested in was the values of both parameters α and β. From equation (7.1), we know that α can be considered the elasticity of total funding, while β is the elasticity of past publications. Values of parameter α (or $\alpha - 1$) reveal the sign of returns to scale in total funding:

- for $\alpha = 1$ (or for $\alpha - 1 = 0$), there are constant returns to scale in funding, and increases in total funding determine proportional increases in unit research productivity;
- for $\alpha > 1$ (or for $\alpha - 1 > 0$), there are increasing returns to scale, and increases in total funding determine more than proportional increases in unit research productivity;
- for $\alpha < 1$ (or for $\alpha - 1 < 0$), the opposite happens, and decreasing returns to scale in funding operate.

The values of β have a similar meaning, and describe the sign of returns to scale in past publications. So, for $\beta = 1$ constant returns to scale operate, for $\beta > 1$ there are increasing returns to scale, and for $\beta < 1$ there are decreasing returns to scale. Both the values of β and α (or $\alpha - 1$) have clear policy implications and affect the capability of a funding programme to obtain a certain level of output. In other words, levels of α and β determine whether a specific scheme of resource allocation can allow the funding agency to maximize the research output of the whole programme. In order to maximize research output, the allocation of available resources to research groups has to take into account whether increasing returns to scale exist and operate. This would justify, on the one hand, policies that 'invest' in groups with the highest past publication tracks (the 'stars'), or, on the other hand, policies that tend to distribute resources more evenly among research groups (Arora and Gambardella 1997).

As far as sample selection problems are concerned, these arise because when we estimate the productivity equation, only information on selected units is available. In this case, simple ordinary least squares (OLS) regressions, run on available (selected) units, give rise to biased results if, as in our case, selection is not a random process. Indeed, equation (7.4) can be estimated only for $D\_GRANT = 1$. In turn, it can be said, that $D\_GRANT = 1$ if:

$$y_j = \delta \mathbf{X}_j + \varepsilon_1 > 0 \quad (y_j \text{ not observed}) \tag{7.5}$$

where $\mathbf{X}_j$ is the vector of regressors influencing the selection process.[5] If the covariance of error terms in productivity and selection equations is not null

(Corr$(\varepsilon,\varepsilon_1) \neq 0$), then OLS estimates of equation (7.4) produce biased results.

In order to overcome this problem, Heckman selection models were used (Heckman 1976 and 1979; Johnston and DiNardo 1997). In the simplest, two-step procedure, this method involves estimating the selection equation with a probit model, and using the inverse Mills ratio function of the probit residuals as an extra variable in the productivity regression over the selected sample. Furthermore, in order to get more efficient estimates, we used the Heckman full maximum-likelihood (ML) procedure as well.

Apart from S_{jt} and P_{jt-1}, we used the following set of variables as the $\mathbf{Z}_j$ vector of equation (7.4): *POTHERS, COLLAB, AGE, D_TRANS1, D_TRANS2, D_TRANS3, D_CNR, D_UNI, D_NORTH* and *D_CENTRE*. Then, in the selection part of the procedure, we defined $\mathbf{X}_j$ with the same set of regressors discussed in the previous section. However, in different specifications, we used only *SCORE* as the regressor in equation (7.5). Indeed, as we noted in Section 3, values of *SCORE* can be considered a synthesis of the variables influencing selection, since referees were required to assess the same dimensions that we considered separately in the selection phase. Finally, in order to test the robustness of this choice, we estimated equation (7.5) by using the $\mathbf{X}_j$ regressors together with *SCORE*. This specification allowed us to assess whether referee evaluations explain something more than the simple dimensions of research groups expressed by $\mathbf{X}_j$. Intuitively, this means assessing whether referees added their personal knowledge of research groups to the objective characteristics of the same groups included in $\mathbf{X}_j$, and whether this overall estimation emerges in *SCORE*.

Parametric Estimations

Before analysing the results of estimations of equation (7.4), it is worth observing the simple relationship between unit levels of research productivity and past quality-adjusted publications. Table 7.7 reports this relationship. We considered four levels of both the variables (*PRODUCT* and *PBEFORE10*), according to their respective quartiles. Table 7.7 shows the existence of a strong, positive relationship between past publications and a unit's research productivity. Units are mainly distributed across the diagonal of the table, and higher levels of productivity are mainly obtained by those research groups with past publications of higher quality.

If we consider research units belonging to the first quartile of *PBEFORE10* – that is, those with the lowest quality of past publications – it is possible to observe that more than 60 per cent have obtained the lowest level of productivity, more than 30 per cent the second lowest level, and no

Table 7.7   Relationship between units' research productivity and past publications

Quartiles of *PRODUCT*	Quartiles of *PBEFORE10*				Total
	1st quartile	2nd quartile	3rd quartile	4th quartile	
1st quartile	22	29	20	9	80
	(61.11)	(42.03)	(19.80)	(7.20)	(24.17)
2nd quartile	11	18	29	26	84
	(30.56)	(26.09)	(28.71)	(20.80)	(25.38)
3rd quartile	3	14	32	32	81
	(8.33)	(20.29)	(31.68)	(25.60)	(24.47)
4th quartile	0	8	20	58	86
	(0.00)	(11.59)	(19.80)	(46.40)	(25.98)
Total	36	69	101	125	331
	(100.00)	(100.00)	(100.00)	(100.00)	(100.00)

units have shown the highest research productivity. At the same time, the opposite can be observed in the case of research groups with the highest level of past publications. While only 7.2 per cent have obtained the lowest level of productivity, more that 25 per cent obtained the second highest, and more than 45 per cent obtained the highest level.

Hence, the level of parameter β can presumably be expected to have a positive value. Results of econometric estimations confirm this assumption. Table 7.8 reports results of seven specifications of estimation of equation (7.4). The first specification refers to a simple OLS that we have run only on selected units. As discussed above, in this case we take account of sample selection problems and the results of this regression can be useful as comparisons with other specifications. Without the Heckman correction, however, it seems that groups' research productivity is mainly influenced by their scientific capabilities – as measured in terms of past publications and collaborations with foreign non-profit organizations – by geographical location, whether the research unit comes from a northern region, and negatively for those research groups in sub-Programme 7.[6] Furthermore, the β coefficient (related to *LBEFORE*) is significantly positive, but lower than 1, while the $\alpha - 1$ coefficient (associated with *LSIZE*) is not significantly different from 0, making the α value of equation (7.1) equal to 1 (constant returns to scale in total funding).

Specifications II to VII in Table 7.8 take account of the Heckman correction and employ either the two-step (II to IV) or the full ML procedure

(V to VII). As in the previous section, in both cases we used different sets of variables in the selection equation (7.5). First, we estimated the productivity equation by including in the selection part all the variables discussed in the previous section. Then, we estimated the same equation by using only the *SCORE* variable as a determinant of selection. And, finally, we considered the single variables together with *SCORE*. In the first case, regressors for selection and regressors for productivity differ only in terms of three variables, namely unit size (*LSIZE*), the amount of budget being requested (*LASK*), and the participation in sub-Programme 7 (*D_PR7*).

Two comments need to be made on this choice. The first is that, as expressed in equation (7.4), unit size is included in this equation as a proxy for the total amount of budget received by the research unit along its life. In the same equation, the amount of budget being asked for has no bearing because it does not influence a unit's productivity. Although the amount of budget received can be thought of as being correlated with the budget requested, the budget received directly from the funding programme under study is already incorporated in $\mathbf{B}_{jt}$, and hence already represented by unit size. Instead, we assumed that the amount of budget asked for was mainly relevant to CNR's selection, and hence we included it in the selection part of the estimations. The second point is that by using different regressors in the productivity and selection equations, estimation problems associated with the Heckman methodology are reduced. Indeed, in principle, the model is identified even when the two sets of regressors are exactly the same. However, when this is the case, identification depends exclusively on the model and on assumptions of normality, which it is difficult to respect perfectly (Johnston and DiNardo 1997). Differentiating between the two sets of variables makes this problem less severe.

Results reported in Table 7.8 confirm what the OLS estimation predicted. By using both procedures (two-step and full ML), and by using the different sets of variables for selection, units' research productivity seems mainly influenced by their scientific capabilities, by their geographical location and by participation in sub-Programme 7. In particular, the PI's past publications and the number of collaborations with foreign research institutions – which in turn can be considered to be directly linked to units' research capabilities and 'quality' – appear extremely relevant in determining research productivity, while specifications III and VI show that a unit's location in a northern region may be relevant as well. In these latter cases the results in Table 7.8 show that being located in the north increases scientific productivity by about 7 per cent. We know, however, that research groups located in the north have a higher average number of quality-adjusted past publications than groups located in the centre and south, and hence these two variables might reflect the same aspect.

Table 7.8   Determinants of units' research productivity

	I OLS ($D\_GRANT = 1$)		II Heckman selection (two-step estimates)		III Heckman selection (two-step estimates)	
	Coef.	Std error	Coef.	Std error	Coef.	Std error
LPROD						
LBEFORE (β)	0.074	0.011***	0.078	0.048	0.076	0.020***
LOTHERS	0.000	0.008	0.001	0.015	−0.001	0.013
LCOLLAB	0.035	0.016**	0.036	0.031	0.036	0.024
LAGE	−0.107	0.071	−0.104	0.231	−0.126	0.228
D_PR7	−0.100	0.037***	−0.100	0.063	−0.108	0.061*
D_TRANS1	−0.047	0.045	−0.049	0.079	−0.044	0.068
D_TRANS2	−0.052	0.046	−0.054	0.079	−0.055	0.069
D_TRANS3	−0.055	0.044	−0.055	0.070	−0.055	0.063
D_CNR	−0.045	0.039	−0.040	0.087	−0.045	0.064
D_UNI	−0.016	0.033	−0.013	0.068	−0.026	0.060
D_NORTH	0.064	0.029**	0.064	0.046	0.071	0.042*
D_CENTRE	0.017	0.031	0.015	0.055	0.024	0.047
LSIZE (α–1)	−0.011	0.029	−0.009	0.053	−0.016	0.046
_cons	0.427	0.286	0.385	1.024	0.486	0.866
D_GRANT						
LBEFORE			0.352	0.051***		
LOTHERS			0.064	0.039		
LCOLLAB			0.135	0.083		
LAGE			0.210	0.220		
LASK			0.354	0.092***		
D_TRANS1			−0.217	0.218		
D_TRANS2			−0.181	0.224		
D_TRANS3			−0.002	0.216		
D_CNR			0.534	0.187***		
D_UNI			0.222	0.143		
D_NORTH			0.135	0.151		
D_CENTRE			−0.107	0.158		
SCORE					0.962	0.073***
_cons			−4.379	1.034***	−2.413	0.173***

	Number of obs = 282	Number of obs = 682	Number of obs = 701
	$F(13, 268) = 7.14$	Censored obs = 400	Censored obs = 426
	Prob > F = 0	Uncensored obs = 282	Uncensored obs = 275
	R-squared = 0.257	Wald chi^2(24) = 109.89	Wald chi^2(13) = 34.65
	Adj R-squared = 0.221	Prob > chi^2 = 0	Prob > chi^2 = 0.001
	Root MSE = 0.174		

Note: * $p < 0.10$; ** $p < 0.05$; *** $p < 0.01$.

IV Heckman selection (two-step estimates)		V Heckman selection (full ML)		VI Heckman selection (full ML)		VII Heckman selection (full ML)	
Coef.	Std error	Coef.	St. Err.	Coef.	St. Err.	Coef.	St. Err.
0.083	0.020***	0.117	0.013***	0.076	0.011***	0.114	0.011***
0.002	0.012	0.013	0.009	−0.001	0.008	0.015	0.009*
0.038	0.026	0.056	0.018***	0.037	0.016**	0.052	0.018***
−0.115	0.258	0.031	0.051	−0.129	0.070*	0.021	0.018
−0.106	0.061*	−0.001	0.009	−0.109	0.036***	−0.021	0.021
−0.050	0.070	−0.062	0.053	−0.044	0.044	−0.088	0.050*
−0.058	0.071	−0.052	0.053	−0.056	0.045	−0.085	0.050*
−0.056	0.065	−0.023	0.051	−0.055	0.042	−0.064	0.049
−0.039	0.068	0.067	0.048	−0.045	0.038	0.046	0.042
−0.023	0.063	0.036	0.039	−0.026	0.032	0.011	0.034
0.071	0.043	0.043	0.034	0.070	0.028**	0.063	0.032
0.018	0.050	−0.029	0.036	0.024	0.031	−0.021	0.035
−0.012	0.048	0.001	0.032	−0.015	0.028	0.016	0.004***
0.406	0.971	−0.575	0.226**	0.489	0.278	−0.499	0.040***
0.254	0.059***	0.463	0.055***			0.424	0.053***
0.096	0.045**	0.052	0.037			0.067	0.036*
0.052	0.096	0.223	0.074***			0.256	0.079***
0.385	0.323	0.120	0.203			0.113	0.118
0.292	0.110***	0.004	0.062			0.067	0.075
−0.302	0.254	−0.233	0.223			−0.260	0.202
−0.146	0.259	−0.199	0.219			−0.250	0.205
−0.080	0.250	−0.081	0.208			−0.112	0.197
0.279	0.223	0.258	0.200			0.237	0.172
0.131	0.169	0.142	0.146			0.112	0.138
0.083	0.176	0.169	0.139			0.164	0.143
−0.165	0.184	−0.111	0.149			−0.087	0.162
0.840	0.085***			0.962	0.074***	0.053	0.013***
−6.095	1.441***	−2.288	0.891***	−2.411	0.175***	−2.542	

Number of obs = 611	Number of obs = 682	Number of obs = 701	Number of obs = 611
Censored obs = 336	Censored obs = 400	Censored obs = 426	Censored obs = 336
Uncensored obs = 275	Uncensored obs = 282	Uncensored obs = 275	Uncensored obs = 275
Wald chi^2(24) = 73.82	Wald chi^2(13) = 143.19	Wald chi^2(13) = 107.91	Wald chi^2(13) = 20405.83
Prob > chi^2 = 0	Prob > chi^2 = 0	Prob > chi^2 = 0	Prob > chi^2 = 0
	Log likelighood = −207.28	Log likelighood = −261.75	Log likelighood = −171.21

It is worth analysing the values of coefficients associated with *LSIZE* and *LBEFORE* (that is, the estimated α and β of equation (7.4)) resulting from Table 7.8. First, from the simple OLS estimation, the value of $\alpha - 1$ is not significantly different from 0 in all specifications, hence bringing the value of α equal to 1. This clearly means that there are constant returns to scale in total funding, and that increases in total budget do not yield more than proportional increases in research output.

At the same time, estimates of β show that past scientific performance is always positively correlated with actual scientific productivity. The estimated values of β reveal that the elasticity of past performance on research productivity ranges from 7.4 to 11.7 per cent, and in most cases is very close to estimations obtained with the simple OLS regression. Although positive, the impact of past publications on productivity is low in value, elasticity is lower than 1, and returns to scale are decreasing. As an example, this means that a 100 per cent increase in quality-adjusted number of publications by a researcher implies about 10 per cent (or even less) increase in productivity. In other words, if we compare two researchers, one with a track of past publications twice that of the other, then the former is expected to produce (less than) 10 per cent publications more than the latter, all else being equal – including the amount of financial resources received.

Note, however, that the distribution of past publications is very skewed. The average value – for both selected and non-selected units – is about 21.35 quality-adjusted publications, but 8.3 per cent of researchers have a publication track of 0 publications, 41.6 per cent have a number of publications lower than half the average value, and 62.2 per cent of researchers who applied to the B&B programme have a number of quality-adjusted publications no higher than the average value. Hence, doubling the number of quality-adjusted publications is very uncommon. Only a small fraction of researchers can be expected to have a high productivity level because of strong scientific background, and most researchers present a similar *ex ante* (expected) level of scientific productivity. Policy implications follow from this result. The strategy of 'picking the stars', that is, those with the highest past scientific performance, certainly becomes an optimal strategy when the objective is to maximize the overall output level of the funding programme. However, the number of 'stars' is fairly limited and most researchers have similar scientific backgrounds, mainly distributed at the lowest levels. Hence, the difference in expected productivity which can be obtained from such researchers is limited.

As far as the methodology is concerned, it is worth noting that OLS and Heckman estimations produce almost comparable results. This shows that the selectivity bias has not been a severe problem in the case of the funding programme under study. Semi-parametric estimations discussed in the following section partly confirm this conclusion. As has been widely recognized by the literature in this field (among others, see Lalonde 1986), programme administrators in the funding agency usually do not have a sufficient degree of freedom to independently influence the selection process. As a consequence, the resulting sample of selected research groups is not statistically different from a pure 'random' sample of the whole population. If this is the case, as the results of our analyses seem to suggest, simple OLS procedures give rise to significant results.

Semi-parametric Estimations

The analyses carried out in the previous section used the Heckman procedures in order to try to reduce the impact of sample selection bias, even though results showed that selectivity bias seems a minor problem, at least in the case of the programme under study. The objective of this section is to confirm this conclusion, by using a different methodology, namely semi-parametric estimation.

In general terms, the selectivity bias arises because the selection decision by the funding agency (CNR) has been based upon expected future publication output, so that when we regress scientific productivity against PI and group characteristics, which are correlated with selection as well, the estimated coefficient of the productivity equation has an upward bias. In other words, this creates a source of 'unobserved heterogeneity'. The Heckman correction can be considered to be a tool to deal with this problem.

However, the problem can be overcome (simply) by using appropriate instruments that affect selection but not research output, or by attempting to control as much as possible for sources of unobserved heterogeneity. This second possibility can be exploited by using non-parametric or semi-parametric procedures, which try to compare groups of research units (or PIs) with similar characteristics. In other words, it is possible to consider separate groups of PIs (or research units, or research proposals) having similar scientific or institutional characteristics (for example, geographical location, institutional typology, PI's age, proposal transferability, past scientific publications and so on). Within each group, it is then possible to suppose that selection and award have been a fairly random process. Hence, estimating the productivity equation for selected units within each group produces results that can be associated with non-selected units within *the same* groups as well. The higher the number of groups that can be defined, and the higher the number of variables that are used in creating groups, the lower will be the problems of unobserved heterogeneity. This, however, will inevitably reduce the number of units within each group and will produce less robust estimations.

We managed this trade-off between reduction of unobserved heterogeneity problems and estimation robustness, by considering only three variables for creating groups of units. We took into account research centres' geographical location (north, centre and south), their institutional typology (CNR laboratories or university centres), and the degree of industrial transferability of their proposal (values 0–3). As far as institutional typology is concerned, we preferred to exclude cases of research centres belonging either to firms or to other non-profit organizations (like hospitals, foundations and so on) because the total share of these organizations is very low in our database compared to others and by including them we would have created several cells with zero or very few units, thus making estimations less significant.

Within each cell, we then estimated the productivity equation (7.4), with the Heckman full ML correction and considering only *SCORE* as the regressor in equation (7.5) of the estimation procedure. In other words, we computed the same estimations of specification V described in the previous section, for each group of units. This methodology allowed us to gain advantages of both parametric estimations and Heckman corrections – thereby reducing problems of unobserved heterogeneity and sample selection – at the cost, however, of reduced robustness of estimates. In the productivity equation estimated for each cell, we used only the PI's past publications and unit size as regressors, so that equation (7.4) became in this case:

$$\ln PR_{jt} = \ln \alpha + (\alpha - 1) \ln S_{jt} + \beta \ln P_{jt-1} + \varepsilon \qquad (7.4a)$$

where the term $\gamma \ln Z_j$ included in the original equation (7.4) has been excluded because in part it is already included in the definition of single groups of units. As in the previous section, we were interested in the values of α (or $\alpha - 1$) and β, that is, in elasticities of total research budget and past publications on research productivity.

The results of this exercise are reported in Table 7.9. We have to note first that cell composition varies significantly and if some cells have no or very few research units included – as in the cases of CNR units located in the centre and with a value of proposal industrial transferability equal to 0, which are not present at all in our dataset – others are composed of a large number of research centres – as in the case of university research laboratories located in the north and with value of transferability equal to 3, which number 82. As a consequence, standard errors are usually very high, and estimates are not evenly significant. Given this general limitation of our estimations, it emerges clearly that the general trend confirms results obtained in parametric analysis.

*Table 7.9 Semi-parametric estimations of **LPROD**, by location and type of research unit, and project degree of transferability (Heckman selection model, full ML)*

Num.	Unit locality	Unit type	Project transf.	Obs.	LBEFORE (β)		LSIZE ($\alpha - 1$)		SCORE	
					Coef.	Std error	Coef.	Std error	Coef.	Std error
1	North	CNR	0	2	0.204	–	–	–	–	–
2	North	CNR	1	7	0.007	0.011	−0.090	0.036	5.200	141.029
3	North	CNR	2	8	0.096	0.083	−0.120	0.129	1.250	0.393
4	North	CNR	3	18	0.112	0.046	0.217	0.120	0.724	0.391
5	North	Univ.	0	15	0.044	0.003	0.133	0.043	0.703	0.335
6	North	Univ.	1	70	0.180	0.041	0.091	0.128	1.235	0.285
7	North	Univ.	2	42	0.053	0.032	0.263	0.093	1.267	0.372
8	North	Univ.	3	82	0.106	0.029	0.054	0.070	1.035	0.215
9	Centre	CNR	0	0	–	–	–	–	–	–
10	Centre	CNR	1	13	0.142	0.220	−0.038	–	1.117	0.284
11	Centre	CNR	2	22	0.120	0.049	0.078	0.112	1.070	0.488
12	Centre	CNR	3	11	0.066	0.017	0.103	0.060	11.359	–
13	Centre	Univ.	0	13	0.124	0.243	−2.044	0.217	2.150	2.769
14	Centre	Univ.	1	36	0.004	0.036	0.084	0.097	1.769	0.546
15	Centre	Univ.	2	41	0.055	0.051	−0.142	0.041	0.452	0.244
16	Centre	Univ.	3	58	0.014	0.044	0.039	0.070	0.009	0.330
17	South	CNR	0	0	–	–	–	–	–	–
18	South	CNR	1	12	0.025	0.050	−0.059	0.046	2.283	1.776
19	South	CNR	2	6	0.446	0.018	1.733	0.078	1.583	0.172
20	South	CNR	3	11	0.221	0.089	0.177	0.121	−0.084	0.401
21	South	Univ.	0	10	−2.882	–	18.645	7.412	0.602	0.926

Table 7.9 (continued)

Num.	Unit locality	Unit type	Project transf.	Obs.	LBEFORE (β)		LSIZE (α − 1)		SCORE	
					Coef.	Std error	Coef.	Std error	Coef.	Std error
22	South	Univ.	1	29	0.014	0.067	−0.049	0.072	1.490	0.638
23	South	Univ.	2	20	0.065	0.057	−0.218	0.130	0.722	0.420
24	South	Univ.	3	25	0.039	0.035	−0.108	0.133	1.618	0.549
Average					−0.0339		0.8928			
Average without case 21					0.1018		0.0052			
Weighted average					0.0018		−0.0049			

At the same time, it is possible to note some interesting differences in estimation values for both $\alpha - 1$ and β coefficients. Concerning the $\alpha - 1$ coefficient, associated with *LSIZE*, cases 13 – university centres located in the centre with transferability equal to 0 – and 19 – CNR laboratories located in the south with transferability equal to 2 – have values that mostly differ from the 0 obtained in parametric estimations. Among others, the case that deviates the most from 0 is case 21 in which the point estimate of $\alpha - 1$ coefficient is 18.64. But here some bigger problem of estimation might have occurred. As a matter of fact, if we compute the average value of $\alpha - 1$ coefficients obtained in different cells, including cell number 21, we obtain a result which differs significantly from 0, and makes elasticity of total budget on research productivity (that is, $\alpha - 1$) very close to 1. However, if we compute the average value by excluding case 21, the results are again similar to what were obtained through parametric estimations (that is, $\alpha - 1$ = 0, and $\alpha = 1$). This seems to confirm that cell 21 produces results that are anomalous compared to the others.

The same conclusion can be made about β coefficients. Cases 19 – CNR laboratories located in the south with transferability of 2 – and 20 – CNR centres located in the south with transferability of 3 – show the highest levels of β coefficients, without considering case 21. As above, estimations in this cell differ significantly from those in other cells. Again, if we compute average values of β coefficients with and without case 21, results first differ and then confirm what was obtained by parametric estimations. Also graphical representations of both $\alpha - 1$ and β coefficients resulting in different cells (see Figures 7.1 and 7.2) help to show the 'strange' behaviour of case 21, and, at the same time, confirm a general trend resulting from estimations reported in the previous section.

In sum, what should be emphasized about the semi-parametric analyses shown in this section is that, even if estimations are less significant because of the lower number of units in each cell, results are strongly coherent with those obtained with parametric estimations, and hence can be considered robust. The advantage of semi-parametric analyses, however, lies in the fact that research centres included in each cell are all very similar, by definition, in terms of the characteristics used to define cells, and this minimizes the risks of unobserved heterogeneity that usually affect *ex post* estimations with selected and non-selected units. In turn, analysis of production or productivity equations computed only on selected units within each cell, even if less significant, can be extended to non-selected units as well, thus making this analysis overall very robust.

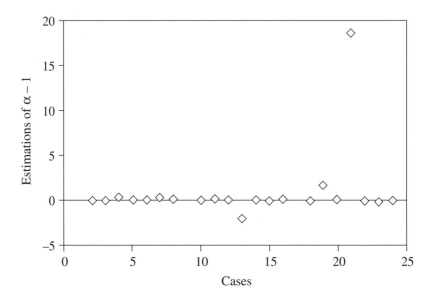

Figure 7.1   Point estimations of $\alpha - 1$ *(*LSIZE*)*

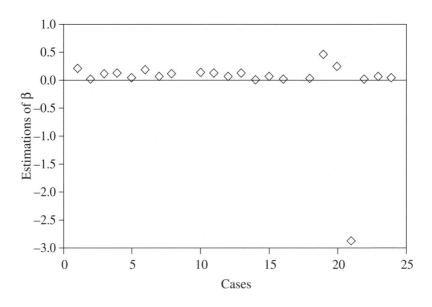

Figure 7.2   Point estimations of β *(*LBEFORE*)*

5 CONCLUSIONS

The overall evaluation of publicly funded research programmes and of the production of outputs by research groups and researchers that have been selected and funded, has become a relevant task in recent years, given the stricter control over expenses that increasing budget constraints impose in developed countries. This task, however, is difficult to perform, especially if conducted at the end of the funding programme, once the researchers have been selected and research outputs obtained. Without the chance to collect all relevant information during the running of the programme, it is usually difficult to carry out accurate estimations.

One of the main problems arising in the course of such exercises is related to the fact that correct 'as if' considerations are difficult to make. Output information is, by definition, only available for the funded units, and this creates problems when trying to assess what the output of the whole programme would have been if resources had been allocated in a different way. As a consequence, econometric estimations performed only on funded research units usually present a selection bias. Indeed, the funding agency's selection decision is based upon expected future output, so that when we regress scientific productivity against PI and group characteristics, which are also correlated with selection, the estimated coefficient of the productivity equation has an upper bias, and creates a source of 'unobserved heterogeneity'.

In order to overcome this problem, we used two different methodologies. First, we used the Heckman selection model, both in its two-step and full ML specifications. Then we performed a semi-parametric estimation, by considering 24 different groups of research units (obtained by dividing the whole sample for values of institutional typology, geographical locality and degree of industrial transferability) and by applying the same Heckman procedure to each group. Indeed, the rationale of semi-parametric or non-parametric estimations lies in the fact that research centres included in each cell are all, by definition, very similar in terms of the characteristics used to define cells, and this minimizes risks of unobserved heterogeneity that usually affect *ex post* estimations with selected and non-selected units. In turn, analysis of production or productivity equations computed only on selected units within each cell, even if less significant, can be extended to non-selected units too well, thus making this analysis robust overall.

The results obtained by the two methodologies are strongly comparable and mainly show that research productivity of research units is mostly influenced by their scientific capabilities and the geographical location of units. In particular, the PI's past publications and the number of collaborations with foreign research institutions – which in turn can be considered as being directly linked to units' research capabilities and 'quality' – appear extremely relevant in determining research productivity. The estimated values show that the elasticity of past performance on research productivity ranges from 7.4 to 11.7 per cent, and is about 10.2 per cent on average among different groups of research units. At the same time, results show that there are constant returns to scale in total funding and, hence, increases in total budget do not yield more than proportional increases in research output. Furthermore, these results are comparable with simple OLS procedures, thus showing that the selectivity bias has not been particularly severe in the case of the funding programme considered in this study and that the final effect of the selection process operated by the funder has been an almost involuntary randomization. All the different methodologies applied in this study confirm this conclusion.

The role of past publications in explaining research productivity needs to be further explored. Past publications is usually used in analysis as a measure of scientific competency and the capabilities of researchers and research centres. In this sense, results obtained by our estimations clearly seem to show that the ability to obtain a research output is mainly and directly correlated to scientific competency – the number of collaborations with foreign research centres used as alternative regressor definitely has the same meaning. It should be noted, however, that using past publications as a regressor of research output – measured in terms of scientific publications – might cause problems of endogeneity that are difficult to resolve. One possibility would be to use referee scores instead of past publications, particularly the subscore which assesses the unit's scientific excellence. Exploring this possibility is part of our future research agenda.

NOTES

*   We should like to thank Aldo Geuna, Ammon Salter and Ed Steinmueller for having patiently waited for us to provide this chapter, and an anonymous reviewer for extremely accurate and useful comments and suggestions on an earlier draft. The usual disclaimers apply.
1.   The IF ratio is calculated as the number of citations of a journal to other journals divided by the number of citations of other journals to that journal. The higher the value of IF, the higher is the 'quality' of the journal, because that journal is cited more frequently than it cites. The lowest level of IF is obviously 0. Articles in books and working papers have a nominal IF of 0, stating that those publications have not been reviewed by the peer review system, existing for scientific journals.
2.   To be correct, 49 more applicants were granted from CNR for less than five years. Some of them entered into the B&B programme, but then exited before the end, and some others started later than the first year. For the purposes of this study, we preferred to consider those units as non-selected.

3. For a complete discussion on this topic based on the same funding programme (B&B), see Arora et al. (1998).
4. It is possible to formulate different hypotheses for this result. On the one hand, it is possible to say that CNR has preferred to give no advantages to industrial units, and considers the B&B programme mainly as a funding instrument finalized to non-profit research centres (especially from CNR and universities). On the other, it is equally possible to say that this result reflects either the late development of a biotech industry in Italy, or the fact that Italian pharmaceutical companies (mainly involved in biotechnologies) are non-R&D-intensive firms.
5. In principle, regressors of selection and productivity equations can be exactly the same.
6. As sub-Programme 7 focused on bio-instrumentation, publications do not represent the most important research output, compared to others such as prototypes. Thus, research groups in this sub-programme show a scientific productivity lower than those groups in different sub-programmes.

REFERENCES

Arora, A. and A. Gambardella (1997), 'Public policy towards science: picking stars or spreading the wealth?', *Revue d'Économie Industrielle* **79**, 63–75.

Arora, A., P.A. David and A. Gambardella (1998), 'Reputation and competence in publicly funded science: estimating the effects of research group productivity', *Annales d'Économie et de Statistique* **49–50**, 163–98.

Dasgupta, P. and P.A. David (1994), 'Towards a new economics of science', *Research Policy* **23**(5), 487–521.

David, P.A. (1994), 'Positive feedbacks and research productivity in science: reopening another black box', in O. Granstrand (ed.), *Economics and Technology*, Amsterdam and London: North-Holland, pp. 65–116.

de Solla Price, D.J. (1963), *Little Science, Big Science*, New York: Columbia University Press.

de Solla Price, D.J. (1976), 'A general theory of bibliometric and other cumulative advantage processes', *Journal of the American Society for Information Science* **27**(5/6), 292–306.

Etzkowitz, H., A. Webster and P. Healey (1998), *Capitalizing Knowledge: University Intersections of Industry and Academia*, Albany, NY: State University of New York Press.

European Commission (1996), 'Good practice in the transfer of university technology', European Innovation Monitoring System (EIMS) Publication no. 26, available at: http://www.cordis.lu/eims/src/eims-26htm – last accessed 30 April 2002.

Geuna, A. (2001), 'The changing rationale for European university research funding: are there negative unintended consequences?', *Journal of Economic Issues* **35**(5), 607–32.

Heckman, J. (1976), 'The common structure of statistical models of truncation, sample selection, and limited dependent variables and a simple estimator for such models', *The Annals of Social and Economic Measurement* **5**, 475–92.

Heckman, J. (1979), 'Sample selection bias as a specification error', *Econometrica* **47**, 153–61.

Jaffe, A.B. (2000), 'Building program evaluation into the design of public research support programs', paper presented at the 'Technological Policy and Innovation. Economic and Historical Perspective' conference, Paris (France), 20–22 November.

Johnston, J. and J. DiNardo (1997), *Econometric Methods*, 4th edn, New York: McGraw-Hill.

Lalonde, R. (1986), 'Evaluating the econometric evaluations of training programmes with experimental data', *American Economic Review* **76**(4), 604–20.

Lotka, A. (1926), 'The frequency distribution of scientific productivity', *Journal of the Washington Academy of Sciences* **16**(12), 317–23.

Potì, B.M., F. Cesaroni and M. Cioppi (1999), *L'Interazione tra Scienza e Industria in Italia. Idee per una valutazione della politica della ricerca*, Milan: Franco Angeli.

Silvani, A. (1998), 'I metodi, le tecniche e le procedure per la valutazione della ricerca', *Università e Ricerca* **3**, 7–17.

Stephan, P.E. (1996), 'The economics of science', *Journal of Economic Literature* **34**(3), 1199–235.

Commentaries

PAULA E. STEPHAN

Both the Llerena, Matt and Schaeffer chapter (Chapter 5) and the Riccaboni, Powell, Pammolli and Owen-Smith chapter (Chapter 6) relate to the issue of why technology transfer from the public sector (PRO) appears to have been more successful in the United States than in Europe. Here I comment very briefly on each chapter and then make more general comments relating to why the US system, particularly in the biomedical sciences, has been so effective in fostering technology transfer between PROs, especially universities, and biotech start-ups.

Chapter 5 discusses the impact of French innovation policies on universities. From a US perspective, a system whereby researchers are allowed to hold an equity position in a firm while being at a PRO should encourage start-ups. So, too, should a policy that permits researchers to leave the academic laboratory for a period of up to six years and then return. Perhaps most important, is a policy that allows researchers to stay in the laboratory and still bring their scientific talents to a firm. These attributes are supported by the US experience in technology transfer in biotechnology, which is characterized by a number of factors. First is the ability of university-based founders of biotech companies to have their cake and eat it too, maintaining their job in the university while founding the company. Audretsch and Stephan (1999) find, for example, that 35 out of the 50 university founders of the publicly traded biotech firms in their sample still held academic appointments at the time the company became public. A second characteristic of the US system is the holding by university researchers of large equity positions in start-up firms. Stephan and Everhart (1998) find that 40 university scientists affiliated with the same sample of biotech firms had sufficient holdings to require disclosure at the time the firm made its initial public offering.[1] The median portfolio value of the beneficial shares held by these 40 scientists at the close of day one of trading was between $3 million and $4 million. Many other faculty members, of course, hold smaller positions. Stephan and Everhart estimate that in 1992 there were over 1,400 linkages between university-based scientists and biotech firms that resulted in an equity position in a publicly traded firm.

A strength of Chapter 6 is that it weaves together, in terms of the story it is telling with regard to university–industry relations, data from the US and from Europe. The figures tell a compelling story of a limited number of players in Europe, the importance of geography and the role of specialized fields. The findings are consistent with those of Gittelman (2000) that commercial connections, when they are made in France, are more likely to be made between pharmaceutical companies and research institutes than between research institutes and biomedical firms.

General Comments

One interpretation of why the US system, particularly in the biomedical sciences, has proved so effective in fostering technology transfer between PROs, especially universities, and biotech start-up firms in the US, is the way that university science is funded in the US, especially in the life sciences. The facts of life for biomedical researchers at US research universities require that the researcher has a lab of his or her own. Indeed, it is common practice in the US for the lab to be named after the university scientist who is directing it. At the time the scientist joins the university, the university provides start-up funds for the lab. Thereafter, it is the responsibility of the scientist to obtain funding for the lab. Such funding is key to the scientist's continuation at the university since a history of funding for one's lab is a necessary condition for a researcher to get tenure at a research university. Grant-seeking activity is also encouraged by the compensation system at US universities. This is because faculty members, who are usually paid on a nine-month basis, are allowed to write-off summer research time on grants, thereby earning up to one-third of their nine-month salary in the summer. Moreover, at many universities, faculty members can buy themselves out of the classroom during the academic year with grant money. While this does not increase their yearly earnings, the buy-out opportunity provides them with more time to do research.[2]

The primary funding agency for research in the life sciences in the US is the National Institutes of Health (NIH). In 2001 its budget was $20.5 billion; the 2002 budget is approximately $23.5 billion and the amount requested for 2003 in the President's budget is $27.6 billion (NIH 2002). More than 80 per cent of this is allocated to extramural programmes; 52 per cent to research project grants (NIH 2002). Despite this large budget, the success rate of applicants is not that high, although with growing budgets it has increased in recent years. In 1994, for example, of the 6,876 first-time unamended, unsolicited applications for the traditional research project grant of NIH (called R01 projects), 12.9 per cent were funded. By 1998, this had increased to about 20.1 per cent due to the large increase in the NIH budget (Mandel and Vesell 1999). When revised proposals are included, the rate in 1998 was 36 per cent. Renewal requests, called continuations (the typical R01 grant has an average term of 3.8 years [National Research Council 1994]), have a significantly higher success rate, in the 40–55 per cent range depending on year.[3]

The grants system results in faculty members spending a great deal of time writing research proposals. 'Some studies estimate that 30 to 40 percent of a researcher's time could be devoted to the grant application process' (Rabinow 1996, p. 28). Such a system of strong competition, and high opportunity costs, results in a natural selection process in academe whereby the survivors – and it is the survivors of the system who are tenured faculty members at research universities – excel at obtaining money. Having honed their skills at government agencies such as NIH, they are in a good position to acquire funding from other places as well, including industry.

It is common practice in the US in the life sciences to receive funding from industry as well as government. Blumenthal et al. (1996) find that 28 per cent of the life scientists in their survey of the top 50 US research universities had research support from industry. It is not just research grants that they receive. Faculty members receive gifts from industry as well. Campbell et al. (1998) find in a survey of the top 50 research universities that 43 per cent of the respondents report receiving some kind of gift from industry, in the form of equipment, biomaterials, discretionary funds, support for students, trips to professional meetings and so on.

It is, therefore, not surprising that we see more and more interaction between industry and academe in the US manifested in a variety of ways including joint authorship as well as scientific personnel who hold positions in both sectors simultaneously.

In conclusion, the US system has not only resulted in creating an entrepreneurial culture among university scientists in terms of grant seeking, but it has also produced a faculty that has become increasingly interested in financial rewards. Was it US government policy that fostered this entrepreneurial culture? Yes, but, as in the case of many other government policies, we argue that it was largely an unintended consequence of government policy. The National Institutes of Health were set up with the idea of improving health. Research that NIH supports in the university sector has undoubtedly contributed greatly to achieving this goal. But, the NIH goal has also been facilitated by the willingness of university staff to forge ties with both start-ups and established companies, thereby facilitating technology transfer. Although indirect, NIH has played a role in this piece of the equation as well, by creating an environment that has fostered an entrepreneurial faculty.

W. EDWARD STEINMUELLER

There are several ways of reading the chapters in this section. The chapter authors propose that their work should be read as evaluative. At the risk of oversimplification, the key questions receiving affirmative answers in the chapters are:

1. Is there persuasive evidence that US university research makes widespread contributions to industrial innovation? (W.M. Cohen, R.R. Nelson and J.P. Walsh, Chapter 4).
2. Is it justified to reach preliminary critical conclusions about French efforts to allow researchers a greater scope of interaction with the public sector? (P. Llerena, M. Matt and V. Schaeffer, Chapter 5).
3. Do differences in institutional rules and division of labour between the US and European research efforts in the life sciences help explain the persistence of US first-mover advantages? (M. Riccaboni, W.W. Powell, F. Pammolli, and J. Owen-Smith, Chapter 6).
4. Are the criteria used to award research grants in Italy robust in predicting scientific output quality when we control for the benefits of having previously received research funding? (F. Cesaroni and A. Gambardella, Chapter 7).

An alternative to reading these chapters as evaluations of specific, situated questions is to take the view that these detailed empirical investigations provide clues as to the operation of the science system. In translating their findings into policy presciptions it is this reading that is likely to be more fruitful for reasons that will be elaborated in this commentary. The commentary begins with a discussion of the difficulties involved in using the type of evidence presented in these chapters, particularly when cast in an evaluative framework, to influence science policy. It then proceeds to a discussion of the managerialist approach to science policy which is becoming a dominant influence and to which these chapters are addressed. The commentary concludes with several observations about the limitations of the methods employed in these chapters for comprehending the scientific enterprise.

Despite the wishes or fantasies of social scientists, social science is not widely accepted as a means for reaching policy conclusions about how the scientific activities of society should be organized. The actors that are relatively privileged in science policy debates include senior scientists, whose authority derives not only from their specific understanding of the subject matter but also from experiences of interacting with funding agencies and other administrative structures and building or maintaining successful and prestigious scientific laboratories. While senior scientists have considerable influence in the establishment of research priorities within specific domains of enquiry, their authority is matched by senior civil servants and, in some countries, longstanding elected representatives with an interest in science policy. Ultimately, the political actors must arbitrate the competing claims for priority and resources among different scientific communities. In several major domains, including the life sciences, aeronautics, chemistry and, in recent years, electronics, industrial research managers in many of the OECD countries have an important, and increasingly stronger, say in science policy priorities. These key actors are influenced by a complex mixture of self- and social-interest. For example, it would be quite surprising if individuals with a lifelong research involvement in particular scientific activities would, upon elevation to a position of influence, argue for reducing the priority for such activities. Similar proclivities may be expected from both government officials with expertise in specific research domains and industrial spokespersons. At the same time, however, those connected with scientific enterprise have a nearly universal commitment to the idea that there exists a quality within research activities that is most commonly called 'good science'. Of course, there is no universal agreement as to what constitutes 'good science', but the common belief in its existence serves to frame the negotiations over the funding and governance of the science system.

Social scientists in general, and economists in particular, enter this debate with the disadvantages of an agnostic at an ecumenical conference. Their view of what constitutes 'good science' is not based upon their own judgements of the relative opportunities offered by different fields for further discovery or the elegance of specific lines of enquiry. All social scientists are forced to rely upon observation of the behaviours and the artefacts produced by scientists and to make the argument that while these byproducts may not capture the faith of adherents they do reflect how this faith is organized and practised. In particular, economists immediately proceed to utilitarian features of scientific practice – the scientific papers and patterns of interorganizational agreements that arise in research practice. From these 'traces' they attempt to divine how the system operates. For scholars who see a unifying principle in the social problem of allocating scarce means among competing interests, the focus on the relation between tangible inputs and outputs is understandable. This does not mean that it is widely appreciated as a proper tool for understanding how to best organize scientific activities.

An important opening of the rather exclusive 'club' of science policy-making arose during the 1970s and 1980s from the increasing interest of policy-makers in the role of science in industrial innovation. This interest was fuelled by the possibilities of replacing industries whose growth had slowed or that were experiencing relative decline, with 'sunrise' or new technology-based industries, bringing virtues such as preserving the jobs of political constituents and tax revenues. It was also supported by a growing attention to and concern about the rate of productivity improvement, which had declined from the very high levels experienced throughout the OECD countries after the Second World War. Towards the end of this period a new and somewhat controversial approach to empirical innovation studies emerged from researchers at Yale (Levin et al. 1987) and the work of Edwin Mansfield and colleagues at the University of Pennsylvania. Both research teams approached the problem of understanding the linkages within the research system as one that could be solved by research managers. Uncharacteristically for modern economists, they proceeded to ask these individuals about the issues they were studying – which were their life work. This particular approach proved very influential for US science and technology policy and was reproduced in the Carnegie-Mellon Survey on Industrial R&D and a variety of surveys conducted in other countries including the Community Innovation Survey in Europe. In this volume, Cohen, Nelson and Walsh (Chapter 4) present the findings of the Carnegie-Mellon survey on the relation between public research and industrial R&D.

The opening of science policy to consideration of issues of innovation and productivity effects had two principal outcomes. The first was to encourage scholars to develop a deeper analysis of the network features of scientific and technological knowledge production and distribution, a theme that is dealt with in the introduction and conclusions to this volume. The second was to stimulate policy-makers' interest in the possibilities of better management of public investment in science. The combined forces of budgetary stringency and the emergence of new priorities had a powerful effect in shaping a particular type of managerial focus for science policy. This focus has disrupted the traditional science governance system and produced new priorities for social science research. The essence of these changes has been a rethinking of the science system in terms similar to other public investments rather than reserving science policy as a distinct speciality in which only a limited number of actors could have a legitimate voice. This rethinking and the entry of actors from treasury ministries and other parts of government have provoked the search for new principles. The solutions that have been devised to date are influenced by the general enthusiasm for markets and market institutions. In this sense, economic reasoning and logic have been introduced into the science governance system. This introduction has, however, been extremely limited as the following discussion will illustrate.

A virtue of the chapters in this section is that they directly engage with the managerial approach to science policy by taking on the questions that naturally arise from this approach and introducing the minimum of additional logic and a healthy dose of data to provisionally answer these questions. A first principle of the managerial approach is to regard scientific knowledge as a commodity that can be purchased through the issuance of research grants and contracts. The fiscal stringency applied to government expenditures generally demands that a standard be established by which projects might be ranked according to 'value for money' considerations. This has provoked renewed questions about what the returns from public research investments might be, with investments in university research receiving particular scrutiny. As Cohen, Nelson and Walsh (Chapter 4) make clear for the US system, the contributions of public research investment including university research are pervasive and significant. In making this finding, however, the authors of Chapter 4 make an important subversion of managerial principle. While the principle would hold that grants and contracts produce discrete quanta of knowledge that are launched against specific targets and have, or fail to have, distinct impacts, the authors of Chapter 4 make it clear that university research produces a cascade of outputs that are filtered, reconfigured and recombined through a variety of different channels in the course of reaching the designated targets. Indeed, this mechanism raises questions about the extent to which it is either possible or desirable to engage in the targeting process. This is the first of several subversions or 'mind expansions' that have been attempted by the authors in this part.

Accompanying the concerns about the returns to public investment in science there is a renewed interest in the criteria by which these monies are allocated among researchers. Applying the 'value for money' style of reasoning leads to the conclusion that limited resources should be allocated to those able to make the most productive use of them. The thorny problem of allocating a diminishing pool of funds can therefore be simplified by identifying scientists that are more productive than the average, and the prevailing approach to identifying these scientists is to look at their historical performance. Applying this criterion is not without its problems, however.

Scientific research is an uncertain undertaking and, like drilling for oil or prospecting for minerals, sometimes produces nothing despite significant investment. Moreover, again like mineral exploration, discovering a worthwhile claim may produce a steady output for a sustained period of time, discouraging further prospecting even though a much more productive resource lies nearby, although far removed from their knowledge. Thus, adopting systems designed to identify 'star' scientists raises alarming possibilities. Are these researchers the beneficiaries of early success, who are given further resources because of their past productivity and, as a result of these resources, are able either to continue to work their claims or to discover new ones? Much of the moral claim to rewarding productivity would evaporate if 'star researchers' were seen merely as having been fortunate young prospectors.

In Cesaroni and Gambardella (Chapter 7) the possibility of 'fortunate young prospectors' is explored for the case of the Italian research system. Their findings indicate that, while the reinforcement of early success might in fact be operating within the system, the scale of research funding is sufficient to extend support well beyond the 'stars' in the system and thus create the diversity in prospecting that might otherwise disappear from the system. However, this finding leads to another alarming (at least for scientists) possibility – should the Italian funding authorities sharply reduce research budgets to achieve more 'value for money'? One answer that would discourage this conclusion is that doing so would reduce the diversity or variety of the system and greatly strengthen the rewards from early success – outcomes that are likely to have costs in terms of the productivity of the system as a whole.

In addition to seeking ways to assess individual researchers, the managerialist approach raises questions as to how to arrange the division of labour among organizations. It would seem at first glance that investing in researchers who pursue their research part-time while undertaking other responsibilities, such as teaching, is likely to be less productive than funding full-time researchers. Similarly, it is appropriate to ask whether a greater concentration of funds might produce efficiencies. At a minimum, researchers in a similar domain of investigation are capable of sharing common administrative and facility overheads. Co-location might even provide further benefits through synergistic interactions among researchers. With respect to these issues, Riccaboni, Powell, Pammolli and Owen-Smith (Chapter 6) are particularly instructive. Their findings do support the conclusion that there are structural advantages in agglomeration in a particular locale, as both Europe and the US exhibit this structure. They conclude, however, that the greater concentration of funding in Europe and the stronger role of large pharmaceutical houses in coordinating the research agenda are a source of weakness. It is regional rather than organizational co-location that provides the advantage.

In a wider context, the findings of Chapter 6 are rather discouraging for the managerial agenda. It would appear necessary to base funding decisions in particular domains upon the specific qualities of the research effort and its relation to processes of innovation. Moreover, as Paula Stephan's commentary to this part emphasizes, it is not only differences in structural configuration between the US and Europe that are responsible for differences in performance, but also what is done within this structure with respect to institutional rules, such as those regulating the participation of researchers in public employment. Further evidence of the 'situated' nature of research systems is offered by Llerena, Matt and Schaeffer (Chapter 5) who examine French efforts to establish a closer tie between universities and industry by relaxing several of the rules that dramatically limit this involvement.

The French experiment is relatively young and the conclusions of Chapter 5 are thus a preliminary evaluation based on much less evidence than the other three chapters in this part. The findings, none the less, offer intriguing facts about attempting to move from one to another institutional configuration. French university researchers have been firmly ensconced in the public sector and bound by unusually strong regulatory conditions such as a statutory requirement regarding the number of hours that must be spent in classroom teaching regardless of the level of research funding. The provisions that have been made in recent legislation for their participation in private sector activities are therefore a remarkable achievement. These provisions accord with the managerial principles of more closely aligning incentives within university and industry research. At one extreme, some would believe that such incentive restructuring would provide a means to reduce the public sector funding of universities as they are transformed into knowledge enterprises, generating a stream of revenues from intellectual property and direct participation in new companies. Unlike the typical model of the US research university, which offers a continuous renegotiation of the terms of engagement of the researchers in university affairs while they are engaged in private sector activities, the French system that has been introduced remains deeply concerned with regulating the activities of public employees. As a consequence, it would seem that relatively few researchers are taking up the new arrangements. An ironic consequence of the continuing control of the university over its employees, noted by Llerena, Matt and Schaeffer (Chapter 5), is that it is more onerous to establish a company than to be taken into an existing company. Instead of creating university entrepreneurs, the new system is likely to make university researchers responsible to two masters. Hence, even when radical managerial reforms are the intended goal of institutional reform, they are likely to be weighed down if not crushed by the burden of institutional history.

The chapters in this part provide a thorough if oblique criticism of several of the main tenets of the managerial reform model that has become the new prevailing paradigm for science policy. Collectively, they suggest that there is much more complexity to the science system than can be accommodated by approaches derived from a managerial perspective, such as viewing public research as procurement of knowledge, allocating research funds on the basis of value for money productivity considerations, or aligning public researcher incentives with those governing researchers in the private sector in order to enhance the linkages between public research and industry. Their results do not suggest a wholesale rejection of the managerial model, but, instead, the need for a more sophisticated approach to implementing its precepts with the possibility that these precepts will, themselves, have to change in order to take account of the nature of the science system. It is in regard to this last point that a few comments are warranted.

While it is quite appropriate to evaluate the claims made by advocates of the managerial approach and to answer the questions that this approach suggests, it is important also to keep in mind the limitations to our ability to understand the science system using existing tools. None of these contributions comes close to providing an operational definition of what 'good science' might mean in terms that would be recognizable to a scientist. The strongest candidates for the claim that research quality can be measured involve examining which scientific papers are taken up in the citations of other scientists or involve international collaborations. The econometric tools employed in assessing these traces of scientific practice rely heavily upon numerous observations to achieve statistically significant results. It is, however, a characteristic of scientific advance that breakthrough results are seldom immediately followed up or appreciated. While there are today several areas of science, such as molecular biology where massive additions to the stock of knowledge have become possible through new types of instrumentation and experimental methods, much of this knowledge remains unarticulated in larger frameworks of understanding. What accounts for a current discovery or a publishable paper may bear only faint resemblance to this larger structure of understanding that emerges only after a prolonged period of reflection and digestion.

It is therefore important not to subscribe wholly to the managerial dicta that science should be measured by the tangible artefacts or traces that it produces. Ultimately, scientific progress involves a transformation of cognition about the phenomena and 'facts' that are produced by experimental method. These transformations are poorly tracked, if at all, by the accumulation of scientific papers as they involve a broad change in the understanding of scientists of their domains of investigation and are incorporated into the training of new generations of scientists. This is one of the many reasons why managerial efforts to improve the productivity of scientists is likely to have unexpected and often untoward effects. In order to better apprehend the reality of scientific knowledge and, therefore, scientific progress, new tools are needed that better capture the cognitive transformation involved in scientific advance and the nature of the scientific frontier that scientists are trying to advance.

NOTES

1. The US Securities and Exchange Commission (SEC) requires that the names and positions of insiders having substantial holdings in a company be listed in the prospectuses concerning the initial public offering. In addition, the SEC records the market activity of insiders.
2. It also provides the university resources. After teaching obligations are covered from these buy-outs, many universities use what is left to invest in research.
3. These success rates come from unpublished NIH data for the 1970–96 period. The success rate of continuations has declined somewhat in recent years as the number of continuation proposals has grown. For example, while in the 1980s the success rate was often over 50 per cent for continuations, in the 1990s it was in the lower 40s, and in one year it was 39.4 per cent.

REFERENCES

Audretsch, D. and P. Stephan (1999), 'Knowledge spillovers in biotechnology: sources and incentives', *Evolutionary Economics* **9**(1), 97–107.

Blumenthal, D., E.G., Campbell, N. Causino and K. Seashore Louis (1996), 'Participation of life-science faculty in research relationships with industry', *New England Journal of Medicine* **335**(23), 1734–9.

Campbell, E., K. Seashore Louis and D. Blumenthal (1998), 'Looking a gift horse in the mouth', *Journal of the American Medical Association* **279**(13), 995–9.

Gittelman, M. (2000), 'Mapping national knowledge networks: scientists, firms and institutions in the United States and France', Ph.D. Thesis, The Wharton School, University of Pennsylvania.

Levin, R., A. Klevorick, R.R. Nelson and S.G. Winter (1987), 'Appropriating the returns from industrial R&D', *Brookings papers on Economic Activity*, special issue, 738–820.

Mandel, H.G. and E.S. Vesell (1999), 'Likelihood of NIH extramural funding', *Science* **285**(5434), 1674–6.

National Institutes of Health (NIH) (2002), 'NIH Press Release for the FY 2003 President's Budget', www.nih.gov/news/budgetfy2003/2003NIHpresbudget.htm.

National Research Council (1994), *The Funding of Young Investigators in the Biological and Biomedical Sciences*, Washington, DC: National Academy Press.

Rabinow, P. (1996) *Making PCR: A Story of Biotechnology*, Chicago: University of Chicago Press.

Stephan, P. and S. Everhart (1998), 'The changing rewards to science: the case in biotechnology', *Small Business Economics*, **10**(2), 141–51.

PART III

Models of Research Funding

Introduction

The four major chapters and the two commentaries in this last part review the conceptual core issues and provide original insights into the rationale for funding of basic research seen as a public or quasi-public good. One of the characteristics of current approaches to public funding of research is the increased use of network funding. Both at the national and at the EU level, funds have been increasingly allocated to (a) collaborative research (research projects where individuals from different institutions are involved forming a network); and (b) networks of researchers to support knowledge exchange rather than research into the production of new knowledge. Several empirical studies have described these new funding/research structures, but little theoretical work to assess their impact and validity has been done. The first two chapters in this part (by Paul David and Louise Keely and Robin Cowan and Nicolas Jonard, Chapters 8 and 9) attempt to redress this. Both focus on networks though David and Keely's work concentrates on the collaborative research configuration while Cowan and Jonard's chapter focuses on the second configuration, that is, networking as a mechanism for knowledge exchange outside the local environment.

The other two chapters (by Peter Swann and Dominique Foray, Chapters 10 and 11) also focus on the fact that knowledge is characterized by strong complementarities in its production and use. However, they concentrate on another aspect of this characteristic: they analyse the possibility of collective production and use of scientific and technological knowledge. Specifically, Swann develops a theoretical framework within which to assess the applicability or otherwise of the club goods approach to funding basic research while Foray presents a review of the advantages and shortcomings of this approach in the case of industry-specific public goods.

Finally, the commentaries of Cristiano Antonelli and Bronwyn Hall provide a broader perspective on the issues discussed in these four chapters. Antonelli presents a critical discussion of the shift that occurred in the understanding of the process of knowledge production and distribution and its relation to public funding of scientific and technological knowledge. He stresses that current understanding of the importance of cumulability and complementarity of scientific and technological knowledge, both on the use and supply side, call for policy action in the area of governance. In his view, public funding of research is aimed not only at the creation of a public good, but also, and mainly, at the management of dynamic coordination issues resulting from the instability of market interactions and multiple funding sources. Bronwyn Hall's commentary highlights many of the key findings of the chapters in this part. She observes the important omission of the role of the university in diffusing knowledge through the education of graduates who carry with them to their industrial employment recent advances in knowledge. Hall also notes that the chapters underemphasize the potentials for using research collaborations to strengthen market power, to form cartels or to raise rivals' costs.

David and Keely's contribution starts from the observation that in recent years a small but growing body of scholarly work has provided useful qualitative and, to a lesser extent, statistical analysis of public resource allocation for collaborative research, but that no formal model assessing, for example, how research competences are affected by the allocation of funds based on network structure, has been developed. Thus, they set out to address this gap. They develop a formal model of coalition-building among research units that seeks competitive funding from both national and supra-national agencies. From this stylized model a set of challenging conclusions emanate, such as the fact that national funding decisions developed in response to the allocation of the supra-national agency do not constitute the optimal strategy. David and Keely offer strong analytical support to the view that, in a science-funding environment involving multiple sources, the assessment of policy action should be framed in a context of interdependence of multiple funding strategies and outcomes.

Cowan and Jonard's chapter contributes to the analysis of the rationale for funding of basic research by examining the impact of networking upon the production and distribution of knowledge. Funding of networks both at the European and national levels has become important for universities at the expense of more traditional methods of funding research activities in single-institution settings. Cowan and Jonard's chapter is an attempt to assess how much networking is 'good'. They develop a model of knowledge creation and diffusion in which innovation in the knowledge stock (knowledge creation) is seen, mainly, as the recombination of existing ideas. They identify two main mechanisms of knowledge distribution and creation: collaboration via seminars or working papers (which gives rise to knowledge distribution and creation via recombination) and job mobility. The results of the simulation of their model point to the fact that too much networking decreases knowledge production; maintenance of only a few permanent long-distance links (such as those developed through networking) produces the optimal outcome.

The traditional justification for public funding of basic research focuses on the existence of positive externalities. Basic research is seen as a public good which it is difficult to appropriate, hence the need for public funding to reach the socially optimal investment. The dissatisfaction with this approach in policy circles has been paralleled by an increased interest in the club goods approach to the funding of basic research. Swann's chapter (Chapter 10) assesses the applicability or otherwise of the club goods approach to funding basic research. The analysis focuses on the ease with which externalities can be internalized within the club in relation to the applied versus basic character of research. If the benefits from research can be easily internalized (with low transaction costs) then club good solutions are preferable. The chapter identifies two specific factors affecting the rate of internalization: (a) the spatial distribution of beneficiaries and (b) the specific character of the diffusion process – that is, epidemic diffusion versus probit diffusion. When the benefits of research are spatially contiguous, with very few beneficiaries from other sectors or regions, that is to say, when a tight-knit socio-economic group benefits from the new knowledge, the club goods solution can be applied. This is more often the case for applied research than for basic research.

Chapter 10 concludes by highlighting a set of circumstances in which public finance of basic research is preferable to club good solutions that are attainable. It argues convincingly that in a world characterized by a large number of innovators (whose specializations are diverse) and a complex economy with substantial intersectoral science–technology relationships, public finance is preferable to a club good solution in most cases.

Foray's chapter (Chapter 11) complements Chapter 10 by Swann. The focus in Foray's work is to assess the feasibility of the provision of industry-specific public goods. The assumption here is that the public good is industry specific and, as such, it is possible to internalize the externalities to the club participants, who are a subset of the industry members. Thus, the chapter reviews empirical and theoretical evidence on the feasibility, advantages and shortcomings of club good approaches to the support of industry-specific goods. On the basis of a set of 'real world' examples – both historical and contemporary – Foray develops a matrix to evaluate the advantages and shortcomings of different provision of industry-specific public goods.

Collectively, the chapters in this part provide important insights into the mechanisms influencing the performance of research networks and collaborative structures. They indicate the possibility of new arrangements in funding and conducting research. However, rather than producing a panacea for the problems involved in governing the science, these mechanisms bring with them new and distinct problems of governance. They also introduce trade-offs and complementarities that are often not immediately apparent from the stated intentions of new programmes or funding mechanisms.

Ignoring the new issues of governance and the trade-offs and complementarities that these programmes may introduce is sure to result in unintended effects, some of which may contravene the original intent of the programmes' sponsor. While this is very good news for researchers, providing ample opportunities for future study, it may not be as welcome either to scientists or to their sponsors.

8. The economics of scientific research coalitions: collaborative network formation in the presence of multiple funding agencies*

Paul A. David and Louise C. Keely

1 INTRODUCTORY OVERVIEW: MOTIVATION, APPROACH AND RESULTS

A global trend towards the formal collaborative organization and conduct of scientific and technological investigations has been promoted by the increasing scale, 'lumpiness' and complexity of research and development opportunities.[1] Understandably enough, there has been a corresponding increase in the attention and effort devoted by economists to describing the various phenomena associated with the proliferation of cooperative R&D agreements among firms, multi-institutional research partnerships, and international scientific consortia; as well as to accounting for the characteristics of the entities (whether business firms, university schools and departments, or public institutes) that exhibit strong propensities to enter into coalitional arrangements of this kind.[2] This is very much in order, in as much as the increasing ubiquity of collaborative modes of research that transcend national boundaries calls for some critical rethinking of traditional national science and technology policies, an undertaking for which there is none too ample a supporting basis of empirical findings and analytical constructs.[3]

The growing recognition of the collaborative context within which individual researchers typically function, and the respects in which their organizational arrangements do not conform to the ideal of a 'perfect team' organization within which the incentives of the constituent agents have been so aligned that the collectivity can be viewed as a monolithic entity, are new and welcome departures from past research approaches in the economics and the sociology of science. Strong traditions in economics analysis favoured accepting the individual researcher, rather than researchers and their colleagues, situated in laboratories, as the relevant unit of analysis. This predisposition was reinforced by the impetus that early studies in the economics of science received from concerns with 'scientific manpower' policy issues; the latter were approached simply as a matter of applying the economic analysis of individual labour supply decisions.[4]

In the more normatively oriented discipline of research management, analysis has been geared to finding the best means of motivating, coordinating and directing the activities of closed teams (comprising employed scientists and engineers) dedicated to achieving specified tasks that serve the externally stipulated goals of a supporting organization, such as a commercial corporation or a public mission agency. The organization and behaviour of more autonomous groups of academic researchers who involved themselves in research coalitions hardly fits neatly into either of these approaches.

Motivating Considerations

Although one might have expected the study of collaborative research to have been a staple in the field of organizational sociology from the latter's inception, such was not the case. On the contrary, the sociology of science, having initially been preoccupied with macro-institutional analyses following the line of inquiry opened by Merton (1973), only belatedly came to concern itself with the microcosm of scientific work groups comprising researchers situated in specific laboratories. But, rather than attaching special significance to formal structures of collaboration, the thrust of more recent developments in the sociology of scientific knowledge has somewhat paradoxically directed primary attention to situating the individual actors and their apparatus and artefacts within larger relational networks, and to 'following scientists and engineers through society' without particular reference to the nature of the organizational structures within which their activities were conducted.[5]

For these and still other reasons, comparatively little systematic attention has been given to the impacts upon the relevant research communities of the recognized trend favouring provision of public funding to scientific and technological research projects that are conducted in formal 'collaborative networks', especially those that assemble research units from a variety of academic institutions and business entities under various forms of contractual agreement.[6] Indeed, the study of research collaborations predominantly or exclusively formed among public sector research entities in the physical, engineering, medical, social and behavioural sciences, remains essentially in its infancy. This is so both in an absolute sense, and in relation to the growing mass of empirical material pertaining to interfirm R&D agreements, and government-sponsored research 'partnerships' involving university- and industry-based research units.

To guide the decisions about resource allocation in all these related areas, obviously, one would hope to draw upon more ample and firmer knowledge than we now possess about the ways in which the terms of such programmes affect the structure and performance of the R&D coalitions that are successfully formed. What is the effect of special programmes targeting the collaborative conduct of scientific research upon the distribution of research competence, scientific reputational standing, and access to resources within the research communities at large? When there are some sources of funding that stipulate particular forms of collaboration as a condition of eligibility to compete for support, how does their influence interact with that of other research agencies that continue to provide research support without imposing organizational conditions favouring the formation of 'collaborative networks'?

The latter query raises a more general problem: non-profit (charitable) foundations, public agencies and government departments which concurrently engage in sponsoring research activities may rarely do so in a tightly coordinated fashion even when all their funding is concentrated within a single national domain. A multiplicity of differentiated goals among the sources of funding, some quite idiosyncratic, some quite mimetic and rivalrous, presents both opportunities and potential conflicts that influence the growth, structure and performance of research communities. Diversity of funding agencies operating in a given field of scientific exploration and application often is a correlate of the sheer extent of the aggregate resources that can be mobilized for research. But, in so far as diversity, and the degree of coordination or decentralization among the programmes run by the different funding sources represent a subject of policy design, we should ask what differences it makes to the effectiveness of any particular agency's strategy that its programmes are not 'the only (funding) game in town'.

Quite patently, it is seriously misleading for science and technology policy-minded economists to go on presupposing that they should devote themselves solely to working out the best advice to give in this sphere to a governmental funding authority that is able to allocate all the relevant resources available to the research groups operating within its domain. Some public agency directorates do resemble the classic corporate executive board that has exclusive responsibility for the company's R&D projects and corresponding control over all of its research resources; and in some of the smaller developing economies, there are unitary, centralized government research boards. But, such a degree of centralization in research funding, where it obtains, is likely to exact a price in terms of the loss of diversity and breadth of vision about matters that are inherently hard to predict. Consequently, even where it is possible to impose a unified structure of coordination and control, it might well not be thought desirable to do so.

What is wanted, therefore, is a mode of policy analysis that takes explicit account of the existence of a multiplicity of R&D funding bodies that are operating in essentially the same areas of scientific inquiry but may be pursuing distinct goals that will be reflected in differentiated criteria for project selection.

Focal Problems for Economic Analysis

In the present chapter we cannot hope to satisfactorily address the entire nexus of issues that are spotlighted by the foregoing questions. Rather, it has the considerably more modest goal of making some headway towards a clearer identification and understanding of the resource allocation problems posed by the two empirical features of the world. Curiously, although these conditions commonly are ignored by theoretical analyses that propose economic rationales for public programmes of research support, it is now ubiquitously apparent that close collaborations may exist among research units, but not necessarily among their potential sponsoring institutions.

The first aspect of reality that we thus must notice explicitly is that, typically, there will be more than one public funding agency whose policies and programmes need to be considered. Within a given national domain there are numerous government agencies, each of which has its own mission and particular goals. It has been noted that competition among rival agencies for the services of experts, including those who are expert in the production of reliable knowledge, in general has the effect of allowing the expert agents to extract better terms of support from their patrons and principals.[7]

While this may well have a direct and important bearing upon the terms and the volume of funding provided for scientific and technological research in the aggregate, that aspect of the influence exerted by the degree of coordination prevailing among sponsoring agencies is not the primary focus of concern here. Instead, we concentrate on the equally interesting, but less studied question of what happens when there are different funding agencies which have quite different objectives, and so might adopt rather different funding criteria. Focusing on such situations deliberately is intended to exclude the entire class of problems that are usually modelled in the economics of R&D, namely the choice of strategies made by funding organizations whose conflicting goals differ in a symmetrical manner. Such is the case in a so-called 'patent race', where rival research sponsors in effect seek to attain the same scientific or engineering objective, but each has the goal of achieving it before all the others.

The second aspect of the observable research scene is that the research units self-organize themselves into coalitions seeking support for proposed projects. Except in the case of public agency procurement contracting, with which we are not concerned here, the sponsoring entity is thus presented with a set of pre-bundled capabilities. Rather than being in a position to assemble the teams that it would wish to fund in a collaborative project, the public agencies responsible for such programmes typically must select among the coalitions that have been constructed with a view to gaining their support. Consequently, in each round of funding an agency's choice set reflects the outcome of the constituent units' efforts to place themselves in as attractive a company as is feasible.

Those efforts, in turn, are predicated upon the research units' knowledge of their own capabilities and those of their peers. They also reflect what is believed about the respects in which appraisal made by their disciplinary peers may diverge from the opinions that are held within the funding body as to the (reputed) abilities and attainments of the pertinent candidates for coalition partnership. Equally influential in the efforts to form coalitions that will prove successful in the competition for support are the researchers' beliefs about the goals of the collaborative research programme and the selection criteria that have been set by the administering agency.

It is no less important to recognize that the research coalitions in question are quite malleable, and in general impose commitments of only rather limited duration upon the members, even when the latter are bound together by formal agreements. The structure of these coalitions may well reflect underlying social relationships among some of the individuals belonging to the constitutive research teams, and the experience they have gained in collaborating successfully on previous projects may induce recurring clusters of participation in successive undertakings.[8] Scientific research collaborations of this variety thus fall neatly into the organizational category of 'networks', being a form more enduring and socially grounded than the canonical anonymous spot-market contract, but more readily formed and dissolved than the canonical business firm.

Their comparative plasticity, or malleability, carries the implication that their composition is more likely to be endogenously determined. The collective characteristics and attributes of the network organizations that compete for funding, therefore, are not fixed by those of the aggregate ensemble of human research agents, or by its individual members, if only because the latter are able to assemble and reassemble in different configurations designed to meet their prevailing perceptions of the properties of the feasible arrangements that will prove most attractive to the sponsoring agency. Research capability, in particular the ability to successfully carry through the project that the network proposes, naturally is likely to be prominent among those properties. But, except where very specific and restrictive research objectives are stipulated (as in procurement contracts), the scientific and

technical goals may be adjusted to accommodate the strengths and limitations of a collaboration which has formed with a view to providing other
'qualities' that are thought to be even more attractive to the funding agency.

In view of the significance that academic research communities attach to
researchers' reputational standing derived from collegiate peer assessments,
not only as a measure of prestige but as a basis for a variety of professional
rewards that include access to research resources, it is reasonable to regard
considerations of scientific reputation as occupying a central role in the
self-organization of research coalitions. Empirical studies of the allocation
of public funding and its impact upon the productivity of research units
points to the importance of distinguishing between the effects of research
competence and scientific standing or reputation. Competence can build
reputation by affecting the record of past experience and achievement, but
in the natural sciences and engineering it is necessary to secure significant
material resources in order for the abilities of an individual or a group to
express themselves in observable accomplishments.

Moreover, the receipt of public funding itself carries a signal that generally augments and rarely if ever diminishes the recipient's scientific repute,
even where considerable uncertainty surrounds the exact nature of the
evaluation criteria upon which the award of support had been based.
Reputation thus figures as a basis of perceived competence, not simply
because hearsay may readily be substituted for knowledge of the true state
of a research unit's capabilities; but because there is a dynamic relationship
through which 'reputation' affects the likelihood of securing access to the
wherewithal for demonstrating those capabilities. In as much as 'reputation' is a property that by definition is readily knowable, and generally will
be widely known within the relevant epistemic community, it is quite understandable that this attribute of a research unit should tend to figure more
powerfully in the competition for research support.

Reputational standing within scientific peer groups thereby occupies the
critical role in the formation of a positive feedback mechanism – described
as 'cumulative advantage' and famously labelled 'the Matthew Effect' by
the sociologist of science, Robert Merton (1968). That type of dynamic
process, which has been found to operate at the level of research units as
well as that of the individual researcher, tends to generate stratification in
the distribution of research productivity and reputational standings.
Competence, by contrast, is a less certain quality. It often has many more
dimensions, but none the less remains difficult to assess *ex ante* by reference
to quantitative indicators. Such 'objective' measures of research competence, not surprisingly, are found by empirical studies to have a less predictable bearing upon the scientific productivity of those units that proved
successful in mobilizing equivalent levels of material support.[9]

Theoretical Approach, and the Principal Findings

The motivation for this chapter therefore derives from the conviction that a useful analytical check can be provided for the intuitive explanations that may be offered for the observed patterns in the organization and conduct of collaborative R&D under the aegis of the European Commission (EC). But, to do so requires developing a more appropriate theoretical framework than those available hitherto. More specifically, what is needed is a formal model of coalition-building ('network' formation) among research units that seek competitive funding from a supra-regional programme, while also drawing support from their respective regional funding agencies. Further, such an analytical structure should admit the possibility that the different governmental entities engaged in supporting research may each follow a distinctive strategy with regard to the project selection criteria they employ. This approach enables one to ask whether there are stable (equilibrium) outcomes in the interactions among the several funding entities, and to investigate what those outcomes would employ for the evolving distribution of scientific performance within the entire region and its national subregions. From the latter, as will be seen, some insights emerge regarding the nature of the optimal strategies that may be pursued by the various funding agencies in such a system.

The analysis of the chapter proceeds in two steps. First, a model is developed to analyse how collaborations are formed under different sets of funding rules of an international funding institution. In this first model, there will initially exist a finite number of research units with an associated distribution of reputed quality, or reputation. The research units may form collaborations in expectation of receiving external funding for their collaboration's research. Collaborations will form in each period according to a set of procedures, described in detail below. Once collaborations are formed, then each of the proposed networks (coalitions) may be awarded some external funding in that period, but not every one of them will be successful in attracting support. The level of funding received is determined according to a rule comparing the distribution of reputations within and across collaborations. Several possible external funding rules are analysed to determine how they impact upon collaboration formation. The evolution of the reputation distribution is tracked with these collaborations.

The first model analysed in this chapter is a repeated non-cooperative game of coalition (or collaboration) formation with the distribution of payoffs within the collaboration according to a fixed rule. Non-cooperative games of coalition formation developed by several authors, including Bloch (1995) and Ray and Vohra (1999), provide a useful framework for this work. Keely (forthcoming) applies this type of game to a multiperiod setting in which a distribution of coalitions is tracked.

The results of this model under various rules are compared with empirical evidence on EC research collaborations to determine which rules are consistent with the evidence. In the second step, various combinations of national and supra-national funding regimes are examined, but all the rules considered stipulate that collaborations are funded as a whole, regardless of the number of members; and that their funding is determined by the absolute level of average reputation, or of the variance in reputation, rather than just the rankings of the proposed networks. To characterize the outcomes, we examine these two moments of the endogenously determined distributions of research 'competence', signalled by the reputation measures. These distributions span the entire ensemble of research units across all countries.

The main conclusions of this simple model of collaboration formation can be summarized in the following way. If the funding institution chooses to fund collaborations of the highest variance in reputation (to promote convergence) rather than collaborations of the highest average reputation (to promote excellence), then leapfrogging in the distribution of reputation by research units becomes possible. Persistence in the collaboration patterns occurs when the funding institution chooses to fund collaboration of the highest mean reputation. Coalitions of a size greater than two are possible only if collaborations are funded on a per unit basis within the network, rather than fixing the level of funding on a per network basis.

The second step of the analysis considers a model with both a supra-national funding agency (such as the EC) and national funding institutions and agencies. For simplicity we abstract from the multiplicity of funding bodies operating at and below the national level, and consider each of the national domains as an integral funding regime. Within each nation there exists a population of research units and an associated distribution of 'scientific reputations' based on current perceptions regarding the units' respective 'competence'. The latter is assumed to be described completely by a cardinal scalar measure. Each of the agencies has a funding rule that can be varied parametrically, and these rules interact to produce a national and supra-national effect on the average and variance of the research reputation of research units within and across nations. Underlying each rule chosen is a supposed goal that the funding entity seeks to attain. It is possible for different sets of rules to work towards or against the goals of the other funding agencies. For example, a funding rule by the supra-national agency may have an effect on the distribution of research competence in the region that is offset by the funding rules chosen by national agencies.

An example is examined, based upon a particular specification of the model in which both multiple national agencies and a supra-national entity provide funding for collaborations within the supra-national domain. This makes it possible to evaluate the consequences of different sets of funding rules, and thus to identify the best response of each agency to the other agencies' funding rules. A Nash equilibrium of funding rules is thus identified for each set of possible national and supra-national agencies' policy goals. Again, the absolute means and variances of the resulting reputation distributions for the ensemble of research units, and for its national partitions, are examined; the corresponding rel-variance measures are also considered.

It is found that when all the funding bodies seek to maximize the average reputation, or to minimize the reputation variance of research units in their respective constituencies, then the best possible outcome for each entity coincides with the Nash equilibrium. The same results obtain when all the funding agencies seek to minimize the respective regions' variance relative to their regional mean levels. Further, it is seen that national agency strategies should involve funding choices that are independent of supra-national funding choices. The outcomes obtained when such (independent) national strategies are followed always dominate those obtained where national funding allocations are conditioned – whether as supplements or offsets – on the allocations made by the supra-national agency. This analysis suggests that further research should focus not on the potential conflict between the EC's own objectives, but, instead, on the policies that national governments have adopted in view of the presence of EC programmes that support research collaborations.

Organization of the Chapter

Section 2 describes a concrete context in which the set of generic R&D policy issues identified by the foregoing discussion are manifestly present: the territory that the Research Directorate of the European Commission recently has begun to refer to as the 'European Research Area' (ERA). The model of research coalition (or collaborative network) formation presented in Section 3 is, in a sense, a caricature of the process through which R&D proposals involving multiple research units are developed. The outcomes of the funding of some among the proposed coalitions over several periods are analysed under the different external agency funding rules and initial reputation distributions, for the case in which individual research units all are sustained by equal fixed levels of internal funding. Particular attention is given to the size, persistence and relative reputational standings of the endogenously formed networks (coalitions). In Section 4, some empirical evidence is reviewed regarding European research collaborations that have been funded under the EU Framework Programmes. These observations are compared with the analytical results obtained with the simple model of Section 3, and they are used to obtain the model presented in Section 5. In the latter, various rules for the funding for transnational research networks under a supra-national agency, are combined with alternative funding policies adopted by national entities for supporting individual research units within their respective national domains. The Nash equilibria corresponding to the various possible policy regimes are examined; a numerical simulation example is presented and the implications and robustness of the results are discussed. Section 6 concludes the chapter, reporting some preliminary results of efforts to ascertain the robustness of the main findings through simulation studies of variant specifications.

2   A CONCRETE POLICY CONTEXT: THE EUROPEAN RESEARCH AREA

Certainly one of the notable features of the institutional arrangements for the public funding of scientific and technological research in the European Union (EU) is the coexistence of a multiplicity of funding programmes that are organized and financed by different levels of government. Such a situation in itself is by no means unique, as it emerges quite naturally within federal governmental structures. Thus, in the United States, both the states and the federal government underwrite research projects; the same may be said in the case of the German Federal Republic and its constituents as well as for the situation prevailing in some Commonwealth countries, for example, Canada and Australia. Actually, this feature appears to be quite ubiquitous, as soon as one looks below the national level: within a number of European states, notably France and Italy, the multilayered structure of support for research activities is manifest in the coexistence of regional and national funding programmes.

The existence of a supra-national governmental entity or agency that allocates public resources to R&D activities undertaken by research units throughout its domain, consequently, is not an idiosyncratic feature that is unique to the EU. A widely shared feature of the situation, however, is the fact that the amount of the funding directly allocated by Europe's national entities (at the sub-ordinate governmental level) is far larger than that which the super-ordinate government authority awards to R&D projects organized in the region. Indeed, the combined level of national funding is approximately of an order of magnitude larger than the RTD (research, training and development) funds allocated by programmes at the regional EU level. Thus, an obvious matter of interest for European science policy is the degree of coordination that exists between the national funding agencies and the programmes devised and implemented from the European Community level, and its consequences for the effectiveness of the goals being pursued at both levels. Furthermore, there are some fundamental questions concerning the alignment of governments' policy goals that underlie many of the practical issues of implementation which, surely, will arise in regard to the recommended programmes for a more coordinated approach to RTD activities under the EU Sixth Framework.[10]

In the European science and technology policy context, therefore, the design of programmes that provide public funding for collaborative research networks – comprising teams that may be institutionally situated anywhere within the EU – is a key strategic vehicle which the European Commission may use to pursue R&D opportunities and challenges that transcend the particular capabilities and concerns of the individual member states. Yet, it must also be recognized that additional, more immediately instrumental considerations of a political and economic kind have shaped the terms and criteria for funding supra-national research. These transient 'coalitions' are the R&D networks, and Targeted Social and Economic Research (TSER) networks that are organized within what the European Commission recently has been referring to as the 'European Research Area' (ERA).[11]

By and large, the research programmes sponsored by the European Commission are designed for strategic explicitly stated purposes. In some instances the aim is to change the objectives and methods of research, or to undertake socially useful lines of investigation that otherwise would be neglected; in many others, the goal is to improve European industry's international competitiveness – by inventing and developing new products and processes, or by forging links between academic and industrial research groups. Still another, more directly political motivation – that of fostering the 'cohesion of Europe', by reducing disparities in its communities' scientific and technical capabilities – has figured in the implementation of some of the RTD programmes organized under the aegis of the Commission.[12]

Thus, since the European Commission's inception, the collaboration among research teams drawn from more than one member country of the EU has been made a necessary condition for funding within the terms of successive European Community Framework Programmes.[13] Of course, the question remains: 'collaborations of which sorts?'. The EC has potentially conflicting goals regarding the criteria for selecting which among the proposed research coalitions (or 'networks') will receive funding under these programmes. In the near term, it seeks to raise the overall R&D productivity of the region as a whole by effectively targeting its support to the collaborative projects that appear best able to make use of the resources. But, at the same time, it has evinced a sustained interest in promoting greater 'cohesion' within the ERA, and specifically the long-term convergence in levels of scientific and technical capability among the member states and provinces of the EU.

More than one observer of European science policy has remarked upon the potential conflict between the strategies that the EC might adopt to achieve the latter goals.[14] Were it to set the selection criteria for project funding primarily with consideration for generating high-quality research findings most efficiently, or with a view to building greater European scientific and technical capabilities on the best foundations, priority would most likely be given to proposals from research units that possessed a higher reputational standing in the relevant scientific area. In the case of network projects, it is thus possible that, with a given overall budget constraint for research funding, the Commission's goal of raising the average level of Europe's scientific and technical capabilities and performance would dictate a strategy of encouraging the strongest research institutions to work with one another. In other words, the selection criterion applied to network projects would give priority to coalitions in which the average reputation level of the members was highest.

Yet, it seems likely that a commitment to attaining that policy objective would preclude adoption of a pure 'pro-cohesion' selection strategy. Under the latter, priority in the allocation of collaborative project funds would be given to proposals from networks in which the variance of the distribution of reputations (for the participating units) was greatest. By encouraging the scientifically strongest research units to collaborate with teams drawn from institutions that currently had much less elevated reputational standings, more opportunities might be created for the occurrence of the sort of knowledge and training spillovers that would promote the convergence of research capabilities across the communities of Europe.[15]

Quite understandably, a considerable amount of attention has been directed to the emblematic tension between these policy objectives and the pure strategies of implementing each in network selection criteria.[16] One might therefore anticipate that the issue will arise anew in connection with discussions of precisely how the contemplated EU Sixth Framework (2002–2006) Programme for funding 'Networks of Excellence' should be implemented. The term 'excellence' might be interpreted variously, for example, as 'present scientific excellence' or as 'promoting the future excellence' of European scientific research.[17]

But, consideration of the matter of conflicts among R&D policy goals takes on special complexity in the European context, where, as has been pointed out, the provision of research support through the EC's collaborative programmes is hardly 'the only game in town'. The national agencies engaged in supporting research activities may also have a variety of objectives, including the improvement of the general level of the scientific prestige and performance of the research units that are based in their respective territorial domains; or they too may be concerned to reduce internal regional disparities in their 'quality', as gauged by scientific and technical capabilities. If EC and national governments choose to focus on one or the other goal, the actual joint impact of their implementation strategies might well yield unexpected outcomes – or at least outcomes that will be unexpected by the agencies if they fail to take account of each other's existence and strategy choices. Correspondingly, the design of rational public funding policies in this realistically complicated context calls for explicit consideration of the effects of the activities being undertaken by the other governmental agencies that have 'jurisdiction' within the territory in question.

3   A MODEL OF COLLABORATION FORMATION WITH AN ENDOGENOUS EXTERNALITY

Notation and Key Assumptions

The model developed here is intended to capture some important elements of the way in which research collaborations form and evolve over time. Academics join departments, research groups join with other research groups in order to work on particular problems together. Part of the purpose of these collaborations can be to apply for funding towards the research undertaken together, or at least with some level of interaction to facilitate individual research. The award of external funding can produce an effect on next period's reputation of each research unit in the group. Reputation is assumed to be cumulative in this model, with reputation measured as a stock and external funding contributing to the stock.

There are a fixed set N of research units,[18] indexed by $n = \{1, ..., N\}$. The research unit's size and composition depends on the particular context. A research unit may denote, for instance, a person, a research department, or an academic agency. In any one context, each research unit is taken to have the same reputation. Each research unit has a reputation at each period t, $r_n(t)$ and a reputation change denoted $\Delta r_n(t+1)$. Initial reputation is denoted as $r_n(0)$. Initial reputation is assumed to be distributed uniformly across research units. This assumption is somewhat special. However, it simplifies and extends the possible analysis. The results of the chapter depend somewhat on this assumption, as they would hold for some other distributions of reputation but not all. Effects of changing this assumption are discussed with the results.

A collaboration[19] structure $\pi(t)$ is a partition on the set N. The set of all collaborations we denote by Π. A collaboration structure $\pi(t)$ consists of a set of $C(t)$ collaborations, indexed by $c = \{1, ..., C(t),\}$ so $\pi(t) = \{c(t)\}$. Each collaboration c contains a non-empty subset of N, consisting of $N_c(t)$ ≥ 2 research units. The payoff vector for each research unit in a collaboration is $\Delta r_n(t+1)$: $\Pi \rightarrow \mathfrak{R}$, where $\mathfrak{R}$ is the set of real numbers. A method for determining the fixed payoff to reputation will be commonly known *ex ante*. Reputation is non-transferable, as there is no bargaining over payoff division within a collaboration. For any subset K of N, the set of partitions of K is Π_K with typical element π_K.

There is a rule of order $\theta(t)$ for N, used to determine the order of moves in the sequential game of collaboration formation. This rule $\theta(t)$ specifies that the order of moves will be descending in the current reputation of each research unit. We will call the game $\Gamma[\Delta r_n(t+1), n = 1, ..., N, \theta(t)]$ because collaboration formation may depend on:

- the specification of reputation building, which derives from any element of Π and the implied $\Delta r_n(t+1)$ given a set N and initial reputation levels for each research unit; and
- the rule of order θ for a given set N.

External Funding Rules

Reputation building $\Delta r_n(t+1)$ is assumed to be equal to at least some minimum greater than zero, and above that it is a direct result of external funding. That is, reputation building can occur due to effort that will occur with or without the external funding, although external funding will increase the reputation building possible. External funding is measured in units of reputation.

External funding to an entire collaboration $E_c[\Pi(t)]$ is non-negative and will be determined by three rules, each of which may vary as described above. These rules are set before the game begins in period 0 and they are commonly known to all research units. To repeat, these variations in the rules are:

- External funding depends on either the average reputation of a collaboration c, $\bar{r}_c(t)$, or the reputation variance, var $[r_n(t), n \in N_c(t)]$, of a collaboration. Denoting the selected measure of a collaboration's reputation as $m_c(t) = \bar{r}_c(t)$ or $m_c(t) = $ var $[r_n(t), n \in N_c(t)]$, the external funding will be non-decreasing in that measure, $\partial E_c[\Pi(t)]/\partial m_c(t) \geq 0$.
- External funding of a collaboration is defined either as per collabor-

ation with equal distribution between research unit members or as per research unit within a collaboration. If external funding is per collaboration, then $\partial E_c[\Pi(t)]/\partial N_c(t) = 0$ (although it is possible that $dE_c[\Pi(t)]/dN_c(t) \leq 0$). Thus, as the size of a collaboration increases then, all else equal, the external funding per research unit will decrease.[20] If external funding is per research unit within a collaboration, then $\partial E_c[\Pi(t)]/\partial N_c(t) > 0$ (and it is still possible that $dE_c[\Pi(t)]/dN_c(t) \leq 0$).

- External funding of a collaboration will be based on either absolute $m_c(t)$ or relative $w[m_c(t); m_k(t) \; k = 1, ..., C]$ measures of its reputation distribution, where $w[m_c(t); m_k(t) \; k = 1, ..., C]$ is the rank of collaboration c relative to all collaborations at a period t. Either $\partial E_c[\Pi(t)]/\partial m_c(t) > 0$ if the absolute measure is used, or $\partial E_c[\Pi(t)] / \partial w[m_c(t); m_k(t) k = 1,...,C] > 0$ if the relative measure is used.

Each of the eight possible forms of external funding is analysed and their outcomes compared.

A Description of the Collaboration Formation Game

The formation of collaborations occurs according to a non-cooperative game. An advantage of using a non-cooperative game is that it allows for explicit analysis of how collaborations form and the strategies of research units. The main drawback of using a non-cooperative game of coalition formation is that additional structure – an order of play – must be imposed on the game in order to define players' strategies. However, in the setting described here, such an order of play seems an appropriate abstraction. When forming research collaborations, it is reasonable that a research unit with a high reputation would have some ability to suggest collaborations in which that research unit would be willing to take part before other research units of lesser reputation. The structure of the non-cooperative game utilized is similar to that developed by Bloch (1995). The identifying details of the agents and the application are specific to this chapter's model.

Collaborations are formed sequentially in each period t according to the game $\Gamma [\Delta r_n (t + 1), n = 1, ..., N, \theta (t)]$. Each player knows the reputation stocks of the set N, $\{r_n (t)\}_{n \in N}$. The first research unit according to $\theta(t)$ proposes the formation of a collaboration T to which it will belong. Each potential member of T responds to the proposal in the order given by $\theta(t)$. If one player rejects the proposal, it makes a counteroffer and proposes a collaboration T' to which it will belong. If all potential members accept, the collaboration is formed. All members of T would then form the collaboration and leave the game, and the first research unit in $N\backslash T$ according to

$\theta(t)$ makes a proposal. Note that once a collaboration is formed, the game is then played only by the remaining players. Once a player joins a collaboration, it cannot leave or propose to change the collaboration in that period.[21] The game is completed in a period t when either all research units are part of a collaboration, or when none of the remaining research units is willing to propose a collaboration.

A history of the game $h_v(t)$ at stage v in period t is a list of offers, acceptances and rejections up to stage v in period t. A history thus implies: the set $\hat{K}[h_v(t)]$ of research units who have formed collaborations, the coalition structure $\pi_{\hat{K}[hv(t)]}$ formed by those research units, any ongoing proposal $\hat{T}[h_v(t)]$, a set of research units who have accepted the ongoing proposal and which research unit proposes at stage v.

A research unit n is active at history $h_v(t)$ if it is its turn to accept/reject or propose after the history $h_v(t)$. The set of histories at period t at which a research unit n is active is $H_n(t)$. A strategy $\sigma_{vn}(t)$ for a research unit n is a mapping from $H_n(t)$ to its set of actions, that is

$$\sigma_n[h_v(t)] \in \{\text{Yes, No}\} \text{ if } \hat{T}[h_v(t)] \neq \phi$$
$$\sigma_n[h_v(t)] \in \{T \subset LS\backslash\hat{K}[h_v(t)], j \in T\} \text{ if } \hat{T}[h_v(t)] = 0.$$

If $\hat{T}[h_v(t)] \neq \phi$ then research unit n must accept or reject the ongoing proposal. If $\hat{T}[h_v(t)] = \phi$ then research unit n is the first research unit in $N\backslash\hat{K}[h_v(t)]$ according to the order rule $\theta(t)$ or else research unit n has just rejected a proposal and it must now propose a new collaboration.

A strategy profile $\sigma(t) = \{\sigma_n(t)\}_{n\in N\backslash K}$ determines the outcome $\pi[\sigma(t)]$.

Equilibrium Definition and Properties

We now clarify the concept of equilibrium in this model. The payoff for a research unit n is given by:

$$\Delta r_n(t+1) = {}^{\max}_{\pi}\Delta r_n(\pi) = \Delta r_n\{E_c[\Pi(t)]; n \in c\} \, \forall n \in N.$$

A subgame perfect equilibrium $\sigma^*(t)$ is a strategy profile such that $\forall n \in N$, $\forall h_v(t) \in H_n(t)$, $\forall \sigma_n(t)$, $\Delta r_n\{\pi[\sigma^*_n(t), \sigma^*_{-n}(t)]\} \geq \Delta r_n\{\pi[\sigma_n(t), \sigma^*_{-n}(t)]\}$.

There exists a subgame perfect equilibrium of the game

$$\Gamma[\Delta r_n(t+1), n = 1, \dots, N, \theta(t)].$$

Proof This result is proved by Bloch (1995, pp. 97–8).

This result is proved by Bloch by showing first that in a game with sufficient time discounting, a subgame perfect equilibrium will exist because players' payoffs will decrease if they wait too long before settling on an outcome. It is then shown that a subgame perfect equilibrium with sufficient time discounting is also a subgame perfect equilibrium of the game $\Gamma\left[\Delta r_n\left(t+1\right), n=1, ..., N, \theta(t)\right]$.

Equilibrium Collaborations

The selection criterion of a given 'funding regime' is defined according to whether the agency will assign priority scores to collaborations according to the average (or the variance) of the partners' reputational standings, and will allocate funds on the basis of these absolute scores (or the coalitions' relative rankings). Combining the binary variants of these two dimensions of the funding regime with the pair of alternative budget-setting rules (fix either the level of funding per collaboration, or per research unit participating in the collaboration), there are 8 different cases of the funding regime to be considered.

For each of these cases the object of this stage of the analysis is the same: to describe the pattern of endogenous coalition formation that represents an equilibrium at a given moment of time, and then to track how that pattern will be modified over time as the effects of funding allocations, and the research outcomes they permit, alter the reputational distribution in the population of research units.

Comparisons of the way that the funding regime's institutional features affect the distribution of reputed research competence is then possible, albeit in a highly stylized sense. Do some sets of funding rules result in a tendency towards reputational convergence within the population as a whole, whereas the effect of other rules is an increase in the variance of the distribution of reputations in absolute terms, or possibly also in relation to the mean of the distribution? Also of interest is the question of whether the equilibrium coalitional is unique for some funding regimes, and whether a multiplicity of equilibria exist in other cases. Then there is the question of the influence of the funding regime's features upon the size of the equilibrium coalition(s) whose formation it will induce: is the number of partners tightly circumscribed by a given regime, or can it vary widely?

In Table 8.1 the eight variants we have considered are identified and assigned 'case' numbers, which are used, in turn, by Table 8.2 to label the summary of the analytical results. The details of the analysis are presented for all 8 cases in Appendix 8A1: Equilibria of the Coalition-formation Game with a Single Funding Agency. From the tables it may be seen immediately that the answer to the questions posed above in every instance is: 'yes'. In 6 of the 8 cases the size of the equilibrium structure of the induced

Table 8.1   Summary of cases

	Maximize average		Maximize variance	
Per collaboration	Absolute	Case 1	Absolute	Case 3
	Relative	Case 5	Relative	Case 7
Per research unit	Absolute	Case 2	Absolute	Case 4
	Relative	Case 6	Relative	Case 8

Table 8.2   Summary of results

	Average		Variance	
Per collaboration	1. Absolute	Size 2; unique; variance increasing	3. Absolute	Size 2; unique; variance increasing under uniform distribution
	5. Relative	Size 2; multiplicity; leapfrogging possible	7. Relative	Size 2; multiplicity; leapfrogging possible
Per research unit	2. Absolute	Size 2; unique; variance increasing	4. Absolute	Size 2; unique, variance increasing under uniform distribution
	6. Relative	Size 2 to *N*; multiplicity; leapfrogging possible	8. Relative	Size 2 to *N*; multiplicity; leapfrogging possible

coalitions is tightly circumscribed, at 2 partners; and in 4 of those 6 the equilibrium structure is uniquely defined. But there are 4 other cases in which a multiplicity of equilibria exists, and for 2 among those more than one coalition size is possible. In 4 of the 8 cases the absolute variance of the reputation-measure among the research units in the population will be increasing unambiguously from one round of the funding competition to the next, but the ordering of reputational standings remains undisturbed. But in the other half of the cases, there can be 'leapfrogging' – in which some units surge upwards in the reputational rankings, while others drop behind. In some instances this can result in convergence in the distribution.[22]

4   THE FORMATION OF SUPRA-NATIONAL RESEARCH NETWORKS

In the model of collaboration formation, when the research funds are allocated towards the highest average reputation collaborations, then the collaboration pattern is a partition of disjoint subsets along the reputation distribution. Further, the variance will unambiguously increase. When the research funds are allocated towards the highest reputation variance collaborations, then the collaboration pattern is no longer a partition and leapfrogging in the reputation distribution becomes possible. The overall variance may not increase.

When funding is allocated on a fixed per collaboration basis, then the equilibrium collaboration size is always the minimum of 2. When funding is allocated per unit, then collaborations become insensitive to the size of the collaboration, and so larger collaborations are possible in equilibrium.

Lastly, if funding is allocated based on a collaboration's absolute measure of average reputation or reputation variance, then the collaboration equilibrium is unique. On the other hand, if funding is allocated solely on the basis of the networks' respective rankings according to whichever measure is appropriate for the agencies' goals, then a multiplicity of equilibria appears in the array of networks which can be formed.

It is of some interest to ask which, among the variety of stylized funding regimes just considered, is the one that should be thought to most closely resemble the general features of recent EU funding for RTD under the Economic Commission's Framework Programmes. Two quite different approaches might be taken to answering this question. One might try to extract the essentials of the complex and not always transparent process of allocating grants and contracts, or, alternatively, make use of the implications of the theoretical model of research coalition formation to extract inferences about the salient characteristics of the regime – reasoning backwards from empirical observations about the outcomes of the operations of these R&D programmes. We take the second option, partly because the purpose here is not to detail the administrative realities of EU R&D funding. A further reason is that, as will be seen, the juxtaposition of available empirical observations and the coalition formation model's implications serve to underscore several respects in which the highly stylized nature of the model limits its direct applicability for the task of designing funding policies in the European Research Area.

A number of empirical points may be cited in support of the argument that publicly funded transnational research collaborations in Europe resemble those that, on theoretical grounds, would be expected to form in a 'regime' corresponding to Case 1: funding priority given to collaborations with higher average reputational standing, allocation of funds on the basis of absolute reputational scores and budget rules that fix the level of funding per collaboration (rather than per partner).

First, the pattern of concentration, or left-skewness, in the distribution of R&D output (such as publications and patents), is evident among European research institutions. A small proportion of research units contribute a large proportion of the research results, just as a small proportion of individual researchers are found to be (at least nominally) responsible for the majority of scientific and technological publications (see David 1994). This may be in part due to the information signalling problem that affects funding decisions: funders may use past success as a signal of future potential success. This criterion leads to the familiar cumulative advantage phenomenon associated with the Matthew Effect in science. The application of such a criterion may not bestow support upon those research institutions that actually have the greatest research productivity potential for the programme in question. Nevertheless, being able to achieve more funding may allow institutions with strong reputations to draw support, and thus reinforce stratification rather than convergence within the distribution of Europe's research units.

The Matthew Effect is consistent with the average reputation funding rule, which implies an increased variance in the reputation distribution. It is also consistent with the use of an absolute measure of average reputation, as the unique equilibrium implies persistence in the units that are funded via collaboration.

Second, the determinants of participation in the European research coalitions that receive EC funding have been identified in empirical work (see Geuna 1999b). Past research success, consistent with the Matthew Effect, appears to be a main indicator. Larger and older universities, in particular, have a higher participation rate in these coalitions than other universities. Finally, country effects appear to be important – some countries (such as Ireland) have a higher rate of participation than others (such as France).

The influence of past research success also supports the use of an absolute measure of average reputation, as use of this measure implies persistence in the distribution of reputation.

Third, the types of participants have changed over time. There has been increased homogenization of research institutions over time, the variety of institutions has decreased. The size of the coalitions has decreased over time. (For details of this, see Garcia-Fontes and Geuna 1999.)

An increase in the homogeneity of funded research units is, again, consistent with persistence in the units that are funded over time. Persistence is a result of a unique equilibrium, as when the absolute level of average reputation is used to determine funding.[23] The decrease in the number of institutions corresponds with a move from funding per unit to funding per collaboration.

The obvious trouble with the foregoing inferences is that, as may be seen by consulting Table 8.2, the implication of the funding regime corresponding to Case 1 is that the equilibrium size of the coalitions should never exceed 2 partners.[24] Yet, both from casual observation and from the systematic studies (by Garcia-Fontes and Geuna 1999 and Geuna 1999b) of the participation of university-based research units in EU Framework Programmes, it is apparent that there typically are many more than 2 partners. Indeed, that is the case even within the recurring subgroups of 'core partners' ('network clusters') that are found to have drawn funding from the successive Framework Programmes.

What the foregoing discrepancy suggests is that those who take the lead in the coalition formation process give due weight to the possibility that other criteria may enter into the process of project selection, so that their own expected funding awards may be raised by the recruitment of additional partners even though doing so tends to reduce the average partner's share of the amount awarded. In as much as many of the research problems undertaken call for a variety of technical skills and expertise, and the population of potential partners is heterogeneous in this respect, this is hardly surprising. It is also reasonable to suppose that applicants for funding do not presume to know with certainty the relative weights that will be given to the various selection criteria in the funding process; rather than 'optimize' on the basis of false certainty, the coalition members are buying a form of 'insurance' by enlarging their collaboration by the inclusion of a more diverse collection of partners whose presence augments the attractiveness of the ensemble to the funding agency. These considerations, however realistic, lie beyond the reach of our present modelling efforts. By the same token, they indicate the limits of applicability of the findings as a basis for advancing specific institutional policy designs.

5   A MODEL OF NATIONAL AND SUPRA-NATIONAL RESEARCH FUNDING

A model of national and supra-national research funding is now developed to determine how the funding rules of these two types of institutions interact. The effects on the distribution of reputation both within nations and supra-nationally are analysed. Different rule combinations on the distribution will be compared.

Behind each of these rules is a goal of each funding agency; rules will be chosen in the light of those goals. It is possible to evaluate each agency's rule choice given the goal of that agency and the goals and rules of the other institutions. After a general analysis under each possible combination of rules is presented, an example will be developed. This example will allow for more exact comparison of different combinations of rules, in order to determine which rules will be equilibrium strategies for each agency in the light of the goals of each agency. These results are used to suggest how national and EC funding institutions should approach funding research. Equilibrium rules are determined in order to draw general lessons for how the national and supra-national institutions should fund R&D in the presence of each other.

It may be noted that the 'either/or' formulation is a convenient simplification that allows us to assess the contrasting effects of the external criteria, so long as it corresponds to the set of beliefs about the agency's goals that are held among the research units when they consider forming collaborations to seek funding. But to the extent that there is uncertainty as to which of the extrema (max the average, versus max the variance) actually best characterizes the funding agency's selection criterion, then the characteristics of the coalitions that formed would differ from those indicated by our model, and the results of the analysis would be correspondingly altered.

In this model, the supra-national agency will continue to fund collaborations, but these collaborations must include research units from more than one nation. National institutions will fund individual research units within their national borders. Each agency will have a goal that it is trying to achieve through its funding. This goal will be either to improve the average reputation of its research constituency, or to decrease the variance in reputation of its research constituency. These goals correspond to the two stated goals of the EC, described in the Introduction and Section 2.

It is assumed that there are two nations, indexed by 1 and 2. They have the same number of research units in each, $N_1 = N_2$ and $N_1 + N_2 = N$ is the total number of research units in the economy. Research units $n \in [1, ..., N]$ are ordered by their reputation and their reputation will be uniformly distributed. In particular, all nation 2 units will be assumed to have a higher reputation than all nation 1 units: $r_n > r_m$, $n \in [N_1 + 1, ..., N]$, $m \in [1, ..., N_1]$.

The number of collaborations funded k will be assumed small relative to the total number of research units in each nation. The funding per research unit from a collaboration will be assumed larger than the national funding per research unit. However, the total amount of funding from collaborations is assumed smaller than the total funding from national institutions, in accordance with empirical evidence referred to in the Introduction and Section 4.

It will be taken as given that collaborations are funded on a per collaboration basis and based on an absolute measure of the collaboration's reputation average or variance. Therefore, as follows from the analysis detailed in Appendix 8A2, and the next subsection and summarized by Table 8.2, a unique set of collaborations, each having exactly 2 partners will be formed and a subset of them will be selected to receive funding according to the criteria of the national and supra-national agencies.

Funding from supra-national institutions and from national institutions will determine the change in reputation for each research unit, Δr_n. The magnitude of the effect of the collaboration c on the increase in average reputation level depends on the functional relationship between the reputation average of a collaboration and its funding level $E_c[\Pi(t)]$ and the functional relationship between the funding level and reputation building $\Delta r_n \{E_c[\Pi(t)]; n \in c\}$. If there is a constant returns relationship in both cases, then the size and number of collaborations will not affect the rate of increase in the overall average reputation level of research units. Empirical evidence from Arora et al. (1998) suggests that the effect of reputation level on the change in reputation level exhibits diminishing returns.

Therefore, this assumption will be adopted; funding will be assumed to have a diminishing returns effect on Δr_n. However, this diminishing returns will be of a special type. It will also be assumed that collaboration and individual funding will increase in the absolute level of the reputation of the funded unit(s). Funding will increase by reputation in such a way that the change in reputation for all units receiving the same type of funding (or both types) will be equal. In other words, Δr_n can be identified from the source of research funding only. The change in reputation due to research funding to a unit from a collaboration will be denoted as Δr_H; from a national source as Δr_L. In the case that neither source of funding is received, it will be assumed that the change in reputation is equal to v:

$$\Delta r_H > \Delta r_L > v.$$

Several combinations of funding rules are to be considered and compared. First, as has been alluded to, the supra-national agency will fund k collaborations that have either the highest average reputation or the highest reputation variance. Each national agency can follow three main rules: it can fund individual research units independently of the funding decision of the supra-national agency, it can fund only research units that have not been funded by the supra-national agency, or it can fund only research units that have been funded by the supra-national agency. If research units are funded independently by the national agency, then it will fund all equally, or fund only the top half of the reputation distribution, or fund only the

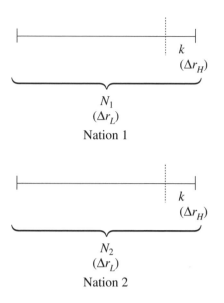

Figure 8.1   Case 1Ai

bottom half of the reputation distribution. It will be assumed that all national institutions follow the same funding rule.

The Interaction of National and Supra-national Funding Regimes

The possible combinations of national and supra-national funding rules generate 10 different 'mixed funding regimes', each constituting a case that must be examined in turn. The first of these is exhibited in the text below, with the explanatory Figure 8.1, in order to give the reader the flavour of the calculations that are involved in determining the outcome of the inter-actions between the funding rules and the equilibrium coalitions whose for-mation they induce. Details of the remaining (9) cases, some of which are considerably more complicated, may be followed in Appendix 8A2.

Before funding takes place, the initial averages and variances in reputa-tion for each nation and for the entire economy are:

$$\bar{r}_1 = \frac{\sum_1^{N_1} r_n}{N_1}; \; \bar{r}_2 = \frac{\sum_1^{N_2} r_n}{N_2}; \; \bar{r} = \frac{\sum_1^{N} r_n}{N}$$

$$\text{var}_1 = \frac{\sum_1^{N_1}(r_n - \bar{r}_1)^2}{N_1}; \; var_2 = \frac{\sum_1^{N_2}(r_n - \bar{r}_2)^2}{N_2}; \; var = \frac{\sum_1^{N}(r_n - \bar{r})^2}{N}$$

The possible combinations of national and supra-national funding rules are now considered in turn.

1. The national agency funds independently of the supra-national agency decision.
A. The national agency funds all research units in the nation to produce an equal change in reputation.
i. The supra-national agency funds the k highest average reputation collaborations.

This case is depicted in Figure 8.1, explaining which units are funded and what their resulting change in reputation is. The illustration is used to calculate the new averages and variances. The new average for each nation is clearly higher:

$$\bar{r}_{1A} = \frac{\Sigma_1^{N_1} r_n}{N_1} + \frac{[(N_1 - k)\Delta r_L + k(\Delta r_H + \Delta r_L)]}{N_1};$$

$$\bar{r}_{2A} = \frac{\Sigma_1^{N_2} r_n}{N_2} + \frac{[(N_2 - k)\Delta r_L + k(\Delta r_H + \Delta r_L)]}{N_2};$$

the new overall average is

$$\bar{r}_A = \frac{\Sigma_1^N r_n}{N} + \frac{[(N - 2k)\Delta r_L + 2k(\Delta r_H + \Delta r_L)]}{N}.$$

The new variance for each nation is also unambiguously higher:

$$\text{var}_{1A} = \frac{\Sigma_1^{N_1}(r_n - \bar{r}_1)^2}{N_1} + \frac{\Sigma_1^{N_1}(\Delta r_n - \Delta \bar{r}_1)^2}{N_1} + \frac{2\Sigma_1^{N_1}(r_n - \bar{r}_1)(\Delta r_n - \Delta \bar{r}_1)}{N_1}; \quad (8.1)$$

$$\text{var}_{2A} = \frac{\Sigma_1^{N_2}(r_n - \bar{r}_2)^2}{N_2} + \frac{\Sigma_1^{N_2}(\Delta r_n - \Delta \bar{r}_2)^2}{N_2} + \frac{2\Sigma_1^{N_2}(r_n - \bar{r}_2)(\Delta r_n - \Delta \bar{r}_2)}{N_2}; \quad (8.2)$$

and the new overall variance is also unambiguously higher:

$$\text{var}_A = \frac{\Sigma_1^N(r_n - \bar{r})^2}{N} + \frac{\Sigma_1^N(\Delta r_n - \Delta \bar{r})^2}{N} + \frac{2\Sigma_1^N(r_n - \bar{r})(\Delta r_n - \Delta \bar{r})}{N}. \quad (8.3)$$

In particular, it is straightforward to show that the third terms of the right-hand side of (8.1), (8.2) and (8.3) are positive.

A Numerical Example

These 10 cases are exemplified through specific assumptions on the variables. The main purpose of using an example is that comparisons between the effects of the rule combinations is simple. It is possible to determine the best strategies to be chosen by each funding agency given its goal and the goal of the other institutions.

The assumptions used in the example are as follows. The size of the two nations are $N_1 = N_2 = 100$; the number of collaborations funded by the supra-national agency is $k = 15$. The initial reputation distributions across the two nations are uniformly distributed and disjoint: $r_n < r_m \ \forall n \in N_1, m \in N_2$. In particular, $r_n \in [50,149]$ and $r_m \in [150, 249]$. The effect of funding on reputation from the different types of funding are: $\Delta r_H = 10$ from supra-national agency funding of collaborations, $\Delta r_L = 5$ from national agency funding of individual research units, and the change in reputation is $v = 2$ if there is no funding from either source. The results of this example under each case are summarized in Table 8.3 and in Tables 8.4a–c.

Using these tables, a Nash equilibrium for each set of institutional goals can be determined. If the supra-national agency wants to maximize the increase in the overall reputation average, and the national institutions each want to maximize the increase in their national reputation average, then the Nash equilibria correspond to each national agency funding all of its research units equally, and the supra-national agency funding either the highest average collaborations, or the highest variance collaborations (cases 1Ai and 1Aii). These strategies not only correspond to Nash equilibria, they also result in the best possible outcomes for each agency *given their goals*.

In the case where the supra-national agency's goal is to minimize variance and the national institutions' goals are to minimize their national variances, the strategies (rules) in Nash equilibrium are for national institutions to fund the bottom half of the research unit reputation distribution and for the supra-national agency to fund the k highest variance collaborations. The Nash equilibrium represents the best possible outcomes for all of the institutions given their goals.

The Nash equilibrium strategies are the same in the case where the supra-national agency's goal is to maximize the overall average reputation, while each nation's goal is to minimize the national variance of reputation. The Nash equilibrium results in the best possible outcome for the national institutions, but not for the supra-national agency.

When the supra-national agency's goal is to minimize overall variance and the national institutions' goals are to maximize their national reputation averages, then the Nash equilibrium strategies are for the supra-national agency to fund the top k variance collaborations and for the national institutions to fund all of its research units equally. This Nash equilibrium again provides a best possible outcome for the national institutions, but not for the supra-national agency.

Table 8.3 Example summary

| | Before | After Rules | | | | | | | | | |
		1Ai	1Aii	1Bi	1Bii	1Ci	1Cii	2i	2ii	3i	3ii
Average region 1	99.50	106.00	106.00	104.50	104.20	104.20	104.50	105.25	105.25	103.45	103.45
Variance region 1	841.67	983.33	725.76	1065.91	821.27	875.82	656.82	909.28	780.49	1030.86	696.01
Var/avg region 1	8.46	9.28	6.85	10.20	7.88	8.41	6.29	8.64	7.42	9.96	6.73
Var/avg sqd region 1	0.09	0.09	0.06	0.10	0.08	0.08	0.06	0.08	0.07	0.10	0.07
Average region 2	199.50	206.00	206.00	204.50	204.50	204.20	204.20	205.25	205.25	203.45	203.45
Variance region 2	841.67	983.33	983.33	1,065.91	1,065.91	875.82	875.82	909.28	909.28	1,030.86	1,030.86
Var/avg region 2	4.22	4.77	4.77	5.21	5.21	4.29	4.29	4.43	4.43	5.07	5.07
Var/avg sqd region 2	0.02	0.02	0.02	0.03	0.03	0.02	0.02	0.02	0.02	0.02	0.02
Average overall	149.50	156.00	156.00	154.50	154.35	154.20	154.35	155.25	155.25	153.45	153.45
Variance overall	3,350.00	3,490.95	3,362.81	3,573.12	3,466.51	3,383.98	3,259.98	3,417.27	3,353.20	3,538.24	3,371.66
Var/avg overall	22.41	22.38	21.56	23.13	22.46	21.95	21.12	22.01	21.60	23.06	21.97
Var/avg sqd overall	0.15	0.14	0.14	0.15	0.15	0.14	0.14	0.14	0.14	0.15	0.14

Table 8.4a Comparison of average reputations across funding regimes

Average after	Supra-national rules	
	Fund k highest average	Fund k highest variance
Overall		
National rules		
Fund independently		
Fund all	156.00	156.00
Fund top half	154.50	154.35
Fund bottom half	154.20	154.35
Fund those not funded supra-nationally	155.25	155.25
Fund only those funded supra-nationally	153.45	153.45
Region 1		
National rules		
Fund independently		
Fund all	106.00	106.00
Fund top half	104.50	104.20
Fund bottom half	104.20	104.50
Fund those not funded supra-nationally	105.25	105.25
Fund only those funded supra-nationally	103.45	103.45
Region 2		
National rules		
Fund independently		
Fund all	206.00	206.00
Fund top half	204.50	204.50
Fund bottom half	204.20	204.20
Fund those not funded supra-nationally	205.25	205.25
Fund only those funded supra-nationally	203.45	203.45

These equilibria can be summarized in the following way: the supra-national agency should always choose to fund the top k variance collaborations regardless of the goals of each agency. The national agency should fund all of its research units equally when its goal is to maximize its national reputation average, and should fund the bottom half of its research units when its goal is to minimize its national reputation variance. The national agencies rules hold regardless of the rule adopted by the supra-national agency.

As a check on robustness, several related exercises are carried out. In short, the result of these exercises is that the results reported above are indeed robust to several alternative assumptions. Alternative assumptions

Table 8.4b   Comparison of reputation variances across funding regimes

Average after	Supra-national rules	
	Fund k highest average	Fund k highest variance
Overall		
National rules		
Fund independently		
Fund all	3,490.95	3,362.81
Fund top half	3,573.12	3,466.51
Fund bottom half	3,383.98	3,259.98
Fund those not funded supra-nationally	3,417.27	3,353.20
Fund only those funded supra-nationally	3,538.24	3,371.66
Region 1		
National rules		
Fund independently		
Fund all	983.33	725.76
Fund top half	1,065.91	821.27
Fund bottom half	875.82	656.82
Fund those not funded supra-nationally	909.28	780.49
Fund only those funded supra-nationally	1,030.86	696.01
Region 2		
National rules		
Fund independently		
Fund all	983.33	983.33
Fund top half	1,065.91	1,065.91
Fund bottom half	875.82	875.82
Fund those not funded supra-nationally	909.28	909.28
Fund only those funded supra-nationally	1,030.86	1,030.86

on the initial distribution of reputations were considered. Both overlap across the two nations' distributions and left-skewness in each nation's distributions were considered. These alternatives do not change the results. Altering the measurement of reputation and change in reputation by using the natural log of each value does not change the results (see Tables 8.5a–c). Variations in k, the number of collaborations funded by the supra-national agency, do not affect the results so long as k is not too large. When k is large (75 or larger) then the results affected are those of the variance/(mean-squared) variable only (see Table 8.3), which is not a variable focused on in our analysis.

The use of the variance of reputation, rather than the variance/mean, for

Table 8.4c   Comparison of reputation variance/mean across funding regimes

Variance/mean after	Supra-national rules	
	Fund k highest average	Fund k highest variance
Overall		
National rules		
Fund independently		
Fund all	22.38	21.56
Fund top half	23.13	22.46
Fund bottom half	21.95	21.12
Fund those not funded supra-nationally	22.01	21.60
Fund only those funded supra-nationally	23.06	21.97
Region 1		
National rules		
Fund independently		
Fund all	9.28	6.85
Fund top half	10.20	7.88
Fund bottom half	8.41	6.29
Fund those not funded supra-nationally	8.64	7.42
Fund only those funded supra-nationally	9.96	6.73
Region 2		
National rules		
Fund independently		
Fund all	4.77	4.77
Fund top half	5.21	5.21
Fund bottom half	4.29	4.29
Fund those not funded supra-nationally	4.43	4.43
Fund only those funded supra-nationally	5.07	5.07

the analysis, may be subject to question. Again, in terms of the results, use of one or the other does not alter our conclusions. This is clear from Tables 8.3 and 8.4a–c. Conceptually, it is the view of the authors that the use of variance is appropriate for at least two reasons. First, variance in reputation here is used to capture inequality in reputation. Controlling variance by the mean causes inequality to be measured relative to reputation level. It is not clear that this is desirable in the abstract, or what policy-makers have in mind. Consider discussions of income inequality. There, a commonly used measure of inequality is the Gini coefficient which, like variance, does not control for the level of income. Gini coefficients are

Table 8.5a   Comparison of average natural log reputations across funding regimes

Average after	Supra-national rules	
	Fund *k* highest average	Fund *k* highest variance
Overall (LN)		
National rules		
Fund independently		
Fund all	4.618	4.631
Fund top half	4.598	4.607
Fund bottom half	4.604	4,619
Fund those not funded supra-nationally	4.613	4.620
Fund only those funded supra-nationally	4.589	4.606
Region 1 (LN)		
National rules		
Fund independently		
Fund all	4.618	4.631
Fund top half	4.598	4.607
Fund bottom half	4.604	4.619
Fund those not funded supra-nationally	4.613	4.620
Fund only those funded supra-nationally	4.589	4.606
Region 2 (LN)		
National rules		
Fund independently		
Fund all	5.316	5.316
Fund top half	4.598	4.607
Fund bottom half	4.604	4.619
Fund those not funded supra-nationally	4.613	4.620
Fund only those funded supra-nationally	4.589	4.606

compared across countries with very different average per capita incomes. Thus, there is precedence for using measures of inequality that do not control for the level of the variable considered.

There is also a connection between the measure of cohesion of research units and assumptions regarding spillovers across research units that collaborate. Implicitly, we have assumed diminishing returns to research funding that depend only on a research unit's own reputation level, and not those of its collaborators. This can be interpreted as assuming spillovers across research units that depend only on the level of supra-national funding and not on the initial levels of reputation. This is where the use of variance or

Table 8.5b   *Comparison of natural log reputation variances across funding regimes*

Variance after	Supra-national rules	
	Fund k highest average	Fund k highest variance
Overall (LN)		
National rules		
Fund independently		
Fund all	0.181	0.163
Fund top half	0.193	0.176
Fund bottom half	0.179	0.161
Fund those not funded supra-nationally	0.179	0.170
Fund only those funded supra-nationally	0.192	0.168
Region 1 (LN)		
National rules		
Fund independently		
Fund all	0.095	0.067
Fund top half	0.107	0.081
Fund bottom half	0.088	0.062
Fund those not funded supra-nationally	0.091	0.076
Fund only those funded supra-nationally	0.104	0.067
Region 2 (LN)		
National rules		
Fund independently		
Fund all	0.023	0.023
Fund top half	0.026	0.026
Fund bottom half	0.021	0.021
Fund those not funded supra-nationally	0.022	0.022
Fund only those funded supra-nationally	0.025	0.025

variance/mean as a measure of cohesion comes into question. The use of variance alone implicitly allows for spillovers to be independent of the level of reputation and to depend only on the collaboration funding. The use of variance/mean implicitly assumes that spillovers will depend on the level of reputation, that it will be easier for a research unit to increase a given amount, all else equal, if its initial reputation is higher. To repeat, this issue is important theoretically. However, its impact in practice is negligible, as our example's results are not dependent on the use of variance, as opposed to variance/mean, to measure cohesion of reputation across research units.

Table 8.5c *Comparison of natural log reputation variance/mean across funding regimes*

Variance/mean after	Supra-national rules	
	Fund k highest average	Fund k highest variance
Overall (LN)		
National rules		
Fund independently		
Fund all	0.037	0.033
Fund top half	0.039	0.036
Fund bottom half	0.036	0.032
Fund those not funded supra-nationally	0.036	0.034
Fund only those funded supra-nationally	0.039	0.034
Region 1 (LN)		
National rules		
Fund independently		
Fund all	0.021	0.015
Fund top half	0.023	0.017
Fund bottom half	0.019	0.014
Fund those not funded supra-nationally	0.020	0.016
Fund only those funded supra-nationally	0.023	0.015
Region 2 (LN)		
National rules		
Fund independently		
Fund all	0.0044	0.0044
Fund top half	0.0048	0.0048
Fund bottom half	0.0040	0.0040
Fund those not funded supra-nationally	0.0041	0.0041
Fund only those funded supra-nationally	0.0047	0.0047

Discussion

This analysis presents three general results. First, it is clear that each agency's outcome depends on its strategy (its rule) and the other institutions' strategies (their rules). Second, in the Nash equilibrium it will be the case either that the supra-national agency does not realize its best possible outcome given its goal but the national institutions do, or that all three institutions do. Third, although each national institution's optimal strategy changes given its goal, that the national agency will always be able to achieve its best possible outcome, while the supra-national agency will be able to do so only when the goals are of the same type across institutions.

The national agency never finds it an optimal strategy to choose its funding based on the funding rule of the supra-national agency. Rather, it should choose its funding rule independently of the funding choice of the supra-national agency. This result is important in the light of evidence that countries, such as the UK, determine which national researchers to fund based on which obtain EC funding. The analysis suggests that such a strategy is not optimal for the UK as a whole, regardless of its ultimate goal.

The supra-national agency may state that its objective is not (only) to minimize the variance but to maximize the overall average reputation. The analysis predicts that which objective the supra-national agency has should not change its strategy, it can always fund the top k reputation variance collaborations. However, even if the national institutions misread this statement to mean that the supra-national agency is going to fund the top k average reputation collaborations, then the national institutions will still choose the same strategy as that of the Nash equilibrium. Therefore, the potential conflict between EC objectives, described in the Introduction, does not present itself in terms of adoption of strategy.

6   CONCLUSION

This chapter sets out a framework to model collaboration formation in a setting of research funding that depends on the collaboration characteristics. The results of this model are used to analyse a setting in which national and supra-national institutions fund researchers. Their goals and strategies interact to yield particular Nash equilibria. The purpose of such a model is to provide a framework in which to discuss the formation and funding of research networks by a supra-national agency, such as the EC, in light of the existence of national funding entities that may be pursuing their own objectives.

The conclusion of the analysis conducted in this particular exercise is that, regardless of whether the supra-national agency's underlying objective is to raise the overall level of R&D capabilities and hence of the average scientific standing of the research units within its domain, or to promote greater coherence (in the sense of convergence) among the capabilities of its research units, the stated rule it should adopt is to give funding priority to the proposed collaboration that has the highest variance in the reputational standings of its members. The supra-national agency's optimal strategy in this regard is not only independent of the weight it assigns to the seemingly conflicting policy goals of ('excellence' versus 'coherence'); it is also independent of the strategies being followed by the national agencies.

The response of the national institutions will depend on their own national objectives. However, the national institutions should fund their own researchers based on rules that do not depend on the funding decisions of the supra-national agency. Rather, the national rules should be free-standing.

Some more obvious, and perhaps more robust conclusions also follow from the analysis. Endogenously formed research networks constrain the selections that funding agencies are able to make without directly intervening in the network-building process. The policy goals of a supra-national funding agency may be more fully attained if it is able to influence the policies of national funding bodies, but discourage them from adopting strategies that cause national funding policies to change if the supra-national funding goal changes. As a rule, however, taking explicit account of the coexistence of a multiplicity of funding agencies introduces significant complications, and raises awareness for policy-makers of the likelihood of the interdependence of funding strategies and outcomes. Understanding these complications is not possible within the terms of the traditional analysis of the economics of R&D project choice, where the array of alternative projects is presumed to be independent of the funding criteria – just as the shape of the marginal efficiency of investment schedule is presumed to be independent of the rate of interest. Where the projects that present themselves for selection are endogenously formed, those that present themselves will both reflect expectations about the intentions and constraints under which the funding agency is operating, and, in turn, constrain the choices that are available to it. This mutual interdependence will, of course, be all the greater in the absence of effective competition for projects among diverse funding agencies.

Both difficult challenges and important opportunities are presented for further theoretical and empirical study of the economics of research networks. Clearly, further work is necessary to understand the institutional intricacies that result in the funding of research in the EU today. None the less, the results of this simple model are quite clear, and suggest that the current strategies of the EC and national R&D funders may not be their best possible strategies. The national strategies, in the presence of a supra-national agency's funding, appears to be the place where concern should focus particularly.

This chapter has provided only a heuristic aid to thinking about a quite complicated class of problems for public finance economics to tackle. But, it has not escaped our notice that the scope for application of the modelling approach taken here is considerably broader than might be suggested by confining our discussion to the provision of public funding for R&D, by a multiplicity of agencies with overlapping spheres of action. Generically, the issues addressed here are ones that will be seen to arise in federal systems where local fiscal entities are able to form coalitions in order to compete for funding from the centre, and where receipt of such funding enhances the attractiveness of those entities as partners in future fund-seeking coalitions.

NOTES

* Presentation of the first draft of this chapter at the NPRnet Workshop held in Paris on 5–6 May 2000, provided numerous comments and suggestions that were useful for improving and tightening the exposition. We wish to express our gratitude to the assembled members of the NPRnet Project and the invited discussants, particularly the paper's designated discussants – Bronwyn Hall and Cristiano Antonelli. Further comments were received, from Jonathan Cave and others at the Warwick Summer Research Institute, where a subsequent draft of the chapter was presented on 14 July 2001 to the session on Modelling Networks and Network Games. The present version has benefited from the comments of an anonymous reviewer, and the liberality of the editors of this volume. David's research in connection with this chapter drew support under the NPR net Project sponsored by the STRATA Programme of the Directorate General of the European Economic Commission, and coordinated by SPRU at the University of Sussex.

1. Although the emergence of research collaboration in 'Big Science' fields was viewed from the 1960s onwards as a significant novelty reflecting underlying tendencies in the organizational structure of modern science, the increasing generality of collaborative organization is now attracting fresh interest as the most recent phase in a broader, longer and more continuous development. See, for example, Katz (1994), Katz and Martin (1997), Etzkowitz and Kemelgor (1998).

2. See, for example, Coombs et al. (1996), Mowery et al. (1996), and Mowery (1998). For recent studies examining these developments in the Western European context, with references to the corresponding literature focused upon US experience, see Gambardella and Malerba (1999).

3. The task is briefly essayed by Hicks and Katz (1996).

4. See the discussion in Stephan (1996), whose early contributions exemplified the focus of economists upon individuals; and also, Stephan and Levin (1997).

5. See, for example, Latour and Woolgar (1986), Latour (1987), Callon and Rip (1986), Callon (1995).

6. This is to say that enough of a beginning has been made (for example, in Gambardella and Malerba (1999, chs 13–15) to suggest both the interest and promise that the subject of publicly funded formal research collaboration holds, and to indicate the enormous amount of work that has yet to be done. In what follows here, it should be understood that the focus is upon formalized collaborations ('coalitions'), as distinguished from informal cooperative actions by individual researchers (whether or not productive of co-authorship, or co-patenting) that may be viewed as particular instantiations of the 'communal ethos of science' discerned by Merton (1973, p. 273): 'The substantive findings of science are a product of social collaboration and are assigned [in the sense of ownership] to the community'. For analyses of the relationship between the Mertonian norms and the micro-level organization and collective performance of epistemic communities as 'invisible colleges', see Dasgupta and David (1994), David (1998b).

7. On the effects of 'common-agency contracting' involving multiple sponsors and research agents, see David (1998a, 2001).

8. Garcia-Fontes and Geuna (1999) present systematic statistical evidence of such patterns of repetitive participation on the part of European university-based research units, notably those drawn from the stronger institutions, who received funding under successive EU Framework Programmes. Evidence from casual empirical observation is more abundant and points in the same direction.

9. For the original formulation of 'the Matthew Effect' see Merton (1968). On the roles of reputation and competence in scientific research productivity see, for example, David (1994), and Arora et al. (1998).

10. Major implementation issues are astutely examined in the recent NPRnet briefing paper by Steinmueller et al. (2001). The pragmatic approach followed in that analysis, however, is one that (doubtless, by design) thoroughly accords with the discussion style of EC public documents. Thus, it rarely refers openly to the possible existence of underlying goal conflicts among the member states, and focuses instead upon the potential manifestation of such conflicts in disagreements over the details of implementing the concept of a European Research Area. See Geuna et al. (2001) for a summary statement of the particular issues of implementation which are identified as most problematic.

11. Among recent EC documents concerning the European Research Area, see European Commission (2000, 2001).

12. The EU Human Capital and Mobility programme is perhaps the one most explicitly designed with such considerations in mind, but their influence extends more widely. See, for example, the discussions by Gambardella and Garcia-Fontes (1996) and Garcia-Fontes and Geuna (1999).

13. On the participation of university-based research teams in the Framework Programmes, see, for example, Geuna (1999a, chs 6–7).

14. See, for example, Sharp (1998).

15. The latter proposition rests on the presupposition that all of the participating researchers would be 'scientifically qualified'; not only in the sense of being able to contribute to the collaboration's scientific work, but also in possessing basic levels of training and experience needed for them to readily absorb knowledge spillovers from all other members of their network. The degree to which such a condition actually has been met in EC Framework Programme collaborations is an interesting and potentially important policy-relevant question that deserves empirical investigation.

16. See, for example, the discussions by David et al. (1995) and Garcia-Fontes and Geuna (1999).

17. The discussion of implementation issues for the ERA by Geuna et al. (2001) and Steinmueller et al. (2001) suggests, by implication, that under this programme the EC intends to give greater autonomy in the control of research objectives to networks formed from the leading research groups in Europe. Whether that strategy will be found to be politically implementable without reference to the national distribution of the participating teams is an issue that remains to be clarified.

18. Research units could be individuals, but for the analysis of EU research networks, they will be teams associated with educational institutions, research institutes, or firms. Research units will be interpreted as each having a single collective reputation, much as academic research departments have a single ranking relative to other departments.

19. A collaboration is commonly called a coalition in the literature; the term collaboration is used deliberately to denote the specific type of coalition under consideration here.

20. As mentioned above, it is assumed that the external funding – and thus contribution to reputation building – is split equally between the members of a collaboration. Other potential rules for splitting the funding exist, such as using a Shapley value. However, using the Shapley value, or any rule based on relative contribution to collaboration's funding, is not possible in this model. This is because relative contribution is not determinable for most or all cases.

21. As noted earlier, no bargaining within a cluster can occur due to the non-cooperative framework and the absence of an enforcement mechanism. For a model of coalition formation with intra-coalition bargaining, see Ray and Vohra (2000).

22. The reader is referred to Appendix 8A1 for further elucidation of the complex forces that give rise to these varied results. In some instances it is not possible to determine, without additional specification of the model, whether the variance (and the rel-variance) tend to increase, or not with the repetition of the funding process.
23. Partially weakening this conclusion is evidence that the internal structure of the coalitions has changed over time. The proportion of small, less-well-known, research institutions in the coalitions has increased. The coalitions have internally seemed to exhibit competitive rather than cooperative behaviour in the division of rewards and in the research process. Nevertheless, the level of technology 'spill-ins' within the coalition appears to have increased.

    In the collaboration model, the churning that occurs in the cases where relative ranking occurs is roughly consistent with this empirical evidence. However, the other evidence described in the body of the chapter all points towards an absolute measure.
24. EC-funded R&D collaborations that are engaged in pre-market research ('indirect actions') have been permitted to have as few as two partners, under the terms of the Framework Programmes up to and including the Fifth Framework (1998–2002). This will continue to be the case under the Sixth Framework (2002–2006), except for the newly introduced 'networks of excellence', which must have 3 partners, at least 2 from EU member states. The proposed 'networks of excellence' represents a radically new mode of funding for the EU, and a departure from the model based upon historical experience, in that it allows non-EU participation, provides contractual flexibility to permit new partners to enter, and original partners to withdraw from these longer-lived collaborations.

REFERENCES

Arora, A., P.A. David, and A. Gambardella (1998), 'Reputation and competence in publicly funded science: estimating the effects on research group productivity', *Annales D'Économie et de Statistique* **49/50**, 163–98.

Bloch, F. (1995), 'Endogenous structures of association in oligopolies', *RAND Journal of Economics* **26**(3), 537–56.

Callon, M. (1995), 'Four models in the dynamics of science', in S. Jasanoff, G.E. Markle, J.C. Peterson and T. Pinch (eds), *Handbook of Science and Technology Studies*, London: Sage, pp. 29–63.

Callon, M. and A. Rip (eds) (1986), *Mapping the Dynamics of Science and Technology*, London: Macmillan.

Coombs, R., A. Richards, P. Saviotti and V. Walsh (eds) (1996), *Technological Collaboration: The Dynamics of Cooperation in Industrial Innovation*, Cheltenham, UK and Brookfield, US: Edward Elgar.

Dasgupta, P. and P.A. David (1994), 'Towards a new economics of science', *Research Policy* **23**(5), 487–521.

David, P.A. (1994), 'Positive feedbacks and research productivity in science: reopening another black box', in O. Granstrand (ed.), *Economics of Technology*, Amsterdam, London: North-Holland, pp. 65–89.

David, P.A. (1998a), 'Common agency contracting and the emergence of "open science" institutions', *American Economic Review* **88**(2), 15–21.

David, P.A. (1998b), 'Communication norms and the collective cognitive performance of "invisible colleges"', in G. Barba Navaratti, P. Dasgupta and K.G. Maler (eds), *Creation and Transfer of Knowledge: Institutions and Incentives*, Berlin: Springer-Verlag, pp. 115–63.

David, P.A. (2001), 'From keeping "nature's secrets" to the institutionalization of "open science"', Discussion Paper 23, Oxford University Discussion Papers in Social and Economic History, March.

David, P.A., A. Geuna and W.E. Steinmueller (1995), 'Additionality as a principle of European R&D funding', *MERIT Research Memorandum*, 2/95–012, MERIT, University of Maastricht.

Etzkowitz, H. and C. Kemelgor (1998), 'The role of research centres in the collectivization of academic science', *Minerva* **36**(3), 271–88.

European Commission (2000), *Making a Reality of the European Research Area: Guidelines for EU Research Activities (2002–2006)*, COM 612 Final Report, Brussels: EC.

European Commission (2001), *Proposal for a Decision of the European Parliament and the Council Concerning the Multi-annual Framework Programme (2002–2006)*, COM 94 Final Report, Brussels: EC.

Gambardella, A. and W. Garcia-Fontes (1996), 'Regional linkages through European research funding', *Economics of Innovation and New Technology* **4**(2),123–38.

Gambardella, A. and F. Malerba (eds) (1999), *The Organization of Economic Innovation in Europe*, Cambridge: Cambridge University Press.

Garcia-Fontes, W. and A. Geuna (1999), 'The dynamics of research networks in Europe', in Gambardella and Malerba (eds), pp. 343–66.

Geuna, A. (1999a), 'Patterns of university research in Europe', in Gambardella and Malerba (eds), pp. 367–89.

Geuna, A. (1999b), *The Economics of Knowledge Production: Funding and the Structure of University Research*, Cheltenham, UK and Northampton, MA, USA: Edward Elgar.

Geuna, A., A. Salter and W.E. Steinmueller (2001), 'Towards a new era in research', *Science and Public Affairs* June, 25–6.

Hicks, D. and J.S. Katz (1996), 'Science policy for a highly collaborative science system', *Science and Public Policy* **23**(1), 39–44.

Katz, J.S. (1994), 'Geographical proximity and scientific collaboration', *Scientometrics* **31**(1), 31–43.

Katz, J.S. and B.R. Martin (1997), 'What is research collaboration?', *Research Policy* **26**(1), 1–18.

Keely, L.C. (forthcoming), 'Exchanging good ideas', *Journal of Economic Theory*.

Latour, B. (1987), *Science in Action: How to Follow Scientists and Engineers through Society*, Cambridge, MA: Harvard University Press.

Latour, B. and S. Woolgar (1986), *Laboratory Life: The Construction of Scientific Facts*, Princeton, NJ: Princeton University Press.

Merton, R.K. (1968), 'The Matthew Effect in science', *Science* **159**, 56–63.

Merton, R.K. (1973), *The Sociology of Science*, Chicago: University of Chicago Press.

Mowery, D.C. (1998), 'Collaborative R&D: how effective is it?', *Issues in Science and Technology* Fall, 37–44.

Mowery, D.C, J.E. Oxley and B.S. Silverman (1996), 'Strategic alliances and inter-firm knowledge transfer', *Strategic Management Journal* **17**, 77–92.

Ray, D. and R. Vohra (1999), 'A theory of endogenous coalition structures', *Games and Economic Behavior* **26**, 286–336.

Ray, D. and R. Vohra (2000), 'Coalitional power and public goods', Working paper, New York University and Brown University, August.

Sharp, M. (1998), 'Competitiveness and cohesion: are the two compatible?', *Research Policy* **27**(6), 569–88.

Steinmueller, W.E., A. Geuna and A. Salter (2001), 'Implementing the European research area: issues brief', NPRnet, SPRU – Science and Technology Policy Research, University of Sussex, April.

Stephan, P.E. (1996), 'The economics of science', *Journal of Economic Literature* **34**(3), 1199–235.

Stephan, P.E. and S.G. Levin (1997), 'The critical importance of careers in collaborative scientific research', *Revue d'Économie Industrielle* **79**, 45–61.

APPENDIX 8A1   EQUILIBRIA OF THE COALITION-FORMATION GAME WITH A SINGLE FUNDING AGENCY

Case 1

The measure of collaboration rank is the average collaboration reputation; external funding is determined per collaboration; external funding per collaboration is based on the absolute measure:

$$m_c(t) = \bar{r}_c(t); \quad \frac{\partial E_c[\Pi(t)]}{\partial N_c(t)} = 0; \quad \frac{\partial E_c[\Pi(t)]}{\partial m_c(t)} > 0.$$

Equilibrium collaborations will be size 2 for two reasons: the division of the external funding between collaboration members and the desire of potential collaboration members to maximize the reputation building via maximizing external funding. Because the measure is absolute, there will be no multiplicity of equilibria. Collaborations will be proposed and accepted that are of the two highest reputation level units still in the collaboration formation game.

This collaboration formation pattern will persist over time. The variance over the distribution of research unit reputation is increasing over time, as shown below. The increase in variance does not depend on an initial uniform distribution of reputation. The average reputation level of all research units will be increasing.

The collaboration formation pattern is size 2, with persistence in the collaboration pattern and collaborations form in order of reputation level. The variance is shown to be increasing between any two periods for the general case of $\frac{k}{2}$ collaborations (k research units). The variance is increasing if the following expression holds:

$$\sum_{i=1}^{k} (X_i - \bar{X})^2 < \sum_{i=1}^{k} (X_i + Y_i - \bar{X} - \bar{Y})^2$$

where X_i is the original reputation of research unit i, Y_i is the reputation building of research unit i as a result of participating in a collaboration, and $\bar{X}$ and $\bar{Y}$ are the corresponding averages across all research units. The expression reduces to:

$$0 < \sum_{i=1}^{k} (Y_i - \bar{Y})^2 + 2 \sum_{i=1}^{k} (X_i - \bar{X})(Y_i - \bar{Y}).$$

The first term on the right-hand side is clearly positive. The second term on the right-hand side will also be positive because the collaborations form in order of reputation. If $X_i > \bar{X}$, then $Y_i > \bar{Y}$ because of the ordering of the collaborations. If $X_i < \bar{X}$, then $Y_i < \bar{Y}$ by the same reasoning. Therefore, the expression must hold and so the variance is increasing.

Case 2

The measure of collaboration rank is the average collaboration reputation; external funding is determined per research unit; external funding per collaboration is based on the absolute measure:

$$m_c(t) = \bar{r}_c(t); \; \frac{\partial E_c[\Pi(t)]}{\partial N_c(t)} > 0; \; \frac{\partial E_c[\Pi(t)]}{\partial m_c(t)} > 0.$$

Equilibrium collaborations would exhibit the same pattern as in Case 1, with two differences. First, the reason for collaborations being size 2 is now purely because of the desire to maximize the absolute average reputation of a collaboration. Second, the size of the reputation building for each collaboration may differ from Case 1 since external funding is per research unit rather than per collaboration. On this matter the model is silent. However, qualitatively the collaboration pattern at a point in time and over time remains the same.

Case 3

The measure of collaboration rank is the variance of collaboration reputation; external funding is determined per collaboration; external funding per collaboration is based on the absolute measure:

$$m_c(t) = \mathrm{var}\,[r_n(t), n \in N_c(t)]; \; \frac{\partial E_c[\Pi(t)]}{\partial N_c(t)} = 0; \; \frac{\partial E_c[\Pi(t)]}{\partial m_c(t)} > 0.$$

Equilibrium collaborations will again be of size 2 in order to maximize the average reputation and to minimize the division of the collaboration-wide external funding. Because external funding is based on the absolute measure of the variance in reputation, equilibrium collaboration formation will be unique. Collaborations that form in equilibrium will maximize the variance of research unit reputation of the research units that remain in the game at the stage of proposal. If others were to be added to the proposed collaboration, variance would decrease. The exact collaboration compositions may change over time, since the variance within collaborations may lead to churning, or leapfrogging, on the lower half of the reputation distribution. However, the structure of collaborations will remain unchanged.

The average reputation across all research units will be increasing over time. This average will be increasing more quickly than in Cases 1 and 2 if $\partial r[E_c(t)]/\partial E_c[\Pi(t)]\ \partial E_c[\Pi(t)]/\partial m_c(t)$ is decreasing in $m_c(t)$. Empirical evidence from Arora et al. (1998) indicates that the effect of reputation level, what they call knowledge, on the change in reputation level, which they call research output, exhibits diminishing returns.[1]

The variance, however, will be increasing if the initial distribution of reputations is uniform as well as under more general conditions. The increasing variance conditions are derived next.

The collaboration formation pattern is size 2, with collaborations forming in order of distance between reputation levels. The variance of the reputation level distribution is shown to be increasing between any two periods for the general case of $\frac{k}{2}$ collaborations (k research unit). The variance is increasing if the following expression holds:

$$\sum_{i=1}^{k} (X_i - \bar{X})^2 \sum_{i=1}^{k} (X_i + Y_i - \bar{X} - \bar{Y})^2$$

where X_i is the original reputation of research unit i, Y_i is the reputation building of research unit i as a result of participating in a collaboration, and $\bar{X}$ and $\bar{Y}$ are the corresponding averages across all research units. The expression reduces to:

$$0 < \sum_{i=1}^{k} (Y_i - \bar{Y})^2 + 2 \sum_{i=1}^{k} (X_i - \bar{X})(Y_i - \bar{Y}). \tag{8A1.1}$$

The first term on the right-hand side is positive. The second term on the right-hand side may be negative. It will be negative if the distances between the mean and the lower half of the reputation levels is large relative to the distances between the mean and the upper half of the reputation levels for those reputation levels near the extreme. That is, $|X_i - \bar{X}|\,|_{Xi < \bar{X},\ Yi > \bar{Y}}$ is large relative to $|X_i - \bar{X}|\,|_{Xi > \bar{X},\ Yi > \bar{Y}}$. Also, it will be negative if the converse is true for those reputation levels near the average $\bar{X}$. That is, it will be negative if $|X_i - \bar{X}|\,|_{Xi > \bar{X},\ Yi < \bar{Y}}$ is large relative to $|X_i - \bar{X}|\,|_{Xi < \bar{X},\ Yi < \bar{Y}}$.

The first term of (8A1.1) may be small relative to the second term if the distribution of reputation building has a smaller mean and/or variance than the distribution of reputation levels. Therefore, in the case where the first term of (8A1.1) is small relative to the second and the distribution of reputation levels is such that the second term is negative, then the reputation level variance can be decreasing. Otherwise, the variance will be increasing. If the distribution of reputation levels is uniform, then the second term on the right-hand side is zero, and so in this case the variance will be increasing.

Case 4

The measure of collaboration rank is the variance of collaboration reputation; external funding is determined per research unit; external funding per collaboration is based on the absolute measure:

$$m_c(t) = \text{var}\ [r_n(t),\ n \in N_c(t)];\ \frac{\partial E_c[\Pi(t)]}{\partial N_c(t)} > 0;\ \frac{\partial E_c[\Pi(t)]}{\partial m_c(t)} > 0.$$

Equilibrium collaborations would exhibit the same pattern as in Case 3, with two differences. First, the reason for collaborations being size 2 is now purely because of the desire to maximize the absolute variance in reputation of a collaboration. Second, the size of the reputation building for each collaboration may differ from Case 1 since external funding is per research unit rather than per collaboration. Again, on this matter the model is silent. However, the collaboration pattern at a point in time and over time is not affected.

Case 5

The measure of collaboration rank is the average collaboration reputation; external funding is determined per collaboration; external funding per collaboration is based on the relative measure:

$$m_c(t) = \bar{r}_c(t);\ \frac{\partial E_c[\Pi(t)]}{\partial N_c(t)} = 0;\ \frac{\partial E_c[\Pi(t)]}{\partial w[m_c(t);\ m_k(t)k = 1,...,C]} > 0.$$

Equilibrium collaborations will all be of size 2 since funding is given to the entire collaboration and assumed to be split equally between them. Collaborations of size 2 which form in descending order of reputation are an equilibrium formation. If the level of reputation building is in the same order as the initial reputation level, this equilibrium may continue in future periods indefinitely, exactly as in Case 1. The variance of the distribution of reputation across all research units would therefore be increasing over time, as in Case 1.

However, because external funding depends only on rank, other equilibria exist. For instance, if the research unit with the highest reputation can choose to collaborate with the second- or third-highest-reputation research unit and still attain the highest collaboration rank, then either collaboration will be part of a possible equilibrium.

Because of the multiplicity of equilibria, it is not possible to specify exactly how the distribution of reputation will evolve. Although the average reputation will be increasing, the variance of reputations may not be. These same issues arise in Case 6 and the issues are discussed in greater detail under Case 6.

Case 6

The measure of collaboration rank is the average collaboration reputation; external funding is determined per research unit; external funding per collaboration is based on the relative measure:

$$m_c(t) = \bar{r}_c(t); \frac{\partial E_c[\Pi(t)]}{\partial N_c(t)} > 0; \frac{\partial E_c[\Pi(t)]}{\partial w[m_c(t); m_k(t)k = 1,...,C]} > 0.$$

Equilibrium collaborations can be of any size from 2 to N. The highest-reputation research unit will choose a collaboration so that it knows it will be first ranked. Therefore, a collaboration structure that is ordered in initial reputation level is a possible equilibrium. The highest-reputation research unit is indifferent about the size of the collaboration since its external funding will be fixed by the collaboration's rank. The absolute measure of average reputation is of no concern. If the highest-reputation research unit proposes a collaboration of size less than N that will be first ranked, all potential members will accept such a proposal by the same logic. Once that collaboration is formed, the research unit with the highest reputation of those left over will choose a proposal according to the same logic as the original proposer did.

In the initial uniform reputation distribution case considered here, these collaborations will again form, roughly speaking, in order of reputation. However, it will be possible that collaborations are proposed and accepted that do not run exactly in order. The proposer may be indifferent between a collaboration that includes, for instance, the first- to fourth-ranked research units inclusive and a collaboration that includes the first-, second- and fourth-ranked research units only. As long as the rank of the collaboration will be unchanged, that is all the proposer and the potential members will care about. This indifference is the reason for multiplicity of equilibria.

Because of the multiplicity of equilibria, it is not possible to specify exactly how the distribution of reputation will evolve. In the case where collaborations do run in order of the current reputation level, then the ordering will remain the same. It is only in the case where collaborations form that 'skip over' some research unit(s) where churning, or leapfrogging, in the reputation distribution is possible. The exact degree of churning depends on the particular distribution of reputation. The larger is reputation building relative to the reputation level, the larger the degree of churning that will be expected. However, since the proposers will be indifferent between having ordered collaborations or not (of the same rank), there is no reason to expect this type of churning to be prevalent.

If there is more than one collaboration that is formed in order of reputation level, then the average reputation level will be increasing, but the variance of reputation levels will be also. If there is a grand collaboration of size N, then the average will be increasing at a higher rate than when there is more than one collaboration. This follows from the fact that every research unit is in the first-ranked collaboration if there is a grand collaboration, but if there is more than one collaboration, then some research units will have lower reputation building. The maximum reputation level will be unaffected by this difference as long as the highest-reputation-level research unit is always in the highest-ranked collaboration, as it will be in equilibrium.

If there is some degree of skipping in collaboration formation, resulting in churning, then the variance may still be increasing. The logic for why this is the case is very similar to that for describing when the variance is increasing in Case 3, as set out above. In the case of a uniform distribution of reputation levels, the variance will be increasing.

Case 7

The measure of collaboration rank is the variance of collaboration reputation; external funding is determined per collaboration; external funding per collaboration is based on the relative measure:

$$m_c(t) = \text{var}\,[r_n(t), n \in N_c(t)];\; \frac{\partial E_c[\Pi(t)]}{\partial N_c(t)} > 0;\; \frac{\partial E_c[\Pi(t)]}{\partial w[m_c(t); m_k(t)k = 1,...,C]} > 0.$$

Equilibrium collaborations will be of size 2 due to the division of external funding between collaboration members. Collaborations will be proposed and accepted to maximize the potential ranking of variance. The variance will decrease if a third research unit is added with a reputation between that of the first two, and is straightforward to prove.

There is, however, multiplicity of equilibria, even for an initially uniform distribution. Only the relative ranking of collaboration variance matters for the level of external funding, so a proposed collaboration may be less than the maximum possible variance as long as the collaboration will retain its first ranking among the remaining available potential collaborations.

Churning is possible due to the variance measure to determine external funding. The degree of churning will depend on the returns of external funding on reputation building. If the returns are decreasing, then there will simply be cycling of reputation ranking among the lower-reputation research units, with no one breaking through into the upper ranks. However, if the marginal effect is sufficiently increasing, then it would be possible for initially low-reputation research units to become relatively high-reputation research units, at least temporarily. The one research unit whose ranking will never change in equilibrium is the highest-ranking research unit. The returns to reputation building of research funding will determine the proportion of research units, from lowest to highest, that will experience a change in rank as a result of collaborations.

The average reputation level of all research units will be increasing over time. Exactly which collaborations of size 2 are chosen will not affect this average. As shown for Case 3, the variance may be increasing, by similar logic. The variance will increase starting from an initially uniform distribution.

Case 8

The measure of collaboration rank is the variance of collaboration reputation; external funding is determined per research unit; external funding per collaboration is based on the relative measure:

$$m_c(t) = \text{var } [r_n(t), n \in N_c(t)]; \frac{\partial E_c[\Pi(t)]}{\partial N_c(t)} > 0; \frac{\partial E_c[\Pi(t)]}{\partial w[m_c(t); m_k(t)k = 1,...,C]} > 0.$$

Equilibrium collaborations are of size 2 and size N in this setting since only the rank matters for external funding, and funding is per research unit. In either case, the potential members of the coalition can be assured of being ranked as relatively high as possible. Equilibrium collaborations of size between 2 and N are also possible, but only if the resulting decrease in variance will not decrease the proposed collaboration's ranking relative to the ranking without more than two members. From an initially uniform distribution, this increase in size without a decrease in ranking is easily achieved by increasing membership in order from the extreme levels of reputation and workings inwards towards the median. The initial proposer and potential members will be indifferent between all of these collaborations and thus each of the collaborations that decrease variance without decreasing rank are possible equilibria.

Equilibrium collaborations that are not ordered by reputation-level distance between members are also possible, as in Cases 6 and 7. This is an additional potential source of churning.

In the case of a grand collaboration of size N, reputation building will be equal across research units, although the reputation distribution will remain of the same variance as the average increases. In the case of size 2 collaborations, then churning is possible as in Case 6 described above. The increase in average reputation will be smaller with more collaborations than with fewer. Again, the variance may be non-decreasing. If there is one grand collaboration, the variance will be constant. If there is more than one collaboration with an initially uniform reputation distribution, then variance will be increasing.

In general, the intuition for variance to be non-decreasing in a wide variety of cases is that for the variance to be decreasing, the lower-reputation research units would have to be building reputation levels faster than the others. There is no guaranteed mechanism for such catching-up here since reputation building occurs by collaboration members together. However, collaborations can lessen or eliminate the increase in variance that might otherwise have occurred. The grand collaboration is an illustrative example. Clearly, the collaborations serve to increase the overall average of reputation, or technological capability, of the research units through the external funding.

NOTE

1. Arora et al. (1998) also measure an effect of reputation on reputation building via the effect of collaboration size. They find this effect to be positive and exhibiting decreasing returns.

   The effect of size on collaboration formation in the theoretical model here can be considered by the comparison between external funding determined per collaboration and determined per research unit.

   The direct effect of reputation on reputation building in Arora et al. is via a technology production function. The collaboration formation model presented here does not consider such a model explicitly, in order to focus on how the presence of external funding affects collaboration formation. This effect alone also exhibits diminishing returns, although of a higher order.

   Arora et al. estimate that the sum of indirect effects of reputation on reputation building yields increasing returns, although of a magnitude of 1.3.

APPENDIX 8A2   OUTCOMES FOR REPUTATION DISTRIBUTION OF INTERACTIONS BETWEEN NATIONAL AND SUPRA-NATIONAL FUNDING REGIMES

(For mixed funding regime 1Ai, see text, Section 5.)

1. The national agency funds independently of the supra-national agency decision.
A. The national agency funds all research units in the nation to produce an equal change in reputation.
ii. The supra-national agency funds the k highest reputation variance collaborations.

This case is depicted in Figure 8A2.1. The new average for each nation and overall is higher, with the expressions the same as those for case 1Ai. The new variance for nation 2 is the same as for case 1Ai. The new variance for nation 1 may decrease. The third term of var_{1A}, $2\Sigma_1^{N1}(r_n-\bar{r}_1)(\Delta r_n-\Delta\bar{r}_1)/N_1$, will be negative. A sufficient condition for var_{1A} to decrease is

$$\left| \frac{2\Sigma_1^{N1}(r_n-\bar{r}_1)(\Delta r_n-\Delta\bar{r}_1)}{N_1} \right| > \frac{\Sigma_1^{N1}(\Delta r_n-\Delta\bar{r}_1)^2}{N_1},$$

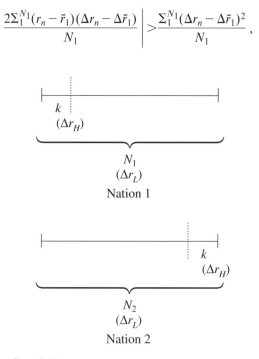

Figure 8A2.1   Case 1Aii

which holds for $(r_n - \bar{r}_1) > (\Delta r_n - \Delta \bar{r}_1) \; \forall n \in [1, ..., N_1]$. That is, the change in reputation is small relative to the level.

Overall variance is unambiguously increasing, as the third term on the right-hand side is equal to zero. This increase in variance will therefore be smaller than that of case 1Ai.

1. The national agency funds independently of the supra-national agency decision.
B. The national agency funds half of all research units in the nation, funding the top half.
i. The supra-national agency funds the k highest average reputation collaborations.

This case is depicted in Figure 8A2.2. The new average for each nation and overall is higher. The averages are:

$$\bar{r}_{1A} = \frac{\sum_1^{N_1} r_n}{N_1} + \frac{\left[\frac{N_1}{2} v + \left(\frac{N_1}{2} - k \right) \Delta r_L + k(\Delta r_H + \Delta r_L) \right]}{N_1};$$

$$\bar{r}_{2A} = \frac{\sum_1^{N_2} r_n}{N_2} + \frac{\left[\frac{N_2}{2} v + \left(\frac{N_2}{2} - k \right) \Delta r_L + k(\Delta r_H + \Delta r_L) \right]}{N_2};$$

the new overall average is:

$$\bar{r}_A = \frac{\sum_1^N r_n}{N} + \frac{\left[\frac{N}{2} v + \left(\frac{N}{2} - 2k \right) \Delta r_L + 2k(\Delta r_H + \Delta r_L) \right]}{N}.$$

These changes in average are smaller than those in cases 1Ai and ii.

The new variances for each nation and overall unambiguously increase, as can be easily shown. Relative to the change in variances for case 1Ai, it is not analytically conclusive which case's variances will rise more.

1. The national agency funds independently of the supra-national agency decision.
B. The national agency funds half of all research units in the nation, funding the top half.
ii. The supra-national agency funds the k highest reputation variance collaborations.

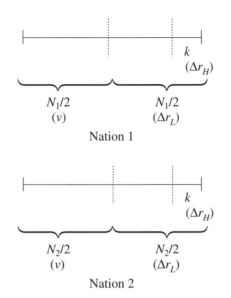

Figure 8A2.2   Case 1Bi

This case is depicted in Figure 8A2.3. The new national averages are:

$$\bar{r}_{1A} = \frac{\Sigma_1^{N_1} r_n}{N_1} + \frac{\left[\left(\dfrac{N_1}{2} - k\right)v + \dfrac{N_1}{2}\Delta r_L + k\Delta r_H\right]}{N_1};$$

$$\bar{r}_{2A} = \frac{\Sigma_1^{N_2} r_n}{N_2} + \frac{\left[\dfrac{N_2}{2}v + \left(\dfrac{N_2}{2} - k\right)\Delta r_L + k\left(\Delta r_H + \Delta r_L\right)\right]}{N_2};$$

the new overall average is:

$$\bar{r}_A = \frac{\Sigma_1^{N} r_n}{N} + \frac{\left[\left(\dfrac{N}{2} - k\right)v + \left(\dfrac{N}{2}\right)\Delta r_L + 2k\Delta r_H\right]}{N}.$$

The average in nation 1 will be smaller than that of case 1Bi; the average of nation 2 will be the same, and thus the overall average is slightly smaller than case 1Bi as well.

The new variance for nation 2 will be the same as for case 1Bi. The new variance for nation 1 may fall from the old variance,[1] and will thus be smaller than the variance in case 1Bi. The overall variance will rise for k sufficiently small.

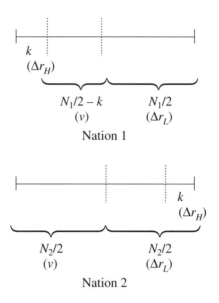

Figure 8A2.3   Case 1Bii

1. The national agency funds independently of the supra-national agency decision.
C. The national agency funds half of all research units in the nation, funding the bottom half.
i. The supra-national agency funds the k highest average reputation collaborations.

This case is depicted in Figure 8A2.4. The new averages are:

$$\bar{r}_{1A}=\frac{\Sigma_1^{N_1} r_n}{N_1}+\frac{\left[\left(\dfrac{N_1}{2}-k\right)v+\dfrac{N_1}{2}\Delta r_L+k\Delta r_H\right]}{N_1};$$

$$\bar{r}_{2A}=\frac{\Sigma_1^{N_2} r_n}{N_2}+\frac{\left[\left(\dfrac{N_2}{2}-k\right)v+\dfrac{N_2}{2}\Delta r_L+k\Delta r_H\right]}{N_2};$$

the new overall average is:

$$\bar{r}_{A}=\frac{\Sigma_1^{N} r_n}{N}+\frac{\left[\left(\dfrac{N}{2}-2k\right)v+\dfrac{N}{2}\Delta r_L+2k\Delta r_H\right]}{N}.$$

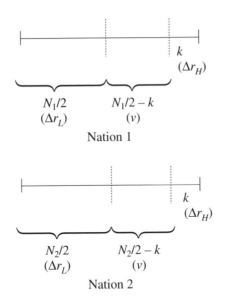

Figure 8A2.4   Case 1Ci

The new average for nation 1 is the same as for case 1Bii. The new averages are thus all smaller than those of case 1Bi, and cases 1Ai and 1Aii.

The variances for both nations and overall can easily be shown to decrease for k sufficiently small, and for the level of reputations r_n sufficiently large relative to the changes in reputation Δr_n. This is the first case considered where both nation's variances can go down.

1. The national agency funds independently of the supra-national agency decision.
C. The national agency funds half of all research units in the nation, funding the bottom half.
ii. The supra-national agency funds the k highest reputation variance collaborations.

This case is depicted as Figure 8A2.5. The new averages are:

$$\bar{r}_{1A} = \frac{\sum_{1}^{N_1} r_n}{N_1} + \frac{\left[\left(\frac{N_1}{2} - k\right)\Delta r_L + \frac{N_1}{2}v + k\left(\Delta r_H + \Delta r_L\right)\right]}{N_1};$$

$$\bar{r}_{2A} = \frac{\sum_{1}^{N_2} r_n}{N_2} + \frac{\left[\left(\frac{N_2}{2} - k\right)v + \frac{N_2}{2}\Delta r_L + k\left(\Delta r_H\right)\right]}{N_2};$$

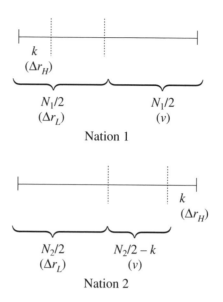

Figure 8A2.5   Case 1 Cii

the new overall average is:

$$\bar{r}_A = \frac{\sum_1^N r_n}{N} + \frac{\left[\left(\dfrac{N}{2}-k\right)v+\dfrac{N}{2}\Delta r_L + 2k\Delta r_H\right]}{N}.$$

The new average in nation 1 is the same as in case 1Bi. The average in nation 2 is the same as in case 1Ci. The overall average is therefore larger than in case 1Ci, and is equal to that of case 1Bii.

The new variance for nation 2 is the same as in case 1Ci. The new variance for nation 1 is easily seen to be unambiguously smaller than the variance in case 1Ci. The new overall variance can be shown to be smaller than the new overall variance in case 1Ci, and smaller than the original variance under similar conditions as those for case 1Ci.

2. The national agency funds those research units not funded by the supra-national agency.
i. The supra-national agency funds the *k* highest average reputation collaborations.

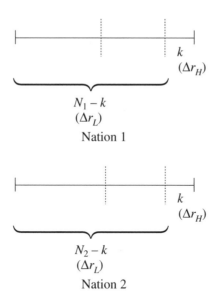

Figure 8A2.6   Case 2i

This case is illustrated in Figure 8A2.6. The new averages will be:

$$\bar{r}_{1A} = \frac{\sum_1^{N_1} r_n}{N_1} + \frac{[(N_1 - k)\Delta r_L + k\Delta r_H]}{N_1};$$

$$\bar{r}_{2A} = \frac{\sum_1^{N_2} r_n}{N_2} + \frac{[N_2\Delta r_L + k\Delta r_H]}{N_2};$$

the new overall average is:

$$\bar{r}_A = \frac{\sum_1^{N} r_n}{N} + \frac{[(N - 2k)\Delta r_L + 2k\Delta r_H)]}{N}.$$

These new averages are unambiguously smaller than those averages of case 1Ai, and unambiguously larger than those averages of case 1Ci. They will also be larger than the new averages of case 1Bi for k small enough and Δr_L sufficiently larger than v.

It is straightforward to show that the variance will unambiguously rise in each nation and overall.

2. The national agency funds those research units not funded by the supra-national agency.

ii.   The supra-national agency funds the k highest reputation variance
      collaborations.

This case is depicted in Figure 8A2.7. The new averages are the same as
those of case 2i. The new variance for nation 2 is the same as for case 2i.
The new variance for nation 1 may decrease. It is not possible to analytically determine whether the new nation 1 variance will be larger or smaller
than that of case 1Cii, the case with the smallest nation 1 new variance thus
far. Overall variance will unambiguously increase.

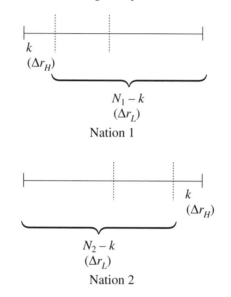

Figure 8A2.7   Case 2ii

3.   The national agency funds only those research units funded by the
     supra-national agency.
i.   The supra-national agency funds the k highest average reputation
     collaborations.

This case is illustrated in Figure 8A2.8. The new averages will be:

$$\bar{r}_{1A} = \frac{\sum_1^{N_1} r_n}{N_1} + \frac{[(N_1 - k)v + k(\Delta r_H + \Delta r_L)]}{N_1};$$

$$\bar{r}_{2A} = \frac{\sum_1^{N_2} r_n}{N_2} + \frac{[(N_2 - k)v + k(\Delta r_H + \Delta r_L)]}{N_2};$$

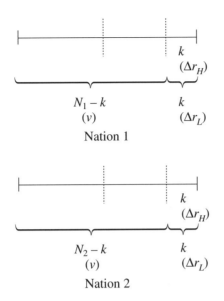

Figure 8A2.8   Case 3i

the new overall average is:

$$\bar{r}_A = \frac{\sum_1^N r_n}{N} + \frac{[(N-2k)v + 2k(\Delta r_H + \Delta r_L)]}{N}.$$

These new averages will be smaller than those of case 2i unless k is sufficiently large and $(\Delta r_L - v)$ is sufficiently small. They are unambiguously smaller than case 1Bi and 1Ci.

It is straightforward to show that variance will increase in each nation and overall. The increase in variance will be larger than that of case 2i.

3. The national agency funds only those research units funded by the supra-national agency.
   ii. The supra-national agency funds the k highest reputation variance collaborations.

This case is depicted in Figure 8A2.9. The new averages will be the same as in case 3i. The new variance for nation 2 is the same as for case 2i. The new variance for nation 1 may decrease. It is not possible to analytically determine whether new nation 1 variance will be larger or smaller than that of case 1Cii. Overall variance will increase unambiguously.

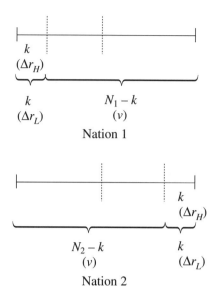

Nation 1

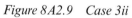

Nation 2

Figure 8A2.9   Case 3ii

NOTE

1. The variance for region 1 and overall may fall for *k* sufficiently large.

9. On the workings of scientific communities*

Robin Cowan and Nicolas Jonard

1 INTRODUCTION

This chapter is about the creation and diffusion of knowledge within scientific communities or disciplines. There has long been a distinction between basic and applied research, corresponding roughly to the distinction between science and technology. More recently, a similar distinction has been drawn between open and closed science, drawing attention to different incentive and reward structures within different loci of knowledge creation. Roughly speaking, the open science model corresponds to what we think of traditionally as university or academic research; closed science corresponding to industrial research, or research aimed at profit-making market activities.[1] In this chapter we are concerned exclusively with the open science model. We focus on single academic disciplines (economics for example) having several subdisciplines (micro theory, applied micro, econometrics, labour economics, industrial organization, macro-economics and so on). Within a discipline individual scientists interact directly with other scientists in a variety of ways – they collaborate; they read one another's working papers; they talk in the corridors; they attend one another's seminars and conference presentations and so on. If these are considered direct interactions, it is clear that all economists do not interact directly with one another. Indeed, any economist will interact directly only with a small number of other economists. Thus we observe a population of individual agents each of whom interacts directly with only a very small number of other agents. We can usefully see this population as organized as a sparsely connected network.

In network analysis each individual has a neighbourhood – the set of individuals to whom he or she is directly connected. In the world of science, this neighbourhood is a metaphor for subgroups of the population who attend the same meetings or conferences, read one another's papers, and talk to one another. But the network here is more than simply a metaphor; it is part of an active policy agenda. The European Research Area has taken on a central role in current research, training and development policy in Europe. The general goal is to integrate the research world and move from 'research done in Europe' to 'European research'. This implies, among other things, bringing together or linking researchers to facilitate both knowledge creation and distribution. On the one hand, Centres of Excellence could create critical masses, and groups of researchers within which synergies can form, and improve the productivity of knowledge creation.[2] On the other hand, networking among 'distant' researchers facilitates the geographic diffusion of new knowledge, thus easing its passage both from one location in Europe to another, and from more basic research towards industrial application (since it could permit research done in one place to be used by industry in another). In both cases, distribution of knowledge or information is at issue. In the first, clustering, or a locally dense network is called for; in the second, a globally dense, randomly connected network would be preferred.

A central concern of this chapter and indeed much of recent science and technology policy, is this transmission of knowledge among a community of researchers. Some codified knowledge is relatively easy to transmit, and can be seen as effectively diffused through general distribution channels such as scientific papers, patents and so on. Transmission of uncodified knowledge, and even some codified knowledge, equally necessary for the pursuit of science, is much more difficult.[3] In this chapter we leave aside formal transmission channels for highly codified knowledge, and restrict our attention more to tacit knowledge and informal transmission mechanisms. Here we focus on two mechanisms. One is ongoing, close (face-to-face) contact among researchers. In this mode, knowledge is transmitted either during the course of normal activities like talking about results with colleagues, members of departments and so on, or through collaborative research. The second transmission mode is the job market. When researchers (or anyone else for that matter) change jobs, they take with them their human capital stock, including their tacit knowledge.[4] In a new environment, this knowledge gets transmitted to a new community of people. Changing jobs is not a common event in the career of a researcher, though, so it constitutes a transmission mechanism that works in different ways. One interesting question is how these mechanisms, close collaboration and job mobility, interact in terms of knowledge creation and diffusion.

There are many ways to approach the issue of knowledge creation. However, we emphasize the idea that much innovation is in fact recombination of existing ideas.[5] Very few new ideas emerge purely from the ether, completely disconnected from existing ideas. In the model we develop below, innovation takes place when an agent receives new ideas from some other agent. Thus innovation is endogenous to a great extent, though because new ideas are combined with the knowledge the agent already holds, innovation is also a path-dependent process.

In what follows we develop a model of knowledge creation and diffusion. It is a network model of sufficient complexity that analytic solutions for the types of effects we examine are not possible, so we perform numerical experiments aimed at understanding how knowledge levels, interagent and intergroup variance, and agent and group specialization respond to changes in various parameters. The goal is to shed light on possible and recent actual policy actions in the field of science and technology.

2　THE MODEL

In this section, we start with a schematic description of the model, before turning to the social network and the details of knowledge circulation and creation. This is a model of open science so we take as given that scientists have no incentive to keep their discoveries secret. Indeed, they have every incentive to circulate them as widely as possible, so at every opportunity they broadcast what they know.[6]

In the scientific discipline we consider, many scientists are located on a graph, each of them having direct connections with a small number of other scientists. Individuals are located within departments, and departments are modelled as very dense, almost complete subgraphs. An individual may, however, also have direct connections with people outside his or her department. These links are fixed, and maintained, unchanging, forever. Each scientist has a knowledge endowment in the form of a real-valued vector, each element corresponding to a particular academic subfield. At random times, a scientist is selected and broadcasts knowledge in his/her area of expertise to the colleagues to whom he/she is directly connected. This is our metaphor for the academic seminar or, even if it sounds slightly more far-fetched, for the circulation of a working paper. The people with whom an individual has a link are the potential (direct) recipients of his/her knowledge. Receiving new knowledge permits an individual to innovate, and produce new related knowledge. Intermittently, at fixed intervals, there is a job market. Individuals enter the job market either if they are unhappy with their department, or if their department is unhappy with them. The purpose of the job market is to reallocate individuals among departments.

Links between agents are in principle one-way. The picture of knowledge diffusion that this entails is that, for example, *i* announces that he/she is giving a seminar, or posts a working paper on his/her website. Some of *i*'s colleagues attend the seminar or read the paper. In the structure of the model, this is formalized in that if i has a connection to j, then j will read i's paper or attend his/her seminar. Agent i will not necessarily (but could) reciprocate. Note that departments are close to complete subgraphs (at least for small numbers of permanent links). What this means in effect is that if i is connected to j, then j is almost certainly connected to i. Thus department links tend to be two-way.[7]

Individuals and Departments

A structured population of N individuals is modelled as a directed graph $G(V, \Gamma)$ where $V = \{1, ..., N\}$ is the set of vertices (individuals or scientists) and Γ is the list of oriented edges connecting one vertex to another. Each vertex has exactly $d - 1$ edges emanating from it, which define the neighbours or connections of scientist i. Formally, the edge from i to j is denoted (i, j) and $\Gamma_i = \{j \in V - \{i\} \mid (i, j) \in \Gamma\}$ is i's neighbourhood. Finally let $\#\Gamma_i = d - 1$. The size of Γ_i is held constant to maintain a constant density of the graph as we vary the nature of the individuals' neighbourhoods. There are $\frac{N}{d}$ departments, each department having exactly d members. A department is denoted δ (with $\#\delta = d$) and Δ is the set of departments. Beside his/her contacts at the department level, each individual has, on average, $p \in [0,10]$ 'permanent connections'. Individuals having more permanent connections have fewer department connections, by equal quantities. This keeps the density of $G(V, \Gamma)$ constant regardless of its architecture. This assumption can be seen as arising from a constraint – any individual has only a certain amount of time and energy to devote to 'networking activity' and if extra-department networking increases, intra-department networking must decrease.[8] In general though, restricting p to the interval [0,10] implies that departments are still very densely connected. We can interpret these connections, in this stylized model, as the source of long-distance networking. They are created through means other than the convenience of location or departmental interactions. They can thus be the links that connect distant parts of the knowledge production structure or economy. Focusing on this variable can be interpreted as focusing on the networking aspect of current science and technology policy.

To illustrate, Figure 9.1 displays two illustrative configurations where at one extreme ($p = 0$) the graph $G(V, \Gamma)$ is a set of $\frac{N}{d} = \frac{16}{4} = 4$ complete, disconnected subgraphs – the Caveman graph, each cave representing a department. Each vertex has $d - 1 = 3$ edges emanating from it, hence a total of $16 \times 3 = 48$ directed edges, and no long-distance links exist. All the links are therefore effectively two-way. The right part of Figure 9.1 is a randomly rewired Caveman graph still having $d - 1 = 3$ edges emanating from each

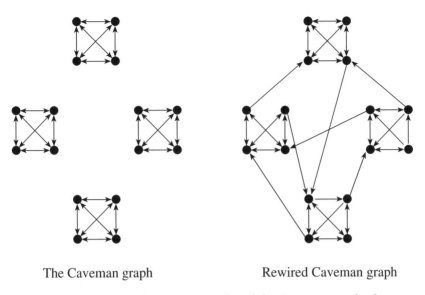

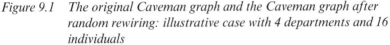

The Caveman graph   Rewired Caveman graph

Figure 9.1   *The original Caveman graph and the Caveman graph after*
random rewiring: illustrative case with 4 departments and 16
individuals

vertex, but now globally connected through a small number of inter-department links. The graph is still locally dense, though no longer locally complete. Some individuals now have more than 3 edges connecting them, though on average everyone still has 3. There are 7 distinct connections between departments, that is to say an individual has an average $p = \frac{7}{16} \approx$ 0.44 long-distance, permanent connections in our parameter space.

Knowledge

Before the dynamics of knowledge are examined, the way knowledge itself is modelled should be discussed. Different types of knowledge exist, and these types are assumed to 'interact'. One of our concerns here is with innovation as recombination, so we model knowledge complementarity explicitly. Since there are several types of knowledge, the complementarities between the knowledge of i and j stem from their having expertise of different types. Given that there are several types of knowledge, it is reasonable to posit that types can be near to or far from one another. To make this explicit, it is assumed a one-dimensional, circular knowledge space in which types of knowledge near to one another combine readily to create innovations. Learning a little more econometrics is more likely to be useful to a labour-economist than it is to a game theorist.

Each individual $i \in V$ is characterized by a real-valued knowledge vector $v_i(t) = [v_{i,k}(t); k \in C]$, with $C = \{1, ..., K\}$ the set of knowledge categories. This vector evolves over time as the individual receives broadcasts from his/her colleagues and as he/she innovates. If i is chosen to broadcast, his/her broadcast is 'heard' by every $j \in \Gamma_i$. Individuals do not broadcast everything they know, however, they only broadcast in the subject of their expertise. Thus, defining the expertise of agent i at time t to be $k^* = \arg \max_{k \in C} v_{i,k}$, individual i broadcasts his/her knowledge of type k^* to all $j \in \Gamma_i$. Individual $j \in \Gamma_i$ is able to use the information if he/she does not already possess it. Thus if $v_{j,k^*}(t) < v_{i,k^*}(t)$, individual j's knowledge increases as

$$v_{j,k^*}(t+1) = v_{j,k^*}(t) + \alpha \cdot [v_{i,k^*}(t) - v_{j,k^*}(t)].$$

The parameter α captures an important aspect of knowledge diffusion and transfer, referred to in the literature as absorptive capacity (see, for example, Cohen and Levinthal 1989). The larger α the easier it is to absorb and use external knowledge. Note that this specification imposes that scientists always give seminars in their domains of expertise, but also includes the possibility of an expertise shift, as j might attend a large enough number of seminars in field k^* to become him/herself an expert in this field.

For individual j, the addition of knowledge of type k^* creates opportunity for recombination with his/her existing knowledge of different types. For simplicity we restrict this recombination to adjacent knowledge types, broadcast yielding

$$v_{j,k^*}(t+1) = (1 + \beta) \cdot v_{j,k}(t), k = k^* \pm 1,$$

where β is a random variable, uniformly distributed over $[0, \bar{\beta}]$ with $\bar{\beta}$ small.

This describes the main, direct, mechanism of knowledge distribution and creation. The second distribution mechanism is the job market.

The Job Market

Every M periods there is a job market. Individuals who are unhappy with their departments, or whose departments are unhappy with them, enter the job market. Intuitively, when individuals evaluate a department (their own or any other) they consider whether they will learn or teach if they are located in that department. From the individual's point of view, learning is preferred, and he/she will learn if in general the members of the department know more than he/she does in many fields. The department asks the same question, namely 'Will the candidate teach or learn, that is give or take?'. But from the department's point of view, teaching is preferred – by employing this individual, the knowledge levels of existing department members will increase any time he/she broadcasts. Put otherwise, individuals want to join strong departments, departments want to attract strong individuals. Formally, the issue is the extent to which an individual dominates the members of a department in the various knowledge types. Consider department $\delta \in \Delta$. For any individual $i \in \delta$, it is possible to calculate a statistic

$$Q_{i,\delta} = \frac{1}{d \cdot K} \sum_{j \in \delta, k \in C} X_k(i,j)$$

where $X_k(i,j)$ is a binary variable such that

$$X_k(i,j) = \begin{cases} 1 : v_{i,k} > v_{j,k}, \\ 0 : v_{i,k} \leq v_{j,k}. \end{cases}$$

Individual i will enter the job market if $Q_{i,\delta} > \theta \in (0,1)$, that is to say the share of potential interactions that would be *unfruitful* is larger than some fixed proportion θ.[9] On the other hand, i will be 'asked' to enter the job market by his/her department if $Q_{i,\delta} < 1 - \theta$. (The symmetry here is unimportant; it is simply a way of keeping the number of parameters manageable.)

The mechanics of the job market are stylized, but do represent features that we see in parts of the academic world. There is a universally agreed ranking of departments. Based on this ranking, the job market is simple. The best department chooses candidates until all of its vacancies are filled. Then the second-best department does likewise, and so on until finally the worst department gets the dregs. Departments are ranked according to the aggregate knowledge they represent, which is simply the sum over members and categories $\sum_{j \in \delta, k \in C} v_{j,k}$. Department δ ranks job candidate i by $Q_{i,\delta}$ as defined above.[10]

3 NUMERICAL ANALYSIS

Network models of any degree of complexity are notoriously difficult to deal with analytically, and the accepted method for examining them is numerical simulation. This is how we proceed. Ultimately, our interest is in knowledge creation and diffusion, and whether there are conditions under which these processes thrive, or the reverse. But we can also examine issues having to do with specialization, namely whether departments and/or individuals become specialists in certain types of knowledge, or whether they retain a diversity.

Statistics

Operationally, several interesting quantities can be recorded. For notational simplicity the time index t is dropped. First the average level of knowledge in the economy is defined as

$$\bar{\mu} = \frac{1}{N} \sum_{i \in V} \mu_i,$$

where

$$\mu_i = \frac{1}{K} \sum_{k \in C} v_{i,k}$$

is individual i's average knowledge level. This is a straightforward measure of the system's efficiency when we assume that more knowledge is unambiguously better. Also of interest is the equity of knowledge allocation, for which an absolute measure is the variance in knowledge allocation across agents

$$\sigma^2 = \frac{1}{N} \sum_{i \in V} \mu_i^2 - \bar{\mu}^2,$$

and a measure in relative terms is the coefficient of variation $c = \sigma/\bar{\mu}$. The coefficient of variation corrects for increases in variance that would arise from a simple global increase in the knowledge level of the individuals, so it is more relevant for our purposes than is the variance. The same calculation can be performed at the department level, with the knowledge endowment of department δ being the sum of its members' endowments,

$$\mu\delta = \sum_{j \in \delta} \mu_j.$$

We are also concerned with the emergence of expertise, both at the individual level (are people becoming experts or generalists?) and at the department level (do we see departments with a single expertise, or are there experts of different sorts in the departments?). To get further insights into the process of specialization, Herfindahl indices of concentration can be computed. At the individual level the concentration index for individual i is written as

$$h_i = \sum_{k \in C} \left(\frac{v_{i,k}}{\sum_{l \in C} v_{i,l}} \right)^2.$$

An individual is specialized if h_i is high. More precisely, index h_i lies in $[\frac{1}{K}, 1]$ and measures how evenly knowledge is allocated across all the categories. When expertise is concentrated in a single knowledge category $h_i = 1$, whereas a homogeneous knowledge profile yields $h_i = \frac{1}{K}$. Averaging over individuals yields $\bar{h} = \frac{1}{N}\Sigma_{i\epsilon V}\, h_i$. The same indicator can be computed at the department level, where again the knowledge endowment of department δ in category k simply consists of the sum of individual endowments $\Sigma_{j\epsilon\delta}v_{j,k}$, so that

$$h_\delta = \sum_{k\epsilon C}\left(\frac{\Sigma_{j\epsilon\delta}\, v_{j,k}}{\Sigma_{j\epsilon\delta,l\epsilon C}\, v_{j,l}}\right)^2.$$

Finally we are interested in knowing whether there is a shared expertise at the economy level: do individuals and departments tend to specialize all in the same few disciplines, or is there persistent diversification across disciplines when things are examined from the macro level? This is measured by pooling all knowledge endowments together and computing again a concentration index

$$H = \sum_{k\epsilon C}\left(\frac{\Sigma_{j\epsilon V}\, v_{j,k}}{\Sigma_{j\epsilon V,l\epsilon C}\, v_{j,l}}\right)^2.$$

Settings

The basic structure of the simulation is as follows. We have $N = 900$ individuals and the department size is $d = 20$ (equally, each individual has $d - 1 = 19$ directed connections). This is a relatively sparse graph as it contains $900 \times 19 = 17{,}100$ distinct edges while the number of possible edges in the complete graph is $900 \times 899 = 809{,}100$ (so roughly 2 per cent of the possible connections are active). There are $K = 8$ types of knowledge, and each individual's knowledge vector has initial values drawn from a uniform $[0,1]$ distribution. We run the dynamic process for 30,000 periods, by which time stable patterns have emerged. All the results reported here concern the state of the world after these 30,000 periods. For each set of parameter values, we run 50 replications, and present average results for the statistics.

The parameters we vary are 3. A job market occurs every M periods, where M takes on values ranging from 300 to ∞. So M is the period of the job market, and the frequency of it is $1/M$, that is to say the market is frequent when M is small. We can compare a very stable world of lifetime tenure combined with indentured servitude ($M \rightarrow \infty$) to one in which individuals are changing jobs 'all the time' ($M \rightarrow 1$). Individuals enter the job market if they are dissatisfied with their current departments, or vice versa. We vary the degree of dissatisfaction θ required before an individual is willing to bear the costs of job search and relocation. With this parameter we can examine the effect of job market frictions. Two values for this parameter are examined: $\theta = 0.625$ corresponds to an active job market (a market with low frictions), whereas $\theta = 0.7$ corresponds to a much less active job market (a market with high frictions). What would be the effect of a policy aimed at reducing (or increasing) the costs of changing jobs in terms of an economy's ability to produce knowledge? Finally, the presence of permanent links represents extra-departmental, long-distance (pan-European?) networking. We vary the number of permanent links p from 0 to 10 on average per individual, with an increment which makes it convenient to display the results on a logarithmic scale. How much networking do we need to create a world of rapid knowledge creation and diffusion?

4   RESULTS

The major concern in this chapter is about the ability of the economy to produce and distribute knowledge. This we measure in an obvious way by observing the average knowledge level in the economy, and examining how this latter responds to changes in parameter values. Heterogeneity at the individual and the department levels (allocative efficiency) is discussed in the second subsection. Expertise is also of interest, and this is examined in the last subsection.

Job Market Activity

The first results we present have to do with job market activity under various parameters. These results are intuitively straightforward, but are useful in understanding other more central results.

Figure 9.2 shows the number of participants, l, in the job market (including both the 'willing-to-leave' and the 'pushed-out' individuals).[11] As in all the figures that follow, the results are shown in two panels. In the left panel, $\theta = 0.625$ which indicates a (relatively) low friction job market. In the right panel, $\theta = 0.7$, a relatively high friction market. Recall the interpretation of θ is that an individual wants to leave when he/she dominates in more than $\theta \times 100$ per cent of all possible (intra-departmental) transmissions, and is asked to leave when he/she is dominated in more than $(1 - \theta) \times 100$ per cent.

There is no ambiguity here: as the time between job markets increases (M increases), the number of agents changing departments in each job market also increases, regardless of the values of p and θ. This could suggest that there is intra-department bifurcation over time: people tend to become more different. This would increase the number of job seekers. It could also indicate inter-department homogenization over time. For people to move, there has to be overlap, for example, the worst person in the best depart-

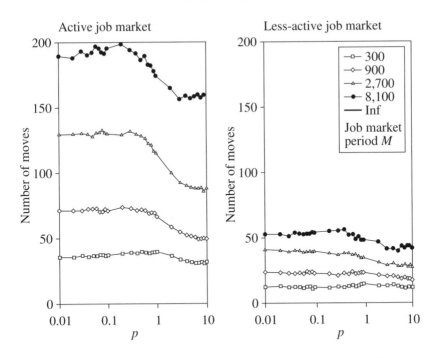

Figure 9.2   Labour mobility: number of agents moving per job market

ment must be eliminated and replaced with the best person in the second department. If departments become very different from each other, this cannot happen. Note that there is a tendency for l to decrease with p, for p larger than 0.5, which probably contributes to the decrease which will be observed in Figure 9.4.

Comparing the two panels indicates three phenomena. First, the dispersion of job market activity is much less in the right, high friction panel. Second, in terms of movement per job market, activity levels at all job market frequencies resemble those of the two highest frequencies in the left, low friction panel. Finally, we can calculate total job mobility over the life (30,000 periods) of the economy by scaling each curve in Figure 9.2 by $30,000/M$, thereby correcting for the time effect.

Total mobility is depicted in Figure 9.3. The rescaling operation inverts the rank order of the curves: the lower the frequency (the larger the period) of the market, the less job mobility there is over the life of the economy. In addition, on this measure the curves in the right panel (for all job market frequencies) resemble the curves for the two most infrequent markets in the left panel, as evidenced by Figure 9.3.

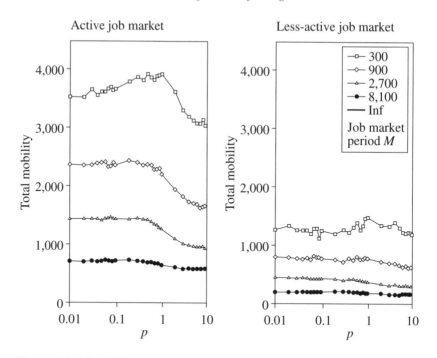

Figure 9.3 Total labour mobility over the economy lifetime

The Production of Knowledge

Two sources of knowledge mobility are at work in the model, directly influencing knowledge creation and diffusion: networking as represented by p, and the job market dynamics (where an increased mobility of knowledge can originate either in a more frequent market – smaller M – or in lower incentives to stay – lower θ).

In Figure 9.4 we depict the evolution of $\bar{\mu}$ as a function of the number p of permanent connections, for two levels of θ, the propensity to move, and a number of values for M, the period of the job market. The leftmost part of Figure 9.4 is obtained for $\theta = 0.625$, while the right part of the figure is for $\theta = 0.7$, that is to say the incentives to stay are stronger in the right-hand panel.

Knowledge levels and networking

An important particular case of the model is when no job market takes place (the no-job-market configuration obtains for $M = \infty$). In that case networking is the only source of knowledge transfer across departments.

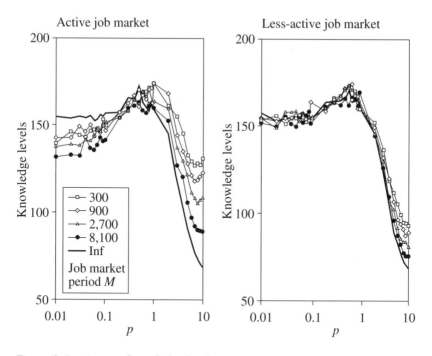

Figure 9.4   Average knowledge levels

As can be seen from Figure 9.4, knowledge levels rise slowly with p, peak in the range $0.5 \leq p \leq 1$, and then dramatically fall off as p is further increased. This pattern is preserved when a job market is introduced, provided its frequency is kept low enough. Above a certain frequency (1/2,700 in the simulations) and only when frictions are low, an increasing relationship with p obtains again when p exceeds 6. There is, however, a clear maximum in the range $0.5 \leq p \leq 1$, for any values of M and θ. Therefore, it seems that an 'optimal' number of permanent links exists, that is, there is an optimal intensity of networking when the goal is to maximize total knowledge. Adding a small number of inter-department (or permanent) links, that is, connecting otherwise isolated departments, raises knowledge levels dramatically in poorly connected communities, but harms diffusive efficiency in denser ones. Therefore knowledge production is maximized when the network structure is characterized at the same time by significant cliquishness and the existence of some (though not too many) permanent connections. As we shall see, the same is true for the distribution of expertise.

Knowledge levels and the job market

The next result concerns the impact of job market frictions (θ) on knowledge levels. First, we observe that there is an ordering of the curves: higher job market frequencies (smaller M) yield higher knowledge levels in the long run. There is significant variance around this trend however, and it becomes marked only for very large numbers of extra-departmental connections, that is, when departments are close to disintegrating. More striking is that the dispersion in the left panel is greater than that in the right panel, in concord with the dispersion in job market activity seen in Figure 9.2. A second difference between the two panels is that to the left of the peak at $p = 1$ the right-hand panel is qualitatively similar to the high frequency curves in the left panel; for $p > 1$ it is similar to the low frequency curves. This suggests that for $p < 1$ having a stable market with little total job mobility is a good thing, but for $p > 1$ high job mobility is a good thing. The interplay between job mobility and networking is clearly complex, and deserves much further attention.

In general there are three sources of knowledge growth: diffusion through broadcast; diffusion through the job market; and knowledge creation. These processes are affected differently by different aspects of the model. Networking favours rapid diffusion through broadcast; an active job market with high turnover favours diffusion through that channel; and a highly coherent department favours knowledge creation. The results here on average long-run knowledge levels suggest that different processes dominate on different parts of the parameter space. This is discussed more fully below (see Section 5).

Note that, intuitively, one might expect that the more frequent the job market (the smaller M is), the higher knowledge levels are, since a job market is a means of knowledge transmission. However, examining Figure 9.4, this seems not to be the case. It takes numerous permanent links before this intuition is confirmed, and a low level of market friction.

Allocative Efficiency

To address the issue of homogeneity of knowledge endowments (are there good and bad individuals or departments, or are they all of equivalent excellence?), coefficients of variation at both the individual and department levels are computed.

Figure 9.5 depicts the coefficient of variation for individuals. The patterns are very similar for departments, except differences are slightly amplified at the individual level. Increasing market frictions (θ) squeezes the distances between curves corresponding to different periods M for the job market, while preserving the pattern with respect to networking (p).

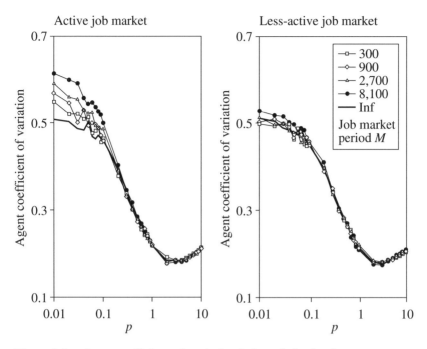

Figure 9.5   Agent coefficient of variation in knowledge levels

Again, this can be explained by the fact that in the high friction market, market frequency has a smaller effect on actual mobility and thus on knowledge diffusion. The effect of p is as follows: networking intensity promotes homogeneity – the more networking there is (the higher p is), the more similar agents are in terms of their total knowledge stocks. The same is true (though not shown) of departments. For large p-values, however, increasing networking tends to increase heterogeneity again.

Both sources of knowledge diffusion are clearly important in the explanation here. With a globally well-connected network (here approximated with large p), diffusion is rapid and thorough (this is a general result in epidemic diffusion theory) and thus heterogeneity (measured by the coefficient of variation) will be low. Job market activity does not exert any significant influence on allocative efficiency in general, nor do market frictions. However, for a low p, the graph is not connected (departments are isolated) and the job market becomes a relatively more important source of long-distance diffusion. One would expect then, that in this circumstance high levels of job market activity (low M) reduce heterogeneity. When the job market is the major source of knowledge circulation (low p), it even seems to promote heterogeneity.

Expertise

The emergence of expertise both at the individual and at the economy level is examined using Herfindahl indices of knowledge concentration. The general idea of expertise is that an agent (or department or economy) has a large amount of knowledge of a few types, and much less of other types. To get at this issue statistically it is convenient to ask about the extent to which an agent's knowledge is concentrated. A standard measure of concentration is the Herfindahl index.

Expertise as heterogeneity in knowledge types
Figure 9.6 depicts the average Herfindahl index for individuals. When measured using a Herfindahl index over knowledge types, agents and departments again look the same so we omit the department graphs.

The curves in Figure 9.6 are averages over agents of the agent-level Herfindahl index for the distribution of knowledge over different disciplines. The population-wide average index $\bar{h}$ lies in the range [0.5, 0.85] for any parametrization, that is to say the equivalent number of categories ($\bar{h}^{-1}$) is between 2 and 1.2 (it can go up to 8). There is therefore evidence that strong specialization takes place.

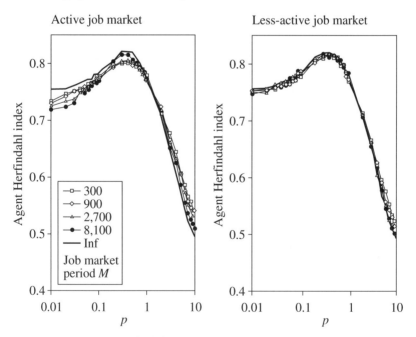

Figure 9.6   Agent Herfindahl indices

Increasing market friction (θ) again squeezes the distance between curves corresponding to different periods M for the job market. This is a very small effect, however. Much more significant is the relationship between networking and specialization. Specialization and networking (p) have a non-monotonic relationship for any period of the job market (M). Specialization rises with the amount of networking to a peak at $p = 0.5$ and then falls over the range $p \in [0.5, 1]$. (This pattern is strikingly similar to the peak in terms of knowledge levels we observed in Figure 9.4.)

That specialization falls as the number of permanent links increases is not surprising. A permanent link tends to be a long-distance one, which thus effectively brings knowledge into a department from distant parts of the economy. When $p > 1$ most agents have long-distance links so they are directly exposed to a wider variety of knowledge. They are further exposed to variety indirectly through the permanent links of the members of their own departments. This broader exposure would, in general, lead to absorption and innovation in an agent's categories of non-expertise. This creates a trend of falling specialization. Note, though, that even with this trend, agents remain relatively highly specialized.

Expertise at the economy level
The last aspect of specialization we examine is the extent to which individuals (and as a consequence departments) tend to develop the same expertise all over the economy, or there is aggregate diversity although we observe specialization both at the individual and at the department levels.

Figure 9.7 depicts the Herfindahl index H of economy-wide specialization. As H obtains by pooling all the existing knowledge in each category, if one category grows more than the others it indicates specialization in this discipline is taking place. Job market frictions do not significantly affect the global patterns; there is a mild influence of the frequency of job markets (in the sense that more markets imply more specialization) and a strong influence of networking. Specialization is a non-monotonic function of the intensity of networking p. Starting from $H \approx 0.65$, concentration rises to 0.75 before falling dramatically below 0.45. Once enough links have been introduced, the more networking there is the less commonality of expertise we see in the economy. It is sensible that isolated departments (p low) specialize on different expertise, so when pooling all the existing knowledge together homogeneity should obtain. When departments are interrelated and cliquishness preserved (p small), a small number of neighbouring dominant disciplines emerge, whose identity is mainly selected by small events taking place at the beginning of the process. As p is further increased, cliquishness is lost so specialization within each department gets weaker, and the overall portrait is a more generalist world.

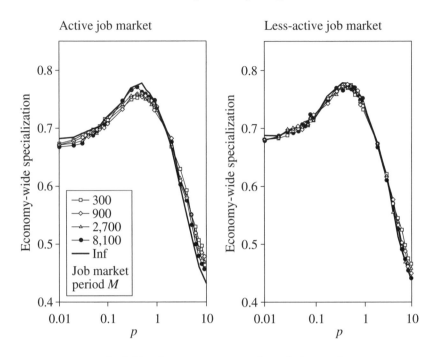

Figure 9.7   Herfindahl index over aggregate knowledge stocks:
specialization at the economy level

5   DISCUSSION

The model considered here is about the production and diffusion of knowledge in networks. We have examined a family of oriented graphs having constant density (each agent is the owner of $d-1 = 19$ directed links) but different architectures, that is, different structural properties. The results that have been presented therefore only arise from changes in graph architecture – how links are allocated between pairs of vertices. At one extreme, the Caveman graph is a disconnected collection of fully connected components. The Caveman graph represents a world in which all the people I talk to also talk to each other, and to me. This is known as cliquishness, a feature which is fairly common in social networks. However, in the Caveman graph, cliques are isolated so no information can travel from one cave to another. At the other extreme, that is, when all the intra-cave links are replaced with long-distance links, caves dislocate and a random graph forms, exhibiting almost no cliquishness but having extremely short path lengths (the friendship chain between any two individuals is short).

A whole spectrum of graphs obtains when intra-cave links can be broken and replaced with 'long-distance' links, that is links going from one cave to another. The objective of this chapter was to investigate the behaviour of graphs that fall between the Caveman graph and the random graph. We saw that knowledge production is maximized when the network structure is characterized at the same time by significant cliquishness and the existence of some (though not too many) permanent connections, and the same is true for allocative efficiency.

Knowledge in the model is circulated via three means: intra-department links, permanent (long-distance) connections and job markets. However these different channels operate on different scales.

Growth, we have seen, takes place on adjacent knowledge categories (due to our assumption about the 'knowledge space'). The general principle is that i transmits to j in say category 3, j absorbs, innovates in categories 2 and 4, and transmits back his/her expertise (say 4). So i absorbs in 4, innovates in 3 and 5, and again will broadcast in 3. This way categories 3 and 4 tend to grow together, feeding each other. But for this to work properly the path between i and j must be very short – the most effective is when the link between them is two-way. As long as p is small, this is true within a department. Departments are close to complete graphs, so most links are effectively two-way. Creating a small number of permanent links therefore does not interfere with cliquishness. But when there tends to be more permanent links (say 2, 3 and above), cliquishness declines and the virtuous cycle we described is weakened. So cliquishness is good in that it permits a local feedback at the department level, and operates most effectively when p is small.

Permanent links are also a good thing, as they permit knowledge to be transmitted to distant parts of the graph in a small number of steps (therefore avoiding degradation due to imperfect absorptive capacity). But the marginal loss in cliquishness tends to be smaller than the marginal gain in path length, as long as p is not too big. Indeed, increasing p while keeping it small retains the desirable cliquishness within a department and adds to it incoming knowledge from distant parts of the economy. Thus total knowledge levels rise. For larger p, departments begin to deteriorate in terms of cohesiveness (cliquishness falls noticeably) and this effect overwhelms the benefits of reducing path length.[12]

The job market also promotes knowledge diffusion, but unless it is very frequent, it does not seem to have a significant effect on the growth of knowledge. The exception occurs when p is very large and M is very small. Under this condition we see that knowledge growth again rises with p. What this suggests is that interactions between job markets and networking can exist, but are only likely to be significant in very special circumstances.[13]

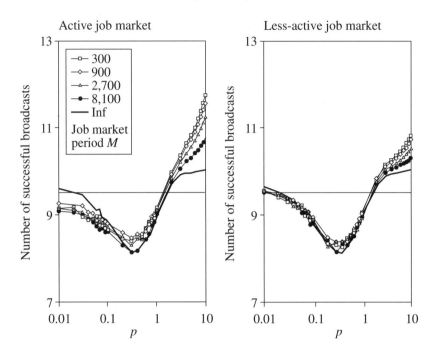

Figure 9.8   Number of successful knowledge transmissions (out of
$d-1 = 19$)

Further insight into the workings of the model can be gained when other micro-economic indicators are examined.

Figure 9.8 depicts the average number n_S of successful transmissions per broadcast episode, out of $d-1 = 19$ possible transmissions.[14] In a world of random knowledge endowments, one would expect that n_S stays very close to $19/2 = 9.5$. However, as evidenced by Figure 9.8, n_S significantly departs from 9.5 (horizontal solid line), being significantly smaller in the range [0.1,1], and significantly larger for $p > 1$. So introducing shortcuts across the graph has a non-monotonic effect on the number of successful transmissions, which falls with p as long as p is lower than 0.5, and increases thereafter.[15] This suggests that less growth should be observed in the region [0.1,1], but the opposite is actually true. The reason is that, although more transmissions take place, they convey less knowledge.

In Figure 9.9, the growth rate of knowledge net of innovation (that is, growth of knowledge due solely to absorption) is plotted against the number of permanent connections. It parallels the evolution of knowledge levels, increasing first, reaching a peak in the range [0.1,1] and then decreas-

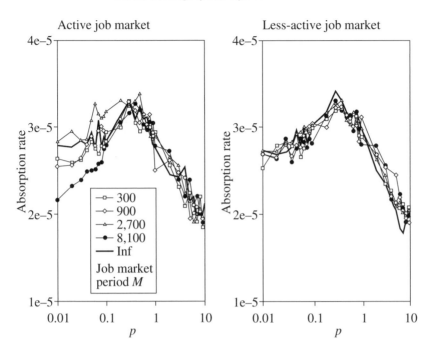

Figure 9.9   Growth rate of knowledge from absorption

ing. This indicates again the importance of absorption as a driver of knowledge growth, but also emphasizes that networking is not the sole driver of absorption.

Finally, it is worth a brief discussion of the assumptions about knowledge transmission and creation. The model assumes that absorption and creation do not depend on the structure of the recipient's knowledge. One might expect, however, that there is an interaction between the type of knowledge transmitted and the nature of the expertise of the recipient that affects both absorption and creation. Regarding absorption, we might think, for example, that a macro-economist could more successfully absorb game theory than he/she could seventeenth-century poetry. Regarding knowledge creation, the macro-economist is likely to make a much smaller innovation in (the neighbouring categories of) eighteenth-century poetry or seventeenth-century prose, than is a literary theorist. Second, it seems reasonable to believe that the size of innovation is related to the amount absorbed. These effects could be integrated into the model, but only at the cost of multiplying parameters. If absorption and creation of knowledge were negatively affected by the distance between what is broadcast and the recipient's expertise, the extent to which individuals become specialized would increase dramatically. This effect would change the way expertise evolves at more aggregated levels. If the size of innovation is affected by the amount absorbed, inter-individual variance in knowledge levels will increase and this effect will spill over to departments. Apart from this there will be few qualitative differences from this change to the model.

Agents in the model engage in little strategic behaviour, neither in link-formation, broadcast timing or content, nor in job market behaviour. Endogenizing these decisions would be an interesting and fruitful extension of the model. None the less it would come at the cost of considerable increase in complexity in the model and its parameter space.[16]

6 CONCLUSION

In terms of knowledge growth, inducing knowledge mobility is a good thing. This can be achieved by establishing an ongoing job market or by promoting networking, that is, establishing inter-department connections among scientists. Both are effective in increasing knowledge production. For any intensity of networking, it is always better to also have a job market, regardless of its frequency, though there is a suggestion that the more frequent the job market (or perhaps more job mobility per period) the better. (It is important to note, in interpreting the last statement, that we have included no explicit transition costs – nothing is lost either for the department or the individual when an individual changes jobs, which is somewhat unrealistic, and would suggest a lower bound to the period of an effective job market.)

The intensity of networking, by contrast, exerts a non-monotonic influence on overall performance. It is possible to have too much networking: having only a few permanent links is optimal. An explanation for this follows from the observation that in our model, adding permanent links implies a move away from a disconnected graph towards a connected random graph. Thus when the number of permanent links gets large enough, the performance of the system should approach that of a complete graph. But because agents' initial knowledge endowments are independent, a complete graph would behave like a single department, and so knowledge levels should approach those obtained in the case of isolated departments (no job market and no networking). Looking at Figure 9.5, we observe that variation in agents' knowledge levels decreases as networking increases – agents become more similar. Since knowledge improvements through broadcasting depend on the difference in level of sender and receiver, as agents become similar, the size of knowledge increments decreases; knowledge growth rates fall. Thus initially, a small amount of networking diffuses information in a sparse enough way so that while agents' knowledge levels grow, the population remains relatively heterogeneous. But when there is a significant amount of networking activity agents start to become too similar, because diffusion is too efficient, and knowledge increments fall, causing a decline in growth rates.

Whether heterogeneity among knowledge levels of scientists or departments is in itself desirable from a policy perspective is not clear. However, in the same region of the parameter space in which knowledge levels are high, agents' knowledge levels are relatively equal. (The minimum in heterogeneity among agents' levels occurs at a somewhat higher level of networking than does the maximum of knowledge levels.) It is also true though, that in that same region agents become more specialized – the intra-agent distribution of knowledge over knowledge categories becomes more unequal. The same is true of the intra-department knowledge endowments. This occurs even though the job market is neutral with regard to promoting specialist or generalist departments. Thus the specialization stems from the networking aspect of the structure, and suggests that networking does create the synergies that it is often presumed to do. When two agents are directly connected, and specialize in adjacent knowledge categories, they can create a strong positive feedback between them in which they improve side-by-side so to speak, each one's improvement directly helping the other. As this happens, the two agents become more and more specialized in their two subdisciplines, as their knowledge there increases fastest.

Should policy focus on job market frictions? Reducing frictions clearly increases the rate of job turnover, but it has other effects as well. Still the relationship is not at all straightforward. If we are beneath the optimal amount of networking, the best structure in terms of knowledge production is no job market at all: lifetime tenure combined with indentured servitude. If we have more than the optimal amount of networking, this structure is the worst possible. Similarly, comparing the panels of Figure 9.4 we see that with 'too little' networking the high friction job market produces more knowledge; with 'too much' networking, it produces less. Curiously, though, within each panel, that is for a given level of job market frictions (or transaction costs) the more frequent the market, and thus the more job mobility per period (as opposed to per market) the better in terms of knowledge production. To conclude more than this would be pushing very hard on the model, though, since it would be resting on implicit assumptions about the nature of the actual transaction costs for both individual and department, and how they affect decisions to move. If the job market is frequent enough, decreasing frictions does not have much apparent effect on knowledge levels. This leaves open an important avenue for policy research, however, in understanding how decisions to change jobs or personnel are made, and how this impinges on the creation and flow of knowledge.

NOTES

*   This research was done while Jonard was a visiting scholar at the International Institute of Infonomics (IIoI) and we thank that institute for its support. This chapter was written as a contribution to the STRATA network 'NPRnet' and has greatly benefited from comments of the members of that network, and from the comments of an anonymous referee.

1.   See Dasgupta and David (1994) for a detailed discussion of open versus closed science and policy implications drawn therefrom. For a general overview of the economics of science, see Stephan (1996).

2.   Note that academic research has been divided into disciplines in part for exactly these sorts of reasons: presumably there are more potential synergies among different types of economists than there would be among an economist, a chemist, a classical scholar and a French sixteenth-century literature expert.

3.   For an extensive discussion of the economics of codified and tacit knowledge see, for example, David and Foray (1995), Cowan and Foray (1997) and Cowan et al. (2000); or the TIPIK project papers in the special issue of *Industrial and Corporate Change* **9**, 2000.

4.   There is now a large literature on network structures and job markets in which the issue has been the role of a social network when an individual is trying to find a job. (See Granovetter 1974; Bian 1997; Fernandez and Weinberg 1997 for very different examples.) This is explicitly not our concern here. Rather, we are interested in job mobility as creating a link in a network of knowledge or information transmission.

5.   See Kogut and Zander (1992), or Antonelli (1999) for discussions of this idea.

6.   See Dasgupta and David (1994).

7.   In practice, what we have called permanent links are likely to be different in nature from department links. Permanent links tend to be created for particular reasons, such as research collaboration, whereas department links are much more like links of convenience. Thus in practice permanent links will, it seems, tend to be two-way. In what follows we have left them as one-way for consistency. But re-running the experiments with two-way permanent links does not make any qualitative difference to the results.

8.   Note that this implies an implicit relative price of 1: department links and permanent links have the same costs to maintain. This could be generalized without qualitatively changing the results.

9.   Recall that if i knows more than j, when j broadcasts, i neither learns nor innovates.

10.   One possible elaboration of the model would be to examine the effects of different job market mechanisms, ranging from the relatively unrealistic random pairing of candidates and departments through the marriage matching algorithm of Gale and Shapley (1962) to the also unrealistic *optimal* marriage matching algorithm proposed by Irving et al. (1987).

11.   Given the structure of our stylized job market, it is possible that agents on the market would be selected by their current departments. Thus there can be a discrepancy between the number of participants in the job market and the number of agents who change jobs. In this section we are discussing the latter.

12.   Our focus in this chapter has not been on the small world phenomenon (see Watts and Strogatz 1998; Watts 1999), but the discussion in this paragraph suggests that it has emerged once again.

13.   When $M = 300$ a job market takes place after every 300 broadcasts. Since a broadcast is 'one agent presenting a paper or posting a working paper' in an economy of 900 agents,

this is essentially a continuous job market. Similarly when $p = 10$ in a world in which department size is 20, the average agent has half of his/her connections with people outside his/her department. This suggests an effective disintegration of the department as an institution. Both of these are extreme situations.

14. Recall that i attempts to broadcast to all $j \in \Gamma_i$. If j knows less than i then j receives information and the broadcast is counted as a success. If j knows more, j receives nothing and the broadcast (to j) was a failure. For any attempted broadcast the maximum possible number of successes is 19, the minimum is zero.

15. Interestingly, in the context of random graphs consisting of cN edges randomly allocated among N vertices, with large N, Erdös and Renyi (1960), have shown that $c = 1/2$ is the critical point above which the graph contains a giant connected component, while only finite-sized connected components exist below $c = 1/2$. If departments are seen as nodes, we are in a similar context, and a qualitative change seems to take place in a similar region (p around 1/2).

16. An extended model would have to address the following issues: how to discount; the structure of expectations; what are the payoffs in non-knowledge terms; prices and value of knowledge; decision rules governing link formation and dissolution; types of links (bilateral, pairwise, one-way . . .); the nature and timing of the job market and job search (whether it is continuous or periodic . . .); the nature of the trade-off between different transmission mechanisms.

REFERENCES

Antonelli, C. (1999), 'Communication and innovation: the evidence with technological districts', paper presented at the International Conference 'Knowledge Spillovers and the Geography of Innovation: A Comparison of National Systems of Innovation', Université Jean Monnet St. Étienne, France, 1–2 July.

Bian, Y. (1997), 'Bringing strong ties back in: indirect ties, network bridges, and job searches in China', *American Sociological Review* **62**(3), 366–85.

Cohen, W.M. and D.A. Levinthal (1989), 'Innovation and learning: the two faces of research and development', *Economic Journal* **99**(3), 569–96.

Cowan, R. and D. Foray (1997), 'The economics of codification and the diffusion of knowledge', *Industrial and Corporate Change* **6**(3), 595–622.

Cowan, R., P. David and D. Foray (2000), 'The explicit economics of knowledge codification and tacitness', *Industrial and Corporate Change* **9**(2), 211–53.

Dasgupta, P. and P. David (1994), 'Towards a new economics of science', *Research Policy* **23**(5), 487–521.

David, P. and D. Foray (1995), 'Accessing and expanding the science and technology knowledge base', *STI Review* **16**, 13–68.

Erdös, P. and A. Renyi (1960), 'On the evolution of random graphs', *Publications of the Mathematical Institute of the Hungarian Academy of Sciences* **5**, 17–61.

Fernandez, R. and N. Weinberg (1997), 'Sifting and sorting: personal contacts and hiring in a retail bank', *American Sociological Review* **62**(2), 883–902.

Gale, D. and L. Shapley (1962), 'College admissions and the stability of marriage', *American Mathematical Monthly* **69**(9), 9–15.

Granovetter, M. (1974), *Getting a Job: A Study of Contacts and Careers*, Cambridge, MA: Harvard University Press.

Irving, R., P. Leather and D. Gusfield (1987), 'An efficient algorithm for the "optimal" stable marriage', *Journal of the Association of Computer Machinery* **34**(3), 532–43.

Kogut, B. and U. Zander (1992), 'Knowledge of the firm, combinative capabilities and the replication of technology', *Organization Science* **3**(3), 383–97.

Stephan, P.E. (1996), 'The economics of science', *Journal of Economic Literature* **34**(5), 1199–235.

Watts, D. (1999), 'Networks, dynamics and the small world phenomenon', *American Journal of Sociology* **105**(2), 493–527.

Watts, D. and S. Strogatz (1998), 'Collective dynamics of small-world networks', *Letters to Nature* **393**(June), 440–42.

10. Funding basic research: when is public finance preferable to attainable 'club goods' solutions?

G.M. Peter Swann

1 INTRODUCTION

One of the most common arguments for public funding of basic research focuses on externalities. The funder of basic research cannot capture all the benefits from that research and some of these spill over to others. As a consequence, there is a risk that some socially viable projects (where *social* benefit exceeds cost) will not be funded, because the cost exceeds the *private* benefit to the funder. Public funding aims to fill that gap. Few economists have questioned this justification for public funding *of basic research*, because basic research is seen as one of the purest forms of public good.

It is recognized, of course, that the club goods solution has a role for the funding of some non-basic research activity. In those areas a common 'club goods' response to the externality argument is to ask, why can the diverse beneficiaries from a project not form a club to fund it? If a sufficient number join together such that their joint benefits exceed cost then the socially viable project will be funded – even if the funding club does not capture all the benefits. In short, the club solution is to internalize (at least some of) the externalities. The club goods approach seems to be attracting ever more interest in policy circles as an alternative to public funding in some non-basic areas – for example, in the funding of standards activity. But for the most part, enthusiasts of the club goods solution have stopped short of advocating this as a solution to the funding of basic research.

However, some are starting to go further and suggest that this model is also appropriate for funding of basic research.[1] In particular, as it gets hard to secure pure public finance for research (and hence publicly financed research is necessarily underfunded research), the club goods route is seen as a potential salvation. Sceptics, however, question the optimality of some of the clubs that it would be feasible to assemble.

The aim of this chapter is simply to look at the applicability or otherwise of the club goods approach to funding basic research. It is not our intention to cast doubt on the role of the club goods solution in funding more applied activities. Romer (1993) has argued that the club goods solution is essentially complementary to public finance: it can help to fill a gap between the funding mechanisms required for basic research and the privately financed research of an individual company.[2] Where does the boundary lie between basic and applied research? The analysis in this chapter offers a partial answer in terms of the ease with which diffuse benefits from research can be internalized within a club. For applied research this is possible; for basic research it is not feasible, or not economic.

2   PUBLIC FUNDING OR CLUB SOLUTION? CONTRASTING RATIONALES

Let us start by briefly comparing the generic rationales for public funding and club solutions. The economic justification for industry policy and public funding tends to be one of three sorts. First, that policy is required because there is *market failure* requiring some sort of correction, or at least some compensating activity. Second, policy is needed to *regulate* private monopolies (though this could be seen as a special case of the first). Third, a 'strategic' rationale – for example, those programmes designed to give a new industry a boost (or kick-start) so that it moves onto a faster growth curve. My assumption from the start is that the justification in the case of basic research is the first sort, so we shall focus on that in what follows.

Economists tend to identify three generic causes of market failure. The first is that *externalities* (whether positive or negative) drive a wedge between private and social returns from a particular private investment. If externalities are positive, some socially desirable investments will not appear privately profitable, so the market does not support enough activity. If externalities are negative, some socially undesirable investments nevertheless appear privately profitable, so the market supports too much activity.

The second is where economic activities are subject to *increasing returns*. In that case there is no unregulated market outcome that is also economically efficient. If perfect competition is sustained, then production does not exploit the increasing returns, so costs are not minimized. If monopoly is allowed to emerge, the monopolist may be able to exploit the increasing returns, but is liable to restrict output to keep up prices. The third is that *asymmetric information* between buyers and sellers can make it impossible to find a price at which to trade that is acceptable both to buyers and to sellers. One example of this is Gresham's law, which asserts that 'bad drives out good'. The presence of 'bad' products in a market, and the inability of the buyer to distinguish bad from good *ex ante*, means that the supplier of a good withdraws his or her produce from the market as he or she cannot raise a satisfactory price (Akerlof 1970).

Our working hypothesis is that the most important source of market failure that arises in this context is the existence of externalities (mostly positive) from basic research. Public funding is required because socially valuable projects do not appear privately profitable.

A typical club goods response to these observations could be this. Why do the project managers not require those third parties that enjoy the spillovers to join the group paying for the project and, hence, *internalize* these spillovers? Indeed, some economists in this tradition argue that there are fewer pure public goods than is commonly supposed. However, it can be a costly business to track down all beneficiaries from spillovers and charge them for the benefits they receive. Moreover, there are always risks of free riding. Sometimes the benefits of seeking to create such clubs do justify the costs; often they do not. While there are indubitably schemes for internalizing some externalities in real worlds, there are in practice still a large number of externalities that evade any levy of this sort.

How can we compare the suitability of a club goods solution to public finance? An answer to this involves discussion of three main issues. The first is transaction costs. Forming a club solution involves transaction costs and, if the requisite club of beneficiaries is large and dispersed, these can be substantial. By contrast, the public finance solution involves relatively light transaction costs. Accordingly, there may be a variety of feasible clubs, all of different sizes: benefits may increase as size increases because of an increasing rate of internalization, but transaction costs will also increase with size. The most profitable club may not be the largest.

The second is economic efficiency, or value for money. For both club and publicly funded activities there is a *challenge of relevance*: how can the researchers demonstrate to their funders the value of what they do? Such a challenge can become much harder in the public context because the constituency is the entire tax-paying public, rather than the select members of a club.

Third, there is the risk of monopolization. It is generally unreasonable to expect clubs to manage their basic research in the same way as the traditional model of publicly funded basic research. (Of course, we should bear in mind that this traditional model has become less relevant as universities assert intellectual property rights with increasing vigour.) Why should clubs allow benefits to spill over to non-members – particularly if these non-members are actual or potential rivals?[3] This monopolization might not matter if those outside the club were not beneficiaries – or, to put it another way, if the club internalizes *all* externalities. But it *will* matter when internalization is incomplete and especially so if a club forms with strategic intent to exclude some potential beneficiaries.

3 TWO SORTS OF ERROR

One popular conception of how the club goods solution compares with a public finance solution can be summarized very succinctly in the following matrix. It compares projects on two criteria: are they profitable or unprofitable (from a *social* point of view)? And are they or are they not funded? In what follows we shall be comparing three solutions:

- public finance;
- the best *attainable* club solution; and
- the optimal or perfect club solution – where the club comprises all beneficiaries who are charged in proportion to their benefits.

Rather like classical hypothesis testing, two kinds of error can be made. A *type I* error (rejecting a true null) occurs if a socially profitable project is *not* funded. A *type II* error (failing to reject a false null) occurs if a socially unprofitable project *is* funded.

Table 10.1   A popular conception of the failings of club solutions and public finance

	Socially profitable	Socially unprofitable
Funded	Correct decision	*Type II error:* Public finance solutions prone to fall here
Not funded	*Type I error:* Club solutions prone to fall here	Correct decision

A common belief is that the (imperfect) club goods solution is more prone to type I errors while the public finance solution is more prone to type II errors. This is a bit too simplistic. We certainly cannot say that public finance never makes type I errors, or that the club solution never makes type II errors – we shall see below that it can. At best, one might assert that the errors of the club solution are skewed towards the bottom left corner, while the errors of the public finance solution are skewed towards the upper right corner. Even that is too simplistic, but it is a useful working hypothesis for now.

What is the justification for the hypothesis? The problems with the club solution are that not all benefits are realized because there may be high transaction costs in assembling a club. In addition there can be free riding. For both these reasons, socially valuable projects may not be funded. And always, there is a natural bias towards projects that bring the highest benefits to the club – regardless of externalities.

The problems with public finance by contrast are that some that pay do not benefit and, more generally, that contributions are unrelated to the size of benefits. Socially unprofitable projects may be funded because the public process is susceptible to lobbying by interested parties. I argued elsewhere (Swann 1994) that patent offices are prone to type II errors in awarding patents. Moreover, some critics are sceptical about selection mechanisms in basic research. A commonly quoted piece of folklore among rejected authors is that, 'Peer review is an excellent system for rejecting the worst 50 per cent and the best 10 per cent'. This suggests a selection mechanism that is prone to many type II errors as well as some, serious, type I errors.

Accepting that the hypothesis distilled in the matrix is too simplistic, what nevertheless does it imply? It means that the appropriate choice between these two methods of research funding depends on the relative weight attached to type I and type II errors. In classical hypothesis testing, the null tends to be *privileged* so the probability of a type I error is kept very small even if that increases the risk of a large probability of type II error. Some critics still interpret the public finance model in this way: they consider that too much mediocrity is funded (type II error) for fear of incurring a type I error. To an insider, however, it seems that while such an attitude to research funding might have prevailed in the golden days of university research funding (mid-1960s), it does not seem to describe the research funding model of today.

By contrast, in popular conception, the club solution is less likely to incur type II errors because the club is more concerned about them. The club takes a hard-nosed approach to funding decisions. By contrast, its members are less concerned about type I errors, perhaps (implicitly) because they accept J.K. Galbraith's (1970, 9:III) maxim that, 'inventions that are not made . . . are rarely missed'. From the perspective of this simple hypothesis, therefore, the choice between public and club funding can be cast in terms of relative concern about type I and type II errors.

We said at the start, however, that this is too simplistic a story. The argument confounds five factors:

- there is a divergence between private and social values, so that socially valuable projects may not seem privately profitable to the club;
- knowledge of spillovers *ex ante* (and even *ex post*) is highly incomplete;
- incentives for due diligence are greatest in the private/club setting;
- public decision-making is a more complex process, more susceptible to special interest lobbying, while club decision-making is more transparent *to insiders*; and
- public bodies are *open in principle* (even if not in practice) while club decision-making is usually insufficiently open.

Table 10.1 compares what we might call the project-funding decisions and any errors therein. It is important to compare public finance and club solutions on three other criteria. One relates to efficient composition: does the funding approach include whom it should and exclude none that would benefit? The second relates to equity: do those who pay really benefit while ensuring no free riding? The third relates to the comparative importance of transaction costs in club formation and political costs of taxation. Table 10.2 illustrates the first criterion.

Table 10.2　Efficiency of club solutions and public finance

	Private benefit	No private benefit
Include	Correct decision	*Type II error:* Public finance solutions prone to fall here
Exclude	*Type I error:* Non-optimal club solutions prone to fall here	Correct decision

Efficiency requires that potential beneficiaries are included while non-beneficiaries can be excluded. Once again there are two potential types of 'error'. The type I error is to exclude a real beneficiary. Non-optimal club solutions are prone to do that by being overly exclusive. The type II error is to include a non-beneficiary, though arguably this is a trivial error. On that basis, the public solution seems unambiguously preferable to the suboptimal club on grounds of efficiency.

Table 10.3 illustrates the second criterion. Equity considerations require that those who are charged are the real beneficiaries while those who benefit pay for the privilege. The type I error is not to charge those who would

Table 10.3   Equity of club solutions and public finance

	Private benefit	No private benefit
Charge	Correct decision	*Type II error:* Public finance solutions prone to fall here
Don't charge	*Type I error:* Club solutions may fall here if non-excludable and hence free riding	Correct decision

benefit; this is the free-riding problem and may be a characteristic of some (suboptimal) club solutions. The type II error is to charge those who do not benefit and, if we look at publicly funded basic research project by project rather than as a bundle of projects, this seems an inevitable characteristic of public finance.

Finally, funding solutions need to be compared in terms of transaction costs. As we shall argue below, transaction costs in club formation can be significant[4] – especially if the club seeks to approach the optimal club membership. By contrast the *logistical* transaction costs involved in raising funding through taxation may be smaller, but there may be very significant political transaction costs.

4   A SIMPLE ANALYTICAL FRAMEWORK

In what follows, Figure 10.1 (and variants on it) will be very useful. It summarizes, for any particular funding arrangement, the net internal benefits of a project (internal benefits less costs) and the externalities.

Any particular project can be located as a point on this map. Projects located above the horizontal axis are privately profitable, while those below the line are not. Projects located to the right of the vertical axis convey positive externalities, while those to the left convey negative externalities. The diagonal line, at 45° to the vertical axis, shows all the projects for which the total social benefit (that is, net internal benefit plus externality) is positive. Projects above and to the right of this line are socially beneficial, while those below and to the left are not.

Immediately, of course, we should stress again that the position of the project depends on where the boundary is drawn between internal and external.[5] Take a project in area (iv) for example. As it stands, it is socially

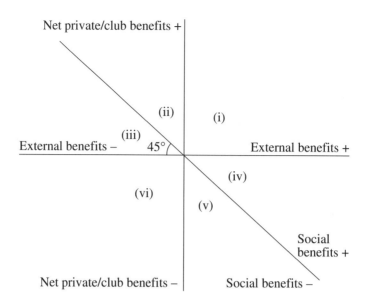

Figure 10.1   Summary of net internal benefits and externalities of a project

Table 10.4   Summary of regions depicted in Figure 10.1

	(i)	(ii)	(iii)	(iv)	(v)	(vi)
Internal	+	+	+	−	−	−
External	+	−	−	+	+	−
Social	+	+	−	+	−	−
Club solution	Fund	Fund	Fund	Don't fund	Don't fund	Don't fund
Public finance	Fund	Fund*	Don't fund	Fund	Don't fund	Don't fund

Note: *May require compensation to external parties.

worthwhile but not privately profitable. In principle, if the funding club is enlarged so that some of the externalities are made internal, then the project will move upwards and to the left in a north-westerly direction. This is a slightly more complex matter than might appear at first sight, so we shall come back to this in a moment.

Figure 10.1 is divided into six regions and these are summarized in Table 10.4. Projects in areas (i) and (vi) are clear-cut. Those in area (i) will be funded by either scheme – and should be. Those in area (vi) will not be funded by either scheme – and should not be. Areas (ii) and (v) are a little more complicated. Those in area (ii) should be funded – and will be unless the external parties have especially strong lobbying power. Even then, there is, in principle, a level of 'damages' that could compensate the external parties and still make funding privately profitable. Those in area (v) should not be funded – and will not be unless, again, the external parties have especially strong lobbying power.

Projects in areas (iii) and (iv) are the problematic ones. Those in (iv) should be funded, but will not be privately funded. Those in (iii) should not be funded (because of the dominant negative externalities), but will appear privately profitable. Immediately, this provides a counterpoint to the simple argument of Section 2: in this case (iii), the private/club solution is more prone to type II errors than the public finance solution.

As indicated, it would appear that if the funding club is enlarged, so that some of the externalities are made internal, then any project will – so to speak – move upwards and to the left in a north-westerly direction. Ultimately, if enough externalities can be internalized, a project will appear profitable to the funding club. However, there are two complications here, captured in Figure 10.2. First, the existence of transaction costs would mean that those former externalities that are now internalized do not accrue costlessly to the club. They have to be bought, thus incurring transaction costs. In Figure 10.2a, this means that the internalization process does not proceed along the (dotted) hypothetical 45° line, but rather along a shallower (solid) line.

Second, however, there is good news for the club.[6] The greater the degree of internalization, then – in many circumstances – the greater the club's ability to extract rents from its more exclusive control of its intellectual property. In Figure 10.2b this means that the actual private/club benefits are greater than those suggested by the post-transaction costs line in Figure 10.2a.

Is the net result in Figure 10.2b a greater or lesser private/club benefit than suggested by the hypothetical line in Figure 10.2a? This is uncertain. But it seems reasonable to argue that a necessary condition for a programme of internalization to take place is that the net result (in 10.2b) is at least as favourable to the club as the hypothetical outcome (in 10.2a). If it were not, then it is unclear why internalization would have any logic. However, we stress that this is just a necessary condition and is unlikely to be sufficient: the exclusive club could have several reasons for preserving exclusivity, even if the net outcome (in 10.2b) seems better than the hypothetical outcome (in 10.2a).

We shall have more to say on the matter of internalization in Section 6.

(a) *Transaction costs*

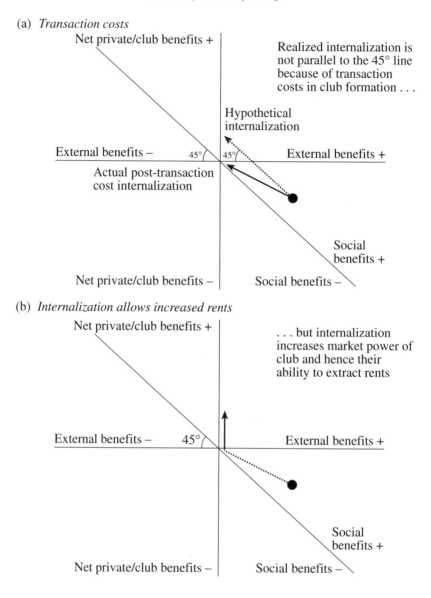

Figure 10.2   Relocating projects in a space of private/club and external benefits

5   DISTRIBUTIONS OF BENEFITS

The seriousness of this difference between club and public solutions depends on the joint distribution of private/club benefits and externalities. One may have little idea about the actual empirical magnitude of externalities. Moreover, as we said before, the shape of this distribution depends on the definition of the club.

Figures 10.3a–d summarize four different sorts of distribution that might be relevant. In each case, Figure 10.1 is overlaid by an ellipse showing the assumed joint distribution of private benefits and externalities. These ellipses show the locus of (say) 99 per cent of all projects.

In Figure 10.3a, the distribution is such that even if the returns on different projects are highly variable, there are few externalities. In other words, those investing in the project are very successful at internalizing these returns – at least, when it matters. From such a perspective, of course, externalities are really not an issue. In Figure 10.3a, 'problem' areas (iii) and (iv) are very small.

In Figure 10.3b, the distribution is such that returns on projects are highly variable, and moreover that the rate of internalization is also very variable. In this case, 'problem' areas (iii) and (iv) are more substantial.

In Figure 10.3c, externalities can be substantial, but the assumption is that the ratio of externalities to private benefits is roughly constant. The distribution of projects is clustered around a line from the origin and the rate of internalization (that is, the slope of this line) is constant. Given this strong positive correlation between private benefits and externalities, the ranking of projects by private value will be similar to the ranking of projects by social value. Areas (iii) and (iv) are small, so there are few problem cases.

Finally, Figure 10.3d illustrates the case where we have a portfolio of projects all of roughly equal social value – hence the projects are all scattered around a line at 45° to the axes. However, the rate of internalization is extremely variable so that, instead of a positive correlation between private benefits and externalities, we actually get a negative correlation. Areas (iii) and (iv) are very large, meaning a large number of 'problem cases'. In those cases with high internalization, we have high private benefits and low externalities, while in cases of low internalization, we have low private benefits and high externalities. It makes no sense to use private benefit as an indicator of social value in setting priorities.[7]

We can compare these distributions in Table 10.5. Which of these figures applies in which circumstances? To answer this at a theoretical level, we need to explore further what factors determine the rate of internalization (see Section 6). Empirically speaking, DTI (1999) has applied the methodology of Swann (1999) to estimate such a distribution, using data from

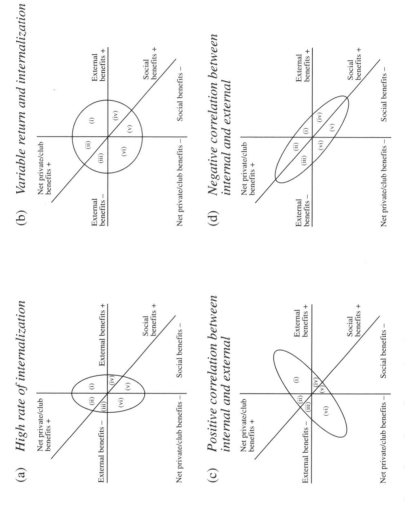

(a) *High rate of internalization*

(b) *Variable return and internalization*

(c) *Positive correlation between internal and external*

(d) *Negative correlation between internal and external*

Figure 10.3   Some hypothetical joint distributions of internal and external benefits

Table 10.5   Comparison of the distribution of benefits depicted in Figures 10.3a–d

	Variability of social return	Rate of internalization	Correlation between internal and external	Size of 'problem areas' (iii) and (iv)
Figure 10.3a	High	High	Nil	Small
Figure 10.3b	High	Variable	Nil	Substantial
Figure 10.3c	Very high	Variable	Positive	Small
Figure 10.3d	Low	Very variable	Negative	Substantial

several case studies of the internal and external benefits from metrology projects, projects involving techniques and standards for measurement. The DTI report finds that the rate of internalization is highly variable and there is no clear positive correlation between internal and external benefits. In terms of Table 10.5, the 'problem areas' are substantial – suggesting that failures in the club goods solution will also be substantial.

6   WHAT DETERMINES THE RATE OF INTERNALIZATION?

What factors influence the rate of internalization that can be achieved? Figure 10.4 is an attempt to illustrate why sometimes it may be easy to track down beneficiaries from spillovers, but sometimes it may not. Suppose that a project will benefit those who seek to introduce a particular characteristic in their product or service. And suppose that among a population of companies about a third would find it helpful to use this characteristic. Suppose also that these companies can be represented in a two-dimensional map. The axes of this map could represent geographical space, or they could represent a more subtle competitive space. But assume at any rate that proximity in this map implies corporate proximity. So, for example, all the members of a particular trade association would be clustered together in a particular part of the map.

Figure 10.4 represents the results of two simulations from a model of diffusion across this population of companies. In this figure, companies that make use of the research project are shown in pale, while those that do not are shown in dark. In Figure 10.4a, diffusion essentially follows an *epidemic* process, where companies are very likely to adopt characteristics and processes that are used by their neighbours. As a result, use is clustered into

(a) *Diffusion to coherent communities*

(b) *Diffusion to dispersed communities*

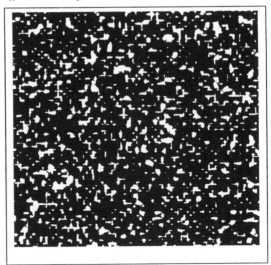

Figure 10.4   Diffusion to coherent and dispersed communities

contiguous or coherent blocks. In Figure 10.4b, by contrast, diffusion is essentially determined by a *probit* (or firm-specific) diffusion process. Here firms are less concerned with the behaviour of their neighbours, and more with the benefits they themselves would enjoy by adopting a new characteristic. As a result, use is not clustered, but instead is spread patchwork fashion across the whole population.

Consider the task faced by those who seek to levy charges on those beneficiaries of a spillover and hence internalize the spillover. If they face a map, as in Figure 10.4a, it would be a relatively easy task to locate beneficiaries. They are almost all in a contiguous block, and some at least may belong to the same trade association. So it looks as though it may be relatively easy to finance this activity by *club* subscriptions. There is still the task of designing a mechanism that excludes these beneficiaries from some related benefit if they do not pay for it, a partial free-rider problem. But at least the task of identifying and negotiating with the beneficiaries is fairly straightforward.

Consider, by contrast, the task if the map is as shown in Figure 10.4b. Here it is very difficult to locate the beneficiaries, let alone to survey them. In such a dispersed collection of companies, it is unlikely that many belong to the same trade association. In such a setting, the inclination would be to give up and accept that this is close to being a pure public good, and that the Coaseian solution is denied by sheer transaction costs. (We return below to the question of whether the Internet makes it easier to reduce such transaction costs.)

We can summarize the club economics in these two cases in Figure 10.5. Figure 10.5a corresponds to Figure 10.4a, and Figure 10.5b to Figure 10.4b. Figure 10.5 illustrates the membership of the profit-maximizing club ($n_{\pi\max}$), the break-even club ($n_{\text{break-even}}$) and the ideal club (n_{ideal}). In Figure 10.5a, because transaction costs – and hence the marginal cost of increasing club size – are quite low, the ideal club is viable and even the profit-maximizing club is quite large in relation to the ideal. But in Figure 10.5b, where transaction costs are high,[8] the profit-maximizing club (and even the break-even club) is small in relation to the ideal club, meaning that the club solution is inefficient. This example is simplistic but it demonstrates two important points. First, the extent to which spillovers can be internalized rather than leaking out as externalities depends on the spatial distribution of the beneficiaries – where we use the term 'spatial' in the broadest socioeconomic sense and not just in a geographical sense. And, second, that just as the spatial pattern of diffusion of use of a new project depends on the precise character of the diffusion process, so also does the achievable rate of internalization of spillovers. In this simple example, it appears that epidemic diffusion leads to a much higher achievable rate of internalization

(a) *Club economics with low transaction costs*

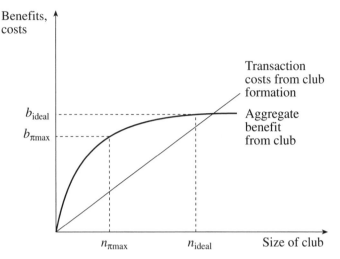

(b) *Club economics with high transaction costs*

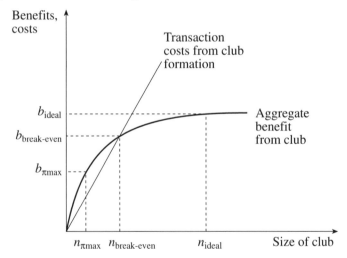

Figure 10.5   Club economics with low and high transaction costs

than probit diffusion. (However, it would be unsafe to generalize from this simple example; these issues need further careful attention.)

Implications

At any rate, these observations offer an interesting angle on how we can assess the importance of externalities. Externalities may be of least concern in stable environments, where the most likely groups to benefit from the project are spatially contiguous and, indeed, where there are very few beneficiaries from other sectors or regions. In short, externalities may be of least significance where beneficiaries are distributed as in Figure 10.4a – because there it is possible to achieve very high rates of internalization.

By contrast, externalities are clearly important in contexts where the beneficiaries are not a tight-knit socio-economic group, where *de novo* entry and cross-entry are important and where, indeed, the benefits from a particular project spread across a number of sectors. In this case, we have a pattern of externalities where beneficiaries are widely dispersed, as in Figure 10.5b. Indeed, the prevalence of these forms of entry may be a good indirect indicator of a project generating important external social benefits.

Where would this second pattern be most common? Certainly, where (in contrast to Jaffe et al. 1993) diffusion is not mediated by socio-economic proximity, and where many firms are innovators in the sense used by Koestler (1964) and Simon (1985) – that is, they bring together insights from diverse knowledge bases. To the extent that those who make use of new projects are Koestler/Simon innovators, then they will be very dispersed in spatial terms – and hence we can expect a very low rate of internalization.[9] In short, the world facing the funders of basic research is becoming more like Figure 10.4b, and less like Figure 10.4a. So we can expect that research funders will have more and more work to do, and that the club goods solution will become ever harder to implement.

We conclude this section by noting an implication of the above that may seem surprising to some. Club solutions presume stability and familiarity. Club solutions, moreover, are only sustainable if they do not promote a pattern of project usage that disrupts this stability and familiarity. Hence, club solutions are likely to exhibit conservatism. In contrast, publicly funded projects encourage the sorts of innovation by outsiders that disrupt this stability and familiarity. Research clubs may be captured by incumbents, who could resist new developments that threaten their competitive position. A public research infrastructure may be necessary for the most radical innovative advance.

7 PUBLIC FINANCE AND CLUB SOLUTIONS COMPARED: I CONVERGENCE

In answer to the question posed at the start of this chapter, there are two broad sets of circumstances in which public finance is preferable to attainable club goods solutions. The first arises when the ideal club goods solution looks very much like the public finance solution – but the former is costly to implement. The second arises when transaction costs are high and the only viable clubs produce undesirable solutions. Section 7 focuses on the former and Section 8 on the latter.

In what circumstances would the incidence of benefits from basic research (in as much as they are known) be similar to the incidence of tax? This is the case of convergence.

One circumstance is where the spillovers from basic research are very widely dispersed as in Figure 10.4b. An extreme case of this is where spillovers are random. In that case it is very hard (and expensive) to assemble a suitable club because that presumes some *ex ante* knowledge of where these beneficiaries are located. This is not available when beneficiaries are unpredictable *ex ante*. This sort of 'club failure' arises when benefits are uncorrelated with obvious firm characteristics, or when it is hard to see *ex ante* how anyone would wish to make use of the basic research project. It is also relevant when benefits from research in one area spill over to another as, for example, in Patel and Pavitt's (1992) observation that companies benefit from patenting in many areas beside their core area.

Another (related) circumstance in which the club goods solution is like public finance is when all taxpayers benefit and benefits are positive and in proportion to tax paid. This might perhaps seem a rather implausible set of conditions. But in the case where the beneficiaries of a project are *ex ante* random and, in particular, where expected benefits follow a uniform distribution *ex ante*, then such a circumstance is not so far-fetched. A variant on this is where internal benefits are perfectly correlated with external benefits. For then, as in Figure 10.3c, the problem areas (iii) and (iv) are very small. These are the problem areas where the club goods solution is at odds with public finance.

A third case in which we have convergence is in a very complex economy – complex in the following sense. If we describe the functioning of the economy with an input–output matrix, a simple economy is where the input–output matrix is diagonal, or block-diagonal, and non-singular, while a complex economy is where the input–output matrix is very non-diagonal and approaching singularity (Leontief et al. 1953; Leontief 1966; Rao and Rao 1998). In such a setting many may benefit indirectly from a research project even if they are not direct beneficiaries. These benefits come around through second round (or subsequent) multiplier effects (see appendix to Swann 1996). Drawing on work by Rosenberg and Nelson (1994) and Feldman and Audretsch (1999), Beaudry and Breschi (2000) illustrate the 'non-diagonal' character of the relationship between categories of academic research and industrial sectors. Table 10.6 shows this relationship for 14 SIC codes and 12 UoA categories of research.[10] An 'X' in any cell indicates that the industry represented by that row (SIC) clearly benefits from research represented by that column (UoA). A rough index of the complexity of this relationship is the proportion of cells containing Xs. As shown, 35 per cent of the cells are so occupied, which is quite a high proportion. If any SIC benefited only from the research of one research UoA, then only 8 per cent of cells would be occupied.

In the light of this, it is worth reflecting on the relationship between the complexity of an economy and the necessity for public finance. In a simple economy clubs can be formed because it is clear who are the beneficiaries from any project. In a complex economy, it is much harder to identify a natural club (because of high transaction costs) and hence public financing may be necessary to fund such projects in a complex economy. Therefore, as the economy gets more complex (in the above sense) we can expect the public sector to grow. Are there any offsetting effects? Some believe that the advent of the Internet makes it easier to achieve club goods solutions. The argument here is that use of the Internet could make it easier to establish who are the potential beneficiaries of any project and, thus, reduce transaction costs in club formation. Superficially that seems right.[11] But we must bear in mind that the Internet is also fuelling globalization and an ever-greater division of labour and that in itself is making the economy ever-more complex. Thus, the Internet is both a factor leading to greater economic complexity and a factor that can help to overcome complexity. The net effect is unclear.

8   PUBLIC FINANCE AND CLUB SOLUTIONS COMPARED: II TRANSACTION COSTS AND EXCLUSION

These are cases where the club goods solution and the public finance solution may be significantly different, but the club goods solution is undesirable. For that reason, public finance is preferable to any attainable club goods solution. There are three broad scenarios.

First, transaction costs are high and the only viable clubs are small clubs. This is unsatisfactory because it excludes many potential beneficiaries. This means that the attainable club solutions are less satisfactory than the public finance solution. This case is illustrated in Figure 10.5b.

Second, there is concern that even if transaction costs do not restrict the

Table 10.6   Which industry actors benefit from research?

Industry	SIC	Chemistry	Physics	Pure Mathematics	Applied Mathematics	Statistics and Operational Research	Computer Science	General Engineering	Chemical Engineering	Electrical and Electronic Engineering	Mechanical, Aeronautical and Manufacturing Engineering	Mineral and Mining Engineering	Metallurgy and Materials
Discipline / UoA		18	19	22	23	24	25	26	27	29	30	31	32
Metal manufacturing	22				X	X						X	X
Manufacture of non-metallic mineral products	24				X	X						X	X
Chemical industry	25	X							X				
Mechanical engineering	32				X	X							X
Manufacture of office machinery and EDP equipment	33		X	X			X	X		X	X		X
Electrical and electronic engineering	34		X	X			X	X		X			X
Manufacture of motor vehicles and parts	35		X	X			X	X		X	X		X
Manufacture of other transport equipment	36		X				X	X		X	X		
Instrument engineering	37			X	X	X	X		X				
Textile industry	43							X					
Timber and wooden furniture industry	46	X					X	X	X				
Manufacture of paper and paper products	47	X					X	X	X				
Processing of rubber and plastics	48							X				X	X
Other manufacturing industries	49		X										X

Source: Based on data created by Beaudry and Breschi (2000), drawing on Rosenberg and Nelson (1994) and Feldman and Audretsch (1999).

size of the club, attainable clubs are too exclusive. One radical manifestation of this is the concern about corporate takeover of science (Monbiot 2000).[12] From a less radical perspective, there are strong grounds for believing that, wherever possible, openness in basic research is the best way to deliver innovation-led growth (Dasgupta and David 1994). Swann (2000) likens this to the growth of a tree: open trees enjoy vigorous innovative growth from each node and this is good both aesthetically and productively.

Third, a related argument is the idea that excessive closure reduces technological variety. A good Schumpeterian innovator does not launch a trajectory that leads to technological change which destroys his or her technological competence. From this perspective, we should maintain a healthy scepticism about the critiques of research projects that they do not satisfy user needs as these can often be disguised anti-competitive arguments. The good Schumpeterian obviously does not want to launch projects that do not correlate with his or her company's own needs, but that does not mean that these projects are of no *social* value.

It is worth commenting on one particular aspect of closure. In some clubs (notably in the standards community) there is strong pressure to restrict membership to leading players in the interests of securing rapid convergence on an accepted standard. Such leading players often reject the involvement of smaller players and customers on the grounds that this slows them down and is anyway redundant. But, as Swann (2000) demonstrates (and Adam Smith said two centuries ago), we should always be sceptical of arguments that large producer interests alone encompass those of the small producer and consumer.

9   CONCLUSION

The main message is clear. Despite the interest in club goods solutions in the context of basic research, we need to be cautious about these. In most circumstances, public finance is still preferable to any attainable club goods solution. But perhaps this chapter has been unduly quixotic? Some (see Pavitt's commentary in Part I of this book) have shown that despite all the rhetoric, and despite the arguments in Kealey (1996), the vast majority of public research is still publicly funded. Club goods solutions for the financing of basic research are still rare. Although the publicly funded university is under pressure its existence is not seriously at risk. Nevertheless, pressures for accountability in the UK (and the Netherlands) are high, and it is often hard to demonstrate the accounting payoff from basic research. In the light of this, we might, in conclusion, modify Table 10.1 to reflect the sorts of errors that occur when the desire for accountability is not matched by an ability to account (see Table 10.7).

Table 10.7 *A revised conception of the failings of club solutions and public finance*

	Demonstrably socially profitable	Socially profitable but *not demonstrably so*	Socially unprofitable but *not demonstrably so*	Demonstrably socially unprofitable
Funded	*Informed correct decision*	*Lucky correct decision*	*Type II error:* Unaccountable public finance and charitable research foundations may fall here through *excess liberalism*	*Type II error:* Unaccountable public finance and charitable research foundations may fall here if *subject to lobby or insufficient due diligence*
Not funded	*Type I error:* Club solutions prone to fall here through *failure to internalize*	*Type I error:* Accountable public finance and club solutions may fall here through *excess conservatism*	*Lucky correct decision*	*Informed correct decision*

NOTES

1. A forthright statement of this position is made by the clinical biochemist, Kealey (1996). His book has received many reviews, some very appreciative (*The Economist* 1996), some cautious (Nelson 1997) and some highly critical (David 1997; Stoneman 1997).
2. There are some important historical examples where the club goods solution has been successful. Temin (1964) and Morison (1966) describe how the Bessemer Association in the US steel industry resembled a club goods solution in which technical expertise was exchanged among members of the association. Allen (1983) describes a similar institutional arrangement in the Cleveland blast furnace industry, but here know-how was shared more widely and not exclusively within the 'club'. A more recent example of a club goods solution is the consortium, SEMATECH (Grindley et al. 1996).
3. It is recognized, however, that clubs sometimes sell their intellectual property to outsiders.
4. A striking (and well-documented) historical example of this was observed in establishing the necessary financial backing for the Great Exhibition of 1851, see Auerbach (1999).
5. There is a natural link here to two other chapters in this book. The different mechanisms for public action and funding described by Callon (Chapter 2) can be represented as different points on this map. The same observation applies to the industry associations and other institutions created to fund industry-specific public goods – as described by Foray (Chapter 11).
6. I am especially grateful to Bronwyn Hall for clarifying this point – though she is not responsible for any remaining errors in this present account.
7. The above observations have an important implication for the choice of an empirical methodology to value research projects. Any technique that focuses on the bottom-line value of a project to the proximate users will make the assessment of any spillover benefits more difficult. As such, it can only generate an incomplete measure of the economic benefits from a research project. Moreover, it is worth drawing out one further implication. Suppose that research project activities are allocated between private and public sectors as follows. Those where the private return is in excess of the cost are purely privately financed, while those where the full social return exceeds the cost but the return to proximate users does not will be funded by the public sector. If an *incomplete* methodology is used, then two results will follow: (a) private sector projects will be measured to have a higher benefit to cost ratio than public sector projects; (b) public sector projects will not appear to be worthwhile. These findings will resonate with some political prejudices, perhaps. But the findings would have nothing to do with the true social merit of the different projects; they would simply follow from the unavoidable measurement errors inherent in using an incomplete empirical methodology.
8. Cristiano Antonelli has made the important point that some government activity can be seen as an attempt to reduce these transaction costs in club formation. In terms of Figure 10.5, this is an attempt to move from case (b) to case (a).
9. The view of R&D as a real option would tend to reinforce this conclusion.
10. These UoA (unit of assessment) categories relate to the UK HEFCE (University) Research Assessment Exercise of 2001. The 14 SIC codes and 12 UoA categories shown in this table are not, of course, exhaustive.
11. Even this must be uncertain, however. Windrum and Swann (1999) argue that the growth of the Internet is not necessarily being matched by a power to search out exactly what the user wants to find.
12. A similar concern surfaced in September 2001 about biases in company-funded research (*The Independent* 2001).

REFERENCES

Akerlof, G. (1970), 'The market for *lemons*', *Quarterly Journal of Economics* **84**(Summer), 488–500.

Allen, R.C. (1983), 'Collective invention', *Journal of Economic Behavior and Organization* **4**, 1–24.

Auerbach, J.A. (1999), *The Great Exhibition of 1851: A Nation on Display*, New Haven, CT and London: Yale University Press.

Beaudry, C. and S. Breschi (2000), 'Does "clustering" really help firms' innovative activities?', Centro di Ricerca sui Processi di Innovazionne e Internazionalizzasione (CESPRI) Working Paper No. 111, University Bocconi, Milan.

Dasgupta, P. and P.A. David (1994), 'Towards a new economics of science', *Research Policy* **23**(5), 487–521.

David, P.A. (1997), 'From magic market to calypso science policy: a review of Terence Kealey's *The Economic Laws of Scientific Research*', *Research Policy* **26**(2), 229–55.

Department of Trade and Industry (DTI) (1999), *Review of the Rationale for and Economic Benefits of the UK National Measurement System*, London: DTI, National Measurement System Policy Unit, 15 November.

Economist, The (1996), 'Review of *The Economic Laws of Scientific Research*', 14 September, **340**(7983), 10–11.

Feldman, M.P. and D.B. Audretsch (1999), 'Innovation in cities: science-based diversity, specialization and localized competition', *European Economic Review* **43**(2), 409–29.

Galbraith, J.K. (1970), *The Affluent Society*, 2nd edn London: Pelican Books.

Griliches, Z. (1992), 'The search for R&D spillovers', *Scandinavian Journal of Economics* **94**(3, Supplement), 529–47.

Grindley, P., D. Mowery and B. Silverman (1996), 'The design of high-technology consortia: lessons from Sematech', in M. Teubal, D. Foray, M. Justman and E. Zuscovitch (eds), *Technological Infrastructure Policy: An International Perspective*, Dordrecht: Kluwer Academic Publishers, pp. 173–211.

Independent, The (2001), 'Drug firms fund biased research, warn editors', 10 September, p. 7.

Jaffe, A.B., M. Trajtenberg and R. Henderson (1993), 'Geographic localization of knowledge spillovers as evidenced by patent citations', *Quarterly Journal of Economics* **108**(3), 577–98.

Kealey, T. (1996), *The Economic Laws of Scientific Research*, London: Macmillan.

Koestler, A. (1964), *The Act of Creation*, London: Hutchinson.

Leontief, W.W. (1966), *Input–Output Economics*, New York: Oxford University Press.

Leontief, W.W., H.B. Chenery, P.G. Clark, J.S. Duesenberry, A.R. Ferguson, A.P. Grosse, R.N. Grosse, M. Holzman, W. Isard and H. Kistin (1953), *Studies in the Structure of the American Economy: Theoretical and Empirical Explorations in Input–Output Analysis*, New York: Oxford University Press.

Monbiot, G. (2000), *Captive State: The Corporate Takeover of Britain*, London: Macmillan.

Morison, E.E. (1966), *Men, Machines and Modern Times*, Cambridge, MA: MIT Press.

Nelson, R.R. (1997), 'Review of *The Economic Laws of Scientific Research*', *Issues in Science and Technology* **14**(1), 90–92.

Patel, P. and K. Pavitt (1992), 'The innovative performance of the world's largest firms: some new evidence', *Economics of Innovation and New Technology* **2**(2), 91–102.

Rao, C.R. and M.B. Rao (1998), *Matrix Algebra and Its Applications to Statistics and Econometrics*, Singapore: World Scientific Publishing Co.

Romer, P. (1993), 'Implementing a national technology strategy with self organizing industry investment boards', in M.N. Baily, P.C. Reiss and C. Winston (eds), *Brookings Papers on Economic Activity: Microeconomics* Vol. 2, pp. 345–90.

Rosenberg, N. and R.R. Nelson (1994), 'American universities and technical advance in industry', *Research Policy* **23**(3), 323–48.

Simon, H.A. (1985), 'What do we know about the creative process?', in R.L. Kuhn (ed.), *Frontiers in Creative and Innovative Management*, Cambridge, MA: Ballinger, pp. 3–20.

Stoneman, P. (1997), 'Review of *The Economic Laws of Scientific Research*', *Economic Journal* **107**(442), 844–5.

Swann, G.M.P. (1994), *Inference from Mixed Bags*, Working Paper, London: Centre for Business Strategy, London Business School.

Swann, G.M.P. (1996), *The Economic Value of Publicly Funded Basic Research: A Framework for Assessing the Evidence*, Report for Technology and Innovation, Department of Trade and Industry, Manchester: Policy Research in Engineering, Science and Technology, University of Manchester.

Swann, G.M.P. (1999), *The Economics of Measurement*, Report for National Measurement System Policy Unit, Department of Trade and Industry, available at: www.dti.gov.uk/tese/swann.pdf, last accessed 31 January 2002.

Swann, G.M.P. (2000), *The Economics of Standardization*, Report for Standards and Technical Regulations Directorate, Department of Trade and Industry, available at: www.dti.gov.uk/strd/fundingo.htm#swannrep, last accessed 31 January 2002.

Temin, P. (1964), *Iron and Steel in Nineteenth Century America: An Economic Inquiry*, Cambridge, MA: MIT Press.

Windrum, P. and G.M.P. Swann (1999), 'Networks, noise and navigation: sustaining Metcalfe's Law through technological innovation', MERIT Research Memorandum 2/99–009, Maastricht: University of Maastricht.

11. On the provision of industry-specific public goods: revisiting a policy process

Dominique Foray*

1 THE CONCEPT OF INDUSTRY-SPECIFIC PUBLIC GOODS AND THE POLICY ISSUE

One way to improve the effectiveness and efficiency of innovation support instruments is to carry out a 'policy experiment'. There is one major reason for undertaking policy experiments, which is that the various international policy forums are quite conservative. Policy-makers do not like 'innovation in policy' simply because the costs and the benefits of any new policy are rather uncertain. As a result, the policy instruments available for promoting innovation and industrial competitiveness are not particularly innovative and do not fit well in local situations. In this chapter I shall give an illustration of the kind of policy experiment that could be carried out in this context and demonstrate that it is important for government to support this strategy.

A particular policy problem arises over the fact that in any industry certain kinds of resources – such as basic research, training programmes, technical services, certification and quality control facilities, generic advertising and commercial information – are critical for the competitiveness of the industry and that small and medium-sized enterprises (SMEs) depend mainly on external infrastructures to access these resources. This policy problem involves several issues: who will pay for these resources and who will decide what kinds of resources must be provided? The problem is one of building and adapting the innovation infrastructure of an industry in which SMEs are predominant, to which there are partial solutions, none of which are 'optimal'.

The Critical Importance of 'Industry-specific Public Goods'

There are several kinds of resources necessary for technological innovation. They might be generic, industry specific, or firm specific.

The generic resources involve public goods, which are necessary in any process of technological development, such as the general infrastructure (transport, telecommunications), the general education system and the system of generic knowledge production (universities). Coordination and coherence, in this case, is a public good problem, which government is the most appropriate institution to solve.

Firm-specific resources are those resources that are localized within the firm, such as particular competences, routines and work organization and practices. At this level, firms are the appropriate institutions to ensure coordination.

By industry-specific public goods (ISPGs), we mean those resources that are both public, in the sense that they are shared by a community of agents, and industry specific. A particular set of skills and training requirement, a particular class of capital good equipment, some applied fields of basic research, a particular group of technical standards, a set of technical services and a programme to support the provision of information about the advantages of a generic product, are typical examples of ISPGs.

These resources – public and industry specific – are at the core of the technological infrastructure and their provision is critical for any regional or sectoral policy.

The types of problem we deal with in this chapter concern not only old industries facing major changes to improve their innovation infrastructure. New industries and services may confront the same kinds of issues as they meet major competitiveness challenges (see Credé and Steinmueller 1999, on financial software, and Steinmueller 1996, on the information technology industry). Industries at a very early stage in their life cycle also have to cope with the problem of creating a knowledge infrastructure (see Swann 1999, on virtual reality).

The Problems

Designing intermediary institutions
The creation of industry-specific public goods is a very complex policy issue: the public good aspect of those resources raises a classical problem of market failure and a lack of private incentives, resulting in underinvestment in ISPGs: small, medium and most large firms cannot individually invest in those resources because they are public goods. (Of course very large companies can and actually do – Toyota, for instance, has an 'in-house' university.) If, overcoming the free-riding problems stemming from the mobility of personnel and knowledge, firms would individually invest, there would still be a great deal of duplication involving high collective costs.

But nor is the government a good candidate for creating such goods. These public goods are also industry specific and, thus, involve a high diversity of situations, which would require from the government the development and maintenance of complex competences that it would not be able to provide. Foray and Llerena (1996) have modelled a policy structure in which this parameter (imprecision in the perception of the needs that are industry specific) determines the choice of the appropriate coordination mechanism. Thus, firms are the best judges of what they need (government cannot help to target policy) but if they operate in isolation, clearly efficiency decreases at the system level.

It is necessary, therefore, to establish a new kind of institution, which would support concerted actions more appropriate for creating ISPGs. An intermediate process that allows firms to take concerted action, is the only way to accomplish what government cannot do successfully (industry-specificity aspect) and what individual firms cannot do (public good aspect).[1] There is, however, concern that such concerted actions do not provide new opportunities for creating cartels.[2]

Finding a consensus

Concerted action by a number of small companies is not easy to manage. There is more than one ISPG and choices have to be made. When the provision of one ISPG clearly emerges as being urgent, creating a consensus is not an issue. However, things are generally not so clear-cut (Romer 1993). Take, for example, the numerous firms encompassed by the textile industry. They decide that there are industry-wide opportunities and problems that independent action by individual firms cannot address. One firm thinks, for example, that universities could undertake useful research for the industry, given the funds and the incentives to do so. Another firm believes that the upstream industry that manufactures textile equipment could be designing more useful specialized equipment; while a third firm thinks that there is an urgent need to improve the technical labour force by establishing some specialized training programmes. These firms face a collective action problem that has no obvious solution!

Introducing flexibility

Finally, there is the necessity to continuously adapt the ISPG infrastructure.[3] It is important to create the proper coordination mechanisms to create ISPGs, but it is just as important to set in place certain mechanisms to allow the industry to adapt its ISPGs to rapid changes in technologies, demands, evolution of the regulatory framework and so forth. This is complex because of institutional inertia and the difficulties involved in trying to change organizations.

The creation and continuous adaptation of ISPGs raises three problems:

- finding proper coordination mechanisms at some kind of intermediate level (between the government and the individual company), that are not just another opportunity to create a cartel;
- finding a mechanism to build consensus among firms which have to decide what kind of ISPGs they would like to create; and
- finding a mechanism to open up some possibilities for adapting the supply of ISPGs, given changes in the environment of the industry.

2   A LOOK AT THE REAL WORLD: HOW SMES ARE ADDRESSING THESE PROBLEMS

We shall look at various solutions that exist in the real world and apply them to the three problems identified above. To do this, we draw upon various case studies concerning 'the modernization of traditional industries' (Kelley and Arora 1996; Sabel 1996; Ynnon 1996), the 'regional policies in Europe' (Asheim and Isaksen 2000), and finally the national institutional systems in various countries (Weder and Grubel 1993).

Industrial Association

The most obvious solution is to have industrial associations (IAs) assume the provision of ISPGs.

Weder and Grubel present the case of the watch-making industry in Switzerland. The companies set up an IA at the beginning of the 1900s. In 1924, this IA established the Swiss laboratory for horological research. In 1962, it created a new institute devoted to the development of the electronic watch movement, sponsored a number of schools with specialist training programmes and supported and maintained an apprenticeship scheme. The association not only finances industry-specific R&D and training, it also provides efficient means for disseminating knowledge relevant to the operations of member firms.

Sabel develops the American example of the National Institute for Standards and Technology which, in the early 1990s, established the Manufacturing Center Programme, later renamed the Manufacturing Extension Partnership. One example of an institution created within this programme is the Textile/Clothing Technological Corporation (TC)[2] which began as a technological development unit. Its mission was then broadened to include educational and demonstration activities. (TC)[2] focuses most of its research efforts on identifying and testing existing technologies and adapting them to textile manufacturing processes.

Finally, Asheim and Isaksen cite the case of the technological institutes in the region of Valencia (Spain). Each institute specializes in one branch of manufacturing (ceramics, textiles, toys and so on). They provide information, technical studies, testing and certification services, consulting on technological transfer and training programmes.

The activities carried out by IAs are in essence very industry specific and are open to all members of an industry. Their activities span a broad range of resources (research, training, technical services) but there is no explicit mechanism to support the building of consensus in the choice of the activities. There are numerous examples of IAs that are heavily influenced by the largest companies, leaving the SMEs de facto excluded from any decision about the agenda.[4] Finally, there is no explicit principle allowing for continuous adaptation of ISPGs. In some cases (the Swiss one) it works well; in others, it does not.

User- or Supplier-driven Mechanism

This solution provides for ISPGs to be supported by a club of 'sophisticated users or suppliers'. This is the vertical relationship that acts as a coordination mechanism.

Kelley and Arora (1996) describe a group of leading companies (Xerox, Motorola, Kodak, Texas Instruments, Digital, Chrysler) which created a consortium for supplier training, established regional training centres to deal with quality control issues and cost-effective production methods for small suppliers.

Asheim and Isaksen (2000) discuss the policy instrument called 'knowledge-intensive industrial clustering', developed in Limburg (The Netherlands), which aimed at supporting policy for upgrading the network of suppliers to a big company (in this case, Océ, a multinational copier producer).

Groups of suppliers can also establish training centres to train users and diffuse technical information in order to gradually introduce new equipment and processes into firms downstream of the industry. This solution provides services that are industry specific but not necessarily beneficial to all members of the particular industry; activities may be limited to a particular class of ISPGs and the selection of activities may address only those issues that are specific to particular vertical relationships. An interesting feature of such an arrangement, however, is that it intentionally addresses the issue of continuous adaptation and improvement.

Uneven Institutional Structure

The third class of solution deals with the unintentional effect of a non-coordinated process of institutional creation: the situation where institutions with different origins and rationales all contribute to the provision of ISPGs.

Ynnon (1996) develops the case of the plastics processing sector in the State of New York where companies have created the Society for Plastic Engineering, which deals with training and technology transfer. At the same time, sophisticated end users launched a programme to increase the level of manufacturing methods in this industry (quality control, just-in-time methods); and finally a local university has set up a centre – the Plastic and Composite Development Center – to address industry-wide concerns in terms of research and development (R&D) and technical services.

In such a system the needs of companies in relation to the provision of ISPGs are more likely to be satisfied. However, some of the activities are not available to all companies and there is a risk of some duplication of activities aiming at the provision of ISPGs. There is no explicit mechanism to build consensus in the industry or to support the process of continuous adaptation.

The Broker Solution

This is a case developed by Asheim and Isaksen (2000). The policy instrument 'technology diffusion from research institutions to SMEs' in Norway includes provisions to increase the absorptive capabilities of SMEs and to improve the ability of the polytechnic high schools to cooperate with industry. Ten country-based technological experts function as brokers, 'animators' or mentors in the SMEs' innovation process. They establish which technological opportunities in SMEs can be met through the R&D activities of the institutes. The main aim is to teach SMEs how to exploit the R&D infrastructure. In one sense, such a scheme would seem to offer very efficient mechanisms to connect SMEs to a particular class of ISPGs (research and technical services). However, because the brokers all come from the polytechnics, the tendency is to orient the demand of SMEs towards projects that fit well within the competences of the polytechnics. This scheme is in fact quite similar to the supply-driven mechanism identified in the second class of solution.

Summary

In Table 11.1 we recapitulate the advantages and shortcomings of each solution with reference to the three problems posed by the provision of ISPGs.

Table 11.1 Summary of advantages and shortcomings of ISPG solutions

	Industrial associations	User- or supplier-driven solution	Complex set of institutions	Brokers
How to create an intermediary mechanism for collective actions that does not present opportunities for the creation of cartels	IAs provide a good mechanism for covering all ISPGs and avoiding risks of cartel's opportunities	Only some ISPGs are covered. Activities are not necessarily open to all	All ISPGs are covered but this is the unintentional result of institutional development. Risk of duplication. Some activities are not open to all	The creation of ISPGs depends upon the ability of the brokers to create collective goods. Risk of duplication
How to build a consensus among companies to choose between various activities	Depends how the committee work. Risk of asymmetric relations	The choice of ISPGs gets away from the industry	Not applicable	Not applicable
How to create a mechanism to support continuous adaptations	Depends how the committee work. Risk of asymmetric relations	The needs of users or suppliers create a force for continuous adaptations	Not applicable	Strong bias towards the agenda of the research institutions

One solution would be to rely on industrial associations while thinking about methods to improve their functioning in terms of their ability to reach consensus in the choice of activities and to introduce mechanisms supporting continuous adjustments and adaptation of the ISPG infrastructure. This is not an easy task and is borne out by the way most IAs function and their inability to adjust their activities to rapid changes in their environment. These questions – how firms can coordinate to change their environment and how they can collectively adjust the supply of ISPG to new priorities and needs – were addressed by Romer (1993) in a very innovative paper to which we now turn.

3   THE POLICY PROCESS (ROMER 1993)

The policy process does not yet exist. A model for it has, however, been designed in a very stimulating paper by Romer (1993), who shares the conviction that one important purpose of technology policy is to provide tools to allow firms to solve collective action problems. Thus, technology policy is considered here as a process of creation and selection of institutions, allowing firms to coordinate changes in their environment.

The Policy Mechanism

The model is based on the establishment of boards within an industry, oriented towards the production of a range of ISPGs which would be financed by means of a compulsory levy (after a process of voting involving all the members of the industry concerned). Each board would have a special connection to a particular ISPG, such as university research, upstream equipment industry, technical standards or training. One board would be specialized in basic research, another in general advertising, another in the provision of technical services and so forth.

Three principles underlie the model:

- the compulsory levy avoids (or reduces) the problem of 'free riding';
- what is produced through the 'boards' is public goods, available to all; and
- above all, the boards compete to capture resources and new boards can be freely set up as required, which limits the effects of inertia and allows firms to structure their environment (skills, basic research, equipment goods) in accordance with their perception of what is lacking, and to compensate for gaps and superfluities in that environment.

This third principle introduces a highly decentralized mechanism for project selection: each firm can devote its contribution to whatever topics it chooses; the unique limitation being that the project deals with common property resources that benefit the entire industry.

Thus each board – on the assumption that it attracts sufficient resources – must carry out the activity and then ensure that the output will be fully diffused within the industry.

BOX 11.1   AN EXAMPLE (ROMER 1993)

Firm A has sales of $100 million a year, so it has to decide where to allocate its annual tax obligation, say $1 million (1 per cent). Firm A is particularly aware of the critical needs of basic science for the industry so it decides to allocate all of the $1 million to a university research board. Firm B has sales of $200 million a year. It can decide to split its $2 million tax obligation – giving $1 million to the university research board and $1 million to an upstream equipment development board because the technological capabilities of the suppliers of manufacturing equipment have to be improved, and so forth. Firms C, D, E have to make their trade-offs so that the boards really compete to capture resources.

Then, every three years firms have to decide how to allocate their tax obligations between the two existing boards and any others that might be created.

In the second period, most of the firms think that it is still useful to support a basic science programme; however, no firms allocate any money to the upstream equipment development board because they consider that this board has achieved its task so it is disbanded. However, some firms take the initiative to establish new boards – one in order to generate voluntary technical standards and another to launch some specific training programmes within high schools to improve skills. Thus new boards appear while others are discontinued.

Advantages of the Schema

At first glance, this mechanism supports a 'simple' process of internalization of externalities, through the development of some kinds of industrial associations. It consists of a number of member firms with common characteristics such as similarity of output, production processes or important inputs. Members pay fees. These fees in turn finance a central administration and a number of activities through which industry externalities are captured by individual firms. This is a rather classical 'club goods approach' where the diverse beneficiaries of one project form a club to fund it.[5] There is, however, a second mechanism, which gives original properties to this policy schema. This mechanism organizes the competition between the boards and maintains the freedom to create new boards. It is designed to allow the industry to cope with changes in their environment: 'the freedom to create new boards and to choose among competing boards is so important that any proposal that did not include these provisions would have an entirely different character' (Romer 1993, pp. 376–7).

There are actually numerous examples of institutions aiming at the provision of ISPGs. However, in most cases the third principle is missing. For instance in the US, the Agricultural Marketing Agreement Act (1937) brought about some coordination. But the principle of competition and free creation of new boards was missing. In France, the technical industrial centres are financed on a para-fiscal basis and produce public goods specific to an industry, but the principle of competition and free creation is absent and problems of inertia and of coordination arise between the changing needs of the firms and the capabilities of the centres. The essence of the mechanism is to introduce some market processes at the institutional level – a mechanism that uses the pressure of competition and a market test to shut down ineffective institutional arrangements and to reward promising ones.

Firms could decide to set up a 'board' to promote a given scientific discipline in universities, support a given type of professional training, aid in the design of new equipment in the upstream sector and so on. Implementation of this pattern could empower firms in various industries to change some of the basic features of their environment: they could act on the patterns of interaction between university and the industry, the system of training, the technological infrastructure and the internal labour market. They could create new institutions for setting standards and so on.

To summarize the advantages of the policy schema, we can stress its transactional, evolutionary and political properties:

- *Solving the problem of generating ISPGs and filling the gap between generic resources and specific firms' needs* It helps to solve the problem of generating ISPGs that cannot be produced either by the independent actions of individual firms or to a large extent by the government; and by focusing on ISPGs, this policy builds bridges between generic resources and firm-specific ones. For example, in the case of R&D, it can support investments that span the gap between the most general forms of basic research and some kinds of use-inspired basic research as needed by the company.

- *Reducing institutional inertia* This model has evolutionary properties in devising a mechanism to support the continuous adjustment of the technology infrastructure to the changing needs of industries, a problem that is in general poorly addressed by traditional industrial associations. If instead the freedom to choose and to create committees is introduced, we will set in motion a dynamic of selection that will serve to curtail ineffective institutional arrangements and promote promising ones, the outcome suggested by Romer (1993) and the experience of the Agricultural Market by Agreement Act (1937). The principle of free entry of new boards is designed to allow the industry to cope with big changes in its environment. It is extremely important to keep some flexibility in the process of creating ISPGs, in order to allow an industry to change its environment according to emerging opportunities and technological transitions. It is, however, a difficult challenge because of inertia and the path-dependent properties of any institution. Institutions generally are less plastic, less malleable than material technologies (on these issues, see David 1994).

The mechanism described could be particularly instrumental in the context of major technological transitions. When an industry is facing such a transition, the problem of providing the new ISPGs quickly becomes acute. In this case, the problem is precisely to create – rapidly – the new environment in terms of the appropriate ISPGs (new training programmes, new basic research capabilities, new equipment supply, new technical services and so forth). The evolution of the local system of innovation of Limoges (France) is a good illustration. Limoges specialized in porcelain products and experienced a major shift towards a new high-tech specialization: technical ceramic.

To manage this transition, the traditional 'porcelain companies' financed various committees with the goal of achieving quickly the appropriate new ISPGs. A new department of basic research was set up in the university and a small centre for technology transfer was created in order to provide firms with the complex measurement services for ceramic manufacturing processes. The possibilities of creating new committees as well as of adjusting committees to the new technological priorities can be very instrumental in the collective management of technological transition. This is not only a problem for old and traditional industries. Credé and Steinmueller (1999) show how the London Insurance Market was facing a problem of collective transition towards a new technological infrastructure involving the creation of new ISPGs.

- *Reducing the cost of entry* It is interesting to contrast this model with SEMATECH from a competition policy point of view. Since its foundation, SEMATECH has shifted from 'horizontal' research cooperation to 'vertical' collaboration between its members – major US users of semiconductor process equipment and materials – and the US suppliers of these goods. In many respects, SEMATECH now resembles an industry association, diffusing information and best-practice techniques, setting standards and coordinating generic research (Grindley et al. 1996). There is, however, a major difference between SEMATECH and the policy process we have described. SEMATECH is a closed network of firms (even if it accounts for over 80 per cent of industry capacity) while the policy process described here is an open one. It is open to any current or future participant in the industry. In the case of SEMATECH, this institution could become the vehicle for preventing new entry into the industry, while in the case of the model described here entry is facilitated; it gives the automatic right to newcomers to access the ISPGs for the payment of a tax.
- *Coping with subsidiarity* Finally, this policy process can help to solve a pure policy action problem, referred to as the delegation problem (Romer 1993). The institutional process we have described belongs to the category of 'private arrangement' between actors, organized under the principle of 'self-discipline' of a professional association. On the one hand, such a process expresses a tendency towards the decentralization of economic regulation. On the other hand, it expresses a tendency towards local coordination. The principle of self-organized committees defines an adequate degree of delegation in the case of the production of industry-specific public goods.

Shortcomings and Problems

The first limitation has been developed by Teubal in many of his recent papers on policy (see, for example, Galli and Teubal 1997). Companies need to have a certain level of 'capabilities' and competences to be able to take part in this process. It is necessary for companies to understand what they need and to make these needs explicit. They must also be able to absorb and exploit the results of the various activities carried out by the boards. When a certain development is required, firms taking part in such a decentralized process of decision-making are able to determine what is good for their industry as a whole. In fact, we can suppose that in hard times, collective action and reorganization must take place locally before firms are able to define projects of general interest to the industry.

A second obvious limitation deals with the issue of defining the boundary of the industry. If the boundaries are not properly defined, some companies that are not subject to the tax will still benefit from the provision of ISPGs.

The third limitation deals with the issue of determining whether a project deals with common property resources and not with problems and objectives that are of interest only to one or a very few companies.

Fourth, the mechanism based on competition among boards can impede the exploration of diversity in an industry. The more resources a board attracts, the more effective it will be and the better recognized by all members of the industry will be its activities and therefore the more it will attract resources. On the other hand, a single firm, which would like to explore new alternatives and new processes will just give up, on the assumption that such a new board would not attract enough resources.

Finally, asymmetry in the size of companies is likely to generate problems. The biggest companies will allocate more resources and will have a big influence on the final 'equilibrium', so that there is a major risk of capture of the policy process by the biggest participants.

4   CONCLUSION: TOWARDS A NEW POLICY RATIONALE

Collective action in the domain of innovation and technology is a key issue. There are a large number of economic opportunities for collective action – not only in some pre-competitive arenas of scientific research but also in many highly competitive markets. Economists know, however, that collective action can be difficult to initiate. The European Union Framework Programmes are good examples of policy instruments, devoted to this kind of purpose. But such instruments have proved to be inappropriate in certain contexts. When this is the case, and if collective action does not spontaneously emerge, there is clearly a need for new policy instruments. New instruments are therefore necessary to allow firms to create institutions for solving collective action problems raised by the production of some kinds of goods, resources and knowledge, usually grouped together in the category 'industry-specific public goods'. There is here a class of instruments that have not yet received the attention of policy-makers and a domain of valuable interactions between economists and policy-makers.

Romer (1993) proposed the creation of 'self-organized industry investment boards', aimed at the production of a range of ISPs, which would be financed by a compulsory levy (after a process of voting involving all the members of the industry concerned). The very innovative feature of the model is that the boards compete to capture resources and new boards can be freely set up as required, which limits the effects of inertia and empowers firms in various industries to change some of the basic features of their environment (qualification, basic research, equipment goods) in accordance with their perceptions of what is lacking.

As manufacturing and innovation processes are increasing in complexity, involving sophisticated resources (knowledge and skills) and complex coordination mechanisms (technical standards, integration of modules), there is certainly a need to develop these kinds of policy tools in order to upgrade the capacity of small and medium firms to coordinate changes in their environment.

NOTES

*   The research for this chapter was conducted at the University of Paris Dauphine; affiliation since January 2001, OECD/CERI, Paris. I gratefully acknowledge the insightful comments and help of Morris Teubal. I am also indebted to Robin Cowan, Attila Havas and Xavier Vence, as well as the participants at the NPRnet Workshop at the École des Mines in Paris, 3–4 May 2001, who gave me feedback to a previous draft. I warmly thank Cynthia Little and Ed Steinmueller for the final touch!
1. For example, in 1930, Ocean Spray Cranberries, Inc. was founded by independent and competing cranberry farmers. Growers own their farms individually but market through the cooperatively owned Ocean Spray marketing cooperative (Nielsen 1988).
2. The case of SEMATECH shows that this is a risk that cannot be ignored (Grindley et al. 1996); see below.
3. On the evolutionary perspectives of technology policy, see Metcalfe (1992).
4. See, for example, the historical work of Mioche (1988) on the Institut de Recherche Sidérurgique (IRSID) in France: small companies complained that IRSID is mainly working for the largest companies and does not pay enough attention to the needs of the smaller ones.
5. See Swann (Chapter 10 in this volume) for an economic analysis of the club goods solution for the support of basic research.

REFERENCES

Asheim, B. and A. Isaksen (2000), 'Regional innovation policies towards SMEs: learning good practice from European instruments', Workshop on 'The regional level of implementation of innovation, and education and training policies', Brussels, November.

Credé, A. and W.E. Steinmueller (1999), *Software in Finance*, Colline WP 09, Institute for the Management of Research and Innovation, University Dauphine.

David, P.A. (1994), 'Why are institutions the "carriers" of history? Path-dependence and the evolution of conventions, organizations and institutions', *Economic Dynamics and Structural Change* **5**(2), 205–20.

Foray, D. and P. Llerena (1996), 'Information structures and technology policies: the case of France and Germany', *Evolutionary Economics* **6**(1), 157–73.

Galli, R. and M. Teubal (1997), 'Paradigmatic shifts in national innovation systems', in C. Edquist (ed.), *Systems of Innovation*, London: Pinter, pp. 342–70.

Grindley, P., D.C. Mowery and B. Silverman (1996), 'Sematech and collaborative research: lessons in the design of high-technology consortia', in M. Teubal, D. Foray, M. Justman and E. Zuscovitch (eds), *Technological Infrastructure Policy: An International Perspective*, Dordrecht: Kluwer, pp. 173–212.

Kelley, M. and A. Arora (1996), 'The role of institution-building in US industrial modernization programs', *Research Policy* **25**(2), 265–79.

Metcalfe, S. (1992), *The Economics Foundations of Technology Policy: Equilibrium and Evolutionary Perspectives*, Policy Research in Engineering, Science and Technology report, University of Manchester.

Mioche, P. (1988), 'Un tournant dans l'histoire technique de la sidérurgie: la création de l'IRSID', *Histoire, Économie et Société* **1**, 119–40.

Nielsen, R. (1988) 'Co-operative strategy', *Strategic Management Journal* **9**(5), 475–92.

Romer, P. (1993), 'Implementing a national technology strategy with self-organizing industry investment boards', *Brookings Paper on Economic Activity: Micro-economics* **2**, 345–99.

Sabel, C. (1996), 'A measure of federalism: assessing manufacturing technological centres', *Research Policy* **25**(2), 281–307.

Steinmueller, W.E. (1996), 'Technological infrastructure in information technology industry', in M. Teubal, D. Foray, M. Justman and E. Zuscovitch (eds), *Technological Infrastructure Policy: An International Perspective*, Dordrecht: Kluwer, pp. 117–38.

Swann, P. (1999), *Collective Invention in Virtual Reality*, Colline WP 05, Institute for the Management of Research and Innovation, University Dauphine.

Weder, R. and H. Grubel (1993), 'The new growth theory and Coasean economics: institutions to capture externalities', *Weltwirtschaftliches Archiv* **129** (3) 488–513.

Ynnon, E. (1996), 'The shift to knowledge-intensive product in the plastics-processing industry and its implications for infrastructure development: three case studies: New York State, England, Israel', *Research Policy* **25**(1), 163–79.

Commentaries

CRISTIANO ANTONELLI*

1 In the Matter of the Knowledge Commons

Important shifts in the economics of knowledge have occurred in recent years. Consensus on the analysis of the public good characters of knowledge has been first contrasted to, and eventually substituted by, the new argument about the quasi-private nature of technological knowledge. The appreciation of demand-side externalities and external knowledge at large has called for renewed interest in the mechanisms of governance upon which the production and the distribution of knowledge builds. The understanding of multiple equilibria and micro–macro feedbacks refocuses attention on the crucial role of economic policy which had important consequences for the institutional design of the organization of the production and distribution of knowledge.

The process by which this shift in the economics of knowledge has occurred can be summarized in three stages. The first recalls the ingredients of the great swing from the build-up of the public knowledge commons to the wave of privatizations and liberalization. Identification of the central role of external knowledge in the production of new knowledge marks the second step, where the discovery of the knowledge trade-off stresses the role of the governance in all interactions and exchanges for knowledge. Understanding of the instability of market interactions in the production and distribution of technological knowledge should pave the way to the third step, where a new scope for an economic policy able to manage dynamic coordination issues is identified.

2 The Great Swing

The seminal contributions of Kenneth Arrow and Richard Nelson had long shaped the debate about the economic organization for the supply of knowledge. In these approaches technological knowledge was seen as a public good for the high levels of indivisibility, non-excludability non-tradability and hence non-appropriability. In this context, markets are not able to provide the appropriate levels of knowledge because of both the lack of incentives, and the opportunities for implementing the division of labour and hence achieving adequate levels of specialization. The public provision of technological knowledge, and especially scientific knowledge, has long been regarded as the basic remedy for underprovision.

The public provision of scientific and technological knowledge through funding to universities and other public research bodies, as well as directly to firms willing to undertake research programmes of general interest, found a rationale in this argument. This led to the actual build-up and systematic implementation of public knowledge commons (Swann, Chapter 10 in this volume).

Alongside this, *ex ante* monopolistic market power was advocated as a proper tool to foster the rate of accumulation of technological knowledge and hence of introduction of technological change. Barriers to entry in existing product markets secure the financial resources to fund research and development expenditures and, most importantly, reduce the risks of uncontrolled leakage and imitation. Competitors have yet to enter, and entry is barred by substantial cost disadvantages.

The creation of intellectual property rights was originally seen as a complementary institutional intervention. Patents and copyrights, if properly implemented and enforced, can reduce non-excludability and non-appropriability. In such an institutional design, intellectual property rights may also favour tradability and thereby lead to higher levels of specialization and division of labour. Intellectual property rights increase the incentives to the production of scientific and technological knowledge (Alchian and Demsetz 1973).

The build-up of an economics of intellectual property rights, however, has resulted in articulation of the stronger hypothesis that appropriate implementation of patents, finely tuned in terms of scope, duration and assignment procedures, can reduce or even erase the problems raised by the public good character of technological knowledge. At the same time, much empirical evidence and theoretical research has shown that appropriability is much higher than was generally assumed. Knowledge is contextual and specific to the original conditions of accumulation and generation: as such natural appropriability conditions are far better than assumed. Imitation costs seem high, as do the costs of receptivity and re-engineering necessary to make use of non-proprietary knowledge. The costs of the not-invented-here-syndrome are appreciated. The assistance of original knowledge holders to prospective users is relevant, if not necessary.

These two strands of analysis, *ex post*, contributed complementary arguments to the new hypothesis that the supply and the demand for technological knowledge can be identified, the actual creation and implementation of markets for technological knowledge is possible and the results of such market interactions are compatible with a workable competitive system operating near to equilibrium conditions.

This new approach led not only to theorizing about endogenous growth but also to significant steps towards the privatization of the public knowledge commons. Universities were solicited to patent their discoveries and often forced to serve the technological outsourcing needs of large corporations. Public funding of research activities declined or was questioned when it was not put under strain. A closer look at the working of the public commons and the actual need to scrutinize the productivity of the resources invested in the public knowledge commons, both at the system and the single unit levels, were advocated. With the divestiture in telecommunications and a new more aggressive antitrust stance (David 1997) some attempts were made to liberalize markets, especially in the new general purpose technology field of information and communication technologies.

3 The Discovery of External Knowledge and the Knowledge Trade-off

The analysis of appropriability made it possible within the economics of innovation to understand the key role of technological externalities and the positive effects of technological spillovers. The discovery of external knowledge, available not only through transactions in the markets for knowledge, but also through technological interactions, marks a new important step in the debate. External knowledge is an important input in the production process of new knowledge. The appreciation of external knowledge as an essential input in the production of new knowledge, has been articulated in the relatively recent systems of innovation approach, where the production of knowledge is viewed as the result of the cooperative behaviour of agents undertaking complementary research activities (Antonelli 2001).

The costs of exclusion associated with intellectual property rights, therefore, should be taken into account. Monopolistic control of relevant bits of knowledge, provided both *ex ante* and *ex post* by patents and barriers to entry in the product markets, respectively, can prevent not only its uncontrolled leakage, and hence its dissemination, but also its further recombination – at least for a time.

The advantages of the intellectual property rights regime in terms of increased incentives for the market provision of technological knowledge are now balanced by the costs in terms of delayed usage and incremental enrichment. The vertical and horizontal effects of indivisibility demonstrate their powerful effects in terms of cumulability. Indivisibility of knowledge translates into the basic cumulative complementarity among bits of knowledge. Complementarity and cumulability, in turn, imply that new bits of knowledge can be better introduced by building upon existing bits, both in the same specific context and in adjacent ones. Exclusion from the knowledge already acquired reduces the prospect for new acquisitions and, in any event, has a strong social cost in terms of duplication of costs.

Here, in the economics of technological knowledge, the issues of externalities on the demand side become relevant and evident. The generation of technological knowledge is now considered to be characterized by demand externalities. The notion of user-interdependence enters the analysis when agents value the levels of usage of other agents of certain goods. As far as scientific and technological knowledge is concerned, interdependence among users, that is, on the demand side, is in fact very strong. The actual chances of an agent generating a new relevant bit of knowledge depend upon the levels of accumulation of skills and competence, education and access to information of other agents in the community.

The amount of external technological knowledge available in a given context, either industrial, technological or regional, becomes – along with the conditions of access to it and the characteristics of the relational set-up – an important endowment. A variety of players contribute to external technological knowledge: firms, universities and research centres, as well as brokers and other undertakings specializing in the spread of technological knowledge, such as knowledge-intensive business service activities. The institutions of labour markets play an important role: job seniority and wage structures can modify the flows of technological knowledge – especially in a regional context (Cooper 2001). Inter-industrial division of labour and outsourcing in general also play an important role as they increase the flows of technological communication. Knowledge-intensive business service activities emerge as providers of technological knowledge and as complementary actors in the trade in patents and other intellectual property rights.

The issue of the distribution of knowledge becomes central to the debate in which the notion of an actual knowledge trade-off is articulated. Uncontrolled leakage and low appropriability regimes reduce incentives and lead to underprovision. Excess appropriability, both *ex ante* and *ex post*, however, may slow down, or even halt, the working of knowledge complementarity, cumulability and fungibility. Governance of the knowledge trade-off is necessary both at the firm and at the system levels (Mazzoleni and Nelson 1998).

The analysis of the governance of both the generation and usage of technological knowledge deserves a careful assessment and scrutiny. The mechanisms of governance include the conditions of access and exclusion to the flows of technological interactions, transactions, coordination and communication that are specifically designed to handle the generation and the distribution of technological knowledge (Menard 2000; Carroll and Teece 1999; Williamson 1985, 1996; Langlois 1986).

Inclusion needs to be coordinated and managed. Free riding can take place, although reciprocity and mutuality in interactions based upon knowledge barters, implemented by repeated and long-lasting exchanges, can help to reduce its extent and effect. Exclusion poses risks that relevant complementary inputs will not be available for the generation of new technologies (Swann, Chapter 10 in this volume).

The identification of the agents holding specific bits of knowledge and the assessment of their complementarity become important functions. This is expensive both in terms of search and opportunity costs: the costs of interacting with the wrong agents in terms of lost opportunities. A specific form of knowledge transaction cost can be identified here. The selection of the firms and agents with whom technological cooperation and technological communication can take place is an important part of the governance process. Once selected, these firms and agents are the basis for creating technological clubs and joint ventures to carry out collective research.

Signalling is also relevant as a means to reduce knowledge transaction costs. Patents are essential tools to signal the levels and the characteristics of the knowledge embodied in each organization. Patents are also more and more becoming bargaining devices used by firms to improve their position in dealings with other firms engaged in complementary research activities. A new chapter in the economics of intellectual property rights emerges here. Patents are no longer regarded only as tools to increase appropriability, but are also seen as devices to increase transparency in the knowledge markets and hence facilitate market transactions. The build-up of reputation, by means of publications and scientific sociality, also plays an important role as a signalling device within the scientific community (David and Keely, Chapter 8 in this volume).

A wide range of choices in terms of governance can be analysed and understood also with respect to the characteristics of the knowledge generation and usage processes. Technological strategies can be implemented by means of internal research and development laboratories, technological outsourcing, locating research and development centres in established technological districts, technological alliances and research joint ventures and, finally, mergers and acquisitions (Antonelli and Quéré 2002).

The firm itself is more and more often being regarded as an island of coordination procedures that facilitate the accumulation of knowledge. The Coase–Williamson argument often applied to the choice between coordination and transaction in the organization of the economic activity, can now be stretched and elaborated to support analysis of the fabric of technological knowledge (Furubotn 2001).

In particular, within corporations the coordination of technological communication becomes a relevant issue. The organization of firms appears to be influenced also by the need to implement and valorize the complementarity of the bits of knowledge possessed and accumulated in the diverse units comprising the firm. In addition, it is also possible to identify further influences stemming from the costs of technological transactions and interactions. The trade-off between knowledge coordination costs and knowledge transaction and interaction costs contributes to the understanding of the technological choices of the firm (Argyres 1995).

In the governance of knowledge not only is the traditional 'make or buy' trade-off relevant; the 'make or sell' choice also has to be considered. The firm needs to assess not only whether to rely upon external or internal knowledge in the production of new knowledge. It also needs to choose whether to try to valorize the knowledge available internally as a good itself and sell it in disembodied form in the markets for technological knowledge, or to use it as an input in the production of other goods (Teece 1986).

The economics of technological knowledge has made important progress in the identification of specific characteristics of technological knowledge. The forms and types of knowledge matter. Different governance mechanisms and governance choices emerge according to the characteristics of technological knowledge.

The forms of the relevant technological knowledge matter: whether technological knowledge is more tacit, articulable or codified has a direct bearing on the governance of the accumulation process. Next to the forms of the technological knowledge, its types play an important role. The complexity, fungibility, cumulability and tradability of technological knowledge contribute to assessing the governance mode of the generation and usage of new technological knowledge.

4 Multiple Equilibria, Instability and the Governance of Knowledge Commons

Technological knowledge can be understood as a collective good characterized by the complementarity both between external and internal knowledge, and the stock of existing knowledge and the flows of new knowledge. The aggregate outcomes of the governance mechanisms at the firm level are unlikely to be attracted to a single equilibrium point.

Once again, markets appear to provide a unique set of incentives to work swiftly; the result of such market interactions, however, may or may not lead the system towards stable and fair solutions.

In assessing the firms' choices underlying these market outcomes, the relationship between external and internal knowledge becomes a key issue.

It is immediately clear that substitutability cannot apply. Unconstrained complementarity, however, also appears inappropriate. The hypothesis of a constrained multiplicative relationship can be articulated. The ratio of internal to external knowledge seems relevant. Also, firms cannot generate new knowledge relying only on external or internal knowledge as an input. With an appropriate ratio of internal to external knowledge, internal knowledge and external knowledge inputs enter into a constrained multiplicative production function. Neither below nor above the threshold of the appropriate combination of the complementary inputs can the firm achieve the maximum output (Audretsch et al. 1996; Cassiman and Veugelers 1999; Bonte 2003).

Assume that the amount of knowledge generated by each firm depends upon the constrained multiplicative relationship between internal and external knowledge inputs. For any given amount of external knowledge available, however, a given amount of internal knowledge inputs and, vice versa, for any given amount of internal knowledge, a given amount of external knowledge, are necessary to generate the maximum amount of knowledge output. The ratio of internal to external knowledge inputs then plays a crucial role. This can be easily modelled as follows:

$$KY = IK * EK * Z$$
$$Z = (IK/EK) \text{ for max } Z = 1, \text{ when } IK/EK = X$$

where KY is the knowledge output for each firm, IK and EK, respectively, are internal knowledge and external knowledge inputs. The actual value of X depends upon industrial, technological and historical circumstances.

An important result is now obtained. Because of the complementarity, between internal and external knowledge, especially if specified in terms of a constrained multiplicative relationship, the aggregate outcome of both market transactions and interactions is unstable and sensitive to interactions and subjective decision-making. When both demand and supply schedules are influenced by externalities, multiple equilibria exist (Marmolo 1999; Autant-Bernard 2001).

The amount of knowledge each firm can generate depends upon the amount of external knowledge available, that is, upon the amount of knowledge that other firms, especially those involved in complementary research projects, have generated, and cannot appropriate or are willing to exchange. The amount of external knowledge available at any point, in time and in regional and technological space, depends upon the amount of technological knowledge generated and upon the conditions of technological communication within modules of complementary technological knowledge. The market provision of technological knowledge is possible, provided appropriate governance mechanisms are in place, but the levels are undetermined.

A further step along this line of enquiry can be made with the full appreciation of the localized character of technological knowledge and of the implications of the key role played in this context by learning processes. The notion of localized technological knowledge in fact makes it possible to stress the role of knowledge as a joint product of the economic and production activities. Agents also learn how, when, where and what mainly from their experience, accumulated in daily routines. The introduction of new technologies is heavily constrained by the amount of competence and experience accumulated by means of learning processes in specific technical and contextual procedures (Antonelli 1999). Agents adopting this approach can generate new knowledge only in limited domains or in fields where they have accumulated sufficient levels of competence and experience. Once again, a strict complementarity must be assumed between learning, as a knowledge input, and other knowledge inputs, either internal (such as R&D laboratories) or external.

A very interesting case now emerges: in the markets for knowledge, both demand and supply externalities, as well as joint production, apply and exert their effects. On the supply side, the amount of knowledge generated depends upon the innovative behaviours of the agents, as well as upon the general production levels of the economic system at each point in time and in the relevant past, because of the role of learning. On the demand side, it is also clear that network externalities among knowledge users play a ubiquitous role. The position and the slope of the demand schedule depend on the position and the slope of the supply schedule and vice versa. The latter, in turn, are influenced by the aggregate conditions of the economic system: learning rates depend upon the amount of output. Needless to say, aggregate output is influenced by the amount of technological knowledge generated in the system, via total factor productivity effects.

At each point in time a solution can be found, but these solutions do not have the standard characteristics of stability and replicability. In the markets for technological knowledge each equilibrium point is erratic. Little shocks, at the aggregate and disaggregate levels, can push the system far away from any particular point and no forces will act to push the system back towards previously experienced levels. At the heart of the market system, the production and the distribution of technological knowledge are characterized by multiple equilibria as well as micro–macro feedbacks and, as such, are sensitive to small and unintended shocks. Macroeconomic or monetary policies can have long-lasting consequences if and when they affect the joint supply of experience and competence and, hence, they have an impact on the supply of technological knowledge. A firm's strategic decision to increase either the demand or the production of technological knowledge can also have long-lasting effects that change the parameters of the system. Thus, entrepreneurial action may have direct consequences for the economic system level in changing the equilibrium conditions. Both failure and success, however, can result – depending on the outcome of a chain of reactions that may occur.

Economic systems may be trapped in a low-knowledge-generation regime, while other systems remain in high-knowledge-generation ones. Path-dependence effects, because of the role of learning and interdependence, are powerful. Small events can cause the system to oscillate from one regime to the other – with long-lasting consequences. In this context, the issues of dynamic coordination among agents and institutions become highly relevant for assessing the general outcome flowing from each individual action.

5 Conclusion

An extended process of idea development has taken place, since the old days of knowledge being considered a public good. A better understanding has been articulated of the dynamics of knowledge accumulation. Appropriability conditions now seem less relevant and demand and network externalities are playing a much stronger role. Transactions do occur in the markets for knowledge, along with systems of technological interaction based upon barter and reciprocity. A variety of governance mechanisms has been designed and implemented, or simply better understood. Eventually, however, the need for economic policy becomes stronger than ever. The governance of the markets for technological knowledge is not sufficient. Multiple equilibria and micro–macro feedbacks affect the working of transactions and interactions in the markets for technological knowledge and their outcome. The dynamic coordination of agents in this context plays a central role.

A credible or reliable announcement of long-lasting major initiatives and the implementation of large research projects, based upon the framed and yet selective participation of a variety of agents in scientific and technological undertakings with direct economic and productive fall-outs, should have large positive effects. In this respect, the consequences of procurement are similar to those that are produced by military or related aerospace expenditures.

The governance of knowledge commons needs to be implemented at the policy level.

BRONWYN H. HALL

All four chapters in this part are concerned with models of the performance of scientific research under various institutional and funding arrangements. Although the questions asked and answered may arise in any economy where the allocation of resources for scientific research is of policy concern, they are particularly important and relevant for those concerned with the design and evolution of a European Research Area (ERA). Such a change in the organization of research brings together basic research that was formerly conducted primarily at the national level and changes the incentives for and organizational structure of the performance of such research. The associated institution-building provides an opportunity to reconsider and re-evaluate the choice and extent of public funding mechanisms.

Economic policy in this area proceeds from a premise that there is a role for government in the provision of funds for scientific research due to the large externalities that such research generates and the difficulty and cost of assembling its beneficiaries into an institution that will provide funding for the research. As was pointed out by Nelson (1959) long ago, the closer research is to basic science and the more diffuse its applications, the greater the argument that the benefits to such research are so diffuse and the beneficiaries so uncertain that funding for it is best provided by a governmental or quasi-governmental entity.

Once we accept this basic premise, several policy questions arise:

1. How much funding should be allocated for basic and scientific research?
2. In what areas? How should projects be chosen for funding?
3. How should we organize the research, especially given its cumulative, interactive and dynamic nature?
4. In making these decisions, how can we ensure that the promised benefits to society from enhanced knowledge are achieved? That is, how can we ensure that spillovers actually take place?

When trying to answer the questions posed above, the researcher confronts the issue of deciding which objectives he or she should try to achieve: what things should be included in the social welfare function.

1. Should he or she maximize knowledge or minimize the variance in access to that knowledge? If so, what is the metric for knowledge?
2. Should the focus perhaps be more directly on quantities subject to economic measurement such as growth or output? If so, how does the distribution of knowledge resources affect growth?

3. What about other goals such as distributional equity or 'social cohesion'? How should they be incorporated? Are they necessarily in conflict with the other goals?

The chapters in this part focus primarily on the third question (the organization of research) posed above, exploring a variety of mechanisms and using a range of methodologies, from game theory to simulation to more qualitative analysis. In evaluating research funding policy, they focus to a great extent on the intermediate output – knowledge – while paying some attention to its distribution, taking the positive effects of this output on growth as given.

Clearly spillover benefits vary enormously across different types of research. Some types of research are not directed towards any particular commercial goal and therefore one might expect the benefits to be rather diffuse. Such research is best funded by government because no individual firm would be able to appropriate enough return from it to pay for undertaking the research in the first place. Other types of research generate results that are only suitable for use in a single industry (for example, the technical development of semiconductor manufacturing equipment or improved electric utility generation equipment). Such research may be best funded by industry consortia, as suggested by Foray (Chapter 11), because such consortia internalize both the costs and all the benefits.

Several of the chapters in this volume do an excellent job of highlighting the trade-offs inherent in the public funding of research: as in any economic system, when there is heterogeneity in initial endowments, the efficient allocation of resources does not necessarily have good distributional properties. In the case of the allocation of resources for knowledge creation, the fact that the production of knowledge has increasing returns properties means that using efficiency as the only criterion may serve to exacerbate differences between and among different geographical regions and research networks. In fact, at some level, the justification for creating an ERA must certainly be accessing the increasing returns available with increasing specialization at larger scales. Exploring the trade-off between this goal and the desire to enhance research productivity in disadvantaged regions and institutions is an important consideration in the David and Keely (Chapter 8) and Cowan and Jonard (Chapter 9) chapters.

However, the research presented in this part occasionally ignores or downplays another important consideration in the design of public policy in this area: the method by which research is funded will often have an impact on the amount and type of research chosen via the incentives created by the funding mechanism. This is because of the fixed cost nature of the research production function, which implies that private incentives to perform research can be increased by granting exclusive property rights to the output or by encouraging the internalization of spillovers via alliances or industry associations. Thus a direct consequence of the attempt to correct the underprovision of basic or generic research can often be to create another drag on social welfare in the form of the monopoly pricing of output. See, for example, Grindley et al. (1994) on the US experience with SEMATECH. The message is that ensuring funding by internalizing the benefits to the research via industry consortia or the patent system may carry with it the cost that these mechanisms facilitate the creation of barriers to entry and monopsonistic behaviour towards suppliers.

The chapters divide naturally into two groups: (i) David and Keely on the interaction of research network funding at different jurisdictional levels and Cowan and Jonard on the performance of research network funding in the presence of scientific researcher mobility; and (ii) Swann (Chapter 10) on the trade-off between club and public provision of goods with positive externalities and Foray (Chapter 11) on the industry-specific club for funding research as a policy experiment. Chapters 8 and 9 are concerned specifically with the trade-offs and complications that arise in structuring funding allocation mechanisms for basic scientific research, using simulation models to explore a number of scenarios, whereas Chapters 10 and 11 are more concerned with the issue of when and where the public funding model is appropriate and only secondarily with the details of its implementation.

Funding Scientific Research

Cowan and Jonard develop a complex simulation model of an open science network with spillovers in order to explore the influence of job market flexibility for scientists, the frequency of job changes and the strength of network connections on the following:

1. total knowledge;
2. heterogeneity across departments in knowledge levels; and
3. specialization across departments/groups.

They find that job market flexibility (the ease with which moves take place and the frequency with which the market opens) increases total knowledge generation slightly and leads to less specialization across departments. The latter outcome is consistent with observations on differences between Europe and the United States.

It should be noted that their model is primarily about non-codified knowledge spillovers and not about the spread of codified knowledge via journal publication. It also ignores the rather important role of teaching and graduate student mobility after training. Nevertheless, properly calibrated, the model should prove useful for analysing the productivity of one aspect of differing innovation systems while being able to hold all other features of the system constant.

David and Keely break new ground in the policy analysis of the 'allocation of resources for invention' by explicitly considering the interaction between two funding agencies with (potentially) different goals. They are concerned with two questions, the second of which follows from the first:

1. What is the equilibrium funding and knowledge 'reputation' in a multi-player game involving researchers, national funding agencies and a supra-national funding agency that awards grants only to collaborations?
2. Given the endogenous response by researchers, how should the two types of agencies achieve their goals where the goals are defined as:
   a. raising the average 'reputation' level; and
   b. lowering the variance in 'reputation'.

The model they use delivers two rather interesting and somewhat provocative results: first, that the supra-national funding agency should fund collaborations with the highest internal diversity in research reputation and, second, that the national funding agencies should not condition their funding on the decisions of the European Commission. In drawing these conclusions, they allow the agencies to have as a goal either raising the average level or lowering the variance. They also find that where the agencies choose different goals, the supra-national agency will not be able to achieve its optimum.

A natural question is whether the set of goals considered is the right set if the ultimate aim is to optimize the contribution of knowledge to economic growth. Several things might suggest that they are not: first, it is not clear what the relationship is between research 'reputation' and research productivity, although presumably they are correlated. Second, and more seriously, minimizing variance while ignoring the average level of reputation may yield a rather poor outcome under some conditions, especially if the knowledge base depends not on some integral over the distribution, but merely on the position of the upper tail. That is, if all worthwhile discoveries come from research groups with very high reputations, minimizing variance may be exactly the wrong thing to do. On the other hand, objective functions of this type may facilitate the diffusion of new discoveries across the region via the learning that takes place.

2 Funding Applied Industrial Research

Swann and Foray tackle a different problem: the provision of industry-specific public goods. Numerous examples of the voluntary formation of research organizations designed to internalize spillovers within an industry exist, although many of the most visible examples are essentially government mandated or instigated, such as SEMATECH in the United States, joint research organizations run by the Ministry of International Trade and Industry (MITI) in Japan or the Electrics and Telecommunications Research Institute (ETRI) in Taiwan. Foray reconsiders the interesting suggestion put forth by Romer (1993) for industry R&D boards and argues for their use at least in an experimental way.

The chapter by Peter Swann addresses the question of when basic research should be provided as a 'club' good paid for by members (of which one example might be an industry R&D board) and when it should be publicly provided. The criterion he uses is the maximization of social economic welfare and he is careful to draw out the distributional consequences of the various types of funding, as well as explicitly considering the transaction costs associated with each. As suggested earlier, the choice of club versus public funding is not a simple one, because the formation of a private organization to fund research may change the allocation of the benefits of that research from external to internal, to the extent that a club is able to internalize and transfer returns to itself via pricing behaviour. That is, at a given level of welfare benefits from innovation, the partition between external and internal benefits of that innovation depends on market structure.

Although the industry-specific funding mechanism for certain types of basic and applied research has considerable appeal, it is fraught with problems in practice. First there is the question of the definition of the industry: all firms within an industry are taxed to support the research and presumably can benefit from it. New entrants will be problematic: either they will be disadvantaged (because they are not members) or they will free ride on existing research, depending on the exact nature of the intellectual property regime and its effectiveness. Existing members of the consortium may be able to direct research towards avenues that ensure barriers to entry for new firms.

A second problem is the one identified so well by Swann in his model of the diffusion of new ideas and discoveries: identification *ex ante* of the type of diffusion likely to occur and the firms that will benefit is very difficult in many cases, but essential if the likely participants in such a club are all to be taxed. This is not to deny that such clubs may not form voluntarily if allowed to, as witness the recent rapid increase in research joint venturing, both within countries and internationally (Hagedoorn and van Kranenburg

2001). But such organizations are usually relatively small and exclude many others in an industry.

Finally there is the issue of appropriability and intellectual property (IP). From the perspective of a firm considering entering into an R&D cooperation arrangement, the trade-off is between benefiting from others' R&D (a 'good') while not spilling over too much of one's own (a 'bad'). There is considerable anecdotal and survey evidence that IP issues are the most contested area in negotiating R&D cooperation agreements. Using data on Belgian firms, Cassiman and Veugelers (1999) highlight the empirical importance of appropriability in determining who enters voluntarily into R&D cooperation, and the connection between this and the spillovers actually achieved. Branstetter and Sakakibara (2002) find that Japanese research consortia have relatively better outcomes for basic research (which presumably generates more spillovers) and worse outcomes when the firms compete in the product market.

In spite of these reservations, there is reason to believe that where beneficiaries can be identified as belonging to a particular industry, and especially where standards are important, so that a single technology trajectory is the preferred one, such industry-specific funding mechanisms might be a policy option, at least on an experimental basis. However, further consideration of the ideal IP ownership structure in such an arrangement might be in order.

NOTE

*   The author acknowledges 'Technological knowledge and localized learning: what perspectives for a European policy?', a project funded through research contract No. HPSE-CT2001-00051 under the European Directorate for Research within the context of the Key Action 'Improving the socio-economic knowledge base'. Thanks are due to Aldo Geuna and Pier Paolo Patrucco for their comments on preliminary versions of this commentary and to Jean Luc Gaffard and Michel Quéré for their comments after its presentation at the Institut de Droit et d'Économie de la Firme et de l'Industrie (IDEFI) workshop 'Innovation and growth: new challenges for the regions' at Sophia-Antipolis, 18–20 January 2002. This commentary also benefited from the stimulation and the discussion following the presentations of Paul David, Peter Swann and Robin Cowan at the NPRnet meeting at the École des Mines, Paris, 3–4 May 2001.

REFERENCES

Alchian, A. and H. Demsetz (1973), 'The property rights paradigm', *Journal of Economic History* **1**(33), 16–27.

Antonelli, C. (1999), *The Microdynamics of Technological Change*, London: Routledge.

Antonelli, C. (2001), *The Microeconomics of Technological Systems*, Oxford: Oxford University Press.

Antonelli, C. and M. Quéré (2002), 'The governance of interactive learning within innovation systems', *Urban Studies* **39**(5), 1051–63.

Argyres, N.S. (1995), 'Technology strategy governance structure and interdivisional coordination', *Journal of Economic Behavior and Organization* **5**(3), 337–58.

Audretsch, D.B., A.J. Menkveld and A.R. Thurik (1996), 'The decision between internal and external R&D', *Journal of Institutional and Theoretical Economics*, **152**, 519–30.

Autant-Bernard, C. (2001), 'Science and knowledge flows: evidence from the French case', *Research Policy*, **30**(7), 1069–78.

Bonte, W. (2003), 'R&D and productivity: Internal vs external R&D. Evidence from West German manufacturing industries', *Economics of Innovation and New Technology*, **12**, forthcoming.

Branstetter, L.G. and M. Sakakibara (2002), 'When do research consortia work well and why? Evidence from Japanese panel data', *American Economic Review* **92**(1), 143–59.

Carroll, G.R. and D.J. Teece (1999), *Firms, Markets and Hierarchies. The Transaction Cost Economics Perspective*, Oxford: Oxford University Press.

Cassiman, B. and R. Veugelers (1999), 'R&D cooperation and spillovers: some empirical evidence', London: Centre for Economic Policy Research Discussion Paper No. 2330.

Cooper, D.P. (2001), 'Innovation and reciprocal externalities: information transmission via job mobility', *Journal of Economic Behavior and Organization* **45**(4), 403–25.

David, P.A. (1997), 'From magic market to calypso science policy: a review of Terence Kealey's *The Economic Laws of Scientific Research*', *Research Policy* **26**(2), 229–55.

Furubotn, E.G., (2001), 'The new institutional economics and the theory of the firm', *Journal of Economic Behavior and Organization* **45**(2), 133–53.

Grindley, P., D.C. Mowery and B. Silverman (1994), 'SEMATECH and collaborative research: lessons in the design of high technology consortia', *Journal of Policy Analysis and Management* **13**, 723–85.

Hagedoorn, J. and H. van Kranenburg (2001), 'Growth patterns in R&D partnerships: an exploratory statistical study', MERIT, University of Maastricht, The Netherlands.

Langlois, R. (1986), *Economics as a Process: Essays in the New Institutional Economics*, Cambridge: Cambridge University Press.

Marmolo, E. (1999), 'A constitutional theory of public goods', *Journal of Economic Behavior and Organization* **38**(1), 27–42.

Mazzoleni, R. and R.R. Nelson (1998), 'Economic theories about the benefits and costs of patents', *Journal of Economic Issues* **32**(4), 1031–52.

Menard, C. (ed.) (2000), *Institutions Contracts and Organizations. Perspectives from New Institutional Economics*, Cheltenham, UK and Northampton, MA, USA: Edward Elgar.

Nelson, R.R. (1959), 'The simple economics of basic scientific research', *Journal of Political Economy* **67**, 297–306.

Romer, P. (1993), 'Implementing a national technology strategy with self-organizing industry investment boards', *Brookings Paper on Economic Activity: Microeconomics* **2**, 345–99.

Teece, D.J. (1986), 'Profiting from technological innovation: implications for integration, collaboration, licensing and public policy', *Research Policy*, **156**, 185–305.

Teece, D.J. (2000), *Managing Intellectual Capital*, Oxford: Oxford University Press.

Williamson, O.J. (1985), *The Economic Institutions of Capitalism*, New York: Free Press.

Williamson, O.J. (1996), *The Mechanisms of Governance*, New York: Oxford University Press.

Conclusions

The system of governance for science, the web of institutions both inside and outside the state that shape the incentives, social norms and priorities of scientific research, is a principal source of external influence on scientific research activities and the organization of scientific institutions. In the last two decades of the twentieth century, there has been a shift away from state-dominated governance systems towards more distributed models of governance. Features of the old model of the governance of science, which emerged immediately after the Second World War and prevailed until the 1980s, included a dominant role for the state support of science and the separation of scientific communities from the rest of society.

This old model was rooted in a high level of public trust or, at least, high levels of expectation for the contribution of science and scientists to society. Public support was based not only on the principle that science could contribute in a major way to the making of a better world, but also that scientific research (and only partially, if at all, technological research) was a public good that would produce the greatest returns for society if it were freely available to all those who might make effective use of it. The public good rationale directly supported the role of government as a principal actor in funding the scientific system. This configuration of purposes and rationales comprised a reference model for science policy and a platform for the extension of funding, as new 'missions' for science in supporting space exploration, medicine and environmental protection were defined.

The forces sustaining the growth of state support for scientific research began to wane in the 1980s. Slowing growth of college enrolments, increased resistance to growth in the share of the public sector and a diminishing appetite for military scientific applications were among the trends that influenced these developments.[1] These trends principally arose out of the broad agenda and levels of funding for specific research programmes.

A more profound influence on the governance of research activity was the move towards achieving more accountability, which involved mechanisms such as the incorporation of user needs as a criterion for funding, the implementation of research programmes to enhance national industrial competitiveness and the quantitative evaluation of such research outputs as scientific publications and patents. While it is incorrect to regard the scientific community as ever having been 'self-governing', these changes further spread control to actors within government, business and, in some countries, charitable, foundation or non-profit organizations, creating a significant adjustment in the governance of the science system.

These changes in governance suggest two basic questions. First, is some part of this change in governance a consequence of fundamental changes in the processes by which knowledge is generated and distributed within the scientific system? Second, is this change in governance the consequence of a more direct stakeholder interest in the research agenda of the scientific system? The tentative answer to both of these questions is yes, as indicated by several of this book's contributors as well as other recent contributions to the research literature.

It appears that the scientific system is evolving towards a greater degree of interorganizational collaboration and exchange, a development that has both disciplinary (see Lerena and Meyer-Krahmer, Chapter 3) and international (see Riccaboni, Powell, Pammolli and Owen-Smith, Chapter 6) consequences. These changes are the consequence of the interrelatedness of scientific knowledge stemming from the convergence of disciplinary paradigms such as the interaction between chemistry, physics and the life sciences in the search for new pharmaceuticals or the definition of materials science as a research domain at the boundaries of physics, chemistry and engineering disciplines. The increasing scope for measurement, modelling and simulation provided by the computer revolution has brought together researchers from previously disconnected disciplines into the processes of knowledge exchange and hybridization. The capacities for international communication afforded by air travel and communication networks have assisted in diffusing both the methods and the results of scientific investigation throughout the world.

These changes in the generation and distribution of knowledge have been accompanied by the growing application of scientific knowledge in industry and other parts of society. It remains true that a relative few industries conduct a disproportionate share of organized industrial research. What has changed is the extent to which industrial processes and methods are subject to systematic scientific research that supports innovations in both the processes they employ and the products that they produce. As Cohen, Nelson and Walsh (Chapter 4) observe, many of the channels for the distribution of knowledge, such as consulting, have not yet been systematically studied despite their importance across a broad range of industries. Similar increases in stakeholder interest are apparent in other parts of society such as the concern for health and the environment. These changes can be summarized in the ironic aphorism, 'science is too important to be left to the scientists', a summary of the increasing desire to influence the agenda and priorities of scientific research.

It is not surprising, therefore, that changes to the historical systems for governing science are being pursued. For example, research projects involving a higher degree of interdisciplinary and international collaboration require a reconsideration of the processes of proposal design and evaluation as well as project assessment (see, for example, Cesaroni and Gambardella, Chapter 7). Similar reconsiderations have led to the incorporation of user needs as a key element in funding proposals and assessment of 'national needs' for scientific research as the basis for setting funding priorities.

The new model of funding and governance is still emerging. Its contours are not as yet fully known. They involve new mechanisms of coordination across individuals and organizations, new forms of networks and new patterns of social interaction. These mechanisms blur traditional distinctions between public and private; science and society; and science and technology. A powerful example of the stresses in the existing governance system is Callon's (Chapter 2) descriptions of the role of research in the wild, the emergence of alternative and competing claims to social legitimacy of research findings and researchers that do not have a 'franchise' within the existing science system. No longer is the public willing to simply 'trust the experts'. A more critical perspective is emerging that sees science as being socially embedded in a range of political and economic institutions.

Even as these new and more critical pressures are being applied to the science system, efforts are being made to harness more directly the existing science system to social needs. Martin (Chapter 1) argues that this involves pressures on the university that are likely to lead to further 'speciation' in its evolutionary development, in which the Humboldt model of mixed research and teaching institutions will no longer be possible, and a new breed of entrepreneurial universities will emerge alongside ones that practise teaching on a massive scale. In contrast, Llerena, Matt and Schaeffer (Chapter 5) argue that in the French system, efforts to improve the flow of university research into industry are having relatively modest effects in transforming the behaviour of universities and are spawning a host of unintended consequences.

As public research institutions, including universities, are being called upon to develop a closer and more instrumental role in advancing industrial competitiveness and innovation, new incentives are being developed to reward this behaviour. At one extreme, it appears that policy-makers are amenable to the argument that if public research institutions are producing value for society then there should be a willingness on the buyers' part to compensate for the costs of the creation of this knowledge. There are several fundamental problems with this view.

Even though a growing share of scientific research may have direct application for commercial purpose, it is far from clear that this is a major share of the total amount of research undertaken (as observed in Pavitt and Wolfe's commentaries to Part I). For some, this may suggest that what is not being directly applied is not worth having. This ignores the consideration that science, like technology, is cumulative. While every line of scientific enquiry has a degree of uncertainty, it is undoubtedly true that ceasing to pursue a line of enquiry guarantees not only that it will not produce results tomorrow but that capabilities for producing results in the future may be lost. In this respect, public investment in scientific knowledge has created an extensible infrastructure that continues to grow – periodically and often unpredictably fertilizing the processes of innovation and commercialization.

Another line of argument against the proposition that a major share of university research funding should flow from commercial contracts for knowledge production arises from a consideration of processes of implementation and their consequences. Regarding implementation, Swann (Chapter 10) develops the implications of a fundamental feature of immediately applicable scientific research, its capacity to be employed by multiple parties, to illustrate the severe limitations to this means of implementing markets for scientific research. The research agenda is still open, as Foray (Chapter 11) and Cowan and Jonard (Chapter 9) indicate. Possibilities for funding the various elements of the knowledge infrastructure of an industry through an explicit competition would, at minimum, provide a clearer understanding of the priorities that industry was willing to assign to different forms of research than does the lobbying process for the allocation of public resources. A more troubling issue, however, that both Swann and Foray mention is the potential for the partial privatization of the knowledge creation process to produce new mechanisms for creating or exercising market power.

Aside from radical proposals for reform involving the internalization of science benefits within 'clubs', there is growing interest in moving towards a research governance system that provides new funding mechanisms, structures and incentives to address the challenges and opportunities arising from interdisciplinarity, internationalization and closer linkages between public and industrial research organizations.

A principal reason for the enthusiasm for research networks is that they address all of these issues. Networks can simultaneously be interdisciplinary, international and involve heterogeneous collections of public and private actors. Within the innovation studies tradition, networks have been identified as a key unit of analysis for analysing innovation performance. Recent works on networks of innovators (Freeman and Soete 1997), systems of innovation (Lundvall 1992), distribution power of innovation systems (David and Foray 1995), the sociology of science (Callon 1994) and regional clusters of technological development (Cooke 1997) all identify the effectiveness of networks for the exchange and distribution of knowledge as a means to support innovation. Prescriptively, many of these works suggest that policies that strengthen the links between network actors in the innovation process can increase innovation.

Efforts to tap the potential of networks have become a major feature of science and technology policy in many of the OECD countries. Funding mechanisms that support exchange, talk and social interaction were all designed to help to diffuse knowledge and achieve coordination between scientific research and innovation. Much of this effort is premised on the principle that the competencies of the single researcher or the solitary research organization are insufficient to ensure the forward movement of technological development. In effect, these policies have been based upon the belief that there was an *interaction deficit* within innovation systems and across national innovation systems, and such policy interventions are attempts to overcome this deficit.

Attention to the role of networks in the innovation process has been extremely useful. It has highlighted the social processes that underlie and shape the direction of technological progress. It has helped to strengthen complementarities between those that create and use knowledge. Pursuing this perspective has demonstrated that the use of knowledge creates positive externalities for others and that to create knowledge, generate ideas and harness new technological opportunities, interaction is required.

This book, however, presents a critical reassessment of the concept of the network in its different applications in relation to public funding of research. Though acknowledging the value of these networks, several contributors (for example, David and Keeley, Chapter 8, and Llerena, Matt and Schaeffer, Chapter 5) highlight some of the consequences of an over-reliance on network forms of public funding for research. We would suggest that a more balanced perspective towards networks is required. From this new perspective networks should be seen simply as one of a number of policy instruments available to governments. We would suggest that a more contextual approach to network development is required. While there are clearly indications that a very broad effort to promote network formation has played an important role in internationalizing research in Europe, the continued promotion of networks as a panacea serves little purpose. The key policy question has become how to manage networks to produce effective outcomes.

A better understanding of networks is needed so that network interventions can take new and more sophisticated forms. Governments need to adapt their research funding to match the emergent properties of the innovation system. Interdependencies and complementarities in the production and distribution of knowledge require a new and more contextual, flexible approach to government funding.

This volume provides a set of tools to assess the impact of the new network model of funding and governance. We can see that the advantages and shortcomings of the network structure for the production and diffusion of knowledge are highly dependent on context. The authors examine the characteristics of networks of support and the opportunities for harnessing the benefits of potential networks. From this perspective, the chapters in this book issue a series of challenges to the next generation of science and technology policy.

One finding from this volume is that research still matters – research is useful not only for producing new ideas but also for enhancing the innovation strategies of private firms. As Chapter 4 by Cohen et al. demonstrates, high-quality research creates opportunities for network development. Research enriches those with the capabilities to exploit its results. Social networking remains the main mechanism of exchange between research and industrial practice. There is a formal network structure that runs alongside informal networks of interaction between university and industry. These interactions are not policy driven: rather they arise out of the desire and need for exchange, a desire to be 'in the know'. This suggests that attempts to overformalize university–industry linkages might have a pernicious impact on the informal patterns of social and economic interaction.

Europe has been more proactive in trying to promote university–industry interactions, while the US seems to have a deeper structure of interaction between university and industry. These interactions in the US have been dominated by a tight network linking leading firms and universities. The European system is, in comparison, a less-defined network. The ideal structure is not achievable merely by increasing the funding for interaction. In the case of the US, it is the need for knowledge that generates network formation rather than the policy actions of US governments. In other words, need creates the interaction, rather than the interaction creating the need.

Another finding of this book is that levels of funding play an important role in shaping research, and the interactions between research and innovation. In many respects, the 1990s were a 'lost decade' for European business-funded research development (Salter et al. 2000). In the 1990s, real expenditures on business-funded R&D declined in Germany, France and the UK. This decline in European private sector R&D capability has had a profound dampening effect on the pattern of exchange between research and innovation. In times of tight or declining R&D budgets, many European firms adopted defensive innovation strategies and these strategies limited opportunities for the development of new relations between science and innovation. Instead of assuming outward and network-creating strategies, many European firms became more inward looking and tightened their network relations.

As has been argued, in the case of the US, it was the combination of high industrial demand for research and the relative high quality of the US science system's outputs that helped to generate the new networks bridging science and innovation (Pavitt 2001). It was demand that created the new networks, rather than the networks that created the demand. In the case of Europe, policy has often created networks that are in search of demand. In some respects, European policy has put the cart before the horse.

There is a need for more structured models that allow an evaluation of when and how networks fail. For example, given the shift from public-dominated funding of scientific research to a more distributed model, the assessment of policy impact requires an approach that takes into account interdependences. Actors, whether individuals or organizations, belong to networks financed by different agencies with possibly conflicting goals. As Cowan and Jonard in Chapter 9 explain, there can be decreasing returns to networking. In their model, these authors find that only a few permanent long-distance links result in the socially optimal production of knowledge. In a world characterized by a large number of innovators – very dispersed in spatial terms – and a complex economy with cross-sectoral input–output science–technology relationships, public finance is preferable to club good solutions.

There are, however, examples of local sectoral club good solutions for more applied research. As Foray suggests in Chapter 11, in these cases, public intervention may facilitate experiments in the development of industry-specific goods. The question here is not whether networks exist, it is rather whether these networks support and sustain technical development in a meaningful way and what role policy can play in shaping these networks.

This book does not provide a new rationale for policy intervention – that is, a new rationale for public funding of research. Rather it is an exploration of the changing context for such a rationale to emerge. In the context of the new systems of governance in science and innovation, the development of a single, all-encompassing rationale for public funding is becoming increasingly irrelevant. The real policy question is the means and mechanisms of intervention – the use of policy to harness, support and expand private activities and to shape public choices. In this new environment, governments will need to become much more effective at *policy management*, selecting and managing a wide range of different and sometimes competing policy instruments. Not only will public intervention need to be justified on a case-by-case basis, but government intervention will need to vary in format and character to satisfy different contexts at different times.

This call for flexibility in policy is not a retreat from the role of the state: it is a call for the development of new capabilities for assessing which interventions to employ and a deeper understanding of the indirect and unintended effects that interventions may produce.

NOTE

1. The relative importance of these forces, of course, differed substantially between countries. In Europe, enrolments in higher education continued to grow with some countries such as Portugal experiencing accelerating growth. In the US, the 1980s witnessed the largest military expansion in history in the US, a surge in expenditure bearing relatively modest dividends for science.

REFERENCES

Callon, M. (1994), 'Is science a public good?', *Science, Technology and Human Values*, **19**(4), 395–424.

Cooke, P. (1997), 'Regions in the global market: The experiences of Wales and Baden-Wurttenberg', *Review of International Political Economy*, **4**(2), 349–81.

David, P. and D. Foray (1995). 'Accessing and expanding the science and technology knowledge base', *STI Review*, **16**.

Freeman, C. and L. Soete (1997), *The Economics of Industrial Innovation*, London: Pinter.

Lundvall, B.-Å. (ed.) (1992), *National Systems of Innovation. Towards a Theory of Innovation and Interactive Learning*, London: Pinter.

Pavitt, K. (2001), 'Public policies to support basic research: what can the rest of the world learn from US theory and practice? (and what they should not learn), *Industrial and Corporate Change*, **10**(3), 761–79.

Salter, A., P. D'Este, B. Martin, A. Geuna, A. Scott, K. Pavitt, P. Patel and P. Nightingale (2000), *Talent, not Technology: Publicly funded research and innovation in the UK*, London: Committee of Vice-Chancellors and Principals and the Higher Education Funding Council of England.

Index